A Resource for Schools, Parents, and Communities

Coping with Crisis

Lessons Learned

Scott Poland and Jami S. McCormick

Proofreading by Beverly Rokes
Cover and Layout Design by Becky Salsgiver
Cover Images © 1999 PhotoDisc, Inc.
Photos p. 23 courtesy of *Jonesboro Sun*
Photos p. 119 courtesy of Steve Adams/Liaison Agency

ISBN #1-57035-218-6

Printed in the United States of America on Recycled Paper

Published and Distributed by:

Sopris West

4093 Specialty Place • Longmont, Colorado 80504 • (303) 651-2829
www.sopriswest.com

dedication

To the healing communities of West Paducah, Kentucky, Jonesboro, Arkansas, and Littleton, Colorado, and to all other school communities that have been so tragically affected by youth violence and other crises. It is our hope that the lessons learned from those tragedies will assist others in coping with school crises in the future.

acknowledgments

I wish to thank the administration of the Cypress-Fairbanks Independent School District for their support and encouragement of my crisis work. A special thank you to my children, Jeremy and Jill, who bring me so much joy, and to my wife, Donna, who provides love and support at all times.

—*Scott Poland*

A warm thank you to our publisher, Stu Horsfall, for his vision, dedication to excellence in education, and also his unwavering faith in my abilities. Thank you to Scott Poland for sharing his experiences with me and welcoming my participation in this gratifying project. Thanks also to Anne Miller for her invaluable research assistance and energy, and to the Sopris West production team. Becky Salsgiver's creativity, design talents, and patience greatly improved both the process and the final product. Bev Rokes' attentive eye and keen mind prevented many errors.

I would also like to thank Michael and Travis for their loving support and patience with my time spent in front of the computer, and my wonderful mother into whose capable hands I entrust my son while working.

—*Jami S. McCormick*

The authors are indebted to the members of the school communities near Jonesboro, Arkansas, and in West Paducah, Kentucky, who graciously reviewed this manuscript, offering suggestions and double-checking the case studies. Their assistance was essential to producing a comprehensive and accurate book.

about the authors

Scott Poland, Ed.D., is director of Psychological Services for the Cypress-Fairbanks Independent School District in Houston, Texas. He also chairs the National Emergency Assistance Team (NEAT) of the National Association of School Psychologists (NASP), and will serve as president-elect of NASP during the 1999-2000 school year. Dr. Poland was selected as a member of the U.S. Department of Education assistance team that advised the superintendent of the Oklahoma City schools in the aftermath of the 1995 bombing of the Alfred P. Murrah Federal Building. He was the team leader for the National Organization for Victim Assistance (NOVA) teams that responded to the school shootings in West Paducah, Kentucky, and Jonesboro, Arkansas, and in 1999 consulted with the Jefferson County schools in Littleton, Colorado, after the shooting at Columbine High School. He has written numerous books, book chapters, and articles on school crisis intervention. In 1998 and 1999 he provided congressional testimony on violent children to the Early Childhood, Youth and Families Subcommittee of the United States House of Representatives' Education and the Workforce Committee and participated in the President's Roundtable on Youth Violence. In May 1999, Dr. Poland was invited to assist Vice President Al Gore in leading discussions concerning school violence in Dallas, Texas, schools.

Jami S. McCormick is a professional writer specializing in education issues (K-12) and youth violence. Formerly the senior editor of an educational publishing house, her business—Tapestry Publishing Services of Nederland, Colorado—currently provides writing, editing, book proposal consultation, and Web site content services to independent writers, publishers, and corporations. She serves on the board of directors of TEENS, Inc., a youth development/violence prevention organization in her community.

contents

foreword

With the current level of violence in America committed by and against children, and the rash of recent school shootings, educators, schools, all levels of government, the faith community, law enforcement, and especially parents are fearful about the safety and well-being of our youth. Much of the rhetoric has focused on "Who or what is to blame?" Everyone is looking for the answer to "why" school violence is impacting communities everywhere, and responsibility is being placed on the entertainment industry, the criminal justice system, school policies and guidelines, parental control, and the gun industry. In the meantime, tragedies continue, such as the recent massacre at Columbine High School in Littleton, Colorado. And the level of fear continues to rise, especially impacting the parents of school-age children.

I have just returned from Washington, D.C., having been invited by the White House to help the government address school violence. I was there to represent the voice of parents who had been directly affected by youth violence and to share with our public policy makers many of the thousands of e-mail messages and phone calls I have received from parents in the aftermath of the recent school shootings. These parents have shared with me that they are afraid to send their children to school whether their children are in elementary, middle, or high school.

A common theme we have heard in the aftermath of publicized school violence is "I didn't think it could happen here." Parents and schools *must* realize that school violence can happen to anyone, anywhere. We must change our thinking from "I wonder if it could happen in my child's school" to "What tools do the school, law enforcement, medical personnel, and the media have in place to use when it does happen here, and what mechanics are in place to help parents deal with such a crisis?"

The problem of school violence is systemic. Bottom line, violence in a school affects not just the individual perpetrators and victims, and not just the school where the violence occurs. It affects the entire school system. Every person within the system is affected through individual experience by living with, working with, or going to school with someone who has been involved in a trauma. This includes parents, the school superintendent, the board of education, and the entire community at large. This is the very reason each of these stakeholders will find *Coping With Crisis: Lessons Learned* an invaluable resource.

Here in America we live in a society that enables nonfatal violence to occur in our schools and tolerates it on an everyday basis. It happens on the playground as elementary children play. It occurs in the cafeteria as students eat their lunch. It happens in the hallways as students move from class to class. And it happens in the classrooms as teachers are trying to instruct and students are trying to learn. Low-level acts of violence such as verbal insults, bullying, hitting and shoving, threats, and destruction of personal and school property don't make the evening news. However, in many cases these are the incidents that lead up to the school violence we do hear and read about.

Sadly, until adults intervene to address these low levels of violence, crises will continue to touch schools throughout our country. In the aftermath of the West Paducah, Jonesboro, Springfield, and other school shootings, thousands of parents have asked me, "What can we do to help our children cope with this tragedy?" Parents, especially, need the valuable information contained in *Coping With Crisis* so they will not compound their children's victimization but, rather, will learn to give their children hope as they reconstruct their lives.

> *Nobody is born with a genetic diathesis to psychic trauma. If you scare a child badly enough, he will be traumatized—plain and simple. But if you combine the trauma with a death or a new disability, then you will see depression, paranormal thinking, and/or character change—count on it.* —Lenore Terr

Death, especially from a violent crime, is a difficult concept to process and integrate for adults and children alike. The finality of loss and dying cannot be fully explained until it is actually experienced. When the injury or death is sudden and complicated by trauma, there is no time to adjust to the shock and pain of separation and finality. Grief is a component of humanity, but the experience of extraordinary crisis can be overwhelming.

Children, for several reasons, are particularly vulnerable to the impact of trauma. Children do not deny trauma; rather, they tend to record its full impact and horror. Trauma terrorizes children, making them feel helpless and unprotected. Their coping skills have not matured. They are still in the process of developing their individual personality and traits.

Adult caregivers, particularly parents and those within the school community, are critical in helping children through the trauma of violent injury and death occurring at their school. Unfortunately, many adults are unprepared for violent crime themselves. Additional stress factors for children and adults alike in the aftermath of school violence are the difficulty in understanding and navigating the criminal justice system and the need to deal with not only the local media but also the national press. *Coping With Crisis* provides invaluable planning and crisis response information to help school staff, parents, clergy, community members, and crisis response team members assist school community members when crises occur. I also encourage key players within law enforcement and the criminal justice system to use this book so they respond in a helpful rather than hurtful manner.

During the 1998 National Organization for Victim Assistance (NOVA) Conference in Orlando, Florida, I was fortunate to have the opportunity to attend several workshops presented by Dr. Scott Poland that focused on the lessons learned from the 1997-98 school shootings. These workshops, in which Dr. Poland shared his knowledge with others and me, were a defining moment in my professional and personal life. I am thankful he and Jami S. McCormick wrote this book so that others may benefit from his experience and wisdom.

—Jenny Wieland, Program Director, *Mothers Against Violence in America*

preface

Introductory Thoughts

by Jami S. McCormick

When my phone rang shortly before noon on Tuesday, April 20, 1999, I was working in my home office putting finishing touches on this book's manuscript. My publisher was calling, and asked if I was following the news. "There's been another school shooting," he told me. When I asked where, he said "Littleton," and it took a second for that to sink in. Incredulous, I realized he was talking about Littleton, Colorado, not an hour away from my home. I turned on the television news, and when I next moved from my couch about six hours later, I was devastated by what I had seen.

Littleton's Columbine High School was under siege by two male students. Bombs were exploding within the school and SWAT teams were assembling outside. The body of a student who had been shot lay unmoving on the sidewalk between the school and a parking lot, yet emergency responders were forced to take cover when shots were fired from within the school. They could not help the fallen boy for quite some time. A Denver news chopper showed another boy reeling near an upstairs window of the school, looking for help, his T-shirt bloodstained. Even the newscaster lost her composure as the limp boy fell headfirst, seriously wounded, from the window while members of a SWAT team in an armored vehicle below scrambled to break his fall.

Just as terrifying was what was happening inside the school: the carnage that the cameras couldn't reach, that the police could not stop. Emergency calls were being placed from within the school. Close to 2,000 Columbine students and staff hid beneath tables and desks, clustered in bathrooms, barricaded themselves in classrooms, and even hid in ventilation shafts in the ceiling (Gibbs, 1999). Fire alarms were blaring, and the school was filled with smoke from explosives and spraying water from the interior sprinkler system. "We heard boom after boom," said one student. "The floor was shaking from the explosions" (Gibbs, 1999, p. 29). The school had become a level of hell Dante could not have imagined, and amidst the chaos two gunmen gleefully slaughtered 12 of their peers and one teacher before shooting themselves.

Throughout the afternoon, groups of students were liberated from the school, running for their lives with their hands on their heads. They took cover behind a protected corner of the school, where they waited for a relay of police cruisers to drive them to safety. Frantic parents gathered at a nearby elementary school and public library, searching for their children's names on circulating lists of survivors, waiting for school buses of rescued students to arrive, praying to see their children disembark. Many students who had escaped earlier had jumped fences and found protection in area homes and the homes of friends, not emerging for hours. Hundreds of tearful reunions were captured by the media, parents and students clinging to each other, saying "I thought I was going to die," "Thank God," "I love you."

Columbine High School, Littleton, Colorado

Other parents were not so fortunate. A triage area had been created on the front lawns of nearby homes, and from that area ambulances transported the more than 20 wounded to Denver area hospitals. Because of the number of live bombs left to be cleared from the school and its parking lot, it would not be until the next day that the coroner would begin confirming and releasing the names of the slain. As the hours passed on the day of the shooting, the strain showed on the faces of the dwindling number of families still waiting for news of their loved ones.

That night, and over the next couple of days, national crisis response team members were poised to depart for Colorado to aid Columbine and the Jefferson County community. A National Organization for Victim Assistance (NOVA) team was put on standby and then on stand-down status. The National Association of School Psychologists' National Emergency Assistance Team (NEAT) members had their bags packed. Yet no invitation was issued from within the school system or community, and the teams' administrators could not reach the local decision makers to offer on-site assistance. Later in the week Dr. Poland, representing the NEAT team, was invited to Littleton by Jefferson County administrators. There, he made presentations directly to the parents and school faculty and provided consultative services at all levels of the school system. Dr. Poland also provided training to Jefferson County mental health professionals.

I have learned a great deal during the research and writing of this book. My co-author, Dr. Scott Poland, and other crisis responders across the country have shared their experiences in responding to school crises and the effects such work has had upon them. (No one involved in a severe school crisis emerges untouched.) What I do not comprehend—and know I never will—is how seemingly decent young people can torture and murder their classmates, teachers, and parents, laughing all the while. In the weeks since the deadliest school shooting in our nation to date I have grieved the shattered potential of the innocent lives lost at Columbine and tried to forget the disturbing images broadcast as the tragedy unfolded. It helps for me to remind myself that most people are good: people like the courageous students who shielded their friends' bodies beneath tables in the Columbine library; the many teachers who risked their lives to save their students; the people who gathered from across the state after the shooting to mourn and support one another; the people in my community who are donating supplies for art therapy and for therapist-guided summer camping trips for student survivors.

It also is comforting for me to remind myself that most schools, most of the time, are very safe places to be. That when I send my son to school, the odds are high that he will never encounter a hate-filled, gun-toting classmate. I don't delude myself that "it could never happen here." It already has. One Columbine student tearfully told a reporter, "This doesn't happen here; this is supposed to happen in the South" (making reference to recent school shootings in such places as Pearl, Mississippi, West Paducah, Kentucky, and the Jonesboro, Arkansas area). I disagree. I would say, "This isn't supposed to happen anywhere, ever."

Yet bad things happen every day to school community members across the nation. Children drown. Teenagers crash their cars and impulsively take their own lives. Beloved teachers die of cancer. And violence continues to occur in our schools. Although we don't yet know entirely how to prevent this growing violence, there is a lot we as a society *can* do and we must do more in terms of prevention. And when a tragedy does occur, people in schools must have guidance in picking up the pieces, in restoring a sense of hope and safety for our children and the adults alike. That's why this book was written.

Fortunately, the research literature on trauma and its effects on people clearly delineates ways to promote healing. Fortunately, there are people like Dr. Poland and many others who are dedicated to putting their helping skills to the test when a school crisis reaches horrific proportions. There have been many hard-learned lessons from school tragedies, knowledge learned not just in college or from research texts but through the pain of real people grieving real losses. These are the lessons we've presented in this book. We hope you will use these recommendations as a guide for supporting your school, children, and community should a school crisis occur. We hope you will also use this book for planning purposes, for the important task of creating a crisis response plan. And we hope that you will never need to use that crisis plan.

Reference

Gibbs, N. (1999, May 3). Special report: The Littleton massacre. *TIME*, pp. 20-36.

introduction

What's Happening to Our Schools?

Why This Book Is Necessary

Every day in America, 15 children are killed by firearms, 13 are victims of homicide, and six commit suicide (Stand for Children, 1996). According to the National Center for Health Statistics, homicide is the second leading cause of death of children under the age of 19 in this country (trailing only accidental deaths, such as those caused by motor vehicles) and suicide is the third (Peters, Kochanek, & Murphy, 1998). Our schools are not immune to these violent acts: Violence committed against and by children is occurring on school campuses nationwide. According to the National School Safety Center (cited in California Association of School Psychologists [CASP], 1998), 40 students, teachers, and other school personnel were killed at their schools during the 1997-98 school year, most as a result of shootings. In the period between February 1997 and May 1998, at least 18 children and school staff members were brutally murdered and 47 were wounded at schools from Alaska to Kentucky. The perpetrators of these highly publicized tragedies were all students, ranging in age from 11 to 18.

Ironically, National School Safety Center data ("School Gun Deaths," 1998) indicate that school gun deaths in 1997-98 were down 27% from 1992, the year in which school deaths reached an all-time recorded high. (In 1992-93 there were 55 school gun deaths; in 1997-98 there were 40.) This slight decrease in school violence is believed to be in part a result of the implementation of tough "zero tolerance" policies and interventions such as metal detectors in inner city and large urban schools. However, the spate of school shootings in 1997 and 1998 illustrates a disturbing new trend in school violence: These incidences were multiple homicides, committed in rural and suburban areas (where schools are less likely to have in place security measures to prevent such acts), by young children with lethal weapons. Additionally, these killings were not aggravated by the drug sales, gang rivalries, or racial tensions that are often found in traditionally high crime neighborhoods. Nor were they necessarily acts of revenge or aggression toward targeted individuals. Instead, they appear to have been indiscriminate acts of destruction: gunfire sprayed across a crowded schoolyard, within a school cafeteria, or into a group of students meeting in the lobby of a school.

In the complete picture of school safety, multiple homicides are rare (although not rare enough). Of importance, however, many of the multiple homicides in America's schools in 1997-98 occurred in communities where residents would have said, "That couldn't happen here." Yet they did happen in the Bible belt, the West, the Midwest, in peaceful towns of fewer than 50,000 residents. Said a school librarian in Arkansas after a school shooting there, "This happens somewhere else. This doesn't happen in Jonesboro, Arkansas. This is something that is supposed to happen in New York or Dallas" (Egerton, 1998). These homicides all occurred in places where the schools and communities were not necessarily prepared to deal with such serious crises and the large-scale emotionality that accompanies them. Noted Frank Sanchez, director of delinquency prevention for the Boys & Girls Clubs of America, "The latest cases reveal that youth violence transcends economic status and ethnicity. No longer are the inner cities and urban settings of America, alone, vulnerable to this type of random violence" (Alexander, 1998, p. 9).

Whereas such serious incidents may be rare, *nonfatal* school violence is much more prevalent. Most schools will not experience a fatal act of violence. Yet statistics indicate that all schools in America will deal with incidents of crime and violence in some form. According to the U.S. Department of Education, during the 1996-97 school year more than 400,000 incidents of crime were reported in public schools, including 10,950 fights with weapons and 187,890 fights without weapons (Cannon, 1998). Nearly one fourth of America's public school students say they have been the victims of an act of violence (MetLife, 1994), and three million children are attacked at school each year (Keen, 1989).

Another frightening trend is the increase in violence toward teachers. Each month about 12% of secondary school teachers nationwide are threatened with harm, and approximately 5,200 teachers are physically attacked (Greenbaum, Gonzalez, & Ackley, 1993); teachers are five times more likely than students to be seriously injured in such attacks (National School Boards Association, 1984).

If you are like many people, you may not fully appreciate the significance of these numbers. These types of statistics, no matter how saddening, often don't sink in because there is too much violence, too often, for them to be shocking any longer. People tend to feel resignation that such violence will continue coupled with a false sense of security: This won't happen to me, to my child, to my coworker, at my school, in my community. But stop for a moment and try to personalize these numbers. According to the National Center for Health Statistics (Peters, Kochanek, & Murphy, 1998), approximately one of every 1,100 high school age students, one of every 3,000 middle school age students, and one of every 4,000 elementary school age students die or are killed each year. As noted previously, the leading causes of death for these age groups are, in order of frequency, accidents, homicides, and suicides. What are the odds that someone you know will be impacted by youth violence or a school crisis? How many students attend your school? How many are in your school district? How many live in your neighborhood? You do the math.

During the 1996-97 school year one in ten U.S. public schools reported at least one serious violent crime (National Center for Education Statistics, 1998). The Department of Education pointed to this statistic as proof of the general safety of America's schools. And one in ten schools may not sound so bad—that's only ten percent. Yet many experts contend that the situation is much worse than the ten percent figure would indicate. The problem, according to Kenneth Trump, president and CEO of National School Safety and Security Services of Cleveland, Ohio, is that "… there has been no consistent reporting on school crises around the country" ("Clinton, Riley Discuss Findings," 1998, p. 6). That's important because the National Center for Education Statistics (NCES) findings are based solely on data *reported to law enforcement agencies*. Stated Trump, "We know that there is gross underreporting of crimes in elementary and secondary schools around the country," making the data inaccurate. Additionally, "The study is relying on institutional [reporting] policies and prevention programs. So the study survey has many influences on it." Concluded Trump, "With the publicity of reports of crime going down in the country, these [reports] can lead to a false sense of security" ("Clinton, Riley Discuss Findings," 1998, p. 6). Realistically, a major organizational crisis can be expected in a moderate-sized to large school district almost every year (Pitcher & Poland, 1992).

The current level of school violence is simply unacceptable. Schools are sacred: No matter what else happens in our society, children are supposed to be safe at school. Thus, school violence violates a national sense of trust and security. As one student in Springfield, Oregon, told the media after a school shooting there, "If it can happen here (at school), it can happen anywhere."

Parents also are shaken by school violence. A recent Gallup poll revealed that more than one third of the parents of school-age children surveyed fear for their child's physical safety (cited in Peterson, 1998). As one parent quipped to Dr. Poland, "The only thing we used to worry about kids dying of at school was embarrassment." And in the wake of highly publicized incidents of school violence, some parents are keeping their children home from school. "Florida education officials," for example, "report[ed] that in the last few years, the No. 1 reason parents gave for home schooling was 'safety'" (Kantrowitz & Wingert, 1998). Others consider sending their children to private or military schools. Said one mother of a first grader in Brandon, Florida, "Maybe this [military] school will be more isolated from some of the things that are going on" (Peterson, 1998).

Private or military schools may or may not be safer than the typical suburban public school. Yet it is interesting to examine the discipline problems now facing teachers in our schools. The following comparison of the top problems in rural Canadian schools in the 1940s and 1980s provided by the Fullerton Police Department (cited in Pitcher & Poland, 1992) clearly illustrates the radically altered school environment:

Top Discipline Problems in the 1940s	*Top Discipline Problems in the 1980s*
1. Talking	1. Drug and alcohol abuse
2. Chewing gum	2. Pregnancy
3. Making noise	3. Suicide
4. Running in halls	4. Rape
5. Getting out of turn in line	5. Robbery, burglary, assault
6. Wearing improper clothing	6. Arson, bombings
7. Not putting paper in wastebaskets	7. Murder
	8. Absenteeism
	9. Vandalism
	10. Extortion
	11. Gang warfare
	12. Abortion
	13. Venereal disease

The trends enumerated for the 1980s have become even more severe in recent years. Obviously murder, suicide, and assaults are much more serious problems than the almost quaint rule infractions of chewing gum and running in the halls. Yet are our children really that much more violent and delinquent today? And if not, then why are these heinous crimes occurring in our schools? Answers commonly offered include lack of parental control, media violence, gun ownership, and the general decline of society and values. While each of these factors may indeed contribute to the problem, youth violence is a complex social issue, making it too simplistic to point our collective finger solely at any one of these factors.

But if we cannot easily blame parents or society at large or the media for youth violence, then whom shall we blame? Many people point to our schools—the same schools that must bear much of the responsibility for coping with youth violence and the crises that ensue. Although it is not reasonable to expect schools to prevent all such crises, they can be expected to respond to them in a competent manner. Unfortunately, most schools are woefully unprepared to handle serious crisis incidents. During his many years of providing training and consultation to schools, Dr. Poland has found that only about one quarter of them have an organized crisis response plan that is understood by staff members—or by crisis response team members! The experience of one Georgia teacher is typical of too many schools in this country: "I am listed as a member of my school's crisis team," she said. "But there has never been a planning meeting and we have no idea what we are supposed to do" (personal communication, August 1998).

The reports of poor crisis responses due to a lack of planning on the part of schools are too numerous to list. The following are a few particularly atrocious examples offered by school personnel from around the country:

- A school principal lined students up in front of (glass) exterior windows when a tornado was sighted near the school.
- An elementary school failed to evacuate the playground when police engaged in a shootout with bank robbers nearby.
- Immediately following the 1995 bombing of the Alfred P. Murrah Federal Building in Oklahoma City, a few school principals planned to keep news of the tragedy from the school community members during the school day, withholding factual information from the students and staff!

Because of the publicity surrounding school violence in 1997 and early 1998, an intensive national dialogue on youth violence was initiated. Prediction and prevention strategies were outlined in all forms of the media, and parental responsibility and gun control legislation were introduced. In the fall of 1998 the White House announced a series of safe school initiatives totaling $80 million, including $12 million to help schools and communities develop plans for responding after violent deaths in schools (Henry, 1998). These all are important, positive steps in curbing school violence. Yet this problem will not be solved overnight. Crises will continue to happen in schools. While some of these crises can be, and hopefully will be, prevented, some school, somewhere, will be faced with violence or another serious crisis incident tomorrow, or next week, or next month. These crises will be dealt with for better or for worse. This book has been written to help school staff, parents, community members, clergy, crisis responders/caregivers, victims' advocates, and law enforcement and judiciary personnel respond to school crises in the safest, most appropriate manner. The information provided also will assist grieving communities in processing what has happened to them so they may heal as quickly as possible, regaining a sense of hope about our schools' future.

> "Half a calamity is better than a whole one."
>
> —T. E. Lawrence

Focus of This Book

For the purposes of our discussion, "crisis" is defined as a temporary breakdown of coping. Expectations are violated, and waves of emotion—such as anger, anxiety, guilt, and grief—surface. Old problems and earlier losses may also surface, as each individual involved has his or her own unique crisis history and emotional equilibrium. By their nature, crises are unexpected and require immediate action. The event's intensity, duration, and suddenness, and the victims' personal stability and ability to understand what has happened, will affect the severity of people's response to a crisis.

There are many types of crises that schools may expect to face. One need only read the newspaper or watch the nightly news to find examples nationwide. Among the most common are:

- Accidental death of a school community member (e.g., drowning of a student, airline crash)
- Car accident (often caused by drunken or reckless driving)
- Homicide
- Suicide (including attempts and threats)
- Death of a school community member by natural causes (e.g., cancer)
- Natural disasters (i.e., flood, tornado, fire, earthquake, hurricane)
- Bomb threat
- Gang violence (including drive-by shootings)

- Attack on a school by an adult (schools are sometimes targeted because disturbed adults have negative school memories, recognize that children and schools are vulnerable, and/or seek national publicity)
- Kidnapping or missing student
- Child sexual abuse or alleged abuse
- Drug-related incidents (e.g., sales of drugs on school grounds, arrests, overdose)
- Death caused by complications associated with HIV/AIDS
- Bullying and aggression (e.g., a student fight resulting in injuries)
- Threatened violence

While the recommendations in this book may be applied to any of the aforementioned crises, most of the examples focus on violent incidents. The American Psychological Association (APA) Commission on Violence and Youth has defined violence as "… immediate or chronic situations that result in injury to the psychological, social, or physical well-being of individuals or groups." That violence may be against one's own self, as in the case of suicide. More frequently it is interpersonal, that is, the "… behavior by persons against persons that threatens, attempts, or completes intentional infliction of physical or psychological harm" (American Psychological Association, 1993).

See the Appendix for resources that specifically address gangs, bullying, kidnappings, etc.

Why are we focusing on violence-related crises? One reason is that levels of youth violence continue to rise. An Office of Juvenile Justice and Delinquency Prevention study cited in Goldstein and Conoley (1997) found that "between 1988 and 1992, all categories of violent crime increased substantially for U.S. youths under age 18 …" (p. 3). These categories included murder and non-negligent manslaughter, forcible rape, aggravated assault, and overall violent crime. Between 1985 and 1995, the number of juvenile murder victims increased 66% (Blank & Cohen, 1997). This trend of increasing violence is apparent in the nation's schools as well. In a National School Boards Association survey of the nation's school administrators entitled *Violence in the Schools*, 54% of suburban and 64% of urban school officials reported more violent acts in their schools in 1993 than the previous five years (Carter, 1998). According to the Children's Defense Fund (1999), a child in the United States is arrested for a violent crime every five minutes.

"We know there is continuing school violence … that incidents continue at an unacceptable rate."

—Albert Shanker, President of the American Federation of Teachers (Greenbaum, Gonzalez, & Ackley, 1993, p. 35)

Another reason for focusing on violence-related crises is that violence often has a more profound effect on people than other forms of crisis. As noted in Pitcher and Poland (1992, pp. 111-112), "… [C]rises or disasters associated with the actions of humans are more traumatic and difficult to recover from than those generated by natural events … [and] aggression and deliberate maliciousness seem to strike the hardest into our psyche."

In addition to the focus on interpersonal violence, one chapter of this book is devoted to suicide (i.e., self-inflicted violence). According to the Centers for Disease Control and Prevention (1989-1994, 1995), the suicide rate among young teens (i.e., ten to 14 years of age) increased 120% from 1980 to 1992, and one of the highest rates of suicide in this country—11 per 100,000—is attributed to 15- to 19-year olds. Because suicide and suicidal behavior are so common among youths today, schools must be prepared to deal with suicide-induced crises and the special considerations associated with them. However, schools have not historically been prepared to cope with the suicide of either students or teachers.

Caplan (1964) described three levels of crisis intervention:

1. *Primary* intervention, which consists of activities devoted to *preventing* a crisis from occurring (e.g., suicide and violence prevention programs, gun safety education, programs such as Mothers Against Drunk Driving [MADD]).

2. *Secondary* intervention, or the steps taken in the *immediate aftermath* of a crisis to minimize the effects of the crisis and to keep it from escalating (e.g., evacuating students, discussing death with witnesses to a crisis incident).

3. *Tertiary* intervention, which involves providing *long-term* follow-up assistance to those who have experienced a severe crisis (e.g., ongoing emotional support and counseling for victims) in order to minimize its debilitating psychological effects.

While all three levels of crisis intervention are important, this book focuses mainly on secondary intervention. Unlike many publications examining youth violence and crisis in purely theoretical terms, this book is intended to be used in a *hands-on format* and is a *quick read*. All of the chapters provide easy to follow information that will be immediately applicable in the wake of a crisis—within an hour of the event and in the days, weeks, and months that follow. This information will be useful both for schools with a functioning crisis response plan (or whose plans address only natural disasters, such as fires and tornadoes) and for the majority of schools without one. It also will be helpful for parents, for members of the clergy and youth leaders, and for those in the judicial system and within community agencies called upon to help after a crisis occurs.

Much of the information covered in the chapters will also be helpful for schools that were not directly involved in the crisis. When a severe crisis occurs at a school, surrounding school systems often underestimate the effects of the crisis on their own school community members. Publicized school crises across town, across the state, or even across the country can significantly affect your students, their family members, and the school staff. To address such "ripple" crisis effects within your school, refer to the material written specifically for other area schools in Chapter Three and Chapter Nine. (In Chapter Eight, parents will find information about how to assist their children if they are upset by news of a school crisis elsewhere.) Also look for sections entitled "For Concerned People Elsewhere…" throughout the chapters, which were written specifically for schools and communities concerned about and affected by another school's severe crisis.

To illustrate the crisis response actions that are recommended, real-life examples are included throughout the book, many from Dr. Poland's district of approximately 60,000 students in Houston, Texas. Two comprehensive case studies, relating tragically fatal school crises, also are presented: the 1997-98 school shootings near Jonesboro, Arkansas, and in West Paducah, Kentucky. Dr. Poland led the national crisis response teams assisting these schools and communities after these murders and provides firsthand knowledge of the events. It is not our intention to exploit the pain of these communities or to sensationalize the events. We have presented the information because we believe Dr. Poland's unique insights will be valuable to other schools attempting to cope with crisis. Finally, tertiary, or long-term, intervention is addressed briefly in Chapter Twelve.

> "Board members, superintendents, principals, and other school leaders can learn valuable lessons from the unfortunate crises experienced by their counterparts in other districts and take … measures to … effectively manage crisis situations which may face their schools in the future."
>
> —Kenneth S. Trump, National School Safety and Security Services (Trump, 1998)

References

Alexander, B. (1998, July/August). White House plugs in to youth workers for school violence remedies. *Youth Today, 7*(5), 8-10.

American Psychological Association (APA). (1993). *Violence and youth: Psychology's response. Volume I: Summary report of the American Psychological Association Commission on Violence and Youth*. Washington, DC: Author.

Blank, J., & Cohen, W. (1997, December 17). Prayer circle murders. *U.S. News & World Report, 123*(23), 24.

California Association of School Psychologists (CASP). (1998, October). Schoolyard tragedies: Coping with the aftermath. *Resource Paper, 2*(4).

Cannon, A. (1998, May 22). Shootings at schools part of new trend that raises many questions. *Houston Chronicle*, p. 10A.

Caplan, G. (1964). *Principles of preventive psychiatry*. New York: Basic Books.

Carter, G. (1998, November). Shooting in Richmond: A teacher's perspective as victim. *NASP Communiqué, 27*(3), 6.

Centers for Disease Control and Prevention (CDC). (1989-1994). Death rates by selected causes: Suicides, by 5-year age groups. In *Morbidity and Mortality Data*. Atlanta, GA: Author.

Centers for Disease Control and Prevention (CDC). (1995). Suicide among children, adolescents, and young adults: United States, 1980-1992. *Morbidity and Mortality Weekly Report, 44*(15), 290-291.

Children's Defense Fund. (1999, February). Moments in America for children. *NASP Communiqué, 27*(5), 6.

Clinton, Riley discuss findings of school violence report. (1998, April). *Practical Strategies for Maintaining Safe Schools: School Violence Alert, 4*(4), 6.

Egerton, B. (1998, March 25). "We had children lying everywhere," paramedic says: Rampage leaves community in shock, tears. *Dallas Morning News*, p. 1A.

Goldstein, A. P., & Conoley, J. C. (1997). Student aggression: Current status. In A. P. Goldstein & J. C. Conoley (Eds.), *School violence intervention: A practical handbook* (pp. 3-19). New York: Guilford.

Greenbaum, S., Gonzalez, B., & Ackley, N. (1993). *Educated public relations: School safety 101*. Malibu, CA: Pepperdine University, National School Safety Center.

Henry, T. (1998, October 16). Clinton announces program to improve safety in schools. *USA Today*, p. 1A.

Jacobson, L., & White, K. A. (1997, December 10). In the wake of tragedy: Kentucky shootings highlight concerns about school safety. *Education Week, 17*(16), 1.

Kantrowitz, B., & Wingert, P. (1998, October 5). Learning at home: Does it pass the test? *Newsweek*, pp. 64-70.

Keen, J. (1989, February 2). USA schools wrestle with kid violence. *USA Today*, p. 1A.

MetLife. (1994). *The MetLife survey of the American teacher 1993: Violence in America's public schools*. New York: Author.

National Center for Education Statistics (NCES). (1998). *Violence and discipline problems in U.S. public schools: 1996-97*. Washington, DC: Author.

National School Boards Association. (1984). *Toward better and safer schools: A school leader's guide to delinquency prevention*. Washington, DC: Author.

Peters, K. D., Kochanek, K. D., & Murphy, S. L. (1998). Deaths: Final data for 1996 *National Vital Statistics Report, 47*(9). Hyattsville, MD: National Center for Health Statistics. DHHS Publication No. (PHS) 99-1120.

Peterson, K. S. (1998, June 23). Worried parents arm schoolchildren with patience. *USA Today*, p. 6D.

Pitcher, G. D., & Poland, S. (1992). *Crisis intervention in the schools*. New York: Guilford.

School gun deaths down. (1998, October 15). USA Snapshots. *USA Today*, p. 1A.

Sleek, S. (1998, August). Experts scrambling on school shootings. *American Psychological Association's Monitor, 29*(8), 1, 35.

Stand for Children. (1996, June 1). *Everyday in America* [Handout]. Washington, DC: Author.

Trump, K. S. (1998, August 5). *Crisis in the classroom: Can your schools' security pass the exam?* Available online: http://www.nsba.org/services/federation/nepn798.htm

Walliser, T. L. (1998, May 24). Why do teens kill? *ABCNEWS.com*. Available online: http://www.abcnews.com/sections/us/DailyNews/teenviolence0325.html

real-life case study

Jonesboro, Arkansas

Dispatcher: "911, where's your emergency?"

A woman's voice is heard. Breathless, frantic, her panic makes her words difficult to decipher.

Dispatcher: "At what?"

Caller: "[There have been] students shot at Westside Middle School."

Dispatcher: "Okay. All right."

Caller: "We need … we need an ambulance as soon as possible."

Dispatcher: "Okay, hold on just a second, ma'am. Do you know who [did] the shooting?"

Caller: "No, we do not. They came from everywhere."

Dispatcher: "They came from everywhere?"

Caller: "Yes, we were … we went out for a fire drill."

Dispatcher: "Okay, was it another student, or do you know?"

Caller: "I don't know, I don't know. Just please send an ambulance as soon as possible."

Dispatcher: "Ma'am, we've got an ambulance in route. Do you know if there was only one shot?"

Caller: "No, there's been several…. there's been … there's been blood loss, there's lots of blood loss."

Dispatcher: "Okay, we *will* get someone out there."

Caller: Sobbing, "Thank you very much."

This 911 call (released by the police) was placed within minutes of the shooting that began on the grounds of Westside Middle School near Jonesboro, Arkansas, at approximately 12:40 in the afternoon on Tuesday, March 24, 1998. The middle school had about 250 students that year in sixth and seventh grades, all from the tight-knit, rural communities of Cash, Bono, and Egypt, which are suburbs of Jonesboro (population 46,000, 130 miles northeast of the capital, Little Rock).

Westside Middle School, near Jonesboro, Arkansas

Shortly after lunch, the fire alarm sounded. Two girls say they saw a boy (believed to be the younger of the two perpetrators) pull the alarm and dash out the door. They thought it was a prank and reported it to the office (Egerton, 1998). Meanwhile, the rest of the school was dutifully filing out the exit doors of the school onto the school grounds, which are partially surrounded by a chain link fence. After the school had emptied and the safety doors closed and locked behind the unsuspecting students and teachers, the ambush began.

Alvin Bonham, who lives near the school, thought he was hearing construction noise. (Another building of the school complex was under construction at the time.) Then he realized he was hearing rifle fire. "At first it was just a few shots. Just bang. Then bang. Bang. Then all of a sudden real fast, bang, bang, bang, bang. It sounded like some deer hunter just picking something off," he explained (Egerton, 1998).

The students themselves did not understand what was happening. Said one student, "When people started falling to the ground, I thought it was all made up. I saw Natalie [Brooks] and Paige [Ann Herring] fall to the ground, and Natalie had blood coming out of her head, but the blood just didn't look real. When Paige fell, I thought she was just diving to the ground." As student Candace Porter was shot and fell against a wall, another student yelled, "Don't worry, don't worry, it's all fake!" (Labi, 1998, p. 33).

Students and teachers, most unable to retreat back into their classrooms, dove to the ground. Some ran or crawled for the safety of the gymnasium building. The scene was one of chaos, the sounds of screaming and crying audible beneath the gunfire. Teacher Shannon Wright shielded one of her sixth grade students—Emma Pittman—from the gunfire with her own body, saving Emma's life. Mrs. Wright later died at the hospital from gunshot wounds to her abdomen and chest.

In less than five minutes, 22 rounds of ammunition were fired from three high-powered rifles by two students of the school, Andrew "Drew" Golden, age 11, and Mitchell Johnson, 13. Dressed in camouflage, the assailants fired from the wooded Cole Hill, about 100 yards away, with a clear shot of the school's playground. They aimed high on their victims' bodies and hit 15 people. Nine students and one teacher were wounded. Five were killed: Shannon Wright, 32; Natalie Brooks, 12; Britthney R. Varner, 11; Stephanie Johnson, 12 (no relation to Mitchell Johnson); and Paige Ann Herring, 12. Only one of the 15 shot was male (Golden's cousin, Tristian McGowan, 13). Golden's grandfather, Doug Golden, speculated after the shooting that the victims were chosen because of their gender. More likely the girls were hit simply because their music class came out of the school first and they clustered together.

One student in particular may have been targeted, however. Candace Porter, 11, who was wounded in the attack (her rib deflected the potentially fatal bullet), had been the girlfriend of Mitchell Johnson for a few days but had broken up with him. Porter's cousin said Candace was really worried about Mitchell Johnson's reaction. One student later remembered, "Everybody was talking about them breaking up [and Mitchell said], 'Nobody's going to break up with me'" (Skiba, 1998). Confirmed a sixth grade girl, "… [Mitchell] said he was definitely going to shoot Candace because she had broken up with him." And one of Mitchell's friends said Mitchell warned students on the day before the shooting, "… tomorrow you will find out if you live or die" (Labi, 1998, p. 36).

While heartbreak may have been Mitchell Johnson's justification for murder, Andrew Golden's motive is still unknown. Fifteen of the 22 shots fired came from the .30-caliber carbine Golden was carrying when he was arrested a short time later; five shots came from Johnson's .30-06 rifle. (The other two shots came from a .44-magnum rifle found near the two boys) (Parks, 1998).

The first responders on the scene were stunned by the carnage. "We had children lying everywhere. They had all been shot," said paramedic Charles Jones (Egerton, 1998). A school staff member later told Dr. Poland that people were in shock, wandering aimlessly about the schoolyard "like cattle," holding hands, not knowing where to go. He and a couple of other staff members began herding people into the gymnasium, where they gathered in class groups.

Concerned onlookers gathered in front of the school, soon joined by the media. Frantic parents poured into the school building searching for their children. Bono mayor Ralph Lee rushed to the school, where his daughter is a teacher and his grandchildren are students. "You [couldn't] believe the chaos," he said. "It was almost impossible to get around, and people [were] just—well, when grown people stand there and cry, there's something bad wrong" (Egerton, 1998). The sheriff, Dale Haas, wept when he publicly announced the shooting. "I've been in this a long time, and it's the worst thing I've ever seen," he said (Egerton, 1998).

One parent who was particularly stunned was Dennis Golden, the father of suspected perpetrator Drew Golden. Reported student Sara Short, 12: "I had gone inside the gym when Drew's dad walked up to me and asked if I'd seen his son. 'The police arrested Drew and Mitchell for shooting at us,' I told him. 'No!' Mr. Golden said. I could see he was in shock. 'Drew couldn't have done that. He wouldn't have done that.' He kept saying it" (Casey, 1999, p. 12).

When teacher Shannon Wright's husband, Mitchell, heard about the school shooting on his car radio, he "sped [to the school], my heart pounding, and ended up blocks away, unable to get any closer …. I jumped out of the car and searched for Shannon. I couldn't find her anywhere. Someone finally told me she'd been taken to the hospital. 'I don't know how bad it is,' he said. 'She's been shot.' When I got to the hospital, Shannon's family was already there, and so was [their son] Zane" (Casey, 1999, p. 12). A maintenance worker at the school later told Mitchell Wright that as Shannon Wright lay mortally wounded on the playground that day, she looked up at him and told him, "Tell Mitch I love him and to take care of Zane" (Casey, 1999, p. 12).

Within 20 minutes of the first 911 call, a local radio station began asking on air for blood donations. Quickly a second facility was also set up to accept blood donations. The response from the community was so overwhelming that, as approximately 100 would-be donors waited at both locations that evening, the station had to ask people to stay home (Labi, 1998).

Immediately following the shooting, a call went out for all doctors to report to St. Bernard's Regional Medical Center in Jonesboro. Emergency room director Robert Beaton said the emergency room was soon filled with people with not only a full range of lethal and mild bullet wounds but also injuries from running and falling (Egerton, 1998). "There was just a horrendous, chaotic scene in the emergency room," Dr. Warren Skaug, a pediatrician, said. "There were tortured faces and churning stomachs, including mine" as doctors worked frantically for an hour and a half to treat the shooting victims. "I truly believe good medicine was done," he continued, "or we would have lost more children" (Associated Press, 1998).

Many parents raced to the hospital, anxious for news of their children. Doctors there were faced with the unpleasant task of identifying two of the dead children who had been carrying no identification. Recounted Dr. Skaug: "Hospital staff and clergy had to go to the holding area for desperate parents and call for wallet-sized photos of their children … then go back and tell those parents whose children were dead. That's one of the most cruel forms of Russian roulette I could ever have conceived" (Associated Press, 1998).

While the race was on to save the lives of those shot in the attack, the police officers responding to the school faced another critical situation: apprehending the suspects. The two boys had run back through the woods toward their getaway vehicle—a van stolen earlier from Mitchell Johnson's stepfather—which was parked about a half a mile away from the school. Construction workers who had seen gun smoke coming from the woods pointed the police in the right direction (Labi, 1998). The boys were apprehended near the van within minutes. They offered little resistance. Police quickly disarmed them of ten guns. Said officer Terry McNatt, who knew one of the suspects, "They didn't say anything," and they remained silent for the entire drive to the Craighead County sheriff's office (Labi, 1998, p. 33).

That morning, the two boys had skipped the bus ride to school as well as first period. During that time, they drove the stolen van to Andrew Golden's home and stole three handguns left unlocked in the house (after failing to gain access to other guns by attempting to break into Andrew's father's steel gun case with a torch and a hammer). The two next drove to Andrew Golden's grandfather's house where they broke in, using a crowbar to pry open the basement door, and stole another seven guns. At some point the boys also loaded the van with food, a large quantity of ammunition, camping gear, a machete, a crossbow, and knives. A classmate later said, "[Mitchell Johnson told me] … after seventh period [the previous day] that he was never going to see me again, and I wouldn't be able to see him again because he was going to run away" (Staff, 1998).

Andrew Golden and Mitchell Johnson were held without bail, and each was charged with five counts of capital murder and ten counts of first degree battery. The public was quickly informed that in a hearing scheduled for April 1998, juvenile court judge Ralph Wilson, Jr., would determine the boys' guilt or innocence. Judge Wilson would have the following options: (1) find one or both not guilty; (2) sentence the boys after they had pled guilty; (3) find one or both boys guilty but let them out of custody before their 18th birthdays; (4) reject one or both of their guilty pleas and hold a trial, complete with testimony and the presentation of evidence; or (5) after mental evaluations, find one or both incompetent to stand trial and place them in a hospital for the mentally ill (Parks, 1998). If convicted, the longest the boys could be held was their 18th birthdays, as they could be charged only in juvenile court. Arkansas law prohibits children younger than 14 to be tried as adults, although federal law does allow for a 13-year old (the age of Mitchell Johnson) to be tried as an adult. A few days after the boys' arrests, however, the U.S. Justice Department announced that no federal charges would be filed against them.

Just six hours after the shooting, the Craighead County prosecutor and the state's attorney general asked the National Organization for Victim

Assistance (NOVA) to send a team to Jonesboro to assist the local caregivers with crisis intervention. As would be expected, the small community was having a difficult time dealing with the fallout of the attack, and hundreds of national media representatives were descending upon them. "We went into it unprepared and cold" and were grateful to have the assistance of a national crisis intervention team, said Jack Bower, school psychologist for the Craighead County Special Education Cooperative in Jonesboro ("Counseling Jonesboro," 1998, p. 10). NOVA immediately organized and dispatched a crisis response team of seven individuals from across the country. The team included clergy members, victims' advocates, a police officer, and psychologists—people chosen from a multidisciplinary arena to help ensure that the many varying needs of the community would be addressed in the wake of the tragedy. Because of his school credentials, the team was to be led at the site by Dr. Scott Poland with guidance from NOVA's executive director and other staff in Washington, D.C.

The NOVA team arrived in Jonesboro on the afternoon of Wednesday, March 25, fewer than 26 hours after the shooting (one of the quickest responses in NOVA's history). Prior to the team's arrival, the local leaders of both the school and community pulled together to handle the initial crisis intervention effort. In particular, three local school psychologists assumed a leadership role and spent extensive time after the shooting helping both staff and students deal with their initial shock and grief. School was canceled for Wednesday, and the Westside staff gathered at the school that day to process their reactions to the crisis and fears about what had happened.

On the day of the shooting, a local school psychologist interfaced with the media, who were quite aggressive and present in the school building and surrounding areas. The Red Cross provided food and drink, and members of the National Guard were strategically stationed around the school. State university psychologists, counselors, and other mental health professionals poured in from all parts of Arkansas to lend their assistance, as did many members of the clergy.

When the members of the NOVA team arrived in Jonesboro at about 4:00 PM on Wednesday, they first met with staff from the prosecutor's office. One member of the staff, the victims' advocate for the county, had already spoken by phone with the victims' advocate in West Paducah, Kentucky (where a NOVA team had provided crisis intervention after a school shooting there the previous December), to learn about the activities of the NOVA team. She had then arranged a meeting with the leadership personnel in the Westside School District, and the NOVA team was warmly received at the school when they arrived there a short time later.

The school leaders and the NOVA team met for about an hour, discussing how to proceed the following day when the school would reopen. The meeting was productive, and specific plans were made regarding such things as counseling for the students and transportation logistics. The school representatives were appreciative of the team's training and assistance and were interested in the ideas suggested.

Next the NOVA team met with the local caregivers—the approximately 150 mental health professionals, clergy members, and medical staff who would be assisting the school community the next day—who were gathered in the school's cafeteria. During that hour-long meeting the NOVA team made some concrete suggestions about assisting victims of a severe crisis and dealing with the large-scale emotionality that accompanies such a tragedy. They also discussed with those assembled the plans that had been made with the school representatives for the next day.

The NOVA team was then asked to address the school's students and parents who were assembling in the school's gymnasium. This meeting would be the most critical, and emotionally charged, gathering of the evening, and the team had had next to no time to prepare for it. They had not even had time to visit the crime scene. However, in a crisis of this magnitude human needs come first, and organizational needs often fall by the wayside; plans of action are often evolving as the situation unfolds. Dr. Poland was advised to simply "tell [the parents and students] what you think they need," and was told that the main goal was "to get the kids back to school."

Red Cross volunteers and various community members were standing at the rear, all the bleachers at the front were full, and chairs were filled on both sides of the room. Between 400 and 500 people—angry, grieving, and looking for answers—were assembled. The sheriff first made some introductory statements, and then the county prosecutor addressed the crowd. The citizens were quite upset that Golden and Johnson could be held only until they turned 18 and were shouting at the prosecutor because they couldn't hear him well. Those gathered were also tortured with the question "Why?" and were saying things like: "If those parents had reported their car stolen …"; "If they had reported that when they knew it, maybe the police would have picked [Golden and Johnson] up …"; "How did they get all those guns?"; and "How could they have done this?" They were very angry with the boys' parents, grandparents, and the boys themselves. They also were angry with the laws in the state of Arkansas. The prosecutor did the best he could in answering the questions of the crowd.

Dr. Poland then took the microphone to introduce himself and the national crisis team and told the audience he had been the team leader in West Paducah, Kentucky, in December. Knowing that their angry questioning was not conducive to helping the parents and students move forward over the next days at school, Dr. Poland attempted to defuse their anger and emphasized that they needed to think about something else. He explained:

You are spending so much time tonight trying to answer the question "Why?" I know that it's been over four months in Paducah, and they do not have the answer "why." You will probably never have the answer to your satisfaction.

You are understandably angry at these boys, their families, and the laws in Arkansas. [The county prosecutor] told you we can't change those laws tonight, but even if we did, it would not affect Mitchell's and Andrew's punishment.

What are we going to do now? Your children are right here. What are we going to do to help them? We're going to have to focus on what we can do tomorrow.

This shift of focus helped the crowd settle down, and everyone was listening. Then the students began asking questions. One girl raised her hand and asked two logical questions: "I want to know, is the fire alarm going to ring tomorrow? And if I come back to school, do I have to go outside?"

Dr. Poland replied, "That fire alarm is *not* going to ring in this building for a long time. When and if it ever rings again, you will know about it because your principal will make you a part of that process. And you're *not* going outside tomorrow."

The next question was: "Why is there still blood on the sidewalk and bullet holes on the side of the building?" The answer was that the blood had now been cleaned up, but the bullet holes needed to remain for a while as a reminder to them all that this tragedy had really happened. Dr. Poland mentioned to the people gathered that they might feel a need to walk around the site of the shooting, look at the bullet holes, and think about where they had been as they tried to understand how the tragedy had occurred.

The most difficult question, which choked up many in the room, including Dr. Poland, was: "I was Shannon Wright's student. She's been killed. How can I possibly face going back to her classroom?" Dr. Poland tried to frame the question in a larger context, saying, "She was a wonderful person, I understand. She gave her life for education. What would she want you to do? She would want you to go back in the classroom to face it and go on with the business of learning." His answer seemed to satisfy her, and probably every other student of Shannon Wright's who were likely listening very carefully to the answer.

The county prosecutor again took the stage to answer some legal questions being posed, this time facing a much calmer audience. Dr. Poland then continued answering questions and advised the parents about specific strategies they could use to assist their children in coping with the trauma.

He asked the students to give their parents a chance and to remember that they wanted to help them.

After about two hours (it was 9:00 PM), Dr. Poland thought it best to adjourn for the night. To end the family/community meeting with a sense of hope, he emphasized the resiliency of the community, complimenting them on their strength, how much they cared, and how well they had worked together in the hours following the shooting. He outlined the next day, stressing what would be done to assist the children, and announced that there would be another family/community meeting with the NOVA team the next night that would be open to the entire community (with the exception of the media). Finally, he encouraged every student to be in attendance the next morning and promised that counselors would be calling on each student who was not in school.

He then asked how many people still had questions. Approximately 40 hands went up, so he asked every counselor in the gymnasium to go stand at center court. About 50 mental health professionals were there, so the parents and students who still had questions were able to speak to those counselors about their concerns as the meeting closed.

After the family/community meeting, the NOVA team spent another hour and a half meeting with the school representatives again, finalizing the plans for the next day. Particular attention was paid to Shannon Wright's classroom. After returning to their hotel, the NOVA team spent some more time planning. By the time they went to their rooms it was about midnight, yet it was very difficult for the team members to sleep (as it must have been for the majority of the community).

The next day, Thursday, school was in session at Westside Middle School, but the regular curriculum was set aside. Almost all of the students were in attendance, despite the fact that the scene was still quite disruptive. The National Guard watched over the school, the media were lined up nearby, and the Red Cross was there to assist again. There were counselors riding on some of the school buses, although most parents brought their children to school themselves that day. As one would expect, there was a great deal of emotion and crying as students returned to the scene of the shooting. To smooth the transition back to school, the majority of the staff were either outside greeting the children as they arrived or in the hallways reaching out to them. The school's principal, the superintendent, and the NOVA team were there meeting the school buses and comforting students.

Before the school day began, Dr. Poland addressed the entire faculty and student body. He told them briefly what they were going to do that day and reminded them that they could pull together to get through this crisis, that they had "the right stuff," that they could help each other, and that they were going to have a good day that day. He pointed out that they were "in the safest middle school in America today" because he knew "there was no other middle school ringed by National Guardsmen and state troopers." He reiterated that the students would not be going outside during the school day and that during first period there would be considerable time set aside for the expression of emotions.

As school began, counselors, NOVA team members, clergy members, and school administrators spread throughout the Westside complex. A counseling team (comprising counselors and a member of the local clergy, with support from NOVA team members) was in every classroom of Westside Middle School. Counselors were also in all the classes at the elementary and high schools in the Westside complex. One of the NOVA team members joined two counselors in Shannon Wright's first period class, and these professionals worked with her students extensively to process what had happened using the NOVA model (*see Chapter Five*). When the students entered Mrs. Wright's classroom, everything was exactly as it had been left on the day of the shooting. No one had moved anything or had tried to erase her presence.

Other NOVA team members began to provide important assistance within the community to the first responders on the scene. For example, three separate sessions were held at the hospital in the following days. Team members used the NOVA model with the hospital staff members, including the surgeons, and elicited a range of natural responses. The hospital staff said theirs had been the "best, most efficient response in the history of a hospital. There was no distraction, all the surgery rooms were free, we did a great job," and yet some cried about their part in the crisis response because not everyone had been saved. It was important for them to have the opportunity to express their conflicting emotions and to realize that they couldn't have done anything more than they did that day.

NOVA team members also met with the families of the victims. The victims' advocate for Craighead County utilized the NOVA team in both a consultative and direct service role to provide services to the families of the dead and injured. Initial work with the families of those who had died provided support through the initial shock and numbness that overwhelmed them. Those five families also needed assistance with practical concerns, such as planning funerals, and they needed to be shielded from the spotlight of the national and international media. The families of the injured also needed support in coping with such issues as the severity of the injuries, medical costs, and rehabilitation services.

The NOVA team was not involved in providing services to the families of the suspected student perpetrators, as none were requested. (The decision about whether to provide such services if requested would be made by NOVA's national office; it is anticipated that such a request would be granted.) The two suspected student perpetrators were in jail and thus were not available to receive mental health assistance.

Working with the Craighead County victims' advocate, the NOVA team helped to lay the groundwork for all the services and questions that were ahead for the families of victims with regard to their rights, the judicial process, and the many services available to them. The victims' advocate later commented on how much the team had helped her extend her services and outreach to the troubled community.

As team leader, Dr. Poland conducted numerous press conferences—many with a local school psychologist and the school's principal—and granted interview requests. Teachers also discussed problems and their concerns about particular students with Dr. Poland and other NOVA team members throughout the school day.

Since there was to be no school on Friday due to a preplanned inservice day, the NOVA team, along with the Arkansas attorney general, conducted a meeting after school on Thursday with the approximately 100 out-of-town caregivers who had assisted at the school that day and would now be returning to their homes. The meeting provided an opportunity for the school to formally thank them for their valuable assistance and, because they had been in every classroom and on the school buses, to discuss with them what had and had not been working and their recommendations for the school. The caregivers gave some very important information for follow-up. Equally important, the meeting gave them a forum to vent about their time at the school that day, which was some of the most difficult work they had ever done. They made such comments as: "I didn't want to come"; "I was so scared"; "I wasn't sure I had the right stuff"; "I was so nervous, but I did a heck of a job and I helped these kids"; and "I'm so sorry this happened but I feel good about what I did." By the time these professionals left that day, they felt appreciated and rightfully proud of their crisis response.

An open family/community meeting was held Thursday night and approximately 45 people attended. The much smaller number, and the much calmer mood, were testament to the success of the previous night's family/community meeting. Dr. Poland addressed the group. Then, because at this meeting the citizens were outnumbered by the counselors, those attending were split into family groups with two counselors assigned to every family. This format worked well and was beneficial to the family members as they could address specific mental health questions and concerns in the one-to-one setting. The NOVA team rotated among the families, checking in with each.

On Friday, although there was no school due to the preplanned holiday, it had been announced that there would be counselors at the school and some students and family members did come to the school to talk with them. The NOVA team spent the day meeting with hospital personnel and police officers, and making contact with the families of the dead and injured. In addition, the minister on the NOVA team was helping plan a memorial service to be held the next week.

Also on Friday Dr. Poland and another NOVA team member, Richard Lieberman, conducted a several hour-long processing and training session with the local caregivers. During the session plans were made for the future support of the Jonesboro community, and the caregivers were given a forum to process their own reactions to the tragedy and their role in the crisis intervention. The local caregivers expressed that they had at first been quite emotional, anxious, and uncertain about what to do but that they had utilized their professional experience to the fullest and were proud of the things they did to assist during the crisis intervention. This final session with the caregivers was a critical step in ensuring the ongoing crisis intervention effort within the community by members *of* the community.

NOVA's work continued with another follow-up meeting with some of the local clergy, and then Dr. Poland conducted an exit press conference. The NOVA team met with the prosecutors and victims' advocates to summarize the team's efforts and to make recommendations for the future. One idea that had been proposed, but was not carried out, was to process the tragedy with members of the local media, who were also affected by the events in their community. However, they were too busy continuing to cover the story and the two funerals that took place on Friday.

The NOVA team departed Saturday afternoon. Before they left Jonesboro they met as a team and processed extensively, an important step for anyone working in these types of crisis situations. Dr. Poland shared with the team that several local caregivers had said they were "the answers to their prayers." The team members knew the school and community had benefited from the objectivity and expertise they had to offer, and they agreed they couldn't have accomplished more in three days.

The following Tuesday, a memorial service was held at the Arkansas State University Convocation Center. An estimated 10,000 people attended this community memorial, which was titled a "Service for Hope and Healing." Governor Mike Huckabee, away on a family vacation, did not attend. However, Attorney General Janet Reno spoke in person, and President Clinton—while on a goodwill trip to Africa—addressed the assembly via videotape. This service did much to bring the citizens of Jonesboro, and of the state of Arkansas, together and to set them on the path to healing. It will be a difficult journey, but the Jonesboro community is a resilient one.

The ongoing support within their community and the spiritual faith of the people will help them to cope. With time, the wounds of this tragedy will not seem as raw. But Westside Middle School will never again be the same.

Natalie Brooks

Britthney Varner

Postscript: On August 11, 1998, Judge Wilson found both boys guilty of the charges filed against them. (Mitchell Johnson had pled guilty to the charges; Andrew Golden had pled not guilty by reason of insanity.) Judge Wilson sentenced them to the maximum penalty possible: incarceration in a juvenile detention facility until their 18th birthdays. Andrew Golden and Mitchell Johnson will spend seven and five years in jail, respectively. But Natalie Brooks will never have the opportunity to try out for the cheerleading squad. Among so many other things, Britthney Varner will never play another softball game, and Paige Ann Herring will never spike another volleyball. Stephanie Johnson will not have the opportunity to overcome her shyness and make more friends in the area where she had just recently moved. And Zane, the three-year old son of Shannon Wright, will continue to look under his bed for his mother, asking repeatedly, "Where's Mommy?" and "When is she going to come home?" (Labi, 1998, p. 37).

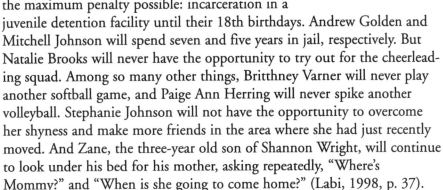

Paige Ann Herring

What We Saw

As the bells started ringing, I started to smile.
I thought it would be the perfect chance to visit with friends for awhile.
We filled the hallway like any other drill.
And exited the metal doors to see our loved ones killed.

The guns sounded like the Fourth of July, but the sight wasn't as nice.
My mind went blank, my heart stopped, and my body froze like ice.
I saw people running and others on the ground.
I just sort of stood there looking all around.

I noticed familiar faces falling down in pain.
Why was this happening? Who was to blame?
I never got to say good-bye to friends that I once knew.
I wish I could go back in time. I wish there was something I could do.

This wasn't supposed to happen. It's hard to believe it did.
I saw some of my best friends get killed by another kid.
The prom and graduation are things they will never get to see.
Their parents won't get the chance to give them car keys.

Stephanie Johnson

Shannon Wright

continued—

They won't be able to cry on our shoulders when someone breaks their hearts
Because a tragedy had to come and tear their lives apart.
It's hard to wear a smile to hide a million tears,
But I'll eventually get over it on through the years.

I know I'll see them once again, but in a sacred place
And we can pick up right where we left off, and my pain will be erased.

—*Tiffany Ishmael, Sixth Grade, Westside Middle School* ("What We Saw," 1998)

References

Associated Press. (1998, April 5). Doctor recounts treating Jonesboro victims: He says many of the injured will need counseling. *Dallas Morning News*, p. 29A.

Casey, K. (1999, March). When the shooting stopped. *Ladies' Home Journal*, pp. 10-13.

Counseling Jonesboro: The role of the school psychologists, the national crisis team, and the strength of the community. (1998, May). *Today's School Psychologist, 1*(10), 1, 10.

Egerton, B. (1998, March 25). "We had children lying everywhere," paramedic says: Rampage leaves community in shock, tears. *Dallas Morning News*, p. 1A.

Labi, N. (1998, April 6). The hunter and the choirboy. *TIME*, pp. 28-37.

Parks, S. (1998, March 28). Investigators outline evidence in shootings. *Dallas Morning News*, p. 1A.

Skiba, K. M. (1998, March 27). Arkansas students get lesson in healing. *Milwaukee Journal Sentinel*. Available online: http://www.onwis.com/forums/shoot/0327ark.stm

Staff. (1998, March 25). Arkansas boys kill 5 in ambush outside school: False fire alarm sent students, teachers outdoors to be shot. *St. Louis Post-Dispatch*, p. 1A.

What we saw. (1998, September). *NASP Communiqué, 27*(1), 31. (Excerpted from a collection of student poems entitled *Gone But Not Forgotten*, published on behalf of Westside Middle School by the National Association of School Psychologist's Children's Fund.)

chapter ONE

When a Crisis Strikes

It is our hope that every school in America will create and regularly practice a comprehensive crisis management plan. If your school has already done so, you will be better prepared than many schools to cope with a crisis when it strikes. Even with a functioning crisis management plan in place, however, most schools are not truly prepared to deal with a severe crisis and the large-scale emotionality that accompanies one. Until you've experienced such an event, you cannot fully anticipate the extent of the response that will be needed and the strength, composure, and even courage that will be required of you. Thus, we believe that you will find the recommendations in this and subsequent chapters a helpful addition to your school's plan. These guidelines represent the best practice in crisis response, as they have been successfully tested in other schools.

If your school, like the majority of schools, is caught unprepared for a crisis, this guide will be invaluable. Beginning with this chapter, which serves as a "blueprint" for the immediate crisis intervention response, this book presents instructions for use by schools and communities otherwise flying by the seat of their pants. No two crises are alike. Nor are all communities and schools. However, all school crises share some similarities, and this common ground forms the basis for the crisis response plan we describe. Incorporating the knowledge of those who have been "in the trenches" of school crisis intervention, the steps we describe are those the average school would not necessarily know to take but are ones that a trained member of a crisis intervention team would quickly identify when responding to a school crisis.

"Nothing in our previous experiences with individual student and teacher deaths prepared us for the magnitude of this horrifying event."

—Cathy Paine, Crisis Response Team Leader, Springfield, Oregon, Public Schools (Paine, 1998, p. 16)

The first section of this chapter, "Less Severe Crises," addresses a few common situations schools may face, such as student fights and bomb scares. These crises are generally resolved within a school day, and they are less likely to have any debilitating long-term effects. The rest of Chapter One (and the majority of the other chapters as well) concentrates on more severe crises: those in which a serious injury or death occurs. When these events occur, a school usually requires a number of days (and sometimes weeks, months, or even years) to regain its equilibrium.

Less Severe Crises

Student Fight

Student fights are the most common violence-related crises most schools will have to deal with. Indeed, physical attacks/fights without a weapon top the list of reported crimes in public schools, with about 190,000 such incidents reported for the 1996-97 school year (National Center for Education Statistics, 1998). If two or more students are physically fighting in your school, follow these tried-and-true guidelines:

- *Do not physically intervene.* Even young children can be dangerous when enraged, and school staff have been hurt and even killed trying to physically intervene in student fights. For example, in March 1997 a middle school guidance counselor in Lowell, Massachusetts, was seriously injured while trying to break up a student fight. During the scuffle he was knocked to the ground and kicked in the head several times by a 14-year old student (causing multiple hairline fractures to his skull). The guidance counselor was hospitalized for his injuries but never fully recovered. He collapsed and died in his home that August ("Injured Mass. Counselor," 1997). You have no legal responsibility to jeopardize your own safety by physically intervening in fights. Don't rush in, particularly if a weapon is involved.

- *Do intervene verbally.* School personnel have a legal responsibility to tell the students to stop and to summon help.

- *If possible, choose who will intervene.* The person who knows the student(s) the best should take the leadership role in interacting with them. For example, if the aggressor is a member of the track team, the track and field coach would probably be the best person to approach the student. In this case the principal should give the coach the space to do so rather than taking over simply because he or she is the principal.

- *When you encounter a student fight, take these steps:*

1. Quickly appraise the situation. Is the fight merely verbal, is there pushing and shoving, or have punches been thrown? Is there a weapon involved?

2. Send a responsible student for help from the nearest teacher, the dean of students, the assistant principal, and/or the principal. Direct this student to alert the adult about any weapon(s).

3. Calmly take charge:
   - Announce your presence so the fighters know a staff member is there. Say, for example, "I'm Jane Doe, the phys. ed. teacher, and you need to stop fighting right now."
   - Call the fighting students by name.
   - Don't invade the personal space of the combatants.
   - Try humor.
   - Do not threaten the combatants with consequences. Instead, give them choices such as, "You may go to the nurse's office or the principal's office."

4. Remove the audience, which often feeds the combatants' aggression. Tell the crowd to back up or disperse. If any students do not listen, give individuals or groups of students any direct instruction (which students are used to complying with), such as, "Sean, go to your locker"; "You girls move over to the fence"; or "Alex, go get your math book."

5. Continue to calmly talk to the fighting students, telling them to stop. If they respond to you, reply with words like, "Okay, settle down" and "Let's talk about what happened."

6. When the students have stopped actively fighting, and if adult assistance is available, physically separate the combatants. Do not use other students to keep the combatants separated.

7. If another teacher is available to cover your class, escort the students to the office. Do not send the fighting students to the office unattended.

   If another teacher is not available to cover your class:
   - Take the students to your class.
   - Separate the fighters in your room.
   - Give them paper and pencils, and tell them to each write their version of what happened. (This exercise is designed to keep the students busy until an administrator arrives rather than as a consequence of the fighting per se.)
   - When help arrives, that person will escort the students to the office.

8. If necessary, obtain medical assistance for the combatants, either from the school nurse or by summoning an ambulance if the injuries are severe. (Students can, and have been known to, break bones and inflict lacerations requiring stitches in fights without weapons.)

9. The school administrator should call the police and follow the appropriate procedures for providing legal consequences.

Threatening Person Outside the Building

If a threatening person (or persons), such as someone with a weapon, is spotted outside your school building, the school administrator should take the following steps:

1. Call the police immediately.

2. Make an announcement over the intercom. If your school has a preestablished warning signal or phrase that will notify the school staff of the threat without panicking the students, then use it. (One example provided in Cypress-Fairbanks Independent School District, 1996, is: "We have a visitor outside the building. I repeat, we have a visitor outside the building.") Otherwise, use a straightforward announcement (such as, "We have an intruder outside the building. Go into lockdown mode."). A benefit of the latter is that substitutes and other legitimate visitors in the building will be able to understand the threat ("What Can We Do," 1998, p. 19).

3. Direct the custodians to quickly lock all the outside doors. If any students are caught outside, and your school does not have a preplanned location (such as an exterior building) at which students have been instructed to gather in such situations, the playground monitor or another staff member should instruct them to take cover behind walls, playground equipment, or other objects, or to drop to the ground and stay there until directed to do otherwise.

4. Alert the school's security staff (if applicable).

5. Instruct all teachers to close and lock their classroom doors and turn off their classroom lights. The teachers should keep all students in their classrooms, away from the door and windows, and take a roll call.

6. Administrators should cautiously walk through the halls to locate any students who may be out of class, giving them directions about where to go.

7. Direct all office personnel to stay away from the front door and windows.

8. Keep the faculty apprised of the situation and give the "all clear" announcement when appropriate.

If gunshots are fired:

- All staff and students in the main building should lie down on the floor or get under a desk immediately and remain there until the "all clear" announcement is made.
- Staff and students in portable classrooms should lie flat on the floor or crouch under desks with lights turned off and doors locked. Attempting to move students to the main building could make them targets for a shooter.
- Staff and students on the playground or in common areas should lie down on the ground or take shelter behind playground equipment and remain there until the "all clear" announcement is made. Running for and clustering in front of the school building doors could make the students targets for a shooter.

Armed Intruder Inside the Building

The first staff member to see or encounter an armed intruder in your building should immediately alert the office (or signal a nearby staff member to contact the office). The school administrator should then take the following steps. (Neither the staff member nor the administrator should confront and possibly provoke the intruder.)

1. Call the police immediately. When the police arrive, provide them with a map of your building.

2. Make an announcement over the intercom. If your school has a pre-established warning signal or phrase that will notify the school staff of the threat without panicking the students, then use it. (One example provided in Cypress-Fairbanks Independent School District, 1996, is: "We have a visitor inside the building. I repeat, we have a visitor inside the building.") Otherwise, use a straightforward announcement (such as, "We have an intruder inside the building. Go into lockdown mode."). A benefit of the latter is that substitutes and other legitimate visitors in the building will be able to understand the threat ("What Can We Do," 1998, p. 19).

3. Direct the custodians to lock appropriate inside doors to isolate the intruder from the students and staff, if they can do this without jeopardizing their own safety.

4. Alert the school's security staff (if applicable).

5. Instruct all teachers to close and lock their classroom doors and turn off their lights. The teachers should keep all students in their classrooms away from the door and windows, and take a roll call.

6. Administrators should cautiously walk through the halls to locate any students who may be out of class, giving them directions about where to go.

7. Direct everyone (faculty, front office staff, and students) to lie down on the floor or get under a desk immediately and remain there until the police have apprehended the intruder.

8. When okayed by the police, make an "all clear" announcement.

For those outside of main building classrooms:

- Staff and students in portable classrooms should lie flat on the floor or crouch under desks with lights turned off and doors locked. Students should not be moved to the main building until the "all clear" announcement has been made.

- Staff and students on the playground or in common areas should lie down on the ground or take shelter behind playground equipment and remain there until the "all clear" announcement has been made.

Bomb Threat

As stated in Goldstein and Conoley (1997), "Bombing is a rare but very serious aggressive act, causing great bodily, site, and psychological damage" (p. 15). Experience has shown that many bomb threats called into schools are made by students themselves. Yet whether the threats are made by students or others, real bombs detonate in schools every year. According to the *School Security Report* (cited in Goldstein & Conoley, 1997), in the school years 1993-1995, for example, there were 42 reported incidents in which bombs were found in schools in 20 states. Of the 47 bombs involved, there were 29 explosions, 12 bombs found and removed, and six fakes. These bombs were placed in all levels of schools, from elementary to high schools. Pipe bombs were the most common type used, as well as Molotov cocktails, chemical bombs, dynamite, live grenades, and even a military shell.

While 47 bombs is frightening enough, that number is a vast underrepresentation of the number of bomb threats received by schools, at least in some districts. In Anne Arundel County, Maryland, for example, bomb sniffing dogs have "... worked full schedules thanks to the more than 100 bomb threats during the past year [1997]" ("What Can We Do," 1998, p. 19). There are thousands of bomb threats made to schools nationwide each year; from practical experience some school representatives have estimated that there are 500-1,000 threats for every real bomb.

Even though the majority of these bomb threats are just threats, each must be taken seriously, as bombs *are* found in schools. If your school receives a bomb threat, don't do what one Texas principal did: He panicked, grabbed the intercom, and yelled for everyone to evacuate the building five minutes before the bell for the winter break. He even forgot to identify himself, so many students thought the announcement was a prank and refused to follow evacuation procedures (Pitcher & Poland, 1992).

Steps for a bomb threat

If your building receives a bomb threat, the following steps should be carried out:

1. The receptionist receiving the call should stay calm and ask for and write down the following information (National School Safety Center, 1989):

   - Where is the bomb?
   - What type of bomb is it?
   - When will it go off?
   - Why was the bomb planted?
   - Who are you?

   He or she should also make note of the following:

   - Characteristics of the caller's voice (i.e., gender, approximate age, any accent, etc.)
   - Background noises
   - Time of the call
   - The number being called from (if "caller ID" is installed on the school's phone lines)

2. While the receptionist keeps the caller on the line, on another line the administrator (or someone else in the office) should call the police.

3. The head administrator must decide whether to evacuate the building or to simply alert the staff. Key factors to consider are:

   - The recommendations of the police
   - The level of unrest and violence in the community
   - Weather conditions the students and staff would be exposed to during the evacuation
   - The information provided by the caller about the specified time of detonation
   - The suspected age and credibility level of the caller

> "Just imagine if you didn't do anything [about a bomb threat] and something happened?"
>
> —Tom Crowley, Dallas, Texas, Bureau of Alcohol, Tobacco, and Firearms (ATF) spokesperson ("Alarming," 1999)

We recommend that school officials err on the side of caution. Even young children can now download from the Internet directions for constructing homemade bombs and can obtain the materials to make a bomb. In Wimberley, Texas, for example, authorities who searched the homes of four 14-year old boys who were arrested in April 1999 for allegedly plotting to blow up their junior high school "… found gunpowder and bomb-building instructions downloaded from the Internet" (Drummond, 1999, p. 29). When police searched the home of a 15-year old boy who opened fire on his classmates in Springfield,

Oregon, in May 1998 they found two pipe bombs, three larger bombs, and bomb recipes the boy had downloaded with his personal computer (King & Muir, 1998). During the nation's deadliest school shooting incident—at Columbine High School in Littleton, Colorado, in April 1999—the two suspects detonated as many as 15 bombs during the massacre (Obmascik, 1999). A bomb squad later found nearly 60 bombs hidden within the school building, many attached to timers (Obmascik, 1999; "Squad Found," 1999). The potentially deadliest was a 20-pound "propane barbecue tank-bomb … packed inside a duffel bag with a wired gasoline can—and surrounded with nails and BBs for maximum killing power." Authorities believe this bomb suggests that the two suspects had plotted to blow up the school (Obmascik, 1999). A federal agent commented that the bombs "… could have been assembled in an afternoon with less than $200 of materials …. All components [could have been] purchased legally and easily at many hardware, sporting goods, and gun stores …" (Obmascik, 1999).

If a decision is made to evacuate the school:

a. The fire alarm should be sounded.

b. The building should be silently (so that any instructions can be heard) cleared, following the exit procedures practiced during fire drills.

c. During the evacuation, one student from each class should be asked to see that everyone is out of the classroom and close the door upon exiting.

d. Each teacher should carry a map of the school during the evacuation.
If an area is barricaded, the next nearest emergency exit should be used.

e. All teachers should bring their grade books and take roll when they reach their designated area outside the building. All teachers should keep their students assembled and supervise them closely.

f. Some schools insist that instruction continue outside the classroom during the evacuation time to both ensure that students do not miss class time and to lessen the motivation for prank bomb calls in the future. (Some schools have even canceled a student holiday to make up lost academic time due to a bomb threat—a real deterrent!)

g. When okayed by the police or bomb team, the school administrator should make an "all clear" announcement.

A common practice is to have crisis team members remain in the school and search for the bomb while the rest of the staff and students are evacuating the building. It is critical that all personnel charged with searching for bombs have training about types of bombs, what they look like, and where they might be hidden in a school. This training should have been provided by law enforcement/bomb squad personnel.

If a decision is made to instead alert the faculty:

a. Your school administrator should make an announcement over the intercom. If your school has a preestablished warning signal or phrase that will notify the school staff of the threat without panicking the students, then use it. (One example is: "We have an item lost inside the building. I repeat, we have an item lost inside the building.") Otherwise, use a straightforward announcement such as, "We have received a bomb threat. Stay calm and await further instructions. Teachers, please carefully search your classrooms." The advantage of the latter is that substitutes and other legitimate visitors in the building will be able to understand the threat ("What Can We Do," 1998, p. 19).

b. Staff members should begin to search for the bomb. When the announcement of the threat is heard, all teachers who are not in class, all administrators, and the custodial staff should meet in the front lobby of the school to help look for the bomb. The most common locations for bombs reported by the *School Security Report* (cited in Goldstein & Conoley, 1997, p. 15) were:

- Boys' bathrooms
- Student lockers/locker areas
- Principal's office
- Parking lots
- Hallways
- Windows/skylights
- Trophy cases
- Planters
- Stairwells
- Water fountains
- Trash cans/dumpsters

Other locations that should be searched are:

- All other restrooms
- Cafeteria and kitchen
- Teacher workrooms/lounges
- Gymnasium
- Coaches' office(s)
- Gymnasium locker rooms
- Heating/utility rooms
- Common areas and playgrounds

c. All searchers should report their findings to the front office.

d. Teachers who are in class should check their rooms in a casual manner (i.e., without alarming the students) for any suspicious items. Filing cabinets, trash cans, cabinets, and so forth, should be checked:

- If any suspicious items are found, the searcher should immediately alert the front office, and should not touch or move the items.

- If an item is found that is obviously dangerous, the searcher should evacuate the area immediately and then alert the front office.

4. When the police arrive, they should be provided with a map of your building and blueprints, if available.

5. When the situation is resolved, the administrator should make an "all clear" announcement.

The First Hour of a Severe Crisis

When a crisis strikes at school—particularly a severe crisis—there will be three "waves" of response: a wave of police/medical personnel, a wave of media, and a wave of parents (Peterson & Straub, 1992). For school personnel trying to cope with the crisis, these waves may feel more like a tsunami than those washing rhythmically onto a shore. They will strike almost simultaneously and with tremendous force! Obviously, one or two people alone cannot deal with this onslaught. The school administrator will need a team of people to help address the various aspects of the crisis.

"Throngs of frightened parents and neighbors filled the sidewalks and pressed past the gathering media to reach [Thurston High School]."

—Cathy Paine, Crisis Response Team Leader, Springfield, Oregon, Public Schools (Paine, 1998, p. 16)

If your school already has a crisis response team in place, you will be ready to address the crisis. But when a crisis strikes in a school without a crisis response team, an impromptu team will need to be quickly organized. Fortunately, members of the school community who can remain relatively calm in a crisis and can assume a leadership role will immediately emerge. In Jonesboro, Arkansas, these people were the school psychologists and school administrators. In your school, these people will ideally be the administrators, counselors and school psychologists, the school nurse (if you have one), and security staff/peace officers/constables (if applicable); they may also include members of the teaching and support staffs. The primary roles these people will need to fill are the following:

- *Crisis Coordinator.* The Crisis Coordinator is preferably the head administrator of your school. Another option is for the administrator and a school psychologist to co-coordinate the crisis response team (Lieberman, 1999). Either way, it is the head administrator of the affected school, as opposed to the superintendent or someone else from the central office, who should lead the crisis intervention effort. This person will coordinate the crisis intervention and remain available and visible to the school community. He or she must be steady by nature, a leader who is able to calm and empower others. In addition, he or she should be an orderly and clear thinker and someone who is able to delegate efficiently.

- *Medical Liaison.* If your school has a nurse, he or she is the logical person to fill this role. This person (or persons) will administer first aid, triage the injured, keep a record of who is injured and where they are transported (and communicate this information to the Parent/Family Liaison), and serve as a liaison between the school and hospital personnel.

- *Security Liaison.* If your school has a security officer, constable, or peace officer, he or she is the appropriate person to fill this role. This person (or persons) will secure the crime scene and evidence until the police arrive. He or she will also limit access to the campus by the media.

- *Media Liaison.* If your school (or district) has a public information/relations (PR) representative, he or she is the logical person to fill this role. This person must be authoritative yet sympathetic and preferably have training in public speaking. He or she will hold press conferences and keep the media updated as the crisis unfolds. Note, however, that at some point in a severe crisis the press will want to hear from the head administrator of your school (and likely the superintendent, as well). If the Media Liaison is not also the head administrator, he or she can help prepare the administrator for the press conference/interview(s).

- *Parent/Family Liaison.* This person (or persons) will provide parents and other family members with verbal and written information about the crisis and make sure the information communicated to them is consistent. (The Parent/Family Liaison will likely need to delegate part of this task to the school secretaries who answer the phones for your school.) The Parent/Family Liaison will deliver injury/death notifications, meet parents and other family members when they arrive at the school, and plan the family/community meeting(s). Because this will be a sensitive assignment, a member of your school's counseling staff or an administrator would be an ideal person to fill this role.

- *Counseling Liaison.* The school psychologist or counselor is the obvious person to fill the role of Counseling Liaison. This person (or persons) will work to calm students, staff, and family members during the crisis. He or she also will provide counseling sessions (both small group and individual) for students and staff after the crisis and advocate for opportunities for staff and students to express their emotions.

- *Campus Liaison*. This person will communicate the specifics of the crisis to the school staff and give the staff guidance on how they can assist in the crisis management. The Campus Liaison will also greet and briefly "interview" any volunteers who come to your school unasked to assist with the crisis response, assign any such helpers their tasks for the day, and coordinate their activities. Further, he or she will help to evaluate the scope of the crisis and the need for outside assistance and will discuss this need with the Crisis Coordinator. A member of your school's counseling staff or an administrator is the logical person to fill this role.

Within the first ten to 15 minutes of a crisis, the head administrator of your school should assign one or more people to each of these roles. This task should not require an inordinate amount of discussion, nor should school bureaucracy or politics play a part. Simply find out what each person feels most comfortable handling, take a few minutes to make sure everyone's clear about who is doing what, and then jump into action. (*NOTE*: The crisis response recommendations in the remainder of this book are written for this crisis response team, with the exception of sections labeled specifically for parents, clergy members, caregivers in addition to your team, and other area schools. In some places the most appropriate team member to handle a task is specified for clarity. In many cases, however, it is assumed that your crisis response team members will generally fill the roles as outlined above. For example, the Media Liaison would likely hold press conferences, and thus would be the person carrying out the recommendations in the media chapter. The Counseling Liaison would likely coordinate counseling sessions for students and staff, thus that chapter section is written with that person in mind. And so forth. Note, however, that any time a certain team member is specified, this specification is only a guideline. By nature, crisis response is chaotic and fluid, and it is often beneficial to set aside rigid perceptions of workplace responsibilities and relationships. It is more important that the tasks we identify be addressed than who, exactly, will address them.)

"Schools are hierarchical and that goes completely against the grain of crisis."

—Mary Margaret Kerr, Director of School and Community Outreach, STAR-WPIC, University of Pittsburgh Medical Center ("When Disaster Strikes," 1998)

Now that your crisis response team members know who is going to be primarily responsible for your school's crisis response, what do you do exactly? The actions taken—or not taken—during the first hour of a crisis will set the stage for the rest of the intervention. They will, in large part, determine the degree of success of the overall crisis response. *There are six main tasks for the first hour, the first two of which will need to happen immediately:*

1. Address human safety and provide medical assistance.
2. Summon help.
3. Secure the crime scene and contain the media.
4. Verify the facts and prepare a Crisis Fact Sheet.
5. Deliver injury/death notifications.
6. Communicate with parents/other family members.

NOTE: These six tasks will probably take longer than an hour. The point is that these are the actions you must start with right away, even if your crisis response team continues working on some of them throughout the entire first day of the crisis. The remainder of this chapter describes these tasks in detail. The amount of material covered may seem at first glance over-whelming, but it is the lion's share of the crisis response. Chapter Two expands on these tasks—outlining the continuing crisis response through-out the day—with some additional information provided about meetings you'll want to hold the evening of the crisis.

Human Safety/Medical Assistance

It's not possible, of course, to detail every conceivable type of violent crisis and school setting in which such crises can occur. Your school's crisis may occur in the cafeteria, for example. In another school, the crisis might occur in the parking lot. The decisions you make must be based upon your school's individual architecture and the unique set of circumstances happening at your school. That having been said, the following guidelines will be helpful.

Disarming the perpetrator(s)

School staff are under no legal obligation to sacrifice their own physical safety by confronting an armed aggressor. However this does not take into consideration the obligations of their own conscience. Your reactions, if you find yourself near an armed assailant, will be spontaneous. It would be easy to make a blanket statement such as "Don't be a hero." Yet in violent crises, heroic actions often save lives. In February 1996, a teacher in Moses Lake, Washington, tackled a 14-year old boy who had just shot a teacher and two students; the teacher was unharmed and likely prevented more injuries (Egan, 1998). Teacher Shannon Wright was not so fortunate when she shielded one of her students from the gunfire at a school near Jonesboro, Arkansas, with her own body (*see the case study*). Her actions cost her her life, but because of what she did a little girl named Emma Pittman is alive today.

These types of actions cannot be preplanned. If you are physically close to an armed assailant, you can't predict how you will react. Follow your heart. Follow your instincts. Know that if you intervene physically, you could lose your life. Also recognize that no matter what you choose to do, or not do, you will likely second-guess your decision later. Many school personnel involved in crises are later tortured by doubts about whether they did the correct thing during the crisis.

As a general rule, first send a responsible student or another staff member to the front office for help. Once you've done that, verbal intervention, when possible, is the safest course of action. And it is best for that intervention to be done by someone the aggressor knows and likes or respects, if possible. During the school shooting in West Paducah, Kentucky (*see the case study*), it was Ben Strong, a friend of the 14-year old shooter, who stepped in front of him and begged him to stop firing. Authorities there say that "… it was Strong's words that persuaded the freshman to let go of the pistol …" and prevented more casualties (Bowles, 1997, p. 1A).

Administering first aid

The Medical Liaison—and others available—should do everything possible to assist victims of crises while waiting for the ambulance to arrive. The first thing to do when people are injured is to send a responsible student or another staff member to the front office and nurse's office for help. If your school has a nurse, he or she will be trained in performing cardiopulmonary resuscitation (CPR) and administering first aid. The Medical Liaison should bring your school's first aid kit(s) to the scene as quickly as possible.

Even if there is only one victim, the Medical Liaison will likely require assistance in helping that person. If others on the staff have first aid skills as well, solicit their help. (It may be necessary to summon them by making an announcement over the intercom.) In Jonesboro, a teacher who found a student shot in the leg and losing blood rapidly ran for a first aid kit and fashioned a tourniquet (Gegax, Adler, & Pedersen, 1998). Her quick thinking undoubtedly saved a life.

If you are witness to a crisis and there is no one with medical training in your building, at the very least offer the victims comfort. Try to keep them warm (covering them with blankets, jackets, etc.) and quiet. Hold their hands and/or touch their faces, and speak in a reassuring manner. Follow these basic first aid guidelines:

- Don't move victims unless they are in immediate danger where they are.
- If you suspect a spinal injury, don't change the position of the body, not even by cradling or turning a victim's head. *Signs of a spinal injury include weakness/numbness in an extremity, inability to move an extremity, and lack of feeling in an extremity.*

- Do not offer victims anything to drink or eat or medicines of any kind.

- *Do not use a tourniquet unless blood loss is so severe and rapid as to be immediately life threatening.* Because it cuts off the oxygen-carrying blood supply to tissue below the wound, a tourniquet may result in the loss of a limb.

- CPR is most effectively and safely performed by someone trained in this procedure. However, if there is no one trained in CPR at the scene and a victim is not breathing, someone needs to begin CPR and continue it until the ambulance arrives. *Do not give chest compressions if there is a heartbeat—doing so may cause the heart to stop beating!*

While waiting for professional help to arrive, it is also important to identify every person who is wounded. The Medical Liaison should put identification wristbands on the dead and injured for use at the hospital or write their names on their hands in ink. If the victims are students, pull their emergency notification forms on file in the front office and photocopy them. Next, make a list of those killed or injured—with the extent/type of injuries, if you can determine this—and give a copy of the list to the Parent/Family Liaison (along with copies of the emergency notification forms). It's important to keep a copy of the list yourself, as you will need it when you accompany the victims to the hospital.

The Parent/Family Liaison will attempt to contact the parents of the wounded children. But if they cannot be reached immediately, it is still crucial to provide medical assistance in a crisis. Do not delay in securing medical attention when an emergency is so severe it suggests immediate hospitalization.

See "Injury/Death Notification" later in this chapter for tips on making these calls.

Protecting students and staff

The safest place for students and staff in the event of a severe crisis will depend upon where the incident is taking place and the unique circumstances. There will be very little time to react, and if crisis drills have never been conducted at your school, you cannot predict what your students and staff will do when the crisis occurs. The following are a few simple suggestions that may be helpful:

- If gunshots are fired, everyone should drop and roll to the nearest cover (e.g., a desk, cabinet, table, other heavy furniture, playground equipment) or wall. Everyone should remain on the floor/ground with their hands covering their heads.

- If shots are being fired from outside the building, people should roll to a position under the window closest to the direction from which the shots are being fired. They should take shelter under a desk if possible and remain on the floor/ground with their hands covering their heads.

- It is natural to want to run. But if shots are being fired, running may make a person a target for the shooter. A fast crawl to safety is a better procedure.

- If you need to evacuate the building, sound the fire alarm and follow the procedures you would use for a fire drill. All teachers should keep their students assembled, supervise them closely, and take a roll call of their classes.

- If told to remain in their classrooms, teachers should lock the doors, turn off the lights, and keep their students away from the windows and door. After quickly taking a roll call of their students, they should instruct everyone to remain quiet and still until an "all clear" announcement is made.

- If students and staff are outside on the playground or in common areas when a violent crisis occurs, they should remain on the ground outside the building or take shelter behind playground equipment until an "all clear" announcement is made.

- If students and staff are in portable classrooms when a violent crisis occurs, they should remain there—with doors locked and lights turned off—until an "all clear" announcement is made.

To begin to regain control after a violent incident, the goal should be to get students and staff back to their classrooms as quickly as possible, as soon as it is safe for them to move. In general, the best place for students and staff to be is in their own classroom (or home room), because: (1) you can better account for the students and protect them in classrooms, and (2) you can begin to deal with the effects of the violence most efficiently at the classroom level. During any severe school crisis, the Counseling Liaison should quickly report to the scene to begin calming students and staff and directing those who do not require medical attention back to their classrooms. If the suspected perpetrator(s) are still on the loose, teachers should lock their classroom doors until an "all clear" announcement is made.

When the police arrive, they will want to question witnesses to the violence. If many people saw what happened, have everyone return to their classrooms, and the police can sort out the witnesses later. If only one or a few people saw what happened, they should wait for the police in the front office or counselor's office. If possible, have someone who is close to the witness(es)—such as a staff member—wait with them, as well as an administrator.

It will be helpful for the Counseling Liaison or another member of the counseling staff to calm and comfort the witnesses. They may need to be "put back together" to some extent before then can make sense and accurately report what they saw. But the counselor should not begin providing in-depth mental health assistance until the police have talked with the witnesses. Note that the police have the authority to question students without either their parents or a counselor present.

Summoning Help

Police/medical personnel

In a severe crisis your first call should be to summon emergency services, period. In most parts of the country, this is done by dialing 911. In some rural areas this is done by dialing the operator—0. The person to make this call should be whoever knows what has happened and can get to a phone first. The person making the call might be directed to do so by the Crisis Coordinator, but that is not necessary. Anyone can make the call—including a student, if necessary—but it must be made immediately. Time is of the essence.

The caller should provide as much of the following information as possible:

- The location of the school (if your area's computerized emergency system does not provide this information to the emergency operator automatically).
- The nature of the emergency (e.g., bombing, stabbing, rape, gang fight, suicide, hostage situation).
- The number of victims and their condition.
- The status of the suspected perpetrator(s).
- Directions to the scene (e.g., "Turn into the back parking lot and go to the end of the building. Come in the south door."). The caller should direct the emergency responders to look for school personnel, who will give them further directions to the site.

Whoever places the call should remain on the line with the emergency operator until directed by him or her to hang up or until the emergency personnel arrive.

Post a staff member outside the entrance the emergency personnel will use. When the police, ambulance, and/or fire engines arrive, he or she can flag them down and direct them to the scene.

When the paramedics/emergency medical technicians (EMTs) finish at the scene, the Medical Liaison (and others, if necessary) should accompany the injured to the hospital. The rule of thumb is to have one staff member per ambulance. You will probably not be allowed to ride in the ambulance itself, so you should quickly follow in your own car. Drive carefully! You will be shaken, and you need to stay in one piece yourself in order to assist others. Remember to bring with you a copy of the pertinent emergency notification forms and the list of those killed or injured.

Throughout the day, the Medical Liaison should keep the school—in particular the Crisis Coordinator and the Parent/Family Liaison—updated on the status of the injured by calling from the hospital. Also, if your school is in a big city, the victims may be taken to more than one hospital (e.g., one may accept only children, another may be designated to receive trauma). The Medical Liaison should be sure to tell the school to which hospital(s) the victims were taken.

Central office

The next call should be to your district's central office. The Crisis Coordinator should alert the following people of the situation:

- The superintendent.
- Associate superintendent(s).
- Any district public information/relations (PR) staff.
- Members of any preexisting crisis team from within your district.
- The school board.
- The facilities/plant manager. This person has keys to all of the district's school buildings as well as blueprints of the schools and can do such things as turn on/off power and water, access the school's kitchen for food (if necessary), and so forth.
- The supervisor of transportation (i.e., of the bus drivers). (The transportation personnel who service your school should be notified so that they have time to process their own reactions to the crisis and are not surprised by the bad news when they arrive to pick up the students.)

After the initial crisis response, you might want to request additional assistance. See "Help to Request" in Chapter Four.

In the best case, the call you make to the office of the superintendent will set in motion the administrative calling tree for your district so that you are not tied up making these other calls. Your central office also should call any appropriate city leaders/agencies (e.g., emergency management personnel, the mayor, the county judge). Next, call any of your administrators and other school leaders (e.g., principal, assistant principal, dean of students, school psychologist) who happened to be away from the building at the time of the crisis.

On October 1, 1997, in Pearl, Mississippi, a 16-year old student shot two classmates and wounded seven others. Said the school's attorney "Skip" Jernigan: "The school board was very visible and accessible and the outstanding job they did was very much appreciated by the community."

("School Officials," 1997)

In a severe crisis, it is critical for the top person in the school system to get involved and to physically go to the scene. Surprisingly, they don't always do that. No matter what the superintendent (or associate superintendent) had on his or her agenda for the day, those tasks should be immediately dropped and he or she should go to the school in crisis. It's not that he or she has to do anything earthshaking at the scene other than obtain the facts and show support. But the presence of the top leader is very important to show the school and community that the district cares about what has happened and is making every effort to deal with the crisis.

Remember that while it is important for the leader of the school system to go to the school and confer with your crisis team, it is your school's head administrator (e.g., the principal) who should publicly "call the shots" during the crisis intervention, for two main reasons:

1. It's your principal's job to run his or her school, and he or she will be the one to continue to deal with the aftereffects of the crisis on a day-to-day basis. Thus he or she must be viewed as the leader of the crisis intervention.

2. The principal knows the strengths and personalities of the staff, the personalities of the students and school climate, and specific school operating procedures better than someone who works in the central office.

Area schools

After summoning help for your school, the Crisis Coordinator should alert all the other schools in the area so they can take safety precautions as well. Incidents have occurred in which more than one school was targeted for violence. In the fall of 1984 in Houston, Texas, for example, an 11-year old boy was shot while raising the American flag in front of his school. The gunman had already fired on another school down the street, shooting at and missing some kids walking into that school. After shooting the 11-year old, he went to a third school and began firing against the side of the building. This situation highlights the need to communicate to your neighboring schools immediately.

When other schools nearby hear that something is happening—or even hear gunfire or an explosion if they are close enough—they will naturally be concerned for the safety of their students. In Jonesboro, Arkansas, when the staff of University Heights Elementary School (12 miles away from the Westside school complex) heard there was a school shooting, they wisely locked their school's outside doors and kept the students in their classrooms. Said school librarian Robin Nichols, "At the time, we just knew it was a shooting. We didn't know if there were going to be other happenings in the city." The school kept their doors locked for about 40 minutes, until it was clear the shooting at Westside was an isolated incident (Egerton, 1998).

Safety measures that should be taken at all area schools include getting everybody inside—and keeping them inside—until school personnel figure out what's really happening, as they did at University Heights in Jonesboro. Then, if the perpetrator(s) have not been apprehended, every event that involves school children should be canceled. Students also should be supervised closely when leaving school. In such situations, it is prudent to advise parents to pick up their children after school.

Besides safety, another reason to alert the other schools in your district is that there may be people in those schools with an urgent need to know what is happening, such as siblings and other family members. In Jonesboro, Joy Rapert, a second grade teacher at University Heights "… spent a harrowing 40 minutes waiting for word about her two grandchildren who attend[ed] Westside, and [her] daughter, a speech therapist there" (Egerton, 1998).

Additionally, there will be more subtle ripples of effect throughout the district that extend beyond family members. For example, a victim's best friend might attend another school in the area, or a teacher elsewhere may have coached a team on which injured students played. Depending upon the severity of the crisis, not every district principal has to stop what he or she is doing to immediately respond to what happened 20 or more miles away, but principals do need to know the facts so that they can respond well should something come up within their schools related to your school's crisis.

Finally, in a major, city-wide crisis—such as the Oklahoma City bombing in 1995—all the city's/district's school principals should meet and communicate about the crisis as quickly as possible. The goal would be to coordinate crisis response efforts on a district-wide basis. This group effort will be helpful any time a crisis directly impacts more than one school, regardless of whether the schools are in the same district.

While it is important to notify other schools when a severe crisis occurs, it may be difficult for you to make all these contacts as your school's phones will be ringing off the hook. Ask staff at the central office to alert area schools, beginning with those closest to you and working their way out from there. Be sure to notify the administration and counseling staff of schools known to have family members of victims and/or potential victims, and "feeder schools"—those with logical connections to victims such as a victim's last-year school or one from which he or she recently transferred.

Regardless of who contacts the area schools, use a communication method that is faster than the phone when possible. Computer e-mail (especially when a distribution list is already in place) will be the most effective choice, if available. "Walkie-talkies" are another option.

Securing the Crime Scene/Containing the Media

To assist the police, the Security Liaison should attempt to secure the crisis area as soon after the incident as possible. Obviously, providing medical assistance to those in need takes precedence over this activity. Do not impede the movements of any medical caregivers at the scene.

Concentrate on protecting from (accidental or purposeful) tampering any weapon used or anything else that could be considered physical evidence (e.g., ammunition casings, personal items of the perpetrator[s] such as ear plugs, etc.). Do not let anyone other than the police pick these items up or accidentally step on them. Keep students, staff, and onlookers out of the critical area.

While these efforts will be a tremendous help in the investigation of any crime committed, it is important to recognize that the police will assume control of the scene when they arrive. Do everything possible to support their activities from that point on, even if that means simply staying out of their way.

Another aspect of securing the scene is to keep the media out of the area. In a severe crisis, the media will arrive almost immediately and it's important to be ready for them. Although your school should cooperate fully with the media later, in the first hour of the crisis response the key is to simply contain them. The Security Liaison (with back-up help, which could include the police and, if absolutely necessary, the National Guard) should quickly seal off the school and gain control by stopping the media's entrance. It may be necessary to set up physical barriers around the school ("Control the Media," 1998).

See "Cooperating With the Media" in Chapter Three.

The best scenario would be to send the media to another location, such as the central office or a neighboring school. Realistically, you'll probably only be able to hold them off across the street. Tell them that a school representative will be out to make a statement as soon as the facts are confirmed and that all members of the school community are no longer in danger and are receiving medical attention if necessary.

In Jonesboro, the scene was too chaotic and devastating after the shooting at Westside Middle School for anyone to intervene with the media, who descended on the school in great numbers. In contrast, after a severe crisis at a Houston high school in May 1998, two news helicopters tried to land on the high school grounds. The school constables anticipated the media response, however, and told the pilots, "No, there's so much going on, we don't want you landing here at the high school." If they had not been so prepared, they wouldn't have been out there quickly enough to wave off the helicopters and the helicopters would have landed in the school's parking lot.

Media representatives may be extremely persistent and argue about staying off the school grounds. They may say such things as because they're taxpayers, they have the right to enter the public school. Arizona has a law specifically protecting schools from such interference and legally gives schools there the right to limit access to their campuses. Regardless of whether your state has such a law—or you know if it does or not—continue to stand firm in the face of media protests. You can borrow language from Arizona's "Interference With the Peaceful Conduct of Educational Institutions" law to help you control the media verbally. That law states:

> *A person commits interference with the peaceful conduct of an educational institution by knowingly … going upon … the property of any educational institution in violation of any rule of such institution or … in such manner as to deny or interfere with the lawful use of such property…. When … an officer or employee designated … to maintain order has reasonable grounds to believe that any person … [is] committing [such an] act …, such officer or employee may order such person to leave the property of the educational institution.*

> *… Such rules shall govern … all members of the public while on the property…. "Property" means all land, buildings, and other facilities owned, operated, or controlled by … [the] educational institution and devoted to educational purposes.*

> *… [This law] may be enforced by any peace officer … wherever and whenever a violation occurs…. Interference with the peaceful conduct of educational institutions is a class 1 misdemeanor* (Arizona Revised Statute 13-2911, cited in Cummings, 1998).

When containing the media, do not behave in a combative manner, and do not engage in a physical scuffle with media representatives. Simply continue to repeat yourself calmly using an authoritative tone of voice. Make clear that "… harassment or exploitation by the media will not be tolerated in any form" (Stevenson, 1994, p. 197).

When the father of a student shot at Westside Middle School near Jonesboro, Arkansas, arrived at the school, his daughter had already been transported to the hospital. "'I didn't know if she was dead or alive,' he said. Traffic was bottlenecked … and he had to walk a mile back to his vehicle at the school. 'It was about two hours of not knowing,' he said [about trying] to make his way to the hospital. 'It was the worst two hours of my life.'"

(Watkins & Hinkle, 1999, p. 15A)

It is extremely unlikely that there would be any negative consequences (e.g., a lawsuit) resulting from your protecting the best interests of the students and the crisis operations of your school in this manner. The school board could back up your actions by citing common policies that state that under certain circumstances (such as an emergency/crisis) the building principal has the right to authorize the clearing of everybody from the grounds except for the students and staff who have a reason to be there.

A final security concern is controlling the flow of traffic. The Security Liaison should immediately send a member of the security staff (or another school staff member) outside to control the flow of traffic in front of and around the school. It is essential that vehicles of family members and media representatives descending on the school not block access by emergency vehicles (Lieberman, 1999).

Verifying Information/Crisis Fact Sheet

It is important to communicate accurate information to your school's staff and students, the central office, other schools in your district, parents, the community as a whole, and the media as quickly as possible.

Getting the facts

A point that cannot be overemphasized is verification. You must get it right. You must be absolutely certain you know who was killed or injured, the exact status of victims' conditions, and other important details about the crisis incident. When dealing with matters of such importance, the information communicated must be accurate.

A verification example: In the Houston school system in April 1987, a kindergarten teacher underwent brain surgery. Her best friend, another teacher at the school, was at the hospital. The surgeon came out and told the teacher they had "lost" her friend. The teacher called the school counselor, who told the school psychologist, and together they went into the kindergarten classroom and told 22 children that their teacher was never returning. The kindergartners went home from their half-day program very sad about their teacher. Then the fellow teacher called from the hospital and said, "She's not really dead. She's on life support." So, the school counselor and psychologist had to pick up the phone and call 22 parents.

Double check the facts, triple check, and think the situation through. You have to make sure that you have the complete set of facts, and an important first step is to consider the source. Admittedly, if an act of violence occurs right in front of you, then you have the facts. You know the date, time, and location of the incident, who the perpetrator was, and who the victim was. What you may not know—because you are not a doctor—is the exact medical condition of the victim.

Rumors fly fast and furiously in a crisis. Accept information as fact only from reputable sources, such as your school's head administrator and/or professional emergency personnel (e.g., paramedics/EMTs, firefighters, police officers, hospital staff). All crisis information must be verified at the highest levels, and *no one should publicly state or repeat what he or she thinks is happening until the information is confirmed* by such leaders. Giving no information is better than giving incorrect information. Don't be afraid to say "I don't know," "We will update you as soon as we know more," or "You need to ask (the Crisis Coordinator) for that information."

For guidelines on speaking with parents and family members of affected students and staff, see "Injury/Death Notification" later in this chapter.

For information about assisting worried parents who arrive at your school, see "Communicating With Parents/Family Members" later in this chapter.

For tips on facing the media, see Chapter Three, "Here Come the Media."

It is particularly difficult to confirm the facts when a crisis incident occurs after or before school (or on a weekend or holiday). In such cases, the information tends to come in from several sources. Although the incident involves the school in many ways, nobody is exactly sure what happened. For such cases, the Crisis Coordinator must verify the facts with either the appropriate local authorities (e.g., the police) or the family of the injured/deceased to ensure that there is no confusion about what happened.

Often, when crisis incidents occur away from the school, it is important to obtain information about the situation directly from the family. School personnel are often hesitant to intrude upon the family of a school community member, but if you've heard that something has happened, you must obtain the facts so you know what you are dealing with and can provide an appropriate crisis response within the school. The Crisis Coordinator and Counseling Liaison (or another school counselor or psychologist) should contact the family in person. This first contact with family members of the injured/deceased is very important as it sets the tone for the continuing relationship with the school. Handle this meeting with delicacy and diplomacy.

Telling the facts

Now that you've got the facts, how should your crisis response team effectively communicate them? The most important point is to share *all* the facts. Tell *everything* you know to be accurate. Administrators often know the facts of a crisis, but will not give them all. This tendency to only give the minimum amount of information actually makes things worse, because instead of everyone concerned beginning to cope with their thoughts and reactions to the crisis, they're expending their energy trying to figure out/find out "What about this?" and "What about that?" If you know that a police officer was shot, for example, say so. Then everyone can deal with that. By providing all the facts, people in the school community can then say, for example: "Okay, we understand. He was shot. He was shot on Plumb Street. Three kids were arrested and they're all in jail. He was shot in the head, and he died two hours later." The more information you give people, the less consternation they feel.

"I think we tend to not want to upset children, so we might avoid talking about [the crisis]. But what that does is it often creates more fears. What kids conjure up in their minds is perhaps worse than what [happened]. So be straightforward and give answers, if you know them. And if you don't, say 'We don't know.'"

—Dinah Graham, Assistant Professor of Psychology, Texas Woman's University, Denton (Thomas, 1998)

Another important point is to tell *everybody*, in age-appropriate terms. *No matter how bad the facts are*, they must be shared with *all* members of the affected school community and with the community as a whole. Again, the tendency to "spare" people who are deemed too sensitive to hear the truth (such as students—especially young students) just makes things worse. By sharing the facts, you actually begin to calm the situation down. Regardless of how awful the truth is, those who have not been told the facts will perceive the situation to be even more severe and complicated that it already is. Note, however, that giving everybody the facts does not mean sharing grisly detail. There's a big difference. And, in fact—especially with students—the less detail provided, the better.

The other key element in sharing the facts is, as previously mentioned, to use *age-appropriate* language. Carefully consider the sophistication of your audience, and adjust your vocabulary appropriately. With high schoolers, for example, you might say there has been a "homicide"; in the event of a suicide, you might say that a knife wound was "self-inflicted." With a primary class, you might explain another incident as: "A bad man shot a gun outside our school. The gun hurt one of your schoolmates, (name). She is at the hospital and doctors are trying to make her better. You are safe. Your parents are coming to pick you up so that we can make sure you stay safe."

Another consideration in sharing the facts in an age-appropriate manner is the forum in which you present the information. For example, it would be appropriate to assemble your entire faculty to alert them of the crisis, but not your entire student body. Students should be given crisis information in their own classroom/home room or in smaller groups, and preferably with their teacher and a member of the counseling staff and/or an administrator present. In this way, the students will receive the news of a crisis situation in familiar surroundings and with people they know and trust (Stevenson, 1994). Grouping two, three, or even more classrooms together is not advised. And gathering hundreds of students together in the auditorium or cafeteria is a very bad idea. Dealing with the intensified emotional response of students in such a large group is not easy, and the situation could quickly get out of hand. Further, these types of large group presentations will be less helpful for individual students needing special attention (Stevenson, 1994).

See "Suicide Postvention" in Chapter Eleven for guidelines on what to say, and what not to say, if your school crisis involves the suicide of a school community member.

When do you share the facts?

In general, your crisis response team should tell everything you know as soon as it is verified as accurate. Then keep updating the information as more becomes available throughout the day.

The only exception concerns sensitive information, such as the names of those injured or killed. Victims' names should not be released outside the school they attended/worked in prior to notification of their family members. For other types of sensitive information, you must take into account what has already been released in the media, what the parents/family members have told you, and what the police have released. There certainly will

See "Injury/Death Notification" later in this chapter.

be times when you will need to say, for example: "No more information is available at this time. When it is available, when such and such is released, we will update you immediately." (Also, do not release a photo of the injured or deceased without permission from the parents/family members.)

When a crisis occurs after or before school hours (or over the weekend or on a holiday), sharing the facts becomes more difficult. Too often, school personnel aren't given enough notice of the incident to assimilate it and prepare themselves for facing their students. A typical scenario is that the morning school bell is going to ring shortly and somebody comes in and says, for example, "Your teaching partner was killed on his way to work. You have ten minutes to get yourself together so you can go help the students." If a crisis occurs outside of school hours, the best plan is to notify the staff while they are still at home, utilizing your prearranged calling tree. That way they can obtain support from their own family members/support network and have time to work through some of their own emotional issues before coming to school. If this is not possible, make every effort to have back-up coverage who can begin the teaching day in classes of affected staff members. This coverage will give the staff members time to deal with their emotions.

What do you say?

One of the most difficult issues confronted by people assigned to share the facts of a crisis is, "What do I say?" In a word: the truth. You cannot go wrong if you state what you know to be the whole truth, and nothing but. You must remember that you did not create the crisis, you're merely reporting on it. And hedging the information will not change the actual event. Not talking about it won't take back what has happened.

Telling the whole truth to a group of people who you know will react poorly to the information is very difficult, but it must be done. For example, the county prosecutor in Jonesboro felt very uncomfortable telling a cafeteria of hundreds of angry parents that the juvenile perpetrators of their school shooting would stay in jail only until their 18th birthdays, at the longest. The crisis team members discussing the content of the meeting with him before it began reminded him that he did not write the law and he couldn't change the law; it was just his job to uphold it. They also reminded him that even if the law could be changed in the future, it wouldn't make any difference in the outcome of this particular case. The county prosecutor knew that he must stick to the facts, no matter how uncomfortable they were for his audience to hear.

You will often be surprised at the positive reaction you receive when you simply tell the whole truth in a plain and uncomplicated manner. You don't need to say anything particularly eloquent or to be cagey about any piece of information. Just state the facts clearly and sincerely. As you prepare your statement, think of all the logical questions that people who have just arrived at the scene would want answered. For example, they might wonder: What is happening with the suspected perpetrator(s)? Tell them they have been taken into custody, if that is the case. They would want to know how a victim was injured or killed. If he or she was shot, tell them that. They would likely want to know where the shooting occurred. Tell them it was in the school parking lot (or wherever the crisis actually occurred). Ask yourself all the logical questions. If you can't give an immediate, logical answer, then you're making your statement too difficult, your answers contrived. Stick with the whole truth, plain and simple.

One important element of telling the whole story is to be as factually complete and exacting as possible. Get the important details correct, and include them in your statement. For example, in Houston in September 1985 a high school assistant principal and a student were shot in front of approximately 600 people. Word went out immediately that the assistant principal had been shot. However, it was not specified *which* assistant principal, so two families were immediately in a great deal of agony. There was a 50% chance the person hit was their dad, their husband. The more accurate and complete story would have specified that Assistant Principal

Webster had been shot in the side and was "life-flighted" to the hospital. Always be precise and remember the details. They will matter a great deal to the family members and friends of those affected.

How do you share the facts?

The Crisis Coordinator and Campus Liaison should communicate the specifics of the crisis as well as crisis response instructions to all school employees. As time allows, they should provide opportunities for the faculty and support staff to vent their emotions, ask questions, and plan how to help the students.

If the crisis occurs outside of school hours, use your preestablished calling tree (if there is one) to alert your faculty and support staff. As mentioned previously, telling the staff while they are at home gives them time to process their own reactions to the crisis before facing their students at school. Invite all the faculty and support staff to a meeting before school to fully explain the loss/crisis and to discuss ways to assist the students with the crisis situation.

If you do not have a calling tree structure already in place, or if it is too late in the day to utilize it, the Campus Liaison should place a written statement concerning the crisis in all staff mailboxes at the beginning of the day. Have a resource person (the Campus Liaison or a member of the counseling staff) stationed nearby to answer the staff's questions.

If the crisis occurs during school hours, the best way to communicate the information is on a classroom-by-classroom basis. Have your crisis team members and/or classroom teachers announce the pertinent information in all affected classrooms. Tell the students what has happened in a quiet, simple, direct manner. Avoid religious symbolism and platitudes, and encourage the expression of natural human emotions and feelings about the event. Answer the students' questions openly and honestly, but do not volunteer unnecessary details.

If there is no time to alert the staff and students on a class-by-class basis, then the intercom can be used. The Crisis Coordinator should deliver any statement made using the school's intercom. Remember that your choice of words, voice tone, and inflection are all very important. Choose your words very carefully, and take a couple of minutes beforehand to rehearse your delivery once or twice. A written statement that you can read word-for-word "live" is the best course of action.

Regardless of whether you provide the information before school or during school, in person or over the intercom, you will need to use a *Crisis Fact Sheet*. This is a written statement to be used to communicate the crisis information to all concerned—the school community, family members, and the media. Create this document within the first hour of a severe crisis, as soon as the facts of the situation can be verified as accurate. (*NOTE*: If your school or community includes people for whom English is a second language or a bilingual population, be sure to produce this statement in all relevant languages.) The Crisis Fact Sheet will guide your communications throughout the crisis; do not deviate from the information contained in it.

Preparing the Crisis Fact Sheet should be a group effort: At least your Crisis Coordinator, Media Liaison, and Parent/Family Liaison should collaborate on its contents. (If someone other than the Crisis Coordinator writes the Crisis Fact Sheet, he or she should carefully check the content and initial the statement before its distribution.) Your superintendent or designee may also need to approve this statement before it is distributed. More heads are better than one, because the accuracy and thoroughness of this statement are critical.

Acknowledge the gravity of the situation and your sincere regret that the events have taken place. Be as positive as possible about your school's crisis response, and be sure to include on the Crisis Fact Sheet:

- All known facts about what happened
- The status of victims and suspected perpetrator(s)
- Whether the school will remain open the rest of the day (*see "Task List" in Chapter Two for guidelines*)
- Whether parents are encouraged to leave their children in school
- Information about the counseling services being made available to students

Another important item that should appear on the Crisis Fact Sheet is the time and location of the family/community meeting to be held the first night of the crisis. Don't worry that right now you have no idea what you will say at that meeting—you have until tonight to figure that out! The important point is that you will need to have a meeting, and you need to make sure that as many parents as possible know you're having the meeting. Simply say, for example, that there will be a meeting for all family members and students at 7:00 PM in the school cafeteria and that important information about the crisis and assisting the students will be given.

See "The Family/ Community Meeting" in Chapter Two for more information about the meeting's format and content.

In the midst of a crisis it may seem impossible to find time to get anything down in writing. But in the majority of cases it will be well worth the effort to take a deep breath, slow down, and use ten to 15 minutes to create a Crisis Fact Sheet (see the sample provided, modified by permission from samples provided by the Los Angeles Unified School District). When it's finished, photocopy the Crisis Fact Sheet for distribution to parents and others arriving at the school. Also send someone to the hospital with copies for the Medical Liaison.

Sample Crisis Fact Sheet

On March 8, 1999, at 3:00 PM, a fourth grade student at Sunnyside Elementary School, Nicholas Kirby (age nine), was killed at the intersection of Vine and Holly near the school. Apparently a car ran a red light at high speed, and Nicholas did not see the car coming. He was taken to Mountview Hospital, where he died at approximately 3:40 of internal injuries.

The driver did not originally stop but later returned to the scene and turned himself in to police. The driver, Matthew Jones, 41, is suspected to have been drinking and has been placed under arrest for vehicular homicide. The results of his blood alcohol level test have not yet been released.

Since the accident happened close to the school, a number of students, including those on Bus #409, witnessed this tragic accident. We have arranged for a team of crisis counselors to be on campus tomorrow morning, arriving before school, and to be present every day thereafter until they are no longer needed to assist grieving and traumatized students.

Normal attendance is expected tomorrow morning, and classes will be in session. A crisis counselor will be on each school bus, and the day will begin with opportunities for the students to talk about their reactions to this tragedy with the support of their teachers and crisis counselors. Crisis counselors will assess the needs of all students riding Bus #409, as well as Nicholas' classmates.

A family/community meeting will be held in the school's auditorium this evening at 7:00 PM. This meeting is free and open to the public (with the exception of members of the media), and all concerned and/or grieving family members are encouraged to attend with their children. Counselors will be available for support, and we will discuss guidelines for parents to use in helping their children understand this tragic death and assist them in coping. Information about the funeral arrangements will be announced at that time.

If you have any questions or concerns about your child's reaction to this tragedy, please contact the guidance office of our school at 452-6783.

Injury/Death Notification

One of the most difficult aspects of dealing with a severe crisis is giving injury or death notifications. You are giving a death notification any time you are the first person to tell another that someone he or she knows has died—whether you relay the information in person or on the telephone. Most people think of death notification as telling the "next of kin" (e.g., calling the parents of a student injured or killed at school). However, it is much more than that. In fact, you may not even know when you are making a death notification. There are other family members besides the next of kin, as well as close friends, colleagues, and even long-time acquaintances who may react with strong emotions when they hear of a victim's injury or death (National Organization for Victim Assistance [NOVA], 1997). When you're untrained or unprepared to give such notification, you're not necessarily going to do it well. Yet it is estimated that every American will give between five and ten death notifications in their lifetime. Obviously, this is something we need to learn to do better and in a more direct manner.

> "Every American will give approximately five death notifications."
>
> —National Organization for Victim Assistance (NOVA)

As the National Organization for Victim Assistance explained: "It is important that death notification be handled as well as possible because it is the critical point of trauma for most survivors. Properly done, it can begin the healing process. When it is done improperly or without insight into the survivor's possible reactions, it may delay the process of reconstructing the survivor's life for years" (NOVA, 1997, p. 5-20).

School personnel generally do not want to give injury or death notifications. They may feel very uncomfortable sharing the information with family members, and so leave this responsibility to the police or hospital personnel. But in the case of a school crisis, you may not have a choice. Your school must try to contact parents when their child is injured at school. Even when you *can* avoid telling the family members, the most humane course of action is to tell them what you know. Otherwise, you put parents in the position of racing to the hospital at 100 miles per hour—in dreadful suspense, jeopardizing their own safety—when you already know what they will be told when they arrive. Don't cop out by saying, "It's serious, it's bad, we don't know." If you *do* know, then say so.

In a school crisis, injury/death notifications to family members of students and staff generally occur on the telephone, in person at school, or in person at the hospital. The following guidelines—many adapted with permission by the National Organization for Victim Assistance (1997)—will assist you in delivering injury/death notifications in each of these three situations in the best manner possible.

A Caveat:

> There could be nothing worse than notifying someone of an injury or death prematurely or mistakenly. You must be absolutely certain of any information you give family members. Only deliver a death notification when a student or staff member is pronounced dead on the scene by a professional emergency responder (i.e., paramedic/EMT, police officer, firefighter) or by the coroner's office and when you've heard this information *firsthand*. If it is uncertain whether a victim will survive, give the family members injury notification but allow the death notification (if necessary) to be handled at the hospital.

Notification on the telephone

As discussed previously, as soon as the injured/killed are identified, the Parent/Family Liaison should pull their emergency notification forms on file in the front office and attempt to make contact with the appropriate family members. Follow these procedures for making the call(s):

1. Before calling, obtain as much information as possible about the injured/deceased—what happened, when did it happen, where, how did it happen, and what is the source of positive identification of the victim.

2. Using the emergency notification form, ensure that the appropriate closest adult relative receives notification first. There may be a legal mandate that governs who that person is.

3. Notification should always be given compassionately, quickly, and with as much accuracy as possible.

4. If possible, try to arrange for a trusted family member, friend, or colleague to be with the survivor when he or she receives your call. However, there may not be time for this, or it may not be possible to make such arrangements without breaching confidentiality in the notification procedure.

5. When you place the call, introduce and identify yourself. Be prepared to offer confirmation of your identity and a reference known to the family member.

6. Confirm the identity of the person you have called to ensure that you are speaking to the appropriate person in the household/family to be notified.

7. Encourage the survivor to sit down while you talk. Say, for example, "I am calling to inform you that a medical emergency involving your son has occurred. Do you have a place to sit while I explain what has happened?"

8. If no other adult is with the survivor when you give him or her notification, ask for permission to call a clergy member, neighbor, friend, or law enforcement officer/victims' advocate (i.e., a person of comfort) to come to the home to stay with the survivor or accompany him or her to the hospital.

9. If possible, have another staff member call the person of comfort while you stay on the line with the survivor. If you need to hang up to place the call yourself, call the survivor back immediately to inform him or her of who will be visiting or accompanying him or her to the hospital.

10. Continue to talk with the survivor until such assistance is available, if possible.

11. Answer all questions honestly, but do not offer unnecessary details.

12. Remain nonjudgmental about the survivor's reaction (whether it involves sobbing, nervous laughter, silence, etc.).

13. If you are notifying a number of family members by telephone, let each of them know whom else you have already notified.

Notification in person at school

In a severe crisis, the Parent/Family Liaison may not have the opportunity to notify affected family members by telephone—panicked parents and other family members will likely arrive at the school within minutes of word of the crisis. As discussed previously, the Parent/Family Liaison should have received a list of those injured or killed—with the nature of their injuries—from the Medical Liaison. The Medical Liaison should also keep the school up-to-date on the status of those injured from the hospital. The Parent/Family Liaison should follow these procedures for notifying family members in person at school:

1. You will need the assistance of other staff members (preferably members of the counseling staff and/or administrators) for giving injury/death notifications in person. The rule of thumb is two additional staff members per victim. Thus, the greater the number of victims, the greater the number of people will be required to help.

2. When parents and other family members arrive at the school, direct them to gather in one quiet, convenient room (e.g., the library). Make sure the room is large enough and is easy for parents to find.

3. As they arrive, ask their names and the names of the student/staff member they are related to. Cross-reference these names with your list of injured/killed. (*NOTE*: Make every effort to notify the possibly legally mandated appropriate adult relative—that is, the person listed on the emergency notification form—first. However, if another family member arrives seeking information about a loved one, do not stall that person or withhold information.)

4. Ask any family members who need to hear an injury/death notification to accompany you to an adjacent room, or at the very least to accompany you outside the room. Do not give injury/death notifications in front of a group of other people.

5. Before giving the notification, obtain as much information as possible about the injured/deceased—what happened, when did it happen, where, how did it happen, and what is the source of positive identification of the victim.

6. Notification in person should be done by a pair of individuals. The pair can be two school staff members—preferably including a staff member who knows the family, a member of the counseling staff, or administrators. (*NOTE*: The pair can also consist of a school staff member and any clergy member who has arrived at the school to help in this capacity. In such cases, the clergy members should merely serve as support. They should not use religious symbolism unless the family members are members of their own congregation.)

7. One person should make the actual notification and take the lead in all conversation with family members. The person who is assisting should remove any obvious objects of danger, monitor the survivors for danger signs to themselves or others, and be prepared to care for any young children who have been brought along, if necessary.

8. If you or your partner have been at the actual scene of the injury/death, make sure your clothes are not bloody and your appearance is not disheveled.

9. Notification should always be performed compassionately, quickly, and with as much accuracy as possible.

10. When giving the injury/death notification, first introduce yourself and your partner to the family member(s).

11. Next, double-check that the person you are talking to is the appropriate person to be notified.

12. Then ask the survivor to sit down, and sit with him or her while you talk.

13. Tell the survivor simply and directly; do not build up to the idea of death. The family member already knows that a crisis has occurred, and your demeanor and the ritual involved with taking him or her outside the room will be clues that something is horribly wrong with a loved one. Do not prolong the survivor's natural anxiety.

14. Do not use euphemisms, and leave no room for false hope if the loved one has been killed. Say, for example, "We need to tell you some

"When [the principal of Thurston High School] read the names of the wounded, he saw shock, disbelief, and tears on the faces before him. Parents who had never before met one another literally helped hold each other up."

—Cathy Paine, Crisis Response Team Leader, Springfield, Oregon, Public Schools (Paine, 1998, p. 16)

terrible news. Your daughter was killed when a student opened fire on the playground this afternoon during a fire drill. I am so sorry."

15. Be prepared to present confirming evidence in a clear and convincing fashion in the face of denial.

16. Answer all questions tactfully but directly. Avoid unnecessary details.

17. Remain nonjudgmental about the survivor's reaction (whether it involves tears, nervous laughter, etc.).

18. Focus on the immediate needs of the survivors:

    • If the survivors want help in notifying others, graciously offer to provide this assistance.

    • Do not leave the survivors alone. Respect their need for privacy, but ensure that they do not injure themselves or others. Ask permission to summon another family member or family friend for support.

    • Escort the family member to the hospital or have a staff member who knows the family do so. The family member may say, "No, no, I'm fine." A staff member who knows the survivor should try to convince him or her that he or she should probably not be driving in such an agitated or shocked state. Simply say, "I'm driving you to the hospital now," and turn a deaf ear to objections.

    • Run interference with the media. The Security Liaison should have the media contained off school grounds, but if they see a family member obviously upset they may try to find out who it is and what has happened to his or her child or relative. Obviously, such media contact is inappropriate and traumatic for the survivor.

Notification in person at the hospital

The Medical Liaison will encounter parents and other family members at the hospital who are seeking information about their loved ones. He or she can be a source of support for these survivors and should assist in coordinating the notification efforts of the hospital personnel. The Medical Liaison should follow these procedures for assisting in the notification of family members at the hospital:

1. If many families are arriving at the hospital in a short timeframe, you will need the assistance of the other staff members who accompanied the injured/dead to the hospital to speak with them all.

2. Since you and your "assistants" were at the scene of the injury/death, make sure your clothes are not bloody and your appearance is not disheveled.

3. Do not assume that family members have already been given an injury/death notification at the school. Once a severe crisis is made public, family members may go directly to the hospital for news.

4. As family members arrive, introduce yourself as a member of the school community. Ask their names and the names of the student/staff member they are related to. Cross-reference these names with your list of injured/killed. (*NOTE*: Make every effort to notify the possibly legally mandated appropriate adult relative—that is, the person listed on the emergency notification form—first. However, if another family member arrives seeking information about a loved one, do not stall that person or withhold information.)

5. Tell any family members whose loved one is not on the list of the injured/killed that their loved one was not brought to the hospital for medical attention. Advise these family members to go to the school and speak with the Parent/Family Liaison about the status of their loved one there.

6. Tell any family members whose loved one is on the list of the injured/killed that you will get their loved one's doctor right away. Ask the family members to sit down while they wait. Immediately alert the hospital staff of any family members who need to hear an injury/death notification, and if possible bring the doctor to the family members and introduce them.

7. Either you or the hospital representative should double-check that the person waiting is the appropriate person to be notified.

8. Stay with the survivor(s) during the injury/death notification by the hospital representative.

9. You can help by removing any obvious objects of danger, monitoring the survivors for danger signs to themselves or others, and assisting in the care of any young children who have been brought along, if necessary.

10. The hospital representative will provide the family members with details about their loved one's medical condition (i.e., the exact nature/severity of injuries or the cause of death). You can supplement these data with information about what occurred at the school. Do not deviate from the information contained on the Crisis Fact Sheet.

11. Provide the survivors with a copy of the Crisis Fact Sheet, if possible. Encourage the family members to attend the family/community meeting that night to obtain more information about the crisis and to share in the support of the community if they feel able to do so.

12. Answer all questions tactfully but directly. Avoid unnecessary details.

13. Remain nonjudgmental about the survivor's reaction (whether it involves tears, nervous laughter, etc.).

14. Focus on the immediate needs of the survivors:
    - If survivors want help in notifying others, graciously offer to provide this assistance.

- Do not leave the survivors alone. Respect their need for privacy, but ensure that they do not injure themselves or others. Ask permission to summon another family member or family friend for support. (That comfort person would ideally drive the survivor home.)
- If the family members of killed students/staff welcome your support, you may accompany them to view the body (which they may choose to do or be required to do for identification purposes). Follow these guidelines:
  - If the body is mutilated or distorted, forewarn the viewer about the nature of the mutilation/distortion. Sometimes survivors decide to let a close friend or family member view the body first and make a recommendation to them about their own decision to view or not to view.
  - If the viewer wants to touch or hold the body, encourage him or her to do so and try to ensure the privacy and time for the viewer to say farewell.
  - Be prepared to advocate for the viewer's wishes with the hospital personnel, medical examiner, coroner, and so forth. Sometimes these professionals try to prevent viewers from having contact with the body because they wish to shield survivors from the impact of death.
- Run interference with any media who have arrived at the hospital. If they see any family member leaving who is obviously upset, they may try to find out who it is and whether they are related to anyone involved in the school crisis. Obviously, such media contact is inappropriate and traumatic for the survivor.

Notification of missing/unidentified loved ones

When people are missing after a disaster (e.g., after a tornado or a bombing), their loved ones should be given a "missing notification." Such notification will be helpful to survivors if the missing are soon determined to be dead. The Parent/Family Liaison or Medical Liaison should follow the same procedures as for giving an injury/death notification outlined previously in this chapter, with the following special considerations:

1. If determination of death is made after a "missing notification" has been provided, notification of the death should be made immediately.

2. If there is doubt about who was killed and the identity of the deceased needs confirmation, make it clear to the person being notified that while you have been given evidence that his or her loved one has been killed, final determination of the identity is being investigated. Say, for example: "I need to talk to you about your son. We think he was in the area that was blown up, but we are unsure. Is there any way you can

help us?" Or, "… Is there a family member or close friend who might help?"

3. If there is a delay in the identification of a family member's loved one believed to have been killed, or a possibility that there will never be a final identification, keep the survivors informed about the circumstances.

Communicating With Parents/Family Members

In the first hour of a school crisis the Parent/Family Liaison will be communicating with the parents of students and the family members of staff in two ways: by telephone calls and in person at school. The main objectives are to share the facts of the crisis, reassure family members about the safety of their loved ones (to the extent possible) and the school's crisis response, and to publicize the family/community meeting.

Communicating by telephone

See "Crisis Effects and Grief" in Chapter Seven and "Helping Your Child Cope" in Chapter Eight for information on helping parents assist their children.

Besides making injury/death notifications by telephone (*see "Injury/Death Notification" previously in this chapter*), the Parent/Family Liaison should contact the parents of other students affected by the crisis. These include students who witnessed the act of violence and were questioned by the police as well as students who may be especially traumatized by the crisis, such as close friends of victims or suspected student perpetrator(s). During the call, take the opportunity to tell the parents a few things about typical childhood reactions to crisis and what they can do to assist their children. Parents will be appreciative of these phone calls.

The Crisis Coordinator/head administrator should contact the parents of the suspected student perpetrator(s), if applicable. (These families may or may not have already been contacted by the police.) These are generally very difficult calls to place. Though news of the crisis is often communicated to these family members by phone, the Crisis Coordinator/head administrator should make every attempt to communicate with the family—both the parents and the siblings (if school age) of the suspected student perpetrator(s)—in person. Use the same sensitivity and care as when delivering injury/death notifications to victims' families (*see "Injury/Death Notification" previously in this chapter*). (If done in person, this communication should be made with two staff members present: the Crisis Coordinator and a member of your school's or district's mental health staff.) This initial contact may help set the tone of the community's attitude toward the suspected student perpetrator(s)' families after the crisis.

The reaction of the family of a suspected student perpetrator will in many ways be similar to that of victims' families upon hearing of their injury or death. The family may react with disbelief, embarrassment, and horror.

They will certainly have many questions about the circumstances and the legal issues. Use the Crisis Fact Sheet to provide details about the crisis but let a law enforcement representative address any legal questions. In addition, prepare the family for the possibility of an extreme amount of media attention. You might offer to drive these shocked parents to the police station or to call a family friend or legal counsel to do so.

Parents and other family members of students and staff will be calling the school in great numbers. They will want to know what exactly happened, the status of their loved ones, whether the school is remaining open, and other pertinent information. It is essential that the school secretaries (and anyone else assisting in fielding these calls) tell all the family members the same thing—the information on the Crisis Fact Sheet. Deviating from the data on the Crisis Fact Sheet, or telling different parents different things, can create a public relations nightmare.

Family members calling to seek information about the safety and medical status of their loved ones should be transferred to the Parent/Family Liaison or staff member(s) assisting the Parent/Family Liaison. The school secretaries/receptionists should simply respond to as many of the incoming calls as possible by providing the information on the Crisis Fact Sheet; they should not give injury/death notifications. The Parent/Family Liaison or his or her "assistants" should be in charge of injury/death notifications whether on the telephone or in person (*see "Injury/Death Notification" previously in this chapter*). The Parent/Family Liaison should briefly (as time allows) document each such parental contact.

Communicating in person at school

Parents and other family members will naturally want to find out if their loved ones are safe. But when parents and other family members come pouring into your school, looking for their loved ones, things can quickly turn to chaos. What you do not want are parents running panicked through the halls, pulling their children out of their classrooms. What you do want it to gather family members together in one place where you can calmly give them the facts of the crisis and reassure them to the extent possible.

When parents and other family members arrive at your school, ask them to gather in one quiet, convenient room (e.g., the library). The room should be large enough and easy for the parents to find. Post one or more staff members (such as "assistants" to the Security Liaison or Parent/Family Liaison) at the main entrance of the school to direct or escort family members to the gathering place.

If the family members of suspected student perpetrator(s) arrive at the school, meet them at the door and keep them separated from the other parents. Emotions will be running high, and no one needs the crisis exacerbated by verbal and/or physical conflict between the families of victims and those of suspected student perpetrator(s). The families of suspected student perpetrator(s) will be shocked and very upset, and harsh words and accusations directed at them by other angry parents could be very painful. Offer to drive these family members home or to the police station.

As will be seen in the West Paducah, Kentucky, case study, the staff did an excellent job of communicating with the students' parents at their school. They had the parents sign in when they arrived at the school and then cross-referenced their names to a list of those students injured or killed.

As discussed previously, the Parent/Family Liaison should immediately ask any family members who need to hear an injury/death notification to accompany him or her to an adjacent room (see "Injury/Death Notification" previously in this chapter). The other parents should be given all the facts about what happened and what is being done to manage the crisis. Use the Crisis Fact Sheet, and provide copies to the family members as well. It works best if you can talk to all the family members as a group. But family members will not all arrive at the same time, and you cannot delay in providing information for more than a couple of minutes because family members will be very anxious and nervous. (If you do try to delay them, they will likely bolt and go see for themselves.) If there is a steady stream of parents arriving, you could say, "In just a minute we're going to get started, because we want to give a few more parents the time to arrive." However, be prepared to repeat the information calmly and with patience many, many times to many different family members.

See "The Family/ Community Meeting" in Chapter Two for more information about the meeting's format and content.

If the crisis is catastrophic, and your school is being closed for the rest of the day (see "Task List" in Chapter Two for guidelines), allow the family members to go to their children's classrooms to collect them after they've been given the facts of the crisis and a copy of the Crisis Fact Sheet. Strongly encourage them to return for the family/community meeting that evening so that they can learn the plan for the following day(s), the counseling services available to their children, and steps they can take to help their children cope.

If the school is being kept open for the rest of the day (see "Task List" in Chapter Two for guidelines), encourage the parents to leave their children in school where they can begin to process the crisis with the assistance of the school staff. Parents will be more likely to leave their children in school if they see an orderly crisis response happening—if they see kids with their teachers, a supportive environment, and safety and security. If any parents are still determined to take their children home, the Parent/Family Liaison should offer to accompany them to their children's classroom to see what is happening there. Often, when parents see for themselves that their children are indeed safe—which is their main concern—they are agreeable to leaving them at school.

Even if your school is remaining open for the rest of the day, school personnel cannot deny an agitated parent the right to take his or her child home. Before they leave, however, be sure to provide parents a copy of the Crisis Fact Sheet and strongly encourage them to return that evening for the family/community meeting so that they can receive some important information.

Ask all family members leaving the school to refrain from speaking with any media representatives gathered outside. Emphasize that although the family members have the right to speak with the media if they choose, it would be helpful to allow the school's crisis response team to provide complete and clear information about the status of the crisis after addressing the needs of school community members. Also ask family members to respect the privacy of other families. If they elect to speak with reporters, they should not provide the names of victims or suspected student perpetrator(s).

Some Final Thoughts on the First Hour ...

The decisions your crisis response team makes should be extremely cautious ones. You need to make sure you have done everything possible. Your attitude during the first hour should be: "Something's happened, and we may not have all the facts yet, but, boy, we've got everyone working on this and everybody is in their classrooms and everybody is now safe. Now we're going to sort it out."

You should provide an over-response to the crisis rather than an under-response. That is, you should make sure you have enough people responding and should really work on the crisis intervention. Drop *everything* else and make sure you have the crisis managed.

A severe crisis is, by nature, unpredictable. Regardless of whether you are using the crisis response instructions in this book, your own crisis management plan, or a combination of the two, flexibility is paramount. There may be times during your school's crisis response when it will be difficult to stick with the sequence of the plan. Being too regimented could get in the way of the most effective response to your school's crisis. In these cases, "go with the flow," monitoring periodically that all critical aspects of the crisis response are being addressed.

If you are one of the key school people responding, you are probably going to be scared. You'll probably feel a lot of other unpleasant things as well, and that is to be expected. The natural initial reaction during a crisis is: "Am I okay? Are my loved ones okay? Now what can I do to help others?" In the first hour of a severe crisis, everybody who is going to be a helper has to quickly deal with his or her own issues. First will come denial: "This could not have happened." Next will come anger: "How could somebody do that?" Then you'll realize that you're needed to help. Forget the denial and the anger, enter panic and anxiety. You may feel that there's extra pressure on you because you are supposed to do something. The classroom teacher will feel it, the counselor will feel it, the assistant principal, everybody involved will feel that pressure. But you'll do what you are responsible for doing in spite of it, because you have no choice: Your school and community are counting on you. You *can* do what needs to be done.

References

Alarming rash of school threats: Dozens of schools closed. (1999, April 30). *MSNBC.* Available online: http://www.msnbc.com/news/264186.asp

Bowles, S. (1997, December 3). Even those closest to teen cannot answer why. *USA Today,* pp. 1-2A.

Control the media but provide information. (1998, November). *Practical Strategies for Maintaining Safe Schools: School Violence Alert, 4*(11), 1, 4-5.

Cummings, J. (1998, July 19-22). *Never say never: Tips for educators on preparing for the unthinkable.* Paper presented at the National School Public Relations Association (NSPRA) Annual Seminar, St. Louis, Missouri.

Cypress-Fairbanks Independent School District. (1996). *Crisis management plan.* Unpublished manuscript.

Drummond, T. (1999, May 10). Battling the Columbine copycats. *TIME,* p. 29.

Egan, T. (1998, June 14). From adolescent angst to school killings. *The New York Times,* p. 1.

Egerton, B. (1998, March 25). "We had children lying everywhere," paramedic says: Rampage leaves community in shock, tears. *Dallas Morning News,* p. 1A.

Gegax, T. T., Adler, J., & Pedersen, D. (1998, April 6). The boys behind the ambush. *Newsweek,* p. 26.

Goldstein, A. P., & Conoley, J. C. (1997). Student aggression: Current status. In A. P. Goldstein & J. C. Conoley (Eds.), *School violence intervention: A practical handbook* (pp. 3-19). New York: Guilford.

Injured Mass. counselor dies. (1997, September 3). *Education Week, 17*(1), 5.

King, P., & Muir, A. (1998, June 1). A son who spun out of control. *Newsweek,* p. 32.

Lieberman, R. (1999, January 22-23). *Crisis Intervention Workshop,* Walnut Creek, California.

National Center for Education Statistics (NCES). (1998). *Violence and discipline problems in U.S. public schools: 1996-97.* Washington, DC: Author.

National Organization for Victim Assistance (NOVA). (1997). *Community crisis response team training manual* (2nd ed.). Washington, DC: Author.

National School Safety Center (NSSC). (1989). *School safety checkbook.* Malibu, CA: Author.

Obmascik, M. (1999, April 23). Bomb evidence points to plot to destroy school. *Denver Post.* Available online: http://www.denverpost.com/news/shot0423a.htm

Paine, C. (1998, November). Tragedy response and healing: Springfield unites. *NASP Communiqué, 27*(3), 16-17.

Peterson, S., & Straub, R. (1992). *School crisis survival guide.* West Nyack, NY: Center for Applied Research in Education.

Pitcher, G. D., & Poland, S. (1992). *Crisis intervention in the schools.* New York: Guilford.

School officials in Pearl, Miss., help community cope with tragedy. (1997, November 11). *School Board News,* p. 4.

Squad found almost 60 bombs at Columbine. (1999, May 7). *CNNinteractive.* Available online: http://cnn.com/US/9905/07/school/shooting.01/

Stevenson, R. G. (Ed.). (1994). *What will we do? Preparing a school community to cope with crisis.* Amityville, NY: Baywood Publishing.

Thomas, K. M. (1998, March 26). When tragedy strikes, kids will want answers. *Dallas Morning News,* p. 1C.

Watkins, A., & Hinkle, B. (1999, March 24). Students who were hurt recall days after tragedy. *Jonesboro Sun,* pp. 1A, 15A.

What can we do about school violence? (1998, September). *NEA Today, 17*(1), 19.

When disaster strikes: Questions schools should consider when developing a crisis management plan. (1998, April). *Practical Strategies for Maintaining Safe Schools: School Violence Alert, 4*(4), 7.

chapter two

Continuing the Crisis Response

The First Day of a Severe Crisis

Throughout the first day of the crisis, your crisis response team may need to continue work on the tasks outlined for the first hour of crisis (*see Chapter One*). This chapter continues discussion of the crisis response from where Chapter One left off, providing a "game plan" for the rest of the first day—and evening. Expect the first day of a severe crisis to be a very long one. If you are a member of the crisis response team, anticipate devoting yourself solely to the crisis response well into the night on the first day. Make whatever arrangements are necessary (e.g., childcare for your own children) in order for you to do so.

Task List

The first four items must happen right away. All the rest will be ongoing throughout the first day and evening of the crisis. As you will quickly see, a team effort is essential for completing the tasks following.

1. *The Crisis Coordinator should organize (or reorganize) your crisis response team—if this was not done in the first hour—and devise a way to identify the team.*

   After the initial, first-hour crisis response, you may need to reorganize your team if a crisis team member "folds." As crisis management specialist Mary Margaret Kerr explained, "If a team member comes to you

See "The First Hour of a Severe Crisis" in Chapter One for information on forming an impromptu crisis response team and the various roles that need to be filled.

to say they can't do their job, don't ask for reasons, let it go and get them replaced. You never know what personal or private issues they have. The best thing is to not ask questions if they say they can't do it" ("When Disaster Strikes," 1998, p. 7). Also do not criticize the team member. Intervention in a severe crisis is an intense experience; respect any team member who finds he or she is not capable of serving in a leadership role.

You might consider asking such team members if they are willing to help in a less demanding manner. For example, in a typical school with six or seven counselors, one or two will likely be uncomfortable with grief and emotionality. Rather than having those individuals serving as the Parent/Family Liaison or working with 15 crying kids, they might be able to work on preparing the Crisis Fact Sheet, write letters, work behind the scenes, or cover the normal scheduling (if appropriate). There is so much to do in a severe crisis; it is vital that you utilize your people in whatever way they feel comfortable supporting the crisis response effort.

Another aspect of this task is to appoint a back-up Crisis Coordinator in case the team leader is occupied for any length of time or becomes ill during the crisis response. As crisis management expert Mary Margaret Kerr advised, it's "… important to know who's number two" ("When Disaster Strikes," 1998, p. 7). An assistant principal would be the logical person to assume this role.

"We were amazed to observe [after our school shooting] that some reporters tried posing as doctors and counselors in their efforts to access hospitals and schools, and therefore ID badges were essential for all volunteers."

—Cathy Paine, Crisis Response Team Leader, Springfield, Oregon, Public Schools (Paine, 1998, p. 16)

Once your crisis response team is set, think of a way to identify your team members and any volunteers authorized to assist in your school. Security is tight in a crisis, the scene is chaotic, and you need to have a way to quickly find your team members and distinguish them from others who shouldn't have access to the scene. Suggestions include having the team members wear badges, armbands, vests, and/or hats. Whatever you choose, ensure that the media can't easily duplicate your form of identification ("When Disaster Strikes," 1998).

2. Decide on the school schedule for the rest of the day.

You will need to quickly decide whether to keep your school open for the rest of the day and, if so, what bell schedule to use. There are arguments in favor of keeping your school open after a crisis. Among them, emotional support must be provided as soon as possible, and staff members and students who have experienced a crisis should generally be kept together. The exceptions to the latter are very young students— such as kindergartners—who should be reunited with their primary caretakers as quickly as possible to minimize the effects of the trauma (Pitcher & Poland, 1992). For older students and staff, however, it is easier to begin providing support if everyone remains at school. Keeping your school open also positions the school as a central source of support for your community.

On the flip side, canceling school for the rest of the day allows your crisis response team to devote all of your energies to the crisis response. It gives you time to meet with the faculty and support staff, allowing them to process their own reactions to the crisis and to formulate a plan for assisting the students. It gives you time to attend to public relations issues with your community and the media and to prepare helpful information to be shared with parents and other family members that evening at the family/community meeting. Potential problems with closing early include the bus schedule and unsupervised children due to parents' work commitments.

Use the following rule of thumb to decide whether to cancel school or keep it open for the rest of the day: If the majority of the staff have it "together" enough to assist your students, it's probably best that the students remain in school, where they will be cared for and assisted in coping with the crisis. But if the staff are significantly affected themselves by the crisis, cancel school for the rest of the day. This will give the staff the time to deal with their own issues and to formulate a crisis response. Realize that this decision will be a nonissue when a catastrophic crisis occurs. In Jonesboro, for example, there is no way anything slightly resembling normalcy could have occurred after the school shooting. And the parents who rushed to Westside Middle School didn't give a second's thought as to whether the school would remain open—they wanted their children with them.

You also will not be able to keep your school open if it is severely damaged in the crisis and/or large areas of the building or grounds are designated a crime scene by the police. After the deadliest school shooting in the nation to date, in which two students at Columbine High School in Littleton, Colorado, shot and killed 12 students and a teacher before shooting themselves on April 20, 1999, federal agents and a bomb squad worked in the closed school for weeks. (The suspects had planted nearly 60 bombs within the high school.) A Jefferson County sheriff's spokesperson said the closed school would "... remain a crime scene until the end of May" ("Squad Found," 1999). The more than 1,500 Columbine students finished the school year by attending classes at another Denver high school.

> "[Grieving students] have to be with their friends. That's the only way the healing's going to begin."
>
> —Principal Bill Bond, Heath High School, West Paducah, Kentucky (Prendergast & Pressley, 1997)

If your school will be closed for longer than 24 hours due to damage or an ongoing police investigation, your first priority must be to arrange an alternate location where your students can gather in classroom groups (e.g., at a nearby school, a community college or university campus building, a stadium, or an auditorium). Your goal should be to return your students to school at some location as quickly as possible—preferably the next day—so that they can receive the assistance of trained school personnel and to decrease the occurrence of "school phobia" among students. Don't worry if you're not very organized; class schedules can be printed and books delivered to the alternate site later. After a severe school crisis, the curriculum will be modified or set aside for a short time anyway to address the effects of the crisis and students' emotional needs (*see "Modifying the Curriculum" in Chapter Six*). Granted, holding school in another location will be disquieting, but it is crucial to provide your students with as much structure as possible and the opportunity to process their reactions to the crisis. Of course, strenuous efforts should be made to reopen your campus as soon after the crisis as is possible.

"The students [were] saying, 'We want to be back in school.'"

—Jane Hammond, Jefferson County schools superintendent (Obmascik, 1999)

If you are able to keep your school open for the rest of the day, and make the decision to do so, you need to determine what bell schedule to use. The staff will need to know whether the students will be expected to move with a normal bell schedule or whether that schedule will be modified in order to help students deal with the crisis. Factors to consider include: Will you need more time than one class period to discuss the crisis with the students and help them process their reactions to it? Will the students be afraid to go outside (or to the cafeteria, or wherever the crisis occurred)? Is it *safe* for the students to go outside or to move within the building? In most cases, it is preferable for students to stay in their first period class (or whatever class was in session when the crisis occurred), their main classrooms, or their home room to discuss the crisis. Then you can ring the bell later, if and when it's clear that the initial effects of the crisis have been addressed and you want the students to move to their next class or activity.

3. *Set (and publicize) the time of the family/community meeting to be held that night, if this was not done in the first hour.*

See "The Family/ Community Meeting" later in this chapter for information about the meeting's format and content.

Post this information on the marquee in front of your school and on your school's Web site (if you have one), and update any telephone "Hot Line" message for your school to include this information ("Crisis Communication," 1998). Some large school systems have their own television stations—if yours is one of them, utilize it to disseminate this and other important information (e.g., guidelines for parents on coping skills for their children) after the crisis.

The Media Liaison or Parent/Family Liaison (or someone assisting these people) should also begin to disseminate this information to your community through key communicators such as student leaders, parent leaders ("Crisis Communication," 1998), the Parent-Teacher Association (PTA), your central office, local churches, other area schools, and so forth. Communication can be made via e-mail (if available), the telephone, and even local ham radio operators in rural areas ("When Disaster Strikes," 1998). Further, your school's front office staff and any volunteers answering the phones of your school should be instructed to provide this information to callers.

4. *Finish (and update) the Crisis Fact Sheet, if this was not done in the first hour.*

   The Crisis Fact Sheet should be a *working document*. Continue to update it as often as necessary throughout the day—whenever additional facts are verified. Clear the photocopy machines and disseminate any new, updated copies to everyone who is concerned about the crisis at your school (e.g., parents and other family members, the media, the Medical Liaison at the hospital, community leaders, area schools).

   > See "Verifying Information/Crisis Fact Sheet" in Chapter One for complete instructions on writing and using a Crisis Fact Sheet.

5. *Communicate the facts of the crisis and your decisions about the day's schedule.*

   As quickly as possible, communicate the complete facts of the crisis (using the Crisis Fact Sheet) and the decisions you have made regarding the schedule for the day to the staff members—both faculty and support staff. The Campus Liaison should inform or update the teaching staff and front office staff and notify the bus drivers serving your school of the situation by calling the director of transportation. Announce the family/community meeting planned for that evening and encourage the attendance of your faculty and support staff.

   > See "Telling the Facts" in "Verifying Information/Crisis Fact Sheet" in Chapter One for tips on communicating about the crisis with the staff.

   The Campus Liaison should clearly communicate to all staff members that only the Media Liaison and Crisis Coordinator are to provide information to media representatives at any time during the crisis. (*NOTE*: This policy will be of particular importance if a lawsuit is filed against your school and/or its employees. Inaccurate statements made to the press could come back to haunt your school later. *See "Liability and Litigation" in Chapter Twelve for more information*.) The Campus Liaison also should outline ways your faculty and the bus drivers can be of assistance to your students.

   > See "Responsibilities of Various School Personnel" later in this chapter for a list of suggested actions teachers can take.

   The transportation personnel serving your school need to know the facts of the crisis so that they can process their own reactions to it before they arrive at the school and can dispense accurate information to the students when they pick them up. The bus drivers should convey

   > See "Modifying the Curriculum" in Chapter Six for activities students can do in class to help them recover from the crisis.

See "Crisis Effects and Grief" in Chapter Seven for information about typical childhood reactions to crisis.

that no matter how bad things are, your students are safe on the bus and that they will be taking the students home to their parents. The bus drivers should model order, with a calm demeanor. Your students should be instructed to load, ride, and unload the buses in their normal fashion, but it is helpful for the bus drivers to communicate concern and an extra measure of control as the students board the buses. To do so, they should speak with the students as they load, making eye contact with each individual. Some students might welcome brief comforting physical contact from their bus driver, such as a pat on the arm or a quick hug.

6. *Announce and hold the first press conference as soon as is feasible.*

See "Cooperating With the Media" in Chapter Three for comprehensive guidelines on working with the media/holding press conferences.

The Media Liaison should then continue to hold press conferences every two to three hours throughout the day, even if there is no new information to announce.

If family members of victims are agreeable to receiving assistance from the school, the Media Liaison also should communicate with the families throughout the day, lending support and serving as a go-between with the media (*see "Containing the Media" in Chapter Three*). The Media Liaison could share with the media the updated medical status of the victims, any statements from the families, and other appropriate information.

7. *Evaluate your need for outside assistance, and assign any volunteers their tasks for the day.*

See "Unasked-For Assistance," "Help to Request," and "General Points When Using Outside Help" in Chapter Four for guidelines on selecting volunteers and utilizing them most effectively.

See "Help to Request" in Chapter Four for a list of available resources and tips on deciding whom to request assistance from.

The Campus Liaison should greet and briefly "interview" any volunteers who come to your school unasked to assist with the crisis response. He or she should then assign helpers appropriate tasks for the day and coordinate their activities.

Additionally, the Campus Liaison should help to evaluate the scope of the crisis and your school's need for outside assistance (e.g., from a state or national crisis response team, through a telephone consultation about your school's crisis response, from counseling/psychology personnel from other schools in your district) and make recommendations about this need to the Crisis Coordinator. Request any additional assistance needed sooner rather than later. Remember, an over-response to the crisis is preferable to an under-response.

8. *If you are keeping your school open for the rest of the day, begin to attend to the needs of your students.*

If your school will stay open for the remainder of the day, your students will need the opportunity to process their reactions to the crisis. As explained in Sleek (1998), "Children were once thought to be largely immune from the type of nightmares and despair that adults experience after suffering psychological trauma. But in the past ten years, psychologists have found that children can suffer from post-traumatic stress disorder (PTSD) …" (p. 12).

Children *are* resilient (more so than adults, typically), but having the opportunity to talk about what happened is very important for their well-being. Research (e.g., Sandall, 1986) has shown that children who verbalize the most after a traumatic event recover the best. By giving them time and permission to express their feelings, they will feel validated, which leads to a return to normalcy more quickly.

It is important to provide the time for your students to discuss the incident and their feelings fully and to encourage them to do so. (*NOTE*: Prior parental permission is not required for this type of counseling/discussion.) The discussion should take place within the students' classroom groups with the assistance of the teacher and at least one counseling staff member (three, if you plan to follow the full NOVA model; *see Chapter Five*) or administrator in each affected class. (*NOTE*: The exceptions are very young students—such as kindergartners—who should be reunited with their primary caretakers as soon as possible after a traumatic event.)

Processing their reactions to the crisis through classroom discussion is a good way for students to start on the road to recovery. However, don't expect the rest of the day to be "business as usual." Modify or set aside the regular curriculum (especially any scheduled tests) at least for the day of the crisis and allow the students to continue to express their feelings through alternate activities, such as artwork and writing, and by listening to appropriate music.

The Counseling Liaison (and a member of any outside crisis response team assisting your school) should follow the schedule of all injured/deceased students and staff throughout the day, as there will likely be extreme emotionality in their classes (such as there was in Shannon Wright's classroom in the school near Jonesboro, Arkansas). While leading processing sessions in these classes, identify any students you are particularly concerned about for follow-up purposes (*see "Providing Counseling Services" in Chapter Seven for more information*).

Before your students leave for the day, have all of your teachers give their classes a quick lesson on media basics. Although you cannot prevent students from speaking with the media if they choose to, you can make sure they understand that they do not *have* to talk to reporters just because they are asked a question. Provide them with a verbal line of defense, such as: "I don't want to talk to you," "Please leave me alone," "Don't take my picture," or, for older students, "No comment."

See **"How Do You Process?"** in **Chapter Five** for a model for this discussion that has proven to be helpful to people of all ages after a crisis.

See **"Crisis Effects and Grief"** in **Chapter Seven** for information about typical childhood reactions to crisis.

For tips on using artwork, writing, music, and drama with students after a crisis, see **"Modifying the Curriculum"** in **Chapter Six**.

Encourage the students to allow *school representatives* to provide the media with the information they need. Discuss the harm that could result from the spread of rumors or speculation.

If you have enough mental health workers from within your school or district, or volunteer counselors assisting your school (*see "Local Caregivers/Agencies" in "Help to Request" in Chapter Four*), assign a counselor to each school bus taking students home at the end of the day. They can assist the bus drivers, and if any students become visibly upset on the way home, can sit and talk with these students.

For Concerned People Elsewhere ...

Supporting Students

A severe school crisis that is widely publicized can affect students across town, across the state, and even across the country from the school experiencing the crisis. Because your students may identify with the student victims of the crisis, and because crises at schools violate a sense of security in general, your students may experience a crisis reaction—such as fear—even though they are in no physical danger. Or they may feel profound sadness or grieve for victims they did not know. After the April 1999 shooting at Columbine High School in Littleton, Colorado, for example, a dozen students from a school elsewhere in the state delivered a 25-foot banner—signed by their school's student body—to the spontaneous memorial that was forming in a park close to Columbine. Explained one of the students, "I didn't know anyone [among the victims] personally, but we can definitely feel it. It hurts us too" (Obmascik, 1999).

Schools often underestimate the effects of a severe school crisis that occurs elsewhere on their students and staff. Be sure to thoroughly address your students' emotional needs whenever a school crisis makes the news. Hearing about the crisis at another school will likely make your students feel afraid, sad, angry, guilty, or any combination of those emotions. (*See Chapter Five, "Processing the Crisis," and Chapter Seven, "Addressing the Trauma," for information about typical crisis reactions and suggestions on supporting students after a crisis.*)

9. Clean up the crime scene.

When the police have finished working in the area in which the violence/crisis occurred—which may be on the first day or not for several days—and give clearance to alter the area, your school's custodial staff should clean up the worst of the damage. In particular, wipe up any splattered or pooled blood and straighten chairs and desks. Neatly gather victims' personal items that may be strewn around the area (scattered across the floor, for example). However, strive to leave other personal belongings of staff and students intact and as you find them. Do not, for example, remove the belongings of a deceased school community member from within his or her desk or rearrange the desks in a classroom to disguise the location where the deceased would normally sit.

Further, do not immediately erase all evidence that the crisis occurred (e.g., patching bullet holes). Many members of your school community may want to visit the scene over the next several days, so it is important that the evidence of the crisis remain for the time being. Seeing the bullet holes (or other physical effects of the crisis) helps people to understand the reality of the tragedy.

See "When Will Things Return to Normal?" in Chapter Six for additional information on this sensitive topic.

10. *Continue to communicate updated information throughout the day.*

It's crucial to continue to communicate with your internal audience as the crisis unfolds. The Campus Liaison should update all school employees on any new confirmed facts that come up during the day. Teachers should then share this information with their students. People will want to know what is new about victims' medical conditions, when a funeral has been set, the status of suspected perpetrator(s), and other such information.

Utilize your prearranged staff calling tree to continue these updates outside of school hours. (If you don't already have a calling tree in place, the Crisis Coordinator should assign a member of your support staff to create one before the end of the day.)

Throughout the day and on subsequent days, the Crisis Coordinator should keep the lines of communication open with the police and/or district attorney's office, the Medical Liaison/hospital staff, and families of victims. He or she also should communicate new information to the superintendent, school board, and other area schools via the central office.

See "Verifying Information/Crisis Fact Sheet" in Chapter One for guidelines on getting and telling the facts of a crisis.

11. *Eat something.*

Don't forget to eat. Try to swallow at least a few bites at what would usually be lunch (and dinner) time. It will be a long day, and you need fuel to keep yourselves going. Also stay hydrated by drinking lots of water, and try to squeeze in a break for a few minutes at least every two to three hours. Deep, "cleansing" breaths during these breaks will help to calm and reenergize you. The Crisis Coordinator should put someone (e.g., from the front office staff, a volunteer assisting your school) in charge of bringing your crisis response team members food and drinks. Whatever food is brought in should be healthful and easy and quick to eat on the run.

12. Plan the family/community meeting to be held that evening.

See "The Family/ Community Meeting" later in this chapter for a list of individuals to include in leading this meeting and for complete information about the meeting's format and content.

See "Providing Counseling Services" in Chapter Seven for suggestions.

See "Crisis Effects and Grief" in Chapter Seven and "Helping Your Child Cope" in Chapter Eight for information to provide parents on these important topics.

The Parent/Family Liaison (or someone assisting this person) should begin planning this meeting early enough in the day to arrange for the attendance of speakers from outside your school. You'll also need enough time to create and photocopy a parent/family information packet. The packet should include:

- The most updated version of the Crisis Fact Sheet.
- Information pertinent to the crisis (e.g., relevant district policies, copies of state laws, etc.).
- A description of the counseling services available to students through your school, as well as the telephone numbers of other community agencies that can assist in counseling the students.
- Information about children's typical reactions to trauma and grief and suggestions for assisting children at home.

13. Send a letter home to parents.

The Parent/Family Liaison, Crisis Coordinator, and any other available crisis response team members should collaborate in writing a letter to parents that can be sent home with the students when school is dismissed. (If the Crisis Coordinator does not participate in writing the letter, be sure he or she signs off on its content before it is distributed.) The letter should clearly explain what occurred and what has been done to resolve the crisis and its effects. It should mention the time of the family/community meeting that night and encourage all parents to attend. It also should specify whether school will be in session the next day. (*NOTE*: If school will be in session, but normal class activities will not be conducted on the first day back after a severe crisis, simply specify that the school will be open, that the effects of the crisis will be addressed, and that regular attendance is encouraged. If you instead state that it will not be a normal school day but that those who would like counseling services should attend, many families will keep their children home and the children will miss the valuable processing sessions to be provided at school.) A copy of the Crisis Fact Sheet also should accompany this parent letter.

The parent letter is a powerful tool for extinguishing rumors that have spread about the crisis and for reassuring parents that the school is doing all you can to assist their children in recovering from the effects of the crisis. The wording of the letter is important, which is why its creation should be a group effort. Double-check the facts, and express your concern about what has happened. A sample parent letter—adapted with permission from the Pasco County Schools in Florida—follows (District School Board, 1994a).

Sample Parent Letter

Date

Dear Parents:

The students and staff of (Your School's Name) experienced a tragedy today with the death of one of our (X) grade students, (name). (He/she) died (state manner of death). A statement providing the complete facts of this crisis accompanies this letter.

All of us are grieving this tragic loss. To assist the students and staff in handling this loss, a special crisis intervention team is serving our school. An increased level of individual and group counseling services has been made available. We will continue to provide these services to students as long as they are needed. You may contact the school directly to request these services for your son or daughter if you feel he or she needs some extra assistance.

Please be aware that your child may experience strong feelings in response to this crisis, including sorrow and depression, anger, fear, or even guilt. He or she may have difficulty sleeping and/or experience nightmares or may temporarily regress in his or her behavior or academically. Your child will likely have a special need at this time for your comfort and support; please try to be available to listen with patience and understanding.

We are holding a family/community meeting at our school tonight at 7:00 PM in the cafeteria. We will be providing updated information about the crisis, as well as discussing many ways you as a parent can assist your child in recovering from the effects of this tragedy. We strongly encourage you to bring your child and other interested family members to the school this evening to participate. The school will be open during the normal hours tomorrow, with time set aside for processing the effects of the crisis. It would be best for your child to attend school as usual tomorrow.

This is a very difficult time for all of us. We want to be sensitive to the needs of your son or daughter. Please call us if we can be of any assistance.

Sincerely,

Principal

If your school or community includes people for whom English is a second language or a bilingual population, be sure to produce this letter in all relevant languages. Also be sure to remind the students to give their parents the information sheets. Elementary students are used to carrying notes, but older students may not take the information home. Anticipate telephone calls from worried parents of older students who may not have been given your information by their children.

For Concerned People Elsewhere ...

Communicating With Parents

After a publicized school crisis, parents of students at other schools may be worried, as well. They might wonder, "What if something like this happened at my child's school?" Their fears are not ungrounded. "Copycat" scares and bomb threats, unfortunately, are rampant after severe school crises. "Since the shooting rampage in Littleton, Colo.," reported NBC News, "threats of violence at schools across the country have become as routine as homework" ("Alarming," 1999). Even schools that received no substantiated threats, such as Valhalla High School in El Cajon, California, received more than 100 phone calls from parents concerned about rumors of threatened violence at the school ("Alarming," 1999).

Take the initiative and send a letter home to parents. Reassure them that you are providing a safe school environment, and detail any precautionary or security measures that are in place at your school. Assure the parents that you will take any threats of violence seriously and will continue to do everything possible to keep their children safe. Stress the importance of regular school attendance.

14. *Supervise the dismissal of the students.*

You will want to handle the dismissal of your students differently depending upon the nature and severity of the crisis and whether your school is remaining open or closing early. For example, with a severe crisis you may need to have staff walk students past the media to their buses and/or parents' cars, and you might implement a "no walkers" policy for the day, contacting appropriate parents to come pick up their children. Many parents will need to be alerted if you close the school early and they have not already arrived at the school after hearing news of the crisis. If your school is remaining open, be sure to sign out any students who leave early because of emotional upset. The bottom line is to take whatever steps are appropriate to safeguard the physical safety and emotional well-being of your students.

15. *Process the crisis with your faculty and support staff.*

See "How Do You Process?" in Chapter Five for a model for this discussion that has proven to be helpful to people of all ages after a crisis.

As you will see in the West Paducah, Kentucky, case study, enabling the staff to process their reactions to the crisis is an important element of the crisis response. Often so much attention is focused on assisting the students that the needs of the adults get overlooked. But teachers are people too, and, like the students, will have been affected by what has occurred at your school. They will be in a better position to fulfill their responsibilities with their students after they have discussed their own reactions to the crisis. By giving them time and permission to express their feelings, they will feel validated, which will lead to a return to normalcy more quickly.

The Counseling Liaison (and members of any outside crisis response team assisting your school) should lead this processing session during the day if school was canceled (perhaps after the Campus Liaison discusses with the staff the facts of the crisis and their role in the crisis intervention) or right after school if the school is remaining open for the rest of the day. The Crisis Coordinator/head administrator should make this meeting mandatory for all school staff (with the exception of bus drivers, who need to maintain their schedule after school lets out, if the meeting is held after school).

During the processing session with the staff members, emphasize that there is no one correct way for them to feel and provide permission for a range of emotions. Remind them that you're "all in this together, and will get through it together." Focus on identifying and reinforcing the resiliency and coping skills of the staff members.

16. *Schedule a mandatory faculty meeting for the next morning and prepare teacher materials.*

The Crisis Coordinator and/or Campus Liaison should meet briefly with the faculty before school the next day. You will want to review the plan for the day (including the bell schedule) and ways the faculty can assist their students in recovering from the crisis. In preparation for this meeting, the Campus Liaison and/or Counseling Liaison should develop a handout for your faculty providing tips for teachers on dealing with a tragedy at school.

See "Responsibilities of Various School Personnel" later in this chapter for a list of suggested actions teachers can take.

See "Modifying the Curriculum" in Chapter Six for activities students can do in class to help them recover from the crisis.

See "Crisis Effects and Grief" in Chapter Seven for information about typical childhood reactions to crisis.

For Concerned People Elsewhere ...

Faculty Meeting

If you anticipate that your students will be affected by the news of a school crisis elsewhere, hold a faculty meeting to discuss ways in which the staff can assist the students. In classroom groups, give the students the complete and accurate facts about the crisis in age-appropriate language (*see "Verifying Information/Crisis Fact Sheet" in Chapter One*). Allow time for the students to discuss their reactions to the crisis, modifying or setting aside the regular curriculum for a short time to address the students' emotional needs (*see "Modifying the Curriculum" in Chapter Six for suggestions*). Refer students who are at risk for a severe crisis reaction (e.g., those students who have recently suffered a significant loss) to the school's counseling staff (*see "Providing Counseling Services" in Chapter Seven*). Additionally, don't ignore the needs of the school staff members to process their own reactions to the crisis (*see Chapter Five, "Processing the Crisis"*). Teachers must be supported emotionally so that they may work with their students from a position of strength and calm.

See "Regrouping With Helpers" in "General Points When Using Outside Help" in Chapter Four for guidelines on the format and content of this meeting.

17. *At the end of the school day, the Campus Liaison should meet with any volunteer caregivers who assisted your school.*

18. *Make emotional support available during the day and evening.*

Even if school is canceled for the rest of the day, keep your school building open and accessible for staff, students, and their family members. Have at least a few counselors (e.g., from your school's staff/crisis response team and/or from any outside crisis response team assisting your school) available to speak with members of your school community who need their assistance. Clergy members and/or volunteer mental health workers who are assisting your school could also work in this capacity.

See "Local Caregivers/Agencies" in "Help to Request," and "General Points When Using Outside Help," in Chapter Four for guidelines on utilizing these volunteers most effectively.

If the day after a severe crisis is a holiday, a prescheduled inservice day, or a weekend, people will still come to the school to talk with others about the crisis and to receive mental health assistance. Caregivers should be available regardless of whether school is in session. Following the shooting at Westside Middle School near Jonesboro, Arkansas, for example, a "crisis center" was established in the school's gymnasium and kept open 24 hours per day for six days. Counselors, clergy members, members of the National Guard, police officers, and Red Cross and Salvation Army personnel staffed the crisis center (Linda Speer Graham and Jack Bower, personal communication, March 1999).

19. *Visit victims and their families.*

Sometime before the family/community meeting to be held the night of the crisis, the Crisis Coordinator, other available members of your school's crisis response team (particularly mental health workers), and members of any outside crisis response team assisting your school should visit with injured members of the school community and families of the injured/deceased. These visits to hospitals and/or the victims' homes should be made *in person*.

Such visits can be very helpful to victims and their families. Not only are they a time for these members of your school community to see familiar faces from school and receive your condolences, but surviving siblings will be pleased to see their counselor, teacher, and/or principal. Further, because the transient nature of our society leaves many students without extended family nearby, school personnel who go to students' homes or the hospital can help fill a real void as it may be the next day or longer before out-of-town family members arrive.

During conversations with the parents during these visits, you can emphasize to them that your school personnel will help plan the school reentry of the surviving siblings, and you can help the parents understand the effect the loss or injury will have on their children. However, do not overwhelm the parents with such discussion if they are distraught. The main purpose of these visits is to simply relate as human beings in sorrow.

20. *Hold the family/community meeting at your school at the appointed time of the evening.*

21. *The Media Liaison should hold the final press conference of the day after the family/community meeting.*

22. *Meet with your crisis response team to plan the next day.*

By this point in your school's crisis response, a lot has happened and you have probably accomplished a great deal. Most likely you are tired, but there are still a few things to wrap up before you call it a night. After the family/community meeting, gather all your crisis team members (and "assistants" if they are still around) to review the day and plan for the next day. (*NOTE*: If an outside crisis response team is assisting your school, be sure to coordinate with those team members as well.) Discuss:

- Each team member's activities during the day. (This brief review will be helpful for the entire team as the individual members will have been going in different directions all day long and probably will not have had many opportunities to check in with one another.)

- What worked well and what didn't.

- Additional assistance you may need and any issues concerning outside agencies.

- The assignments/main tasks of all team members (and volunteers) for the next day, in particular the ways you will assist the students.

- Updated information about the crisis and updates required to the Crisis Fact Sheet.

- Media/public relations strategies and any "damage control" that may be necessary.

- Emotions experienced by team members throughout the day and how well team members are holding up (i.e., if you have eaten, whether your families are being supportive of your crisis work at the school, etc.). Process your own reactions to the crisis and the crisis response as necessary.

During meetings of your school's crisis response team, the Crisis Coordinator should be very warm and complimentary toward the team members. Offer suggestions for how team members can cope with the stress of the crisis response and help identify coping skills and resources. Take the time to thank the team members for their extraordinary effort.

See "The Family/Community Meeting" later in this chapter for complete information about the meeting's format and content.

See "How/Agenda" in "The Family/Community Meeting" later in this chapter for information about the final press conference of the day.

See Chapter Four, "Help Is at Hand," for more information on outside agencies.

See "The Mornings After" in Chapter Six for suggestions on each team member's assignments/main tasks.

See "How Do You Process?" in Chapter Five for a model.

Finally, while meeting with your team members, don't be afraid to allow the use of humor. Making a tasteful joke or two about something unrelated to the tragedy does not make you an insensitive or evil person. Humor is an excellent tension reliever and may be beneficial for you after such a difficult day.

> "Life does not cease to be funny when people die any more than it ceases to be serious when people laugh."
>
> —George Bernard Shaw

Discussing all of these issues may mean staying at the school until ten or 11 o'clock at night, and then being back at the school the next morning by 6:30 or 7:00.

This is a demanding schedule, but this will be time well spent. The more time you spend managing the crisis in the beginning, the more you gain control of the situation and the more confident your team members will feel.

Responsibilities of Various School Personnel

The following are summaries of the main responsibilities of various school staff members on the first day of a severe crisis and in the days that follow:

Crisis Coordinator

- Take charge of the situation and direct the crisis response team.
- Be visible, available, and supportive. Empower the team members and staff.
- Decide whether to keep your school open for the rest of the day or to cancel school. If the school is remaining open, decide what bell schedule to use.
- Communicate all of the decisions you make to the staff (through the Campus Liaison).
- Dispel rumors by providing everyone concerned about the crisis with all of the facts in age-appropriate terms. Update everyone concerned on all new facts confirmed throughout the crisis.
- Communicate with your central administration and the school board.
- Direct the faculty in writing and verbally (through the Campus Liaison) to modify/set aside the curriculum for a short time to address the emotionality of the situation.

See "Memorializing Victims" in Chapter Six and "Suicide Postvention" in Chapter Eleven for memorializing guidelines.

- Follow the comprehensive plan outlined in this book (and/or in your school's own plan) to resolve the crisis and its effects.
- Do not hesitate to request outside assistance.
- Ensure that any memorials that are planned are appropriate.

Crisis response team members

- Stay calm.
- Follow the directions of the Crisis Coordinator.

- Follow the directions for your assigned role in the comprehensive crisis response plan outlined in this book (and/or in your school's own plan).

- Make any necessary arrangements (e.g., childcare for your own children) so that you can devote yourself to the crisis response well into the night on the first day.

- Unless you are the Media Liaison, do not speak with the media. Refer all questions/interview requests to the Media Liaison and/or Crisis Coordinator.

- Do not speculate about the crisis or repeat any unconfirmed information to anyone at any time during the crisis.

- Don't forget to eat something, drink plenty of water, and take a few minutes' break every few hours during the crisis response.

- Be visible in hallways and classrooms so that you can be of assistance to staff members, students, and their families.

- If you are having difficulty fulfilling your role in the crisis response, for whatever reason, notify the Crisis Coordinator immediately.

Support/front office staff

- Stay calm.
- Follow the directions of the Crisis Coordinator/head administrator.
- Follow any school procedures already in place for crises.
- Do not speak with the media. Refer all questions/interview requests to the Media Liaison and/or Crisis Coordinator.
- Do not speculate about the crisis or repeat any unconfirmed information to anyone at any time during the crisis.
- Tell all callers about the family/community meeting.
- Share the facts printed on the Crisis Fact Sheet.
- Refer any family members who need to hear an injury/death notification to the Parent/Family Liaison.

Teachers

- Stay calm.
- Follow the directions of the Crisis Coordinator/head administrator.
- Follow any school procedures already in place for crises.
- Do not speak with the media. Refer all questions/interview requests to the Media Liaison and/or Crisis Coordinator.
- Do not speculate about the crisis or repeat any unconfirmed information to anyone at any time during the crisis, including your students. (Tell your students that they need to stay calm, that rumors can get out of hand, and that you will tell them the facts of the crisis as they are confirmed.)

See "How Do You Process?" in Chapter Five.

- Share the facts printed on the Crisis Fact Sheet with your students. Lead a class discussion in which you assist your students in processing their reactions to the crisis.

- Dispel rumors by answering questions truthfully and providing only accurate information to your students in age-appropriate language. Openly and honestly acknowledge what has happened, but avoid unnecessary details.

- Do not be impassive about the crisis. Discuss your own reactions to the crisis, and allow as much time as necessary for discussion with your students about crisis reactions (District School Board, 1994b).

See "Modifying the Curriculum" in Chapter Six.

- Modify/set aside the regular curriculum (especially tests) as appropriate in order to address the emotionality of the situation. Allow your students to express their feelings through alternate activities, such as artwork and writing, and by listening to appropriate music.

- Give permission for a range of emotions (even nervous laughter or seeming indifference). Everyone deals with trauma differently and at different rates—there is no one correct way to feel at any one time. Note that students may express their emotions through "acting-out" behaviors. If the crisis involved a death, for example, some students may "… act out noisily and physically as a way of affirming that they are still alive" (District School Board, 1994b).

- Allow for a wide variety of religious beliefs (including atheism).

- Identify for the Counseling Liaison students who you believe need counseling or are at risk. (You will probably be able to assist approximately 95% of your students yourself.) Students to monitor closely include those who were close to the victims or suspected student perpetrator(s) and those who have had a recent loss in their lives.

See "Containing the Media" in Chapter Three.

- Brief your students on media procedures. Make sure they understand that they do not *have* to talk to reporters just because they are asked a question, and provide them with a verbal line of defense (e.g., "No comment," "Please leave me alone"). Encourage your students to allow *school representatives* to provide the media with the information they need, and discuss the harm that could result from the spread of rumors or speculation.

See "Funerals" in Chapter Six for complete guidelines.

- Discuss with your students (if applicable) visitation/funeral procedures, including etiquette and appropriate denominational customs. Emphasize that students have a choice about attending funerals and that if they choose to attend it is a good idea for them to go with their parents.

- Discuss appropriate memorials or remembrances of the deceased (if applicable).
- Make appropriate physical contact if you feel it would comfort some of your students.
- Continue to monitor your students' progress in resolving their reactions to the crisis.
- Be prepared to lead follow-up discussions, as needed, as more information about the crisis is verified and at appropriate times in the future. Reactions to the crisis may last a long time.

See "Memorializing Victims" in Chapter Six and "Suicide Postvention" in Chapter Eleven for more information on memorials.

See "Long-Term Effects" in Chapter Twelve.

For Concerned People Elsewhere ...

Teachable Moments

When a severe school crisis is publicized city-wide, state-wide, or nationally, students who are exposed to this coverage will be talking about the incident. Teachers can seize this teachable moment to discuss prevention with their students. Appropriate discussion topics include:

- *Teaching students to tell.* Emphasize the difference between "tattling," which is designed to get a peer into trouble, and "warning of a threat" (e.g., of violence, of suicide), which might save lives. Encourage the students to tell an adult (and continue telling adults until someone listens) whenever they are threatened or hear about threatened violence and whenever they see or hear about a weapon on campus. Emphasize that all threats of severe acts must be taken seriously and require adult assistance.

- *Suicide prevention.* If the crisis elsewhere was suicide-related, discuss how suicide is a bad choice and talk about alternatives that students have. Note that the content and tone of any discussions about suicide must be carefully considered due to the danger of "suicide contagion." (*See "Suicide Postvention" in Chapter Eleven for additional information.*)

- *Causal factors of violence.* Discuss some of the societal factors many believe are related to youth violence today, such as viewing violent movies and television programs (including cartoons), listening to violent music, desensitization to violence through frequent playing of violent video games, coverage of violence in the media, easy gun access, and Internet access (e.g., accessing bomb recipes). Emphasize the finality of death, and discuss how the media often inaccurately portray violence without permanent consequences. Talk about how this portrayal might blur the lines of reality for many youth, and brainstorm ways people in our country might decrease their exposure to violent content.

- *Unknown motives.* Students may wish to focus on the suspected perpetrator(s) (particularly if they are students) or on the motive for the violent act (or suicide). Because children are attention-seekers, some may be excited by the attention paid to suspected student perpetrator(s) and wish to imitate their actions (*see "'Copycat' Incidents" in Chapter Twelve*). Point out

continued—

Chapter Two: Continuing the Crisis Response **87**

that the question "why?" will never be fully answered and that the students could better spend their energy thinking about how similar incidents could be prevented in the future. While being careful not to glorify or excuse the actions of suspected student perpetrator(s), you might also discuss with students how a school climate in which certain groups or types of students are tormented and rejected might, in some cases, contribute to such students committing violence and/or killing themselves. Ask your students to think about the climate of their school and what they might do to improve it. After the school shooting at Columbine High School in Littleton, Colorado, in April 1999, for example, the members of a Boulder, Colorado, youth group decided that they would each attempt to befriend three students at their school whom they had never talked to before (Betsy Albright, personal communication, May 1999).

The Family/Community Meeting

Why

On the evening of the first day of the crisis, it is important to hold a family/community meeting. The parents of your students and family members of the staff will be very concerned about what happened and what you are going to do about it and will expect to be talked to. Schools are often hesitant to hold a meeting for all the parents, but there is really no better way of ensuring that all of their questions are answered, that your school's crisis response plans are communicated, and that the parents will learn ways that they can support and address the emotional needs of their children. By taking the initiative and holding the family/community meeting, not only will your school rightfully look caring and responsible, you will be doing a great service to your school community. The goal of the family/community meeting is twofold: (1) to impart information, and (2) to assist the family/community members in processing their reactions to the crisis.

When/Where

Hold this meeting during the evening hours, when most parents can attend. (Six or seven o'clock is best—this is usually late enough for parents to have arrived home from work and early enough that they can bring their children back to the school with them.) Allow approximately two hours of time for this gathering. You may anticipate needing only an hour or so, but the extra time will ensure that all audience members' questions can be addressed. In a severe crisis, two hours or a little longer may not be enough time to satisfy the needs of the parents and other family members. If this is the case, schedule another meeting for the following evening to continue the discussion. Do begin wrapping up the meeting after about two hours have elapsed—continuing for a longer period of time will likely overwhelm and exhaust those participating.

Hold the family/community meeting at school, not in an off-campus location such as a parent's home. If a large crowd attends, a private residence or smaller facility will not accommodate everyone wishing to participate. The school also is a known location that is easy for all the parents and other family members to find. More important, the meeting should be a *school* event. The school should plan and lead the meeting activities and be perceived as responsive to the community's needs by hosting the meeting.

Who

All of your students' parents and other affected family members (e.g., siblings), the family members of the faculty and support staff, and other concerned community members (e.g., your school's staff, people from other schools, caregivers) should be invited to attend the family/community meeting. All of your students also should be made welcome to accompany their parents to the family/community meeting.

Do not allow media representatives—even the local media—to attend. The students, staff, and family and community members who will be in attendance will need a safe forum in which they can speak freely and express their emotions without worrying about being either quoted or photographed. Have everyone attending the meeting enter through one main door, and have the Security Liaison (with back-up assistance, if necessary) posted there to deny entrance to the media. The Security Liaison should tell all the media representatives who arrive that the Media Liaison will hold a press conference immediately following the adjournment of the family/community meeting.

(*NOTE*: Your local media may be severely affected by the crisis that has occurred in your community and will likely benefit from assistance in processing their own reactions to the crisis. Such processing should be done in a separate session, however. *See Chapter Five, "Processing the Crisis," for additional information*.)

Make facilitating this meeting a group effort. The exact participants will vary by situation and community but in general would include the following:

- The highest representative from the school system available (e.g., the superintendent or associate superintendent) to open the meeting. He or she will briefly express the district's concern about what has happened and introduce the Crisis Coordinator/head administrator of your school.

- The Crisis Coordinator to facilitate the rest of the meeting, introducing the other speakers and setting the pace of the event, and to outline the plans of the school.

- A police spokesperson (e.g., the county sheriff) to handle all discussion related to any crime committed, the suspected perpetrator(s), and evidence.
- The district attorney (or a designated representative from the D.A.'s office) to discuss prosecution of any suspected perpetrator(s) in custody, the relevant laws of your state, and the legal process in general.
- A victims' advocate to explain the services available in your county, city, and state for victims and their families.
- A hospital/medical representative to update the community on the medical condition of those injured during the crisis. (If it is not possible to arrange for a hospital spokesperson to attend, the Medical Liaison or the police spokesperson can provide this information.)
- The Counseling Liaison—with the assistance of any outside crisis team members assisting your school, or the rest of your school's counseling staff—to discuss typical reactions to crisis and what parents can do to assist their children and to lead those attending in processing their reactions to the crisis.
- The Security Liaison (with back-up, if necessary) to bar the media from entering the meeting.
- The Media Liaison to hold a press conference after the meeting.
- The Red Cross, if that organization responded to your school's crisis (*see Chapter Four, "Help Is at Hand"*), to provide food and drink to those attending.

In general, the higher the level of the people leading this meeting, the more concern will be communicated to the audience. For example, the sheriff himself or herself is preferred to a random police spokesperson. The district attorney for your county, rather than a lower level attorney from his or her office, will garner more respect when addressing the crowd. Encourage those at the highest levels to attend this meeting. If the crisis was catastrophic, consider asking your state's attorney general and/or governor to speak.

How/Agenda

As people arrive for the meeting, give them the parent/family information packet created earlier in the day (*see "Task List" previously in this chapter for more information*), which should include the most updated Crisis Fact Sheet and any other pertinent information (e.g., copies of relevant district policies, state laws, etc.). The more helpful information you can provide to parents and other community members in black and white, the better off they'll be at home after they've left the supportive environment of the meeting or need to refresh their memory about something they heard there.

Plan to spend the first half of the meeting providing information, and make the second half an open forum. Let the audience do most of the talking in the second half; they'll need plenty of time to ask questions and vent their emotions. Administrators often balk at this aspect of the family/community meeting. They're generally more comfortable simply giving the audience the facts, stating the time of any funerals, mentioning that the school will be open the next day, and thanking everyone for coming. Many are uncomfortable delving into the emotionality of the situation. But the more you address the emotionality, the more you can help your community. Providing the opportunity to "let off emotional steam" is important: It helps people begin working on a new start.

At the family/community meeting in Jonesboro, Arkansas, the national crisis team suggested that the parents and other adults meet in one room and the students in another to process their reactions to the crisis. They thought it would be more appropriate to work with those two age groups separately. However, the crowd reacted with boos and hisses. During a severe crisis, shaken parents and students may not want to be out of one another's sight. If this is the case with your audience, it's certainly fine to address the adults and students (even young students) together.

Use the following agenda as a guideline:

7:00-7:10

> The superintendent opens the meeting, expresses the district's concern and sadness, and briefly reviews the plans and goals for the evening. He or she then introduces the Crisis Coordinator and turns the floor over to him or her.
>
> The Crisis Coordinator thanks everyone for coming and asks any media representatives in the room to please leave the meeting. After giving them a chance to leave, he or she asks, "Now is there anyone here not known to someone else from our community?" This question will weed out any persistent media representatives. The Crisis Coordinator then encourages everyone present to pick up a copy of the parent/family information packet (*see "Task List" previously in this chapter for more information*), if they haven't already done so, and asks that all questions be held until after each speaker has finished. He or she then introduces the first speaker and serves as the "timekeeper" throughout the meeting.

7:10-7:20

> The county sheriff reviews all the facts of the situation in sequence, in particular discussing any crime committed, the suspected perpetrator(s), and evidence. The sheriff then answers questions from the audience (if necessary, with the assistance of the Counseling Liaison and/or the team leader of any outside crisis response team assisting your school).

7:20-7:30

The district attorney discusses the prosecution of any suspected perpetrator(s) in custody, the relevant laws of your state, and the legal process. The district attorney then answers questions from the audience (if necessary, with the assistance of the Counseling Liaison and/or the team leader of any outside crisis response team assisting your school).

7:30-7:40

The victims' advocate from the prosecutor's office explains the services available in your county, city, and state for victims and their families. He or she then answers questions from the audience (if necessary, with the assistance of the Counseling Liaison and/or the team leader of any outside crisis response team assisting your school).

7:40-7:50

A hospital/medical representative (or the Medical Liaison, or police spokesperson) updates the community on the medical condition of those injured during the crisis. The medical representative then answers questions from the audience (if necessary, with the assistance of the Counseling Liaison and/or the team leader of any outside crisis response team assisting your school).

7:50-8:00

The Crisis Coordinator outlines the plans for the school for the next day and the days following. He or she emphasizes that the school will be open the next day and encourages all students to be back in school (explaining to the audience that a counselor will be contacting the family of any student not in attendance the next day). The Crisis Coordinator then discusses the schedule for the next day (including any special security measures, such as students not going outside for recess), planned activities (i.e., explaining that the regular curriculum will be modified/set aside and time will be given for students to process their reactions to the crisis), and counseling services that will be available to the students. (*See "Modifying the Curriculum" in Chapter Six and "Providing Counseling Services" in Chapter Seven for more information.*) He or she also announces the times of any funerals that have been set.

8:00-8:15

The Counseling Liaison (with the assistance of the team leader of any outside crisis response team assisting your school) discusses how the parents and other family members can help their children (and themselves) deal with the effects of the crisis. Using the parent/family information packet your team has prepared as a guideline, he or she discusses children's typical responses to a tragedy and what parents can do to assist them. The Counseling Liaison then reviews the counseling services available to the students at your school and mentions other resources and agencies in the community that may be of assistance in dealing with the trauma. He or she also asks the students to have patience with their parents and to try to open up to them and let them help.

For information about children's and adults' common reactions to crisis, see "Crisis Effects and Grief" in Chapter Seven.

Next, the Counseling Liaison discusses stress management, the importance of maintaining family routines, the need for increased supervision of their children (i.e., watching to see whether their crisis effects are increasing in severity), and the importance of family members taking good care of themselves (e.g., by going to bed at a reasonable hour and eating proper meals). It is beneficial to point out that during periods of high stress, such as after a crisis, people often stop doing the positive things they were doing previously to help them cope with their lives. When asked, they'll say, for example, "Well, no, I'm not getting out and walking," or "No, I'm not doing things with my friends." During a crisis people tend to pull back and stop doing the very things that help them cope, and help them to be a strong support person for their children.

See "Helping Your Child Cope" in Chapter Eight for tips to communicate to parents.

"Getting back into routines will be an attempt at regaining whatever passes for 'control' of individuals' lives."

(Lieberman, 1998, p. 15)

8:15-9:00

The various speakers then spend the remaining time answering audience members' questions and helping them to process their reactions to the crisis. The most appropriate speaker should answer each question (e.g., legal questions would be addressed by the sheriff or D.A., questions about trauma by the Counseling Liaison, etc.). The Counseling Liaison, with the assistance of any outside crisis team members and/or the rest of your school's counseling staff, then facilitates the "processing" portion of the meeting, using the NOVA model.

See "How Do You Process?" in Chapter Five for complete instructions on this technique and the NOVA model.

Depending upon the number of parents attending (and the number willing to discuss their reactions to the crisis), the Counseling Liaison may or may not be able to follow the NOVA model exactly. The NOVA technique takes a good bit of time and calls for the participants to be seated in a circle in order to talk and express their emotions. This format may work for 50 or so participants but obviously would be impossible in a meeting with hundreds of participants (as they had in Jonesboro)—in the latter case a standard "lecture" format would be preferable. The point is to simply do your best to deal with the emotionality. The Counseling Liaison should use as many of the NOVA principles as are feasible, and remain flexible. It is important to let the audience members set the pace for this portion of the meeting; they need to feel they are being listened to.

When answering questions, all speakers should attempt to shift the focus from the past (i.e., "If only such-and-such, then this tragedy wouldn't have happened") to the present and future needs of your community. Recall from the Jonesboro case study that Dr. Poland asked the audience: "What are we going to do now? Your children are right here. What are we going to do to help them? We're going to have to focus on what we can do tomorrow." It may take a concerted effort to defuse the anger of the audience.

The Counseling Liaison should end this portion of the meeting on a positive note. When the allotted time is about up, he or she should emphasize the resiliency and coping skills of the audience and the assistance available within the community. He or she should try to instill a sense of hope about the future. He or she also should reiterate that it is important for all the students to be back in school tomorrow.

The Counseling Liaison should encourage anyone in the audience who wishes to visit the site of the tragedy to do so. (Of course such visits will have to wait until the police have opened the area and the worst of the physical evidence, such as bloodstains, has been cleaned up.) Visiting the site of the tragedy helps survivors understand that the event was real and makes it easier for them to recall sensory perceptions, which is helpful in processing their reactions to the crisis. Children, in particular, may distort the actual event or physical surroundings and in their minds make the event even worse than it really was. Adults, too, often feel the need to revisit the site of a severe crisis to try to make sense of it and get the facts straight so that they can move on to other stages of recovery. School personnel (and/or mental health volunteers) should monitor these visits and offer assistance to those who become overwhelmed with emotion.

"I never returned to the area where I was shot. I'm not going to. I heard there were bullet holes in the gym, but that's not something I want to see."

—Crystal Amanda Barnes, 13, shooting victim from Jonesboro, Arkansas (Barnes & Martin-Morris, 1998, p. 110)

Next, the Counseling Liaison should ask for a show of hands of who in the audience still has questions and would like to speak with a counselor. Ask these individuals to come to the front of the room at the end of the meeting to speak with your crisis response team members. If they are outnumbered by audience members still needing assistance, ask any mental health workers in attendance to come to the front of the room as well to help in assisting these people.

9:00-9:05

The Crisis Coordinator closes the meeting. He or she announces that there will be another family/community meeting the next night as well (in the case of a severe crisis) and asks those in attendance to please not speak with the media about the meeting when they leave the school. In particular, they should respect the privacy of those who expressed their emotions in the safe environment of the meeting. The Crisis Coordinator should emphasize that a school representative will be holding a press conference right after the meeting, and it would be helpful for the media to receive their information from just one source. He or she should assure the audience that their privacy will be respected by the Media Liaison.

9:05

The Media Liaison holds a press conference about the meeting outside the school, as far away as possible from the door from which the audience members will be leaving. He or she emphasizes to the media the positive effects of meetings like the family/community meeting just held for beginning the healing of the community. The Media Liaison also explains the school's plans for the next day and the following days and the counseling services that will be available to the students. The Media Liaison can report on any and all facts provided at the meeting but does not provide information about any private emotions or reactions communicated by the audience members.

The Media Liaison concludes this final press conference of the day by providing all the media representatives with a copy of the parent/family information packet used in the family/community meeting. He or she then reiterates the boundaries being enforced for the media personnel and announces the time and location of the first press conference the next day.

See "Cooperating With the Media" in Chapter Three for tips on holding press conferences.

For Concerned People Elsewhere ...

Community Meetings/Memorials

When something terrible happens to people in this country, especially when it happens in a school, those who hear about the tragedy often feel the need to gather together, to express their sympathy, and to process their own fears and anger about the incident. During the horrific shooting massacre at Columbine High School in Littleton, Colorado, in April 1999, in which 15 people died and many more were injured, people all over the state (indeed, the nation) gathered together to listen to the coverage of the unfolding crisis and to express their shock and grief. When events seem to be spinning out of control, it is comforting to gather with family members, friends, and neighbors.

Community meetings such as that described in this chapter section are helpful not just for those who have personally experienced the crisis, but for people elsewhere, as well. The information

continued—

presented here can be used as a basic guideline for meetings across the country (if applicable), with the format modified to best suit the needs of each community. You might invite your school administrators, local government representatives, mental health workers, and local clergy members to speak. In a supportive environment, it is important to allow sufficient time for community members of all ages to express and process their fears, anger, and sadness (*see Chapter Five, "Processing the Crisis"*). Provide information to parents to help them support their children during the crisis aftermath, including information about the mental health resources available in the community for those who need additional assistance in dealing with their crisis reactions. Finally, depending upon the intensity of the emotions being expressed, you may want to include a "problem-solving" portion of the meeting. Some communities may wish to progress quickly to discussion of prevention strategies. Others, perhaps closer to the crisis scene or communities that have experienced their own recent loss or tragedy, may need time simply to cry with one another and receive reassurance that the thoughts and emotions they are having are common and natural after hearing about a severe crisis.

One touching community meeting, sponsored by the Peak to Peak Healthy Communities Project (PPHCP), was held in the mountain town of Nederland, Colorado, five days after the shooting at Columbine High. Many in the audience were families. When the teens in the room were asked if they felt afraid after hearing about the shooting, about two thirds of the young people stood up to acknowledge that they were feeling fearful. The town's mayor then told them that adults who cared about them and wanted to help keep them safe surrounded them. He stated, "We love each and every one of you." The principals of the local elementary and secondary schools talked about what their staffs had done to assist their students and discussed briefly the focus on school safety on their campuses. Local clergy members provided inspiring and comforting words.

The teens and adults then gathered in separate rooms to process their crisis reactions. (The counselors working with the young people followed aspects of the NOVA model; *see Chapter Five*.) Those attending the meeting created a community altar, placing such items as a blooming Columbine plant, photos, and a small statue of Kuan Yin (the Chinese goddess of compassion and protector of children) upon it. After all the community members who wished to speak were provided the opportunity to do so, candles were lit in memory of those killed at the school and as an expression of hope for the future. A large banner was signed with words of sympathy to be delivered to the school, and then the meeting closed with the presentation of a bloom from the altar bouquets to each child and teenager in attendance to signify how precious these youth are to their community. There were many tears and hugs, and most people left the gathering feeling better for having experienced the sense of community and healing that the meeting provided.

References

Alarming rash of school threats. (1999, April 30). *MSNBC*. Available online: http://www.msnbc.com/news/264186.asp

Barnes, C. A., & Martin-Morris, D. (1998, September). I was shot at school. *Teen*, pp. 108-110.

Crisis communication: Preparing an effective response. (1998, June). *NSPRA Bonus*, p. 4.

District School Board of Pasco County. (1994a). *Crisis intervention team program rationale and structure*. Land O'Lakes, FL: Author.

District School Board of Pasco County. (1994b). *Handling a class after a student dies* [Handout]. Land O'Lakes, FL: Author.

Lieberman, R. (1998, Fall). Schoolyard tragedies: Coping with the aftermath. *School Safety*, pp. 14-16.

Obmascik, M. (1999, April 23). Bomb evidence points to plot to destroy school. *Denver Post*. Available online: http://www.denverpost.com/news/shot0423a.htm

Paine, C. (1998, November). Tragedy response and healing: Springfield unites. *NASP Communiqué, 27*(3), 16-17.

Pitcher, G. D., & Poland, S. (1992). *Crisis intervention in the schools*. New York: Guilford.

Prendergast, J., & Pressley, D. S. (1997, December 2). Third student dies from rampage. *Cincinnati Enquirer*. Available online: http://enquirer.com/editions/1997/12/02/loc_kyshoot.html

Sandall, N. (1986). Early intervention in a disaster: The Cokeville hostage/bombing crisis. *NASP Communiqué, 15*(2), 1-2.

Sleek, S. (1998, June). After the storm, children play out fears. *American Psychological Association's Monitor, 29*(6), 12.

Squad found almost 60 bombs at Columbine. (1999, May 7). *CNNinteractive*. Available online: http://cnn.com/US/9905/07/school.shooting.01/

When disaster strikes: Questions schools should consider when developing a crisis management plan. (1998, April). *Practical Strategies for Maintaining Safe Schools: School Violence Alert, 4*(4), 7.

chapter three

Here Come the Media

A school crisis will almost always draw some media attention. The amount will depend upon the severity of the crisis and what else is happening in the news that day. The media coverage may be limited to local television and/or radio stations and newspapers. Or affiliates of the major television networks' news divisions from around the country, CNN (Cable News Network), journalists from prominent national newspapers, and reporters for national newsmagazines could quickly set up camp outside your school. There could be literally hundreds of media representatives assembled on the first day of a severe school crisis, as described by Cathy Paine (1998), a crisis response team leader in Springfield, Oregon:

> Throughout the first day and night [of our school shooting], the media vans and satellite trucks rolled in from across the nation. Before the first hour had passed, a CNN helicopter hovered overhead, transmitting images of our new-found horrific "fame." Reporters from as far away as Japan, Portugal, England, and Australia quickly took on a larger-than-life presence in our normally quiet community. ABC, NBC, CBS, NPR, Inside Edition, Hard Copy, USA Today, TIME, Life, Newsweek, People, Rolling Stone, and Psychology Today all made their appearances. Before long, a surrealistic scene developed as the street in front of the high school was reduced to a one-lane road, with cars forced to crawl between the constantly humming generators and blazing lights of 20 white satellite vans (p. 16).

A media presence at your school when you are trying to deal with a traumatic or frightening situation may feel very intrusive to you. The media may get in the way of your school's crisis response (if you let them), report unsubstantiated or incorrect information (unless you provide them with accurate facts about the crisis), and intimidate you with a barrage of difficult questions (unless you're prepared to address them). In general, having the media observing the actions of your school will turn up the heat another notch in an already pressure cooker-type situation.

You may wish that the media weren't there, but *you can't make them go away.* Media coverage of events deemed newsworthy is simply a fact of life in our democracy. The media have a job to do and will do it with or without your help. For the most part, you cannot control who covers the story, what they say, whom they talk to, or what they film or photograph—such is the nature of a free press. If the media show up at your school, they will leave with a story. Just what story they will tell will be in large part determined by your response, and you may not have a lot of time to formulate an appropriate response because within 24 hours (or less) the media may be on to another story. Thus, it is in your best interest to cooperate with the media to a reasonable extent as quickly as possible on the first day of the crisis. Treating the media like the enemy will only result in your looking bad in your community and possibly to the nation.

> "When the President of the United States phoned, we realized that this tragedy would affect not only the 11,300 students and 1,200 employees of the Springfield School District, but the entire Eugene-Springfield community, the state of Oregon, and even the entire nation."
>
> —Cathy Paine, Crisis Response Team Leader, Springfield, Oregon, Public Schools (Paine, 1998, p. 16)

To best balance the media's need to report on the event with your need for the time and space to respond to the crisis, we recommend using a two-pronged approach when working with the media that involves "containment" and "cooperation" (Pitcher & Poland, 1992). This approach is detailed in the following sections.

Containing the Media

The first aspect of the media plan is containment. Essentially, containment means setting appropriate limits for the media. The media, especially national television and newsmagazine reporters, cannot always be counted on to cover a violence-related story in your community in an appropriate manner—that is, without excess or gratuitous footage of carnage, mourning students, and agitated family members. Although not a school example, the following account of the actions of some Los Angeles news choppers covering a story in their competitive media market in May 1998 illustrates the lack of taste and judgment sometimes displayed by the media.

A 40-year old maintenance worker in Los Angeles who was apparently distraught about his HIV-positive status and bureaucratic difficulties he was encountering with his HMO commandeered a heavily traveled section of freeway in the city over the lunch hour. With thousands of people watching on television, he shut his dog in the cab of his pickup truck and set the vehicle on fire. He then "pick[ed] up a shotgun, place[d] its butt against a wall, ben[t] his head to the barrel and pull[ed] the trigger" (Chua-Eoan,

1998, p. 30). The news choppers filmed his fatal shot and clearly showed the burnt-out truck (the dog died too) and a river of blood that ran from the victim's head, where he lay dead near the center lane line, almost to the side guardrail. As reported in Chua-Eoan (1998), "Local stations [there] were inundated with phone calls; station managers … broadcast apologies and toll-free numbers for viewers to call for psychological counseling" (p. 30). In today's intense competition for ratings, the line between reporting and sensationalizing can be easily crossed.

Containment of the media was discussed briefly in Chapter One. (*See "Securing the Crime Scene/Containing the Media" in Chapter One for information about denying the media access to your campus.*) Now let's define more clearly what constitutes "inappropriate" media coverage of a school crisis. The media should not:

- Be on the grounds of your school.
- Be in the school itself, particularly roaming the halls and/or surrounding the crime scene.
- Film injured and/or deceased members of the school community.
- Film mourning members of the school community or their family members.
- Release names of victims and/or suspected student perpetrator(s) prior to family member notification.
- Obtain and/or use photos of victims or suspected student perpetrator(s) without their family members' permission.
- Bother victims' or suspected student perpetrator(s)' families with painful questions and requests for personal information.
- Intimidate or overwhelm students with questions about their reactions to the crisis, either at school or at their own homes.
- Attend family/community meetings held at the school, where their presence would likely inhibit family members from speaking freely and obtaining the assistance they and their children need.

To prevent these types of abuses from occurring in your situation, your school and the Media Liaison should take the following steps:

- Deny the media access to your campus, utilizing your school's security personnel/Security Liaison, the police, and, if absolutely necessary, the

"I think 95% [of the hundreds of media representatives who covered the story of the shooting at Westside Middle School near Jonesboro, Arkansas] acted properly, but there was that five percent that would sneak around to try and get on the campus…. [I was] fielding calls at all hours. [The media] would shove a microphone in your face anytime you moved. Some showed a lack of sensitivity. I realize it was just five percent, but when you take into account there were 300 plus here, five percent can be very troublesome."

—Grover Cooper, the now retired superintendent of Westside School District (Fugate, 1999, p. 1A)

"… [N]o media were allowed on the [Thurston High School] campus until after school resumed, and then only briefly late at night. This was done to minimize the filming of traumatic images and to allow the students' first view of campus to be in person, not on television."

—Cathy Paine, Crisis Response Team Leader, Springfield, Oregon, Public Schools (Paine, 1998, p. 16)

National Guard (*see "Securing the Crime Scene/Containing the Media" in Chapter One for more information*).

- Make every effort to direct the media to gather in a location away from the school—such as a room in the central office or a nearby school—for a press conference during which they will receive information about the crisis. After a May 1998 school shooting in Springfield, Oregon, for example, "The media center was set up in Springfield's City Hall. City, county, school, and hospital officials were available to speak. Press conferences were held there throughout the day to update the information" ("Control the Media," 1998, p. 4).

  The media will probably resist relocating, as they prefer to interview with a shot of the school/crime scene in the background. Plus, they will not want to miss any new developments at the scene. You will likely only be able to detain the media across the street. In Jonesboro, for example, the media were "... moved to a hill within sight of the school grounds, but not within shouting distance" (Lieberman, 1998, p. 15).

- Announce that any media who show up early for the press conference and are trying to obtain their stories from those you do not wish to be exposed to the media, such as your students, will be denied admittance to the press conference when it begins (Lieberman, 1999).

See "Injury/Death Notification" and "Communicating With Parents/Family Members" in Chapter One for more information.

- Do not provide the names of victims or suspected student perpetrator(s) outside the school they attend(ed)/work(ed) in before all family members have been notified.

- Do not provide photos of, or personal information about, such people without parental/family member permission. (The media will likely obtain these things anyway with a little digging—such as by scanning photos from the previous year's yearbook—but they shouldn't come from the school, in any event.)

- Do not provide the names of witnesses to the violence, the names of friends/family members of victims or suspected student perpetrator(s), or the names of students/staff in nearby classrooms.

See "Liability and Litigation" in Chapter Twelve for more information.

- The Campus Liaison should clearly communicate to all staff members that *only you, the Media Liaison, and the Crisis Coordinator are to provide any information to any media representative at any time during the crisis.* Staff members should refer any media representatives who approach them to the appropriate crisis team members. (*NOTE*: This policy will be of particular importance if a lawsuit is filed against your school and/or its employees. Inaccurate statements made to the press could come back to haunt your school later.)

- Students, in particular, may feel violated by media scrutiny. (Some of the students of Westside Middle School near Jonesboro "flipped off" the media representatives from the windows of their school buses on the last day the media were outside their school, expressing their anger at the intrusive nature of the reporting.) Ask the faculty to instruct all their students in media basics before they leave school on the first day of the crisis. Teachers should make sure the students understand that they do not *have* to talk to reporters just because they are asked a question and provide them with a verbal line of defense, such as: "I don't want to talk to you," "Please leave me alone," "Don't take my picture," or, for older students, "No comment."

- To help shield students from the media when leaving the school, the Security Liaison and police should direct the students off campus from side entrances of the school building (Cummings, 1998).

- The Parent/Family Liaison should advise all family members who arrive at the school not to discuss the crisis with reporters as they leave. In particular, the family members should not provide personal information about victims or suspected student perpetrator(s).

  See "Communicating With Parents/Family Members" in Chapter One.

- If the families of victims and suspected student perpetrator(s) welcome your assistance, "run interference" for them with the media. For example, accompany the family members from the school to the hospital, waiving off the media. Also communicate with the families later in the day as well as in the days following the crisis to see how the school can help with regard to the media. If your family member was injured or killed, or your child was suspected of perpetrating violence at school, you would likely not be pleased about television news vans pulling up in front of your house. The school's role would be to lend support and even to serve as a go-between with the media, if that would be helpful for the families. The Media Liaison could say, for example: "This incident is generating all this media attention. How can we help you? Perhaps we can share some information or a statement from you. If we can take care of the media here at school, then maybe they'll leave you alone." (The media, for the most part, would rather get most of their story from the school anyway, because then they would not have to bother family members for details.)

- Deny the media access to all family/community meetings held after the crisis.

  See "The Family/Community Meeting" in Chapter Two for more information.

- If you, the Media Liaison, are also the head administrator, the central office may need to manage media requests so that you can attend to the rest of the crisis intervention.

- Most important, do not stay silent! You must provide the media with the information they need, as quickly as possible. (*See the next section, "Cooperating With the Media" for guidelines.*)

Cooperating With the Media

Cooperating with the media means providing them with the information they need to accurately report the story. Do not even contemplate refusing to speak with the media. For the good of your school and your community, you must work with the media who are reporting on the crisis at your school.

If you do not speak with the media, the following will likely be the result:

- The media will be scrambling to get something on the air or in print—fast. If they are not provided with the facts from a reputable source (i.e., you), they will do the best they can with what they have, piecing together a story based upon rumors, half-truths, and any other snippets of information they can gather from other sources. The release of inaccurate information could be both painful for family members of victims/suspected student perpetrator(s) and detrimental to your school and community.

- Your faculty, support staff, students and their parents, and family members of victims/suspected student perpetrator(s) will be harassed by media representatives who will feel forced to obtain their information wherever and however they can.

- The media may find sources who portray your school in a negative light. For example, in May 1998 a student brought a gun in a backpack to a Houston school, and the gun accidentally discharged in a classroom. The bullet hit another student in the leg. While the district administrators discussed what to do about the media, a former student who had been expelled from the school showed up and basically told the media gathered outside the school: "Man, there are guns everywhere in that school. That's an unsafe place and I'm really glad I don't go to school there." You must proactively counter these types of negative statements.

- The media will draw comparisons between your school crisis and other incidents of school violence in the news. Take the prior example of the gun accidentally discharging in a Houston classroom: This incident coincidentally happened on the same day as the nationally publicized shooting rampage in Springfield, Oregon, in which a 15-year old student shot and killed two others and injured 22 after killing his own parents. The two events were quite dissimilar, yet the media drew comparisons. It was up to the Houston administrators to emphasize that their school shooting was accidental and not fatal.

- You're going to waste valuable time and energy focusing on something you can't do anything about. That is, the media *will* report on the story.

An agitated school principal might say, for example, "We're going to make the media get out of the neighborhood. We're not going to let any of the kids talk to them." But realistically, you can't make the media leave. And if your students walk or drive home from school, it's likely the media will approach them. You have so little time to respond appropriately in a crisis. It's essential that you use the time you do have productively.

- When the school and/or district has no official response after a crisis, you will appear uncaring at best. At worst, you may appear defensive and negligent. It is crucial for you to represent your school and district positively, to go out there and acknowledge what has happened, explain that you have a crisis plan, tell the media what you're doing and that you're doing everything possible, and state that you regret that the event has occurred. (Remember, you have a responsibility to communicate directly to your school community members; don't abdicate that responsibility by allowing a police spokesperson to handle all the press requests after a school crisis.)

- You will miss an opportunity to provide valuable information to your community about such things as coping strategies, messages of prevention, and such practical matters as the time and location of the family/community meeting to be held that evening.

Unfortunately, media relations is not a part of most school administrators' training. Thus, many school administrators fail to take action with the media because they lack confidence, they're uncertain about what to say, and they worry that they might make things worse. Many also are worried about being blamed for the incident. "If I stay in the background here," they think, "I might be blamed a little bit, but if I get out there, then people see me …." Yet consider what one Houston superintendent told a school principal there: "I will not hold you accountable for what you say to the media. I'm going to hold you accountable for what they *say* you said."

> "Often, leaders lose the confidence of their communities not because of the crisis, but because of the way they handled the crisis."
>
> —Rich Bagin, Executive Director, National School Public Relations Association (Bagin, 1998)

A joke in this country is that many Americans fear public speaking more than they fear death. While that may or may not be true, a fear of speaking to the media is quite common. Doing so can be very intimidating, especially if national media have gathered. Given that the Media Liaison, head administrator, and/or superintendent must address the media, however, the pointers in the remainder of this chapter will make the process smooth, (relatively) painless, and productive.

Before the Press Conference

- As soon after your initial, first-hour crisis response as is feasible, the Media Liaison should announce the time and location of the first press conference. Make it clear that your school will be cooperating with the media as long as they "play by the rules." The number one rule is that the media leave your students alone ("Control the Media," 1998).

- Continue to hold press conferences throughout the day. Hold a press conference every two to three hours, even if there is no new information to announce. The first press conference will likely address only the facts of the crisis. The second and later press conferences will provide you with the opportunity to emphasize your district's policies and programs and information about the crisis management steps your school is, and will be, taking (e.g., increased security) (Cummings, 1998).

- If you, the Media Liaison, are not also the head administrator, the media will at some point want to hear from the building principal (and likely, in severe crises, the superintendent as well). He or she should use the same procedures recommended for you, the Media Liaison (which follow). Help the administrator prepare for the interview(s), if appropriate.

- In addition to press conferences, grant reasonable interview requests. Your school's administrators, counseling staff, and crisis response team members should be made available at some point for interviews. Students and staff members should not.

- When granting interview requests, require prior knowledge of the interview's subject matter. You might also require that your district's attorney be present during all interviews ("Control the Media," 1998).

- Before press conferences, media representatives may approach you individually, trying to get their own story first. They might say, for example, "I know there's a press conference in a few minutes, but could you talk to me, just me, for a moment?" Instead, give all the media the same story at one time—through press conferences—so conflicting information is not provided to the various media, and all your time is not taken up with individual interviews.

- Provide a sign-in sheet and identification stickers for media representatives who attend press conferences ("Control the Media," 1998).

See "Verifying Information/Crisis Fact Sheet" in Chapter One for more information.

- Prepare a written statement to be read to the media. The basis of this statement should be the Crisis Fact Sheet. Also include in your press release pertinent district policies and procedures, particularly those pertaining to weapons or any "zero tolerance" policies ("Crisis Communication," 1998; Cummings, 1998; Stevenson, 1994).

- Develop three to five key messages. Ask yourself, "What are the messages the school needs to drive home?" (Staggenborg, 1998).

- Gear your statements to a broadcast audience, rather than to print. A 1998 *Newsweek* poll (cited in Cummings, 1998) showed that more than 65% of people obtain their news from television, so when there is an incident at school, the majority of parents will be tuning in that evening (Cummings, 1998). To best address a broadcast audience, speak in short, clear, fact-filled sentences and use catch phrases that quickly and clearly communicate the school's message and are appropriate for broadcast "*sound bites.*"

- Before releasing the press release, have more than one person double-check the accuracy of the information and have the Crisis Coordinator/head administrator (if he or she is not also the Media Liaison) sign off on its content. Also be sure the press release contains only medically and legally correct information (Stevenson, 1994).

- Before the press conference, take the time to rehearse what you are going to say. As one public relations professional cautions, "One misspoken phrase can be 'replayed' over and over again by all your local and even national media" (Bagin, 1998). Have someone on your crisis response team fire some questions at you to "warm you up" before you address the media.

During the Press Conference

- The Media Liaison should begin the press conference by asking the media to hold all questions until after you've made your statements.

- Always release information regarding student and staff safety first (Cummings, 1998).

- Remember not to release the names of victims or suspected student perpetrator(s) before their families have been notified, and do not provide personal information about such individuals.

- Give all the known facts of the incident in a complete and truthful manner. Warned the National School Public Relations Association (NSPRA): "Tell the truth even when you feel it may damage the district's reputation…. Reporters will find the truth—one way or another. They'll talk to students, police, staff members, and others to get to the bottom of the story…. You don't want to be placed in a position of covering up an incident. Once you lose your credibility, you have lost any chance of bringing everyone together to solve the problem" (Bagin, 1998).

- The NSPRA continued, "Tell the truth and in the same breath tell them what you are doing to fix the problem" (Bagin, 1998). Explain in brief the crisis plan, emphasize that you're doing everything possible to respond to this crisis in an appropriate manner, and emphasize that your district and school care about the situation.

- Emphasize any preparatory actions being taken by your school/district and mention the support being provided to staff and students. Stress that the school was not caught completely unaware and unprepared by the crisis. Mention counseling services available to students, their families, and staff, and the extended hours the school will be open to provide those services.

See "The Family/ Community Meeting" in Chapter Two for information about the meeting's format and content.

- Remember that you can utilize the media to dispense important information about assistance available to the community. Be sure to state the time and location of the family/community meeting and encourage all family members and affected community members to attend. Highlight actions parents can take to help their children cope with the effects of the crisis. Also emphasize that the school will be open the following day and that it would be beneficial for all students to be in attendance.

- Detail the school's plan for the following day. By providing this type of specific information, you help make the school look responsible and on top of the situation.

If the tragedy is a suicide of a school community member, see "Media Coverage of Suicides" in Chapter Eleven for additional information.

- After providing all the pertinent facts, take a few minutes to focus on prevention (especially in the case of a suicide). For example, when an Austin, Texas, student committed suicide in October 1991, the school's media spokesperson asked the media to come back in a few weeks to work on a story on suicide prevention. Also talk to the media about any appropriate prevention programs your school/district has, such as character education, conflict resolution, anger control, "bully-proofing," drug/alcohol education, and peer mediation ("Crisis Communication," 1998).

- Emphasize that violence is a societal problem—not just a school problem—and that violence prevention involves a *community-wide* effort ("Crisis Communication," 1998). Phrase an answer by saying, for example, "In our society we have a problem with kids having access to guns (or whatever is relevant)."

- When taking questions from the media, repeat the question before giving your answer. That gives you a moment to formulate your statement and also clarifies to which question you are responding. Take a deep breath before speaking.

- If you are asked a question that really "throws you," ask the reporter to repeat the question. This buys you a few seconds to compose yourself and think of an appropriate answer.

- Don't be hesitant to set the pace of the press conference. Take the time you need before answering media questions to think clearly about your answers. Do not blurt out the first thing that comes into your mind because you are feeling pressured by a rapid succession of questions. Remember, no one will leave until you're done speaking. The media want your information; you're at the helm.

- Answer only one question at a time, and ignore interruptions. If you stop and start in the middle of your responses, jumping from question to question, you'll appear disjointed. No matter how chaotic the scene, remain calm and communicate clearly.

- Don't lose your temper ("Advice on Managing," 1998).

- Just because a question has been asked doesn't mean that it must be answered. Ignore inappropriate questions, if possible. Or say, for example, "That's not what we need to focus on at this time," or "I'm sorry, I can't provide that information."

- You can also rephrase inappropriate questions posed by the media and then answer the rephrased questions by providing your key points. This technique is helpful for working in important information and messages that you wish to convey.

- "Skip" Jernigan, attorney for the Pearl (Mississippi) School District, found that if there was information he wanted emphasized in the media he should use the reporter's name in his statement. He discovered that, most of the time, television reporters wouldn't edit out their own name ("Control the Media," 1998).

- *Answer all questions related to student safety*, so that community members will understand that the school is acting to protect all students and staff (Stevenson, 1994).

- As advised by the NSPRA, "Limit your comments to school issues. Don't get trapped into comments that should be answered by police officials" (Bagin, 1998). Likewise, ask that the police not make statements on behalf of your school (Cummings, 1998).

- Do not speculate. Discuss only the facts of the crisis. Advised Karen McCuiston, PR director at McCracken County School District in West Paducah, Kentucky, "There is nothing wrong with saying we are conducting an investigation" ("Control the Media," 1998, p. 5). You could also say, "That information has not been confirmed. We will update you when we know for certain."

- If asked about something you do not know, simply say so. Do not answer "No comment" ("Advice on Managing," 1998, p. 5).

- Be yourself. Talk in your normal tone of voice using your everyday vocabulary.

See Chapter Twelve for more information on "copycat" crimes.

- Be sincere, and express your sadness and dismay about what has happened.

- If the press conference has gone well, and the Media Liaison has developed some rapport with the media representatives assembled, he or she should ask them to make every effort to avoid glamorizing the suspected perpetrator(s) or glorifying them with excessive attention. Remind them that children are attention seekers and that a focus on the perpetrator(s) could contribute to "copycat" incidents in the future. At some point you may need to do what Principal Bill Bond did in West Paducah, Kentucky—that is, refuse to answer any more questions about a suspected student perpetrator. In such cases tell the media that you would like to focus instead on what can be done to assist survivors and to work on prevention in our society.

"Journalists tend to turn to where the noise is. One of the things [the death of the victims of the April 1999 Columbine High School shooting in Littleton, Colorado] bequeaths is a reminder to look where the noise is not.… The only question that ever ought to matter to my colleagues and our customers is the one we do not ask except in retrospect, after the guns or the scandal: Who are we all in silence—at a table in the cafeteria, at a table in the library? What can journalists tell others about the mind we all share, the innocent mind and the murderous?"

—Journalist Roger Rosenblatt (1999, p. 102)

- Also remind the media that there are approximately 37 million public school children (grades K-8) in the country (U.S. Bureau of the Census, 1997) who could potentially be exposed to their coverage of the story, which might be very frightening for the children (and their parents). Children pick up newspapers, see and hear television and radio news, access the World Wide Web (WWW), and, in the cases of catastrophic crises, watch the news bulletins that interrupt their television programs. Encourage the media to use restraint in publicizing details that could terrify young viewers.

- Reiterate to the media that you intend to cooperate fully in providing them with any and all pertinent information as it becomes available and direct them to leave your students and their families alone. Announce the time of the next scheduled press conference.

- Before you leave, provide all the media representatives with copies of the Crisis Fact Sheet to support and clarify your verbal statements. Also provide them with a fact sheet about your campus/district, if such information is available ("Crisis Communication," 1998).

After the Press Conference

- Throughout the day, attempt to build rapport with the media representatives to reinforce the importance of privacy/confidentiality for all parties (e.g., victims and their family members) (Stevenson, 1994).

- As Suzette Heiman, University of Missouri public relations professor advised, "… [I]f you feel like you are in over your head, don't be afraid to call in a professional public relations firm that has the experience and expertise in dealing with the media" ("Advice on Managing," 1998).

- Further, a former president of the National School Public Relations Association advised, "The media will inevitably speculate. Visit the editorial board of [your] local paper[s] within 48 hours to give your side of the story" (Staggenborg, 1998).

- Throughout the day and evening, keep a television set and/or radio tuned to a news station to monitor the media coverage of your school's crisis (Cummings, 1998). Verify all of the facts reported, and call the appropriate party to correct any inaccuracies aired. Ask for a correction to be broadcast.

- As mentioned previously, the media will be barred from attending the family/community meeting later in the evening. After the family/community meeting, hold a short press conference at the meeting location. Doing so will:
  - Help prevent the media from approaching students and their family members.
  - Allow your school/district the opportunity to emphasize the steps being taken to assist your students and their families and to provide information about what parents can do at home to help their children cope with the crisis.

Other Area Schools

The media may contact other schools in the district or state, asking them to give their reactions to the crisis or advice about what should be done to prevent other such situations from occurring. The National School Public Relations Association has advised: "Avoid commenting on the response actions taken by the [school or] district involved in an incident since you cannot know all the details of what occurred. Instead, make a positive, generic statement about education and your own prevention programs" ("Crisis Communication," 1998, p. 4).

The media may also contact representatives of the central office. These people should refrain from speaking with the media and refer the media contacts to either the superintendent/associate superintendent or the Media Liaison of the affected school.

After the Crisis

Days immediately following the crisis

Both the Media Liaison and the Security Liaison should beat the news crews to your school on the day after the crisis, according to Jim Cummings, Public Relations Director of the Phoenix High School District, the largest urban school district in Arizona (Cummings, 1998). Arriving at the media "staging area" by no later than 7:30 AM should assure that you arrive there first. Getting there first enables you to contain the media as on the first day and practically ensures that whatever you say will make the morning news (and probably the noon edition as well), because you will be the media's only news source until the students arrive at school (Cummings, 1998).

If there is any new information for the media, the Media Liaison should brief them on these facts. If there is no new information, take the opportunity to again:

- Note your school's concern for safety and record of school safety (if appropriate).
- Review the steps being taken to secure the campus and assist the students (Cummings, 1998).
- Discuss the positive results of the family/community meeting the evening before.

Typical media coverage will last anywhere from one day to a week or more, but in smaller communities, the local media may follow up with human interest stories for a time after the crisis. Be sure to shift the focus of any of these later interviews from the suspected student perpetrator(s) to prevention efforts, the need for healing, and the need for a resolution to the incident within the community.

Long after the crisis

Your school's notoriety will likely take longer to diminish than the hours, days, or weeks that you're in the spotlight immediately following the crisis. The media may return to your school on "milestone" dates, such as the end of the school year, the beginning of the next school year, graduation/commencement, and anniversaries of the crisis. After a school shooting at Thurston High School in Springfield, Oregon, in May 1998, "... reporters and media trucks surrounded the school once again [on the first day of school in the fall] as students entered the campus filled with much excitement and some apprehension" (Paine, 1998, p. 16).

After the school shooting in West Paducah, Kentucky, Karen McCuiston, the PR director for McCracken County School District, let television crews report from in front of Heath High School only "... early in the morning before the students started to arrive and then again after 2:30 PM when the students were gone for the day" ("Control the Media," 1998, p. 5). Heath High has maintained that policy even today. Explained McCuiston, "We still have certain children [who] need extra counseling. If we have cameras on campus, even for a good reason, it could cause these kids more problems." ("Control the Media," 1998, p. 5).

Depending upon the severity of the crisis at your school, you may be approached by the media each time there is a similar incident in your district, city, state, or even elsewhere in the country. In 1989, for example, a gunman shot and killed five children on the playground of a Stockton, California, elementary school. Although it's been ten years, "Every time there is a [school] shooting elsewhere, the principal gets as many as 20 phone calls from reporters seeking comments" (Johnston, 1998, p. 29).

For the emotional recovery and long-term benefit of your school, you may wish to follow the policies of Cleveland Elementary in Stockton. The school routinely denies interview requests. Explained Principal Patricia Busher, "The media get the story and move on, but the wound is repricked and people are left helpless" (Johnston, 1998, p. 29). If the media come to the school with cameras, the school leads the students inside the school building. "We've learned that when there's no photo op, the media go away," said Busher (Johnston, 1998, p. 29).

It bears repeating: If you do speak with the media about a crisis incident elsewhere, "Avoid commenting on the response actions taken by the [school or] district involved in an incident since you cannot know all the details of what occurred. Instead, make a positive, generic statement about education and your own prevention programs" ("Crisis Communication," 1998, p. 4). Principal Busher, for example, limits her interview comments to topics she believes will be helpful to other schools (Johnston, 1998). A focus on prevention efforts—both at your school and within society as a whole—is always a helpful area to emphasize with the media.

References

Advice on managing the media after a tragedy. (1998, November). *Practical Strategies for Maintaining Safe Schools: School Violence Alert, 4*(11), 5.

Bagin, R. (1998, June). Incidents of violence call for seasoned responses by school leaders. *NSPRA Bonus*, p. 5.

Chua-Eoan, H. (1988, May 11). Too many eyes in the sky? *TIME*, p. 30.

Control the media but provide information. (1998, November). *Practical Strategies for Maintaining Safe Schools: School Violence Alert, 4*(11), 1, 4-5.

Crisis communication: Preparing an effective response. (1998, June). *NSPRA Bonus*, p. 4.

Cummings, J. (1998, July 19-22). *Never say never: Tips for educators on preparing for the unthinkable.* Paper presented at the National School Public Relations Association (NSPRA) Annual Seminar, St. Louis, Missouri.

Fugate, L. (1999, March 23). "Kind of like having a nightmare." *Jonesboro Sun*, pp. 1A-2A.

Johnston, R. C. (1998, May 27). Hope in the mourning. *Education Week, 17*(37), 26-31.

Lieberman, R. (1998, Fall). Schoolyard tragedies: Coping with the aftermath. *School Safety*, pp. 14-16.

Lieberman, R. (1999, January 22-23). *Crisis Intervention Workshop*, Walnut Creek, California.

Paine, C. (1998, November). Tragedy response and healing: Springfield unites. *NASP Communiqué, 27*(3), 16-17.

Pitcher, G. D., & Poland, S. (1992). *Crisis intervention in the schools*. New York: Guilford.

Rosenblatt, R. (1999, May 10). A note for Rachel Scott. *TIME*, p. 102.

Staggenborg, R. (1998, July 19-22). Crisis communications: Expecting the unexpected when the most is expected. *Extra! A Newsletter for the 45th Annual NSPRA Seminar*.

Stevenson, R. G. (Ed.). (1994). *What will we do? Preparing a school community to cope with crisis*. Amityville, NY: Baywood Publishing.

U.S. Bureau of the Census. (1997). *Statistical abstract of the United States, 1997: The national data book* (117th ed.). Washington, DC: Author.

real-life case study

West Paducah, Kentucky

"I'm sorry," said 14-year old Michael Carneal as he calmly walked down the hallway with his school principal. Principal Bill Bond, guiding the boy by the arm to his office, did not answer (Prendergast & Pressley, 1997). Really, what could he have said? The freshman was not in trouble for chipping graffiti into the walls of his West Paducah, Kentucky, high school or accessing the Playboy Web site from a school computer—his only prior disciplinary infractions (Bowles, 1997). Michael Carneal had just gunned down eight of his peers within approximately five seconds.

On the Wednesday before Thanksgiving, 1997, Carneal approached his friend Ben Strong—a popular senior who led an informal daily prayer group at Heath High School—between classes. He warned Strong to stay away from Bible study on Monday, saying, "Something big is going to happen" (Bowles, 1997, p. 1A). Carneal had a reputation as a jokester, so his friend and fellow bandmate didn't take him too seriously. "'I asked him what was going to happen,'" said Strong. "'He wouldn't tell me. Then I joked that I'd beat him up if he tried anything.' Carneal remained serious. 'You're not going to be able to beat me up after this,' he said, walking off quietly" (Bowles, 1997, p. 1A). Strong did worry about his friend's strange warning over the weekend, but he thought that whatever Carneal had planned, "… there would be time to negotiate or something" (Grace, 1997). Strong was wrong.

On Monday, December 1, 1997, Michael Carneal got a ride to school with his older sister, Kelly. He brought with him some bulky items taped up in a quilt, a bundle he told his sister contained props for a science project. In reality, the quilt was wrapped around two rifles and two shotguns. Carneal had stolen these guns, and a handgun, on Thanksgiving Day from the garage of a neighbor who didn't realize they were missing until deputies contacted him after the shootings (Prendergast & Pressley, 1997).

Heath High School,
West Paducah, Kentucky

Michael Carneal entered Heath High School as he did every morning through an unlocked door to the band room (Jacobson & White, 1997) and at about 7:40 AM walked to the front lobby of the school where a circle of approximately 35 students held hands, heads bowed in prayer. He stood about ten feet away, inserted shooters' earplugs into his ears, and pulled the stolen .22-caliber Ruger semiautomatic handgun from his backpack. As the student prayer group Agape said their final "Amen," Carneal opened fire, spraying bullets into their midst (Pedersen & Van Boven, 1997).

There were three loud pops, followed by a pause. When the group's leader Ben Strong heard the first shot, he "... thought it was probably Mike." He twice commanded Carneal, "Put down the gun." But he received only a momentary glance from Carneal, who aimed the gun to Strong's left and continued firing. Carneal fired a total of 12 rounds at the students (Grace, 1997).

Many students ran, terrified, out the front door of the school, while others flung themselves to the ground or hid behind walls. Sixteen-year old Emilee Miller was standing just a few feet away from Carneal when he began to fire. When she heard the gunfire, she "whirled around to see what was happening" (Collins, 1997). "He was going real slow, with no expression on his face ... just hitting anybody and everybody he could hit," she said. Panicked, she ran down the hallway, ducking into the counselor's office just as Carneal pointed the gun in her direction (Collins, 1997). Ben Strong reported that during the shooting, Carneal was "... wide-eyed. He didn't blink or anything" ("Crisis Counselors," 1997).

Another student, senior Ben Heady, was standing in front of his locker before first period when he heard the shots. "It happened real fast," he said. "I just thought they were fireworks." Then he heard screaming and saw another boy on his hands and knees, trying to get up. "He raised his head up [and] I could see where the bullet had grazed the side of his head.... That's when I figured out someone had been shot" (Prendergast & Pressley, 1997).

The first student to fall was a close friend of Carneal's, 14-year old Nicole Hadley, who may have been phoned by Carneal over the weekend and warned to stay away as well (Bowles, 1997). Nicole was pronounced dead late that night at Western Baptist Hospital when she was removed from life support. Her organs were donated. Also fatally shot were 17-year old Jessica James and 15-year old Kayce Steger. Kayce died at Lourdes Hospital in Paducah about 45 minutes after the shooting, and Jessica died during surgery Monday afternoon at Western Baptist Hospital ("Third Student Dies," 1997). Three other girls were seriously wounded, including 15-year old Melissa "Missy" Jenkins, whose spinal cord was injured in the shooting and who will likely remain paralyzed ("Carneal Indicted," 1997). Two boys—ages 15 and 17—were treated for injuries and released from the hospital ("Third Student Dies," 1997).

Principal Bond was on the phone in his office when the attack began. "Recognizing the sound of semiautomatic gunfire, Bond jumped from his desk. He could hear crying and moaning. Dashing into the lobby, he saw bodies and blood on the ground—and by the cream-colored walls … two students face to face" (Grace, 1997). Ben Strong had stood his ground against a shower of gunfire. "What are you doing? Don't shoot. Just put the gun down," he implored Carneal. When Principal Bond arrived in the lobby, Carneal pointed the gun in his direction but then put the gun down at Strong's urging (Bowles, 1997). Ben Strong rushed the younger boy, pushing him against the wall (Grace, 1997).

Principal Bond thought Carneal had laid the gun down because he was out of ammunition. But when he picked up the gun, he saw that there was still a bullet in the chamber. "That was meant for me, I know" he later said (Bowles, 1997). Reflecting on the sequence of events, he also said, "If it had not been for Ben, I'm sure I would have taken that bullet. I feel certain he saved my life" (Holliman, 1997).

As Ben Strong held the slight and passive Carneal against the wall, the younger boy seemed disoriented. An earplug fell from his ear, and his voice cracked as he spoke, looking into his friend's eyes (Grace, 1997). He was shaking as he told Strong, "I can't believe I'd do this," and asked him to "kill me now" (Hewitt, 1997). Principal Bond assigned a male teacher to watch Carneal while school personnel called for the police and ambulances. As Carneal waited for the authorities without resistance, he told the teacher, "It was like I was in a dream, and I woke up" (Hewitt, 1997).

Meanwhile the school secretary, a counselor, and teachers jumped into action, donning latex gloves (to help prevent infection) and tending to the fallen students (Prendergast & Pressley, 1997). "[Injured students] were lying all up and down the blood-stained corridor. Many students were crying and screaming. Others were huddled over the bodies of friends who'd been hit" (Collins, 1997). The county nurse assigned to Heath High was in another school that day, and because the school is in a rural area of far western Kentucky more than ten minutes passed before the first ambulance arrived to assist them. Thus some Heath High School staff members and students witnessed a great deal of trauma.

News of the shooting at Heath High was quickly broadcast on a local radio station and spread like wildfire—some parents arrived even before the paramedics. Soon family members' cars were lined up and down the road outside the school for a mile in both directions. A school staff member met all the parents at the door as they arrived. With a list of the injured, she was able to immediately inform them whether their children were on the list (Collins, 1997).

Ann and John Carneal, Michael's parents, were shocked to learn that he was the perpetrator of this tragedy. When she first heard about the shooting, Ann Carneal began gathering blankets, water, and cups to bring to the school to help. Then she heard that Michael was the shooter. When John Carneal heard word of the crisis, he went straight to Heath to check on the safety of his two children. A guidance counselor first told him that his daughter Kelly was okay, but then said, "You need to come with me." John Carneal assumed he was going to be told Michael was dead. Said Tammie Pierce, the wife of John Carneal's law partner, "John said he'd give anything if he himself could have been a victim, rather than being on the other side" (Pedersen & Van Boven, 1997). Carneal's parents later told their minister "… that they were stunned and couldn't explain what might have motivated their son to shoot the other students" (Holliman, 1997).

All the students from Heath elementary, middle, and high schools were dismissed at mid-morning Monday (Collins, 1997). On Monday night, a crowd of approximately 600 adults and teenagers attended a prayer service at Paducah's Olivet Baptist Church that was held to comfort the grieving and pray for the injured. Most sobbed throughout the brief service, and groups of teens huddled together afterward to continue to pray. Commenting about the feelings of shock and disbelief permeating the community, a youth director from another Paducah church said, "Some of us don't even know if it's real or not" (Collins, 1997).

On the advice of Kentucky's experienced state crisis response team—based in Frankfort—the school reopened the next morning with counselors and ministers available to assist the students and staff (Prendergast & Pressley, 1997). More than a hundred students gathered in the lobby of the high school before classes, "… praying silently for their classmates shot a day earlier" (Holliman, 1997; "Paducah Students," 1998). They were joined by a group from neighboring Graves County High School (Walker, 1998). "Students need to be with other students. They need to grieve together. That is why we made the decision to be in school today," said Principal Bond (Holliman, 1997).

In the days following the shooting, security remained high at the school. At least two deputy sheriffs were on duty at Heath High School and two other high schools in the county (Holliman, 1997). On Tuesday, the day following the shooting, teachers were posted at the front door of the school, and the other doors were kept locked as a security precaution ("Crisis Counselors," 1997). Principal Bond reported that "… faculty members checked students' backpacks as they arrived in an attempt to reassure both students and their parents" ("Investigators: Student May Have Told Others," 1997). However, this was the first shooting ever to occur in the 7,000-student McCracken County School District (Jacobson & White, 1997). And, since its inception in 1910, the 550-student Heath High School has never had to suspend a student for bringing a weapon to school (Bowles, 1997; "Third Student Dies," 1997). When asked by reporters about whether some students would be afraid to return to school, Principal Bond replied, "I still believe in Heath High School" (Holliman, 1997).

Kayce Steger

Members of Kentucky's legislated state crisis intervention team were present at the school in the days immediately following the shooting. They assisted the students in beginning to process their reactions to the tragedy. However, they did not have the opportunity to process the crisis with the Heath High faculty.

On Friday a joint funeral service was held for Kayce Steger, Nicole Hadley, and Jessica James at Bible Baptist Heartland Worship Center, Paducah's largest church. Kelly Carneal—Michael's older sister—was invited to sing with the school choir at the funeral (Pedersen & Van Boven, 1997). During the girls' wake thousands of people had paid their respects, waiting up to two hours to view the bodies and comfort the girls' family members. Fellow students wrote touching messages—such as a simple "I love you"—on the three identical, unfinished white caskets (Mead, 1997).

Nicole Hadley

Many of the casket messages reflected the special qualities and shattered potential of the three slain girls. Nicole Hadley, who had moved to Kentucky from Nebraska, had hoped to attend college in North Carolina to study medicine and later to play basketball in the WNBA. She played the clarinet in the school band and was described as a kind, bright student. Jessica James enjoyed teaching a Bible course and performing in a musical interpretation group sponsored by her church youth group. Jessica was accomplished on the French horn and mellophone. She loved the Loony Tunes character Tasmanian Devil, and a doll of Jessica's "trademark" character adorned her casket. Kayce Steger knew from the age of seven that she wanted to be a police officer, and she was buried with a toy police car on her casket. Kayce played the clarinet in the school band, played softball, participated in the Explorers club, and "always had a smile." She was engaged to be married to Mark Blair (Hewitt, 1997; "The Agape Fund,"

Jessica James

1998). All three girls were loving individuals, active in their community and respective churches, and will be sorely missed by their family members, friends, school, and community.

On Saturday, the annual holiday parade was held in Paducah. The holiday spirit was of course tempered by grief. Because the three slain girls—as well as Michael Carneal—had played in the school's marching band, the band "… walked silently, under a memorial banner, as church bells rang" (Nagy, 1998). Each band member carried a rose rather than his or her instrument (Goodwyn, 1997). "When the band passed by John Carneal's law office, the kids paused for a moment of silent prayer—and then marched on" (Pedersen & Van Boven, 1997). Demonstrating a noble spirit of forgiveness, the band later "… had pizza and soft drinks [in] the band room. The Carneal family was there and met with the kids and families involved. There was a lot of forgiving and loving," said band director Roger Hayes (Nagy, 1998).

Evidence of the community's strong Christian spirit was seen and heard almost everywhere, such as on a placard hanging in the school reading "We forgive because God forgave us" and one hanging next to a photograph of Michael Carneal that read "We forgive you Mike" (Pedersen & Van Boven, 1997).

Late Sunday night, six days after the shooting, a NOVA team led by Dr. Scott Poland arrived in Paducah. NOVA had been invited into the community by the county judge. The team was told that their work would focus primarily on the community, as Heath High School had already received an initial intervention from the state's crisis response team and was uncertain about the need for any additional outside assistance.

The victims' advocate from the prosecutor's office was invaluable in orienting the national team to the community, arranging transportation and other logistics, and participating in the team's planning sessions. Through her work with the NOVA team, she kept the community actively involved in every step of the national team's crisis response.

From left: Crisis responders Thomas Hoehner, Kenneth Coleman, Carl Grimes, Scott Poland, and Rev. Charles Lindsey

On Monday morning the NOVA team met at the courthouse with the mayor, the county prosecutors, and judges to identify the community members who needed the team's help. (The sheriff cleared the room of the media.) The people identified for assistance included the victims and their family members and the first responders on the scene (i.e., medical, police, and fire personnel). After identifying the people at risk, the group scheduled two community meetings.

The first meeting—for the local caregivers—was to be held that very evening. Because the team would not be meeting at Heath High, assistants to the mayor made a number of calls and found a meeting room available at Paducah's community college. People then got busy, quickly calling the school counselors and school psychologists, all the local mental health workers, and members of the clergy to invite them to the meeting.

It is estimated that 150 media representatives came to cover the story after the shooting ("Control the Media," 1998). Dr. Poland held a press conference to explain the purpose of the national team and their activities. The local radio and television stations were helpful in publicizing the times and locations of the scheduled meetings. A reporter asked how the national team interfaced with the state team that had been there last week, and Dr. Poland explained: "The NOVA team manager has been trying to reach the chair of the state team all morning. We're only here to complement the excellent work they started."

That night, the caregiver meeting was particularly well attended by the local clergy. There were many mental health workers in attendance as well. The NOVA team provided support to these professionals who were themselves affected by the tragedy. The NOVA team also gave the local caregivers a refresher on crisis intervention principles.

The NOVA team members then began contacting the victims and their families and the first responders on the scene. They were doing some valuable work within the community, but Dr. Poland was not comfortable ignoring the needs of the school. He asked for a meeting with the superintendents of both county and city schools and other top school administrators. A meeting was scheduled for the NOVA team after school Monday at county headquarters.

The initial response from the school representatives was that after six days they were "doing just fine at Heath," and "didn't need anything." Their position was that the school would recover best if the school community moved on and maintained a stiff upper lip, so to speak. Dr. Poland emphasized how much experience the team members had with severe crises, and stressed the importance of processing a crisis of that magnitude. The NOVA team and school representatives discussed the fact that the Heath High School staff had dealt with the wounded and dying students on their own for more than ten minutes and since then had not formally talked about how they were feeling with their principal or anyone else at the school. Principal Bond realized how important it was for the school staff to have the chance to talk about their involvement in the crisis response and decided to let the NOVA team hold a processing session with the school staff the next afternoon.

Principal Bond also agreed to let the two ministers on the NOVA team go to the school the next morning to offer assistance to the Agape prayer group. (Because of the separation of church and state in public schools, adults cannot be involved in the prayer group itself. However, these ministers could be nearby and available to the students when they finished their morning prayer.)

On Tuesday morning a representative from Kentucky's state crisis team arrived and stayed to collaborate with the NOVA team for the duration of their stay in West Paducah, including attending the staff meeting at Heath High School. A local school psychologist was also instrumental in helping the NOVA team members provide their crisis response, working with the NOVA team and attending all the meetings. During the early part of the day on Tuesday the team continued their work in the community and planned the staff meeting to be held that afternoon. The school arranged the meeting room—the school's library—exactly as the team requested in order to use the NOVA model. All the tables were removed, and chairs were placed in a large circle. The entire school staff—both support staff and faculty—would be attending.

To begin the staff meeting, Dr. Poland introduced the NOVA team and explained how the session would work. He told the staff that the meeting was a safe forum in which they could speak and that anything they wanted to say that day would be all right. He assured them that what they said would be confidential,* even though one of the team members would be writing some of their exact phrases on sheets of paper on an easel. They could decide what they wanted to do with the papers at the end of the session, including destroying them if they chose to do so. (Principal Bond saved the papers from the session as a "blueprint" of coping and hope for the days following the crisis.) Dr. Poland also explained that one of the ground rules was that if somebody left the circle, one of the team members would go with the person and check on his or her condition.

Utilizing the NOVA model, Dr. Poland first reviewed sequentially all the facts of the crisis. He began, "Seven days ago, Michael Carneal opened fire…." He listed the names of the dead and the injured and noted that one of the school's own students had been arrested for the crimes. He expressed that the NOVA team was saddened by the situation, saying, "I am so sorry that this has happened to you."

After reviewing all the facts, Dr. Poland began exploring the group's sensory perceptions (i.e., the senses of sight, hearing, and so forth). He asked them, "Who will go first and tell me where you were and what you were doing, what your sensory perceptions were when you first heard about this terrible

---

* The authors received permission from the appropriate staff members at Heath High School to share here a few of their comments made during this session.

event?" There was silence. Dr. Poland looked around the circle and kept repeating the question, waiting for a volunteer. Before long, one of the Heath High staff members spoke. She launched through her whole story, and Dr. Poland helped to validate what she was feeling. He explained that after a tragedy it is not uncommon to experience the feelings she was having. He then helped her to predict what she might face in the immediate future and to identify her coping skills.

This person's story opened the floodgates. Soon a number of people talked about where they were when the shooting happened and what they were doing at the time. People who were in other parts of the building spoke about feeling guilty because they hadn't experienced as much of the trauma as their colleagues. Many were second-guessing themselves. They said things such as, "I just stayed with my class. I should've done more." Dr. Poland pointed out that they had done the right thing by staying with their classes and keeping their students and themselves safe.

For quite a while, nobody mentioned the blood they had seen, the horror of the event, the helplessness they felt. But as soon as one person did, many more began talking about these troubling aspects. One staff member said, "I … ran around … and then I was clamping down and trying to stop the bleeding and I got the blood all over." Many wondered, "Did I do the right thing? Did I go to [help] the right person?"

During this portion of the discussion the staff got into incredible detail— these were the terrible memories they had been bottling up inside themselves that they needed to bring into the open. They held each other's hands, and put their arms around each other. Almost everyone was crying. It was very difficult for Dr. Poland to hold back his own tears while listening to their grief and pain. (An important element of the NOVA model is that whoever is leading the discussion is not supposed to emote a great deal. You can show your concern with your body language and by making eye contact, but it doesn't help the participants if you start crying yourself. If this happens, another team member must take over for you.)

Dr. Poland said reassuring things such as, "It's not uncommon for people to second-guess themselves. No one is certain what to do and everybody wishes they could have somehow prevented it. It sounds like you did everything possible," and "Everybody questions, 'Did I do it right?'"

Dr. Poland continued encouraging the group, asking, "Who else would like to talk? It's not necessary that everybody talk, but if you would like to, we're listening." He would be looking in one direction, asking these questions, and all of a sudden somebody in another part of the room would begin to pour out the emotions he or she had been holding in all those days. Dr. Poland and the rest of the group would then focus totally on the person speaking at the time. Everyone who wished to speak had the opportunity to tell his or her story. After each person spoke Dr. Poland asked him or her, "Is there anything else you would like to say?" Then he told each person, "I am so sorry this happened to you at your high school." Hearing that helped the staff genuinely feel that they had been heard and that there was a commonality to their feelings.

This processing continued for an hour and 45 minutes. (There was no time limit set for this meeting.) Approximately 20 of the 50 people attending spoke. Principal Bond listened to his staff very intently. He reassured people and passed them tissues. He was a great source of comfort and strength to his staff during this difficult session.

Dr. Poland then focused the group on predicting what they might face in the future. He asked them, "What are you worried about right now? What are you facing here at Heath High School today, tomorrow, and in your immediate future?" The staff expressed some very practical concerns, such as how to help the injured students when they returned to class. They had concrete questions about the legal process and the fate of Michael Carneal. Some also admitted having some uncomfortable feelings such as, "I feel afraid every morning when I get up, and I don't want to come to school. How long is that going to last?"

Many models of intervention overlook these practical concerns, but NOVA's theory is that if you get these types of issues "out on the table" people can begin to plan for their own recovery. The NOVA team assisted the Heath High staff in problem solving on their concerns, helping them to create a concrete plan for their immediate future and also showing them that "I'm not the only one worried about such-and-such." This assistance was helpful to the group.

Because NOVA strives to end counseling sessions on a note of hope, Dr. Poland then facilitated the group's identification of their coping skills. The staff listed many people, beliefs, and actions that helped them to cope with the effects of the tragedy, including "religion," "faith," "my husband," "my spouse," "the faculty," "the students," "Bill (the principal)," "I exercise," "I try to eat right," and "I called my mother." They talked about the kinds of coping skills one would expect, but it was a positive exercise for the group to hear all the resources available to assist them. Dr. Poland was impressed with the importance of religion to this community. The staff members' strong religious faith would be a source of healing for them in the months to come.

Dr. Poland told the group, "Those of you who did not talk, I know you were listening, and I know you had many of the same feelings." It was fine that not everyone spoke—it was both comforting and therapeutic for them to simply hear so much commonality of feelings that they might also have identified with.

Finally, Dr. Poland turned his attention to the notes from the session, which had been written down by another team member. He stood up and reviewed the sensory perceptions described, the emotions expressed, the challenges the staff members were facing, and the coping skills they identified. He emphasized the staff members' resiliency and strength and the solidity of their community.

He then announced the other meetings to be held—including an open family/community meeting to be held that night—and told the group that the team would remain in the room to speak with any of them who wanted some more individual assistance. At the conclusion of the session Principal Bond rose and stood next to Dr. Poland. He told everyone assembled that he had at first been uncertain about the need for the session but that now he saw they had needed it very much. He thanked the NOVA team warmly for assisting his staff. His words did a great deal to validate all that his staff had expressed that afternoon.

After the meeting broke up and the staff left the library, Principal Bond called the school board president to tell him how well the meeting had gone and thanked the team again for their assistance. He outlined some other services he wanted the team to provide to the school (including processing the crisis with members of the staff who had missed that processing session). He then decided to tell them about his own sensory perceptions from the crisis and described what he had witnessed that day.

Principal Bond then discussed the effect that the crisis had on him not as an administrator (because he had acted superbly during the crisis itself) but as a human being. He told the team he wasn't sleeping well at night and asked, "How could this happen in my school?" The team reminded him that he had done everything that he could, that he could not have prevented what had happened, and that feelings such as his were to be expected and were quite common after a tragedy.

Later that night the NOVA team facilitated an open session for the entire community (with the exception of the media, who were denied entrance). Unlike the family/community meeting in Jonesboro, Arkansas, fewer than 50 people attended the meeting in West Paducah. The lower attendance was due to the fact that the meeting was being held a week after the crisis and was held at the community college rather than at the school itself. The people who did attend were those who still felt the need for assistance, and they benefited greatly from the opportunity to vent some strong emotions and identify their coping skills. Because fewer people attended this session, the team was able to use the full NOVA counseling model with them. They sat in a circle and followed the same procedures used earlier in the day with the Heath High School staff.

On Wednesday, the NOVA team's last day in Paducah, the team members continued working with the families of the victims and did follow-up in some of the area schools. One interesting session was held for the staff of a "feeder" school to Heath High School, a school that all of the victims and the suspected perpetrator had attended. At this before-school session many staff members expressed feeling dismay that they had not done something differently when Michael Carneal had attended their school, that they somehow should have known. A lot of people wanted to speak, and Dr. Poland was concerned that they would not be able to conclude the meeting before the school day began. Noticing Dr. Poland looking at his watch, the school's principal leaned over and said, "Take all the time that you need." They continued the processing for another 45 minutes. During that time the school's principal took all the students into the gym and played Simon Says!

The NOVA team had an exit meeting with the county school psychologist, who expressed that the NOVA team had been of assistance to the local caregivers like himself who would provide ongoing support to the school and community. The team next met with city leaders such as the mayor and the prosecutor to detail their activities and to discuss whether the community representatives thought an additional NOVA team was needed. They also held an exit press conference in which they emphasized the availability of continuing assistance to the community from a variety of sources, including the state crisis team. The NOVA team left West Paducah very impressed with the leadership shown by Principal Bond and Heath High School and with the desire to forgive within the community.

The people of Paducah, Kentucky, received emotional support in their time of crisis from people around the country and the world. Messages of support came from as far away as South Africa, Germany, Japan, and Australia (Walker, 1998). The Reverend Bobby Strong (Ben Strong's father) reported: "We have received a lot of calls [from] all over the country from other churches, teen groups, letting us know that … 'We are praying for you and your community'" (McRee & Bergeron, 1997).

These sympathies did much to comfort the residents of Paducah. But they remained mystified about why such a seemingly average, nonthreatening kid—a B student, immature but generally well behaved, described by some as "fun loving"—would commit such a heinous act. When questioned by police after the shooting, Michael Carneal began to cry, reported McCracken County Sheriff Frank Augustus. "He really seemed sorry for what he did. He told us it wasn't out of revenge or anything like that. He just said he doesn't know why he did it" (Hewitt, 1997). In a videotaped statement Carneal made to police authorities, "… [his] demeanor indicated he did 'not know the gravity of what he had done,'" said McCracken Commonwealth Attorney Tim Kaltenbach ("Investigators: Suspect May Have Told Others," 1997).

On October 5, 1998, Michael Carneal pleaded guilty but mentally ill for the murder of the three girls. (Carneal's attorney explained that he suffered from paranoia and a personality disorder.) Prosecutors and the victims' families had at first opposed the mentally ill plea because it carries a possibility of parole after 12 years, whereas a verdict of guilty to murder without a finding of mental illness warrants a life sentence without the possibility of parole for 25 years. But under a plea arrangement, Judge Jeff Hines of McCracken County Circuit Court agreed to accept the mentally ill plea on the condition that the maximum penalty—life in prison without the possibility of parole for *25 years*—would be imposed ("Teen-Ager Pleads Guilty," 1998). In the state of Kentucky, a person under 16 years of age cannot be given the death penalty ("Investigators: Student May Have Told Others," 1997).

Kentucky law does, however, allow juveniles who have committed violent felonies to be tried as adults, and Michael Carneal, though 14 at the time of the murders, was charged as an adult with three counts of murder, five counts of attempted murder, and one count of burglary (resulting from the theft of the weapons used in the attack). At the hearing, Carneal told Judge Hines that he understood the pleas and agreed to enter them. His attorney said that neither the paranoia nor personality disorder affected Carneal's decision to enter the pleas. "You are fine today, in terms of your mental health?" the judge asked him. "Yes, sir," Carneal replied ("Teen-Ager Pleads Guilty," 1998, p. A15). Carneal was formally sentenced on December 16, 1998.

As reported in *Newsweek*, "… [F]or the most part, the town of Paducah … resisted assigning blame. Citizens and churchgoers prefer[ed] to talk about the victims—the 'good kids,' as [Principal Bond] says—rather than the shooter" (Pedersen & Van Boven, 1997). Since the murders at Heath High School, the Agape prayer group has been "… committed to claiming victory over the tragedy." Said one student, "The whole school is now turning to God. It's not just a little circle anymore…. I don't want [the public] to say, 'Yeah, I remember Heath. They're the [school] where all those kids died. I want them to say, 'Yeah, I remember Heath. They're the one with the prayer group of 400 [that] didn't let one incident ruin their life'" ("Paducah Students," 1998).

References

Associated Press. (1997, December 2). Carneal indicted for shootings. *ABCNEWS.com*. Available online: http://www.abcnews.com/sections/us/shootings1212/index.html

Bowles, S. (1997, December 3). Even those closest to teen cannot answer why. *USA Today*, p. 1A.

Collins, M. (1997, December 2). Stunned school: Why? *Cincinnati Post.* Available online: http://www.cincypost.com/news/n120297.htm/

Control the media but provide information. (1998, November). *Practical Strategies for Maintaining Safe Schools: School Violence Alert, 4*(11), 1, 4-5.

Crisis counselors at Ky. school. (1997, December 2). *United Press International (UPI).* Available online: http://biz.yahoo.com/upi/97/12/02/general_news/usschools_4.html

Goodwyn, W., & Simon, S. (1997, December 6). Paducah murders. *Weekend Edition, National Public Radio (NPR).*

Grace, J. (1997, December 15). When the silence fell: A tragic shooting in Kentucky reveals a curious and poignant friendship—and the faith of a small town. *TIME,* p. 54.

Hewitt, B. (1997, December 22). Marching on: Stunned by tragedy, the people of Paducah search their hearts and find the healing grace of compassion. *People Weekly,* 42-47.

Holliman, J. (1997, December 2). School gunman's advance warning ignored. *CNNinteractive.* Available online: http://www.cnn.com/US/9712/02/school.shooting.2/

Investigators: Student may have told others of shooting plan. (1997, December 4). *CNNinteractive.* Available online: http://www.cnn.com/US/9712/04/school.shooting.folo/

Jacobson, L., & White, K. A. (1997, December 10). In the wake of tragedy: Kentucky shootings highlight concerns about school safety. *Education Week, 17*(16), 1, 12.

McRee, L., & Bergeron, T. (1997, December 3). Paducah reflects on tragedy. *ABC Good Morning America.*

Mead, A. (1997, December 4). Caskets bear written farewells. *Lexington Herald-Leader.* Available online: http://www.kentuckyconnect.com/heraldleader/

Nagy, S. (1998, February). A place where mercy dwells. *Life,* p. 12.

Paducah students learn forgiveness. (1998, August 10). *Maranatha Christian Journal.* Available online: http://www.mcjonline.com/news/news2333.htm

Pedersen, D., & Van Boven, S. (1997, December 15). Tragedy in a small place. *Newsweek,* p. 30.

Prendergast, J., & Pressley, D. S. (1997, December 2). Third student dies from rampage: Five wounded in school prayer shootings. *Cincinnati Enquirer.* Available online: http://enquirer.com/editions/1997/12/02/loc_kyshoot.html

Teen-ager pleads guilty in fatal shooting at Kentucky school. (1998, October 5). *The New York Times,* p. A15.

The Agape fund: For the parents of our departed classmates. (1998, August 10). Available online: http://www.apex.net/agape/

Third student dies in Kentucky school shooting. (1997, December 2). *CNNinteractive.* Available online: http://www.cnn.com/US/9712/02/school.shooting.on/

Walker, K. (1998, August 10). Paducah teens face tragedy with faith. *Charisma.* Available online: http://www.charismamag.com/issues/cm298/cm2987.htm

chapter four

Help Is at Hand

Unasked-For Assistance

The help that arrives at your school soon after a crisis is publicized may or may not be the help you need. In addition to parents pouring into the school, many mental health professionals and clergy members may rush to the scene to lend their assistance. You need a plan for when, when not, and how to utilize these people.

Most likely, those who come to your school to help will have good intentions. Even so, they may not be the most qualified people to assist you in the crisis response, and well-meaning but misguided helpers can often do more harm than good. In addition, some people who respond to school crises simply do not have your best interests at heart. Some therapists in private practice may come with the agenda of building up their practice or garnering publicity for their efforts. If your school's crisis is nationally publicized, opportunists in the form of for-profit organizations of various kinds—particularly security specialists—may try to profit from your tragedy. Warned Kenneth Trump, president and CEO of National School Safety and Security Services: "Be alert for 'overnight experts' and others who claim that they can easily solve all of your security concerns for a price. Experienced school security specialists are few, and the qualifications and experience of all consultants and trainers should be reviewed prior to bringing them into your district" (Trump, 1998). A school system in Sheridan, Arkansas, experienced such a "sales pitch" after a number of student suicides there in 1991. A mental health organization from California told the school administrators they wanted to come help. The school system declined, but they showed up anyway!

It may seem that it would be difficult to tactfully determine the agenda and/or experience level of helpers who are standing before you, ready to serve. However, you should not blindly accept the help of any warm body who walks through the door, telling you he or she is a great counselor. The Campus Liaison (with the assistance of the Counseling Liaison and/or other members of your school's counseling staff, if necessary) can use the following guidelines to quickly determine whose help to accept and whose to turn away:

- The best people to assist with a school crisis are other school people, since they understand the school climate and operating procedures. In a large school system, you may have all the help you need (with the exception of a specially trained state or national crisis response team) within your own district. For example, the Cypress-Fairbanks Independent School District in Houston has 150 counselors and 20 psychologists. An event would have to be truly catastrophic for that district to need extra assistance. However, in a smaller school district, that number of internal mental health workers would likely not be available. Both large and small school systems should accept the help of anyone from within their district.

- Accept the assistance of any county or regional mental health association without checking references. It is safe to assume that representatives from an agency funded by the county or state are aboveboard and fully qualified.

- Do not use private therapists unless you already have an established relationship with these people (i.e., before the crisis) and they are well known to and familiar with your school. There are certainly many therapists who are very good at what they do, and if given the opportunity would do the right thing. However, you cannot allow those in private practice to work in your school without close scrutiny.

- By the same token, psychiatrists are not necessarily the answer during a school crisis. Sometimes schools think these highly trained individuals will make a tremendous impact, or that the community would really listen to such a person because they are medical doctors. They may be fine individuals, but unfortunately they usually have no hands-on experience working in schools. During a school crisis, this is problematic.

- If you think you will need the assistance of private mental health practitioners who have come to the school to help, ask the following questions to determine if their presence would be beneficial: "How well do you know adolescents (or the age group of your students)?" "What does your practice specialize in?" "Have you helped any other schools when there has been a crisis?" If so, "Whom did you help?" Then take the time to call the school(s) where the practitioner has assisted in the past.

Insist upon a recommendation or referral, as you must know who you are allowing into your school in order to protect both the students and the school. After a May 1998 school shooting in Springfield, Oregon, for example, "There were media and some weirdos who pretended to be counselors" (Johnson, 1998, p. 5).

Another option to a lengthy screening process is to closely supervise private practitioners' work within your school. That method worked well for the Springfield school. Explained a crisis responder, "… we never let anyone [from outside the school] be alone with a student and in each of the safety rooms there was always a faculty member, usually two, with normally two counselors" (Johnson, 1998, p. 5).

> "Our district psychologists … managed the monumental task of screening, scheduling, and monitoring [more than] 200 outside counselors [for] three weeks [after our school shooting]."
>
> —Cathy Paine, Crisis Response Team Leader, Springfield, Oregon Public Schools (Paine, 1998, p. 16)

If the private practitioners' answers to your questions are all satisfactory, and they have a trusted reference, they may truly be of assistance in the crisis intervention. (Those specializing in grief counseling, child development/therapy, trauma, or post-traumatic stress disorder will be most helpful.) If their answers indicate that they might not be of help, politely tell them that you cannot allow unapproved private practitioners to work within the school, and thank them for their offer and kindness. If at that point someone insists on participating, summon the Security Liaison.

- In smaller communities, many of which do not have a strong mental health cadre available for emergency assistance, members of the clergy can help to fill this role. For example, local clergy played a significant role in the crisis response of the town of Montoursville, Pennsylvania (population 5,000), in July 1996. When 16 members of the high school's French team and five adult chaperones were killed in the explosion of TWA Flight 800 bound for France, the community was devastated by the loss. David P. Black, the superintendent of the 2,450-student district, said: "We will be utilizing clergy, the high school student assistance teams, coaches, and teachers [for the crisis response]" (Gamble, 1996, p. 10).

Even communities with sufficient mental health resources available may still choose to prominently involve their local clergy in the crisis response. In the Jonesboro area, for example, where the community has very strong religious ties with local clergy and churches, a local minister was a part of every classroom team following the shooting at Westside Middle School. School psychologists there explained, "We believed this to be a most effective way to utilize their influence" (Linda Speer Graham and Jack Bower, personal communication, March 1999).

It is important for clergy to minimize the theological aspect of their work, especially if the numerous clergy members who arrive at your school have different perspectives on the afterlife. These helpers must refrain from imposing their religious beliefs upon those at the school (particularly if yours is a public school), unless the staff/students/family members are members of their specific congregations. Instead, they can serve in a supportive role: a shoulder to cry on, someone to listen, a calming presence.

If clergy members are to participate in your school's crisis response, pair each with a counseling staff member from within your school system. Certainly, if a student or staff member calls his or her clergy member for support, you should welcome that clergy member to meet with the student or staff member at the school. You can also support the clergy's valuable work in your community by announcing their various counseling/assistance efforts related to the crisis that will take place within their own houses of worship.

If you invite local clergy members to participate in your school's crisis response, give some thought to the *denominations* of clergy that would be most appropriate for your school. In this regard it's important to know your school community and the denominations represented within the faculty and student body. If you have Buddhist students, for example, you wouldn't provide them a Baptist minister for assistance! Including the appropriate clergy members can also help to address the needs of a diverse school community. When a school shooting occurred in 1989 in Stockton, California, for example, "… school officials brought in local religious leaders, including … Vietnamese elders, to conduct traditional ceremonies to promote healing in the greater Cleveland Elementary community" (Johnston, 1998, p. 30). Facilitating these ceremonies within the school demonstrated respect for the beliefs of many of the Cambodian and Vietnamese immigrants within the school community who were deeply affected by the crisis.

Help to Request

Caution in accepting outside assistance during a school crisis is prudent. But a problem arises when school administrators close their doors to *everyone*, which is not necessarily appropriate. Some administrators are quick to say, "We've got it covered. We don't need anyone." But in a severe crisis, there will be people who can really help you. It may be easier initially to refuse any outside help, but it makes more sense to carefully consider the scope of the crisis and evaluate the need for additional resources.

Schools may also hesitate to ask for help during a crisis because of the mistaken belief that their crisis isn't important enough or severe enough to warrant the attention of others. One elementary school principal in Houston, for example, told a crisis interventionist there: "This is nothing like what you've been involved in, but to us, it's a big deal." People's emotions are always a big deal, regardless of whether one person was hurt or ten. If one person was killed, well, that person was the teacher, student, friend, or loved one of others. For them, that one person's injury or death is as important a situation as what happened near Jonesboro, Arkansas, or in West Paducah, Kentucky. Never belittle the effects of a crisis on your community.

Further, schools may not ask for outside assistance because they fear that they will lose control of their own school. There is a defensive atmosphere of "circling the wagons" in these schools, of trying to isolate themselves from the outside world. But such schools still want—and need—the assistance of their central office, the police/emergency responders, and possibly others as well. It is unlikely that anyone from outside their immediate school community would attempt to take charge of the crisis response unless the school clearly had no plan of action. By following the guidelines in this book, that is guaranteed not to be the case.

One of the things the people in Jonesboro, Arkansas did best following the shooting at Westside Middle School was to quickly mobilize all their resources and immediately determine that they needed some additional assistance. Obviously, the more severe the crisis, the more assistance will be required. *Do not hesitate to ask for additional help.* It's almost impossible to have too much assistance during a crisis. And, as mentioned previously, an over-response is preferable to an under-response to a crisis. Asking for outside assistance does not mean that you "can't handle it." It means that you are capable enough—and caring enough—to do whatever it takes to best meet the needs of your school and community in your time of crisis. Many resources are available to schools and their crisis response teams when a crisis occurs, as described in the following sections of this chapter.

Local Caregivers/Agencies

In addition to emergency responders (e.g., local and state police officers, paramedics/EMTs, firefighters), the following are people and organizations from within your community that you may want to call upon for assistance, particularly if yours is a small community.

School psychologists/counselors

As mentioned previously, the best people to assist in a school crisis are other school people, because they understand the school climate and operating procedures. Nationally certified school psychologists (NCSPs), in particular, will be invaluable after a school crisis as they have specialized training in child development and trauma. In many areas of the country,

> "I will always be grateful to the school psychologists who helped us through this crisis. I [had] never worked very closely with one before but I now have a new appreciation for what they do. Our best hope to avert another crisis is prevention … there needs to be one (school psychologist) in every school district due to the problems our students are facing."
>
> —Principal Karen Curtner, Westside Middle School, Jonesboro, Arkansas (Stockton, 1998, p. 12)

> "We want to make sure that important support staff in our nation's schools— social workers, counselors, and school psychologists—are not solely focused on testing and evaluation but also directing their expertise to … violence."
>
> —Secretary of Education Richard Riley (1998)

however, school psychologists may be spread thin. In some parts of Arkansas (including Jonesboro), for example, school psychologists are assigned to multiple small districts. Thus, it is critical to share human resources among districts in the event of a severe crisis.

Unfortunately, the central administration and administrators in other buildings may not realize the need to mobilize all the human resources available within and between districts when a severe crisis occurs in a school. For example, several school psychologists in Oklahoma City said they were told immediately after the 1995 bombing, "Don't get involved [with the crisis response in affected schools]; you might fall behind in your testing." When a severe crisis strikes a school, any district school psychologists and counselors willing and able to help the affected school should be released to go to the scene immediately. Even scheduled special education meetings should take a back seat to an emergency response for the affected school. District administrators must quickly assess the situation and commit to assisting the school in crisis.

School-based teams

Some schools, particularly middle and high schools, have student assistance teams, student/staff support teams (SSTs), or teacher assistance teams (TATs). Members of these school-based teams often have training in conflict resolution, mediation, listening skills, and other affective skills that would be beneficial in a crisis. Whether from your school or neighboring schools, these teams can not only help with the counseling during a crisis but can also assist your crisis response team in many other capacities (e.g., by answering phones, making copies). Members of your PTA might also be willing to help with various administrative tasks.

Other schools that have experienced a similar crisis

Particularly when a crisis is severe, you might benefit from speaking to staff members of another school in your town or state (or even in another state) who have gone through a similar ordeal. These people may be able to give you some practical advice about the crisis response. For example, the victims' advocate in Jonesboro, Arkansas, called the victims' advocate in West Paducah, Kentucky (the site of a school shooting three months earlier), before the NOVA team arrived to learn more about the team's activities. The school superintendent of the Westside School District said the best advice he received during the crisis near Jonesboro came from the superintendent of schools in West Paducah (Fugate, 1999). Similarly, as the year anniversary of the school shooting in West Paducah, Kentucky, approached, Principal Bond contacted the principal of a school in Pearl, Mississippi, that had experienced a school shooting to discuss what that school had done to recognize the anniversary date.

Perhaps even more important than their ability to provide concrete information, such people can provide emotional support. Someone at another school who has survived something similar to what you are presently experiencing can offer a unique perspective—he or she has been there and has come out the other side. For example, after the 1989 shooting at Cleveland Elementary School in Stockton, California, in which five children were killed, the elementary school staff members were visited by teachers from a Winnetka, Illinois, school where the previous year a woman had shot an eight-year old boy and wounded five other children before committing suicide (Johnston, 1998). Explained one of the Stockton school teachers, "For me personally, that was the turning point. They said, 'You're going to get over it.' … It was a ray of hope. They knew what we went through. They were okay." Added the teacher, "I'd always be willing to go somewhere else as proof that life goes on" (Johnston, 1998, pp. 30-31).

Regional/state mental health workers

Having an allegiance with your region's or state's mental health resources is vitally important. If you do not have such an allegiance and do not know a specific individual to call when a crisis occurs, begin by contacting your local mental health association (e.g., for the county). The victims' advocate in your county's prosecutor's office will also be able to assist you in locating appropriate mental health assistance for working with your school community members in the event of a severe crisis.

Emergency management services for your city/county

Each county or municipality has an emergency management agency. People often think of this agency only in the event of catastrophic natural disasters, such as floods, hurricanes, tornadoes, and earthquakes. However, this agency can also be helpful to schools after an act of violence. Among other things, the agency is familiar with medical facilities, crowd control, and coordination with law enforcement and other agencies.

City officials

Coordinating the crisis response with appropriate city officials will benefit not only your school but your community as a whole. During the crisis response to the May 1998 school shooting in Springfield, Oregon, for example, the school district and city officials "… formed a joint 'command center' at City Hall, which was a clearinghouse for inquiries from both the press and the public" (Paine, 1998, p. 16).

University/college psychologists

Your local university or college likely includes a psychology program, and members of its faculty might be willing to assist you. Contact the dean of the appropriate school or a department head there.

Public relations (PR) firm

If your school and/or district is unprepared or understaffed to manage the media onslaught, you might consider hiring a reputable PR firm that has experience in school systems and expertise in dealing with aggressive media ("Advice on Managing," 1998). Or, you might consult with the National School Public Relations Association (NSPRA) in Rockville, Maryland, which can be reached at (301) 519-0496 or www.nspra.org.

Telephone company

Your local telephone service company might provide you with additional equipment (e.g., pagers, telephone lines, and cellular phones) on a temporary basis, if necessary. In Jonesboro, for example, when the regular phone lines became jammed for hours after the shooting at Westside Middle School, the telephone company "… immediately installed two dedicated lines to handle the swarm of incoming calls [to the school]. The phone company also gave [the crisis response team] seven cellular phones to use, which allowed [the team members] to move about freely" ("Counseling Jonesboro," 1998, p. 6). In fact, the school's crisis responders relied completely on cellular phones for telephone communication throughout the first evening of the crisis (Linda Speer Graham and Jack Bower, personal communication, March 1999).

"Additional phone lines set up by 10:00 AM the day of the tragedy were staffed 24 hours per day through the four-day holiday weekend by city and school district employees."

—Cathy Paine, Crisis Response Team Leader, Springfield, Oregon, Public Schools (Paine, 1998, p. 16)

While cellular phones are invaluable during a crisis response, there are two cautions when using them. First, before using cellular phones it is important to ensure that they cause no interference for police and other emergency responders' communication systems ("When Disaster Strikes," 1998). Second, be aware that calls made on cellular phones are not secure and that the media may monitor and use whatever you communicate during such conversations. Shortly after the shooting at Westside Middle School, media representatives, using a network satellite truck, monitored a cellular phone conversation between a school psychologist and the distraught parent of an autistic child. A reporter then called the parent and asked, "How is your handicapped child handling everything?" (Linda Speer Graham and Jack Bower, personal communication, March 1999).

Judicial/Governmental Involvement

Red Cross

Volunteers from your local Red Cross chapter can be a tremendous help during a serious school crisis. In Jonesboro, these volunteers were present during the day, and also at the large family/community meeting held in the evening, providing food and drinks. Red Cross workers can also provide emotional support to survivors. If the Red Cross does not automatically come to your school after a crisis occurs, look under "American Red Cross" in the business white pages of your telephone book for the number of your local chapter.

Victims' advocates

Every community should have at least one victims' advocate available, generally on the staff of the prosecutor's office. The services of the victims' advocate are usually organized by county and funded by the state. The specific services available will vary by state, but generally state (and/or federal) funding is available to assist the family members of victims in many ways.

Victims' advocates are an invaluable asset. Trained to respond efficiently and with compassion during crisis and crime situations, your victims' advocate will help coordinate services for victims' families and explain their rights to them. A main service is helping victims and their families to navigate the legal process and to translate "legalese." The victims' advocate will support the families step-by-step throughout the entire legal process and often for a long time afterward with many practical issues, including paying medical bills, making mental health referrals, and assisting with day-to-day living concerns through the ups and downs of grieving. One victims' advocate commented that in her position "you are never really done supporting the family of a homicide victim."

After the school shooting near Jonesboro, the victims' advocate provided services for approximately 115 family members of the injured and deceased. These services included, among other things, providing transportation (by bus) to a memorial service held at the state university, helping to find personal items the victims were wearing at the time of their death, and serving as a go-between with the media. The victims' advocate in West Paducah, Kentucky, was instrumental in convincing the judge to allow the family members and friends of the victims to have an opportunity to speak directly to the perpetrator in the courtroom during his sentencing hearing.

Victims' advocates will usually contact victims and their families automatically when criminal charges have been filed against a suspected perpetrator or perpetrators. However, you may contact a victims' advocate directly by calling the prosecutor's office of your local courts.

National Guard/state police

The National Guard is available to assist with security in times of domestic crisis, providing both personnel and specialized military equipment (e.g., armored vehicles for SWAT team use) if appropriate. In Jonesboro, National Guard members (in uniform but without visible weapons) were present outside the school for two days after the school shooting. They were there primarily to assist in barring the media and other unauthorized persons from accessing the Westside campus. Their presence also instilled an atmosphere of order and protection for the people at the school whose sense of security was threatened after the violence.

In some situations, however, the presence of the National Guard might enflame the fears of the community. In a less severe crisis, for example, having the military ringing your school could give the impression that the school is under siege and still in danger.

The decision about whether to call in the National Guard is made by the governor of your state and will depend upon the level of chaos outside the school. Your superintendent should speak with the governor to either request such assistance or ask that the National Guard not be sent.

Regardless of whether the National Guard assists your school after a crisis, the state police can provide a great deal of support at the site. The presence of the state police at the school near Jonesboro, for example, provided a much needed sense of security for students and staff. The state police helped contain the media and provided transportation for school administrators and members of the NOVA team.

Governor/state attorney general

As noted previously, the governor of Kentucky sent the state crisis team to Heath High School, where they provided invaluable assistance immediately after the shooting. In Arkansas, the attorney general went to Jonesboro to personally express his sorrow after the school shooting there. He attended meetings with caregivers and thanked them for their efforts. He also assigned several of his staff members to assist the NOVA team and the victims' advocate for the county. In addition, the governor of Arkansas met with the Westside Middle School faculty at the school.

It is likely after a severe school crisis that your state government will offer assistance, and you should accept this help. Your school might also ask for assistance from the state government leaders, such as the governor or attorney general. Your state's government can provide much needed support for your school, and will do so without calling media attention to themselves. The government leaders in Arkansas, for example, called ahead to ask permission to come to Westside Middle School to offer their support and planned their visit in such a way as to minimize media attention.

National Crisis Response Teams/Organizations

National Organization for Victim Assistance (NOVA)

Founded in 1975 in Washington, D.C., the National Organization for Victim Assistance (NOVA) is a private, nonprofit organization working on behalf of victims of crime and other crises such as natural disasters. This organization both serves as a national advocate in support of victims' rights and provides direct services to victims. To provide direct services, NOVA's Victim Services Division sends Community Crisis Response Teams (CCRTs)—such as those that responded to the school shootings in West Paducah, Kentucky, and Jonesboro, Arkansas—to places in crisis both nationally and around the world.

According to NOVA (1994), a CCRT's mission is to serve as *consultants* to the leaders and caregivers of a community in severe distress. Not only individuals but your entire community will suffer trauma in the aftermath of a gruesome crime. Your community may experience a sort of paralysis immediately following the incident. Almost everyone may be in emotional shock, including your local caregivers, and though they may wish to help, they may themselves be affected by the crisis. Additionally, they may be unsure about what to do, since *few people (including school psychologists and counselors) are trained specifically in using their helping skills in catastrophic situations.* For these reasons it often helps to have trained outsiders come into your community—even if yours is a large school district with plentiful resources—for a short period of time to offer information and suggestions on how to respond to your community's distress.

> "We [were] extremely grateful for the invaluable advice and assistance we received from the two NOVA teams.... They supported us with wisdom and caring during the most dreadful experience we could imagine."
>
> —Cathy Paine, Crisis Response Team Leader, Springfield, Oregon, Public Schools (Paine, 1998, p. 16)

A NOVA Community Crisis Response Team is composed of service professionals from around the country, typically including victims' advocates, members of the clergy, law enforcement representatives, and psychologists. The team for each disaster is formed with consideration of what is known about the crisis and the community's demographics. (The team responding to the school crisis near Jonesboro, for example, was composed of two school psychologists, three victims' advocates, a police lieutenant, and a minister. The team responding to the crisis in West Paducah included a 72-year old victims' advocate from Indiana who got involved with NOVA after the murder of four children in a close friend's home in his community.) Regardless of the exact composition of the team and number of people who respond, all NOVA team members will understand what you are experiencing and will be able to compassionately and efficiently help you to deal with the aftereffects of crisis in your community.

All NOVA team members are volunteers, with only their travel and lodging expenses covered by the local community or by donations to NOVA. NOVA teams are sent only when they are invited. NOVA will send a crisis response team to any community in crisis that requests NOVA's assistance.

To Contact NOVA:

- Call (202) 232-6682 (232-NOVA). This number is staffed 24 hours per day to assist those requesting assistance or information.
- Additional contact methods for NOVA include FAX and online:
  - (202) 462-2255 (FAX)
  - nova@access.digex.net (e-mail)
  - www.access.digex.net/~nova (Web site)

When a NOVA team responds to a crisis in a community, they will perform three main tasks:

1. Help your local decision makers identify those most affected by the crisis (including victims and their families; students; school staff; and first responders on the scene, such as police and medical personnel).

2. Provide support and training to your local caregivers (such as counselors, psychologists, and clergy) who are to reach out to those most affected by the crisis.

3. Lead one or more community-wide forums (e.g., the family/community meeting and hospital staff sessions in Jonesboro) to enable community members to begin to process their reactions to the tragedy and cope with their distress. The NOVA model emphasizes helping individuals become survivors rather than victims.

The second task is of particular importance. NOVA recognizes that the ongoing support of a community recovering from crisis must come from within that community. The CCRT will not try to supplant your caregivers; instead, the team will offer your local caregivers support in their time of greatest need. In fact, to avoid dependency upon the CCRT, NOVA will limit the team members' stay in your community to no more than three or four days. (In the event of a catastrophic event, such as the April 19, 1995 terrorist bombing of the Alfred P. Murrah Federal Building in Oklahoma City, multiple teams may be sent consecutively.)

National Emergency Assistance Team (NEAT)

The National Association of School Psychologists (NASP) formed the National Emergency Assistance Team (NEAT) in November 1996. (Creation of this national team was spurred by the needs of schools in

Oklahoma City and its surrounding areas following the bombing of the Alfred P. Murrah Federal Building.) The goals of the NEAT team are to help save lives, reduce trauma and injury, facilitate the psychological well-being of students and school staff, and enable schools to resume their regular activities in a timely fashion following a large-scale emergency.

The seven-member crisis team includes one person from each of four geographical regions of the United States, two at large members, and a chairperson. All NEAT members are nationally certified school psychologists, and all are NOVA-trained.

At press time, NASP has budgeted funding (at the discretion of the Executive Board) to dispatch the NEAT team to only one crisis per year nationally, although this allocation may increase in the future. (Further, additional funds can be requested and approved by the NASP Executive Board in a timely manner following a severe crisis.) The criteria the NASP Executive Board uses in determining whether to dispatch the team in a crisis include the declaration of a national emergency by the Federal Emergency Management Agency (FEMA) and the American Red Cross and the effects of the emergency on children and school districts in the area (Crane, 1998).

Even if the team is not dispatched, upon request from a school district NEAT will provide telephone consultations to crisis teams, individual schools, and school districts and will disseminate information, resources, and handouts pertaining to crisis intervention.

A NOVA/NEAT professional alliance has been formed to better serve schools and children after crises. NOVA has extensive experience in disaster work to help victims, and every NEAT member has been through NOVA training. And as school psychologists the NEAT members also have a background in the needs of children as well as important knowledge about how schools work. Consultation services are always available to schools from NEAT. (The National Association of School Psychologists, NEAT's parent organization, has 21,000 members who can assist the regional representatives in providing such services.) The NEAT team may also be able to provide direct, on-site assistance in the aftermath of a major crisis, probably in partnership with NOVA. To request on-site assistance, schools are advised to make two calls—to NOVA and to NEAT. The two organizations will then work together to provide a comprehensive response for your school.

To Contact NEAT:

To consult with a NEAT team member about handling your school's crisis, call your region's representative during business hours. (*See the Appendix for a current phone number for each state's NEAT representative.*)

Or contact the National Association of School Psychologists (NASP) office, in Bethesda, Maryland, at (301) 657-0270.

Community Crisis Response (CCR)

A division of the U.S. Department of Justice, the Office for Victims of Crimes (OVC) established a Community Crisis Response (CCR) program to improve services for victims of violent crime in cases in which there are multiple victims. The CCR provides direct assistance and training to communities that have been significantly impacted by criminal incidents (and the federal, state, and local agencies assisting them) by funding "… individuals or teams of trained responders to assist victims through debriefings and training in the aftermath of [severe crises]" ("Community Crisis," 1999). For example, the CCR program provided assistance to the Dryden, New York, community after the brutal murder of two high school girls there, and after the 1995 bombing of the Alfred P. Murrah Federal Building in Oklahoma City, a nine-member CCR team arrived on the day of the blast. The CCR "… funded crisis response teams that provided training and debriefings for thousands of [Oklahoma City] school children, teachers, and medical emergency personnel …" ("Community Crisis," 1999).

In addition to providing short-term (usually one- to three-day duration) direct assistance and training to communities, the CCR works to facilitate coordination among federal, state, and local agencies in delivering crisis response services. The CCR strives to maximize the resources available to communities in crisis as well as to reduce duplication of service delivery efforts.

Requests for CCR assistance must come from an agency that regularly assists victims of crime. The following are some of the agencies that could request assistance on behalf of your school: victim service agencies; federal, state, and local criminal justice service agencies; U.S. attorneys' offices; and Native American tribes (when appropriate) ("Community Crisis," 1999). (Requesting agencies can obtain details about the information that must be included in such requests from the OVC Web site: www.ojp.usdoj.gov/ovc/help.ccr.htm.) The OVC will approve or disapprove requests for assistance within two working days.

To Contact CCR:

Timothy J. Johnson, Community Crisis Response
Office for Victims of Crime
U.S. Department of Justice
633 Indiana Avenue, NW, Room 1352
Washington, D.C. 20531

(202) 305-4548
(202) 514-6383 (FAX)

National school organizations

The following national school organizations would be appropriate sources of advice and support after a severe school crisis:

- American Association of School Administrators (AASA)— Arlington, Virginia; (703) 528-0700; www.aasa.org
- National Association of Elementary School Principals (NAESP)— Alexandria, Virginia; (703) 684-3345; www.naesp.org
- National Association of School Psychologists (NASP)— Bethesda, Maryland; (301) 657-0270; www.naspweb.org
- National Association of Secondary School Principals (NASSP)— Reston, Virginia; (703) 860-0200; www.nassp.org
- National School Boards Association (NSBA)— Alexandria, Virginia; (703) 838-6722; www.nsba.org
- National School Public Relations Association (NSPRA)— Rockville, Maryland; (301) 519-0496; www.nspra.org
- National School Safety Center (NSSC)— Malibu, California; (805) 373-9977; www.nssc1.org

State Crisis Response Teams

At press time, Arkansas, Florida, and Kentucky are the only states we're aware of with state-level crisis response teams.

Arkansas

The Arkansas Crisis Response Team was formed in 1998 and is coordinated by the Outreach Division of the Office of the Attorney General (Ginger Bankston-Bailey, personal communication, May 13, 1999). The team responds to both natural disasters (e.g., tornadoes) and severe acts of violence throughout the state. The multidisciplinary team—with many members trained by the National Organization for Victim Assistance (NOVA)—includes school personnel, law enforcement representatives, health department and hospital personnel, mental health practitioners, and other service professionals. Besides providing direct services after a crisis, the team has undertaken a coordinated effort to deliver training in crisis response state-wide. Within Arkansas, contact the team through the Office of the Attorney General, Outreach Division at (800) 448-3014. (For additional information, contact the office of the Arkansas Deputy Attorney General at [501] 682-6073.)

Florida

In 1998 the Florida Association of School Psychologists (FASP) formed the Florida Emergency Assistance Team (FEAT), a response team for schools that is composed entirely of school psychologists trained by the National Organization for Victim Assistance (NOVA) and with extensive experience in school crisis intervention. The team's objective is to provide schools and districts with consultative and direct services as necessary when a major crisis occurs (Lazarus, 1998). To request assistance from the FEAT, contact the team's chair, Frank Zenere, at (305) 995-7319.

Kentucky

The Kentucky Emergency Response Team, administered through the state's Department of Mental Health, is mandated and funded by the state legislature. The Kentucky Community Crisis Response Board directs the statewide team of more than 150 volunteers to "... assist communities, schools, and other agencies in times of natural disasters, violence, and other crises" ("Kentucky Community," 1998, p. 12). Contact executive director Renelle Grubbs or assistant executive director Penny Gaffney at either (502) 564-0131 or (888) 522-7228.

To find out whether your state, region, or county has any sort of crisis response team to assist you, you might contact:

- The president of your state's school psychology association, or your state delegate to the National Association of School Psychologists (NASP)
- NASP's central office, located in Bethesda, Maryland, at (301) 657-0270
- Your state's department of education
- Your county's victims' advocate through your local prosecutor's office
- Your state's attorney general's office

Financial Support

In the event of a severe crisis, your school will receive financial assistance from many people and places. Most likely, members of your own community will begin to collect emergency funds of their own volition. In Jonesboro, for example, many stores set out collection jars labeled "Westside Crisis Fund" ("Arkansas Buries Its Dead," 1998). If your school's crisis is nationally publicized, you may be surprised at the generosity and sympathy directed to you from around the country and the world. Approximately $362,000 in donations poured into a Jonesboro, Arkansas community fund from across the country and internationally (e.g., from Norway, Germany, and Italy) after the Westside Middle School shooting.

Your local bank(s) or savings and loan officer can help your school's administrators to establish accounts, trusts, and scholarship funds to manage such donations. Your local United Way organization might also be of assistance in this area (sometimes even matching donated funds). A representative committee of school personnel (including teachers) and parents should monitor the account(s) and decide together how to spend the money. School personnel, students, and teachers all should be surveyed for ideas about how to spend the funds. Of course, the needs of victims and their families must come first. Spending remaining donations on a lasting memorial (such as a soccer facility or a children's museum) will probably satisfy the largest number of people, as communities like to see a gift of hope for a better future arise from funds donated after a tragedy. The issue of how to utilize such funds is a sensitive one that requires careful planning. Your school might want to consult with another school in your state or nationally that has experienced a severe crisis for additional advice on this issue.

See "Memorializing Victims" in Chapter Six for suggestions on utilizing such funds.

Besides unsolicited support, financial assistance is often available for schools if they request it. Your state's Board of Education might provide funds for the ongoing crisis response, or funds might be allocated from your state's disaster fund, if appropriate. One potential source of federal funding for intervention services is the Department of Education. The Westside school system near Jonesboro, Arkansas requested funding and received $100,000 from the Department's Safe and Drug Free Schools monies. These dollars in large part funded the services of counselors from a mental health agency in Arkansas who worked with the Westside students and school staff throughout the summer.

In some instances, another potential funding source is the Federal Emergency Management Agency (FEMA). FEMA money is usually allocated in the event of a natural disaster, but requesting FEMA assistance may be appropriate for a catastrophic crisis not caused by a natural disaster. For example, when the Alfred P. Murrah Federal Building was bombed in Oklahoma City in April 1995, the school system was written into the FEMA grant. The money received funded 42 counselors who worked in the Oklahoma City schools for a year and a half after that tragic attack. FEMA funds were justifiably necessary in this case, because with more than 900 injuries resulting from the bombing, more than "… 300 of the district's students said that a family member or someone else close to them had been killed or injured" (Poland, 1997, p. 147). (Additional information about FEMA grants is available online at www.fema.org.)

As authorized by the Victims of Crime Act (VOCA) of 1984, the U.S. Department of Justice's Office for Victims of Crime administers the Crime Victims Fund to support state-level services for victims of crime. A unique aspect of this federal program is that the fund "… is derived from fines and penalties paid by convicted federal offenders [as specified by the courts]— not from tax dollars" ("Grants and Funding," 1999). All 50 states, the

District of Columbia, Puerto Rico, and the U.S. Virgin Islands receive a VOCA victim assistance grant annually and are authorized to award such funds to agencies and nonprofit organizations that meet the needs of crime victims. One priority funding area is the support of direct services to crime victims and their families, such as the survivors of victims of homicide. (For example, funds may be made available to cover medical or burial expenses.) Such funds are distributed through each state's Crime Victims Compensation Board. Compensation boards are usually administered through the attorney general's office; in some states, they are administered through the governor's office or state department of health (Ginger Bankston-Bailey, personal communication, May 13, 1999). Information about this funding may be acquired from one of these offices or from the Office for Victims of Crime, which can be reached at (202) 307-5983.

If federal financial assistance is needed, your school should request that assistance as quickly as possible, since delays are common in processing and approving such requests. Your state's department of education, governor, attorney general's office, local and state legislators, and/or congressional representatives could all be helpful in expediting such a request. Your school superintendent and school board should contact these federal and state representatives, as well as city and county personnel (such as your county or municipality's emergency management agency) for advice about and support in requesting financial assistance after a severe school crisis. Questions to address include what funds are available, under what conditions, and how to access those funds (e.g., whether applications are necessary, appropriate contact persons and their telephone numbers, and so forth).

Politics of Crisis Response

The more crisis planning that has been done in advance in your school or district, the less chaos and the fewer competing factions there will be regarding what should be done and who can do it when a crisis occurs. A crisis by definition violates expectations, and everyone involved is flooded with waves of emotion. It is difficult to think clearly, even for those in charge of your school and the crisis response. Thus, conflicts and misunderstandings often arise. Be more patient than usual, and be very clear in your communications and intentions.

The principle guiding the crisis response should be: "What do those affected by the crisis need, and who in the school and/or community has previously demonstrated competency in meeting such needs?" A NOVA team (*see "National Crisis Response Teams/Organizations" previously in this chapter*) is often extremely helpful, since one of NOVA's main goals is to guide, support, and train local caregivers to assume responsibility for the crisis response and the ongoing support of the school and community.

For that reason, NOVA teams stay in a community for only a few days (although they are available to local caregivers for consultation by telephone after leaving the community).

A crisis will exacerbate any communication problems and tensions between competing factions in your school and/or community, but it also has the potential to help improve such situations. For example, prior to the shooting at Westside Middle School, the Jonesboro, Arkansas, area had two Ministerial Alliance groups due to a split in the organization about 20 years ago. The split had occurred because of strong differences of opinion about whether the county should be "wet" or "dry" (i.e., allowed to sell liquor). After the shooting at Westside Middle School, however, the two groups reformed into one alliance so that a cohesive faith-based group could address the healing of the community (Linda Speer Graham and Jack Bower, personal communication, March 1999).

A key to remember during the crisis response is to take the high ground: Do whatever must be done to help the victims and survivors get better, regardless of your own motivations and the political or agency concerns influencing you. If everyone involved is truly working toward that goal, the politics of crisis response will be much less disruptive.

It is important for all key school, community, and agency leaders to sit down together early in the crisis response to discuss the specifics of the situation and how best to work collaboratively to address the crisis. Following almost every crisis situation, there will be problems and concerns including the potential for lawsuits. Early discussion and continued collaboration among school and community leaders, coupled with an overriding focus on what needs to be done to assist those traumatized by the crisis, will help to reduce such problems.

It also is important for the school and district administrators to keep the school personnel who provided assistance in the immediate aftermath of the crisis involved in the decision making in the weeks and months ahead. Some key personnel have reported that their input was no longer valued and appreciated six months or so after a major community tragedy.

General Points When Using Outside Help

There are three main points for your school's crisis response team to keep in mind when utilizing crisis response assistance from outside your school: (1) stay involved yourselves, (2) make sure your helpers are providing an appropriate type of assistance to your school community, and (3) regroup with any outside helpers before they leave your school.

Staying Involved

Regardless of who helps you, but particularly if an outside crisis response team comes to your school, it's important for your school's team members and staff to remain involved and to actively participate in each step of the crisis response. Even a highly trained state or national team will prefer to lend their expertise with your school's personnel "calling the shots" and leading the crisis response effort.

Sometimes, when others come into a school to assist, the school's counseling staff seem to just "disappear." It's often a relief to receive such expert assistance—especially when you're feeling overwhelmed by the needs of your school community—and you might think: "Here are six people who have come in who are really great at this stuff. They can take over now and handle the crisis, and I can just go ahead and do my normal things." This is a natural response, given that severe crises are not part of most school counselors' or psychologists' training programs. Plus, it's difficult to serve as a calm, objective caregiver when you are personally affected by the crisis occurring in your community. Regardless of your own crisis response skill level, it is important to hang in there. The outside team will be there for you to lean on, and will share their knowledge with you, but remember, they need you too.

How does an outside team need you? You know the staff, your students, and your community, and you need to communicate with the "outsiders" about them. Crisis response professionals may have specialized training in trauma and caregiving, but only you know the people involved, their strengths, weaknesses, and viewpoints, and all the nuances that are so critical in crisis intervention.

You're also needed to pick up the pieces when these helpers leave. (As mentioned previously, NOVA, for example, limits its on-site assistance to no more than three or four days per team so that your community will not become dependent upon the team[s].) Don't assume that crisis response professionals will come into your school, take over the crisis response, handle the trauma, and leave. While they may be qualified to do just that, in the long run doing so wouldn't be best for your school or community. The school community will be counting on you for continued support for a long time to come. Thus, one of the main goals of an outside crisis response team will be to train school personnel in the best ways to assist your school and community after the crisis.

Providing Appropriate Assistance

To best utilize outside assistance, your crisis response team will need to give helpers some direction about what they are needed to do. For example, if a group of local clergy members, an SST from a neighboring school, or university psychology faculty come to help, they will probably not have training specifically in crisis intervention. Have your team direct these people to whatever areas need more coverage at the time and provide each helper with a pad of paper and a pen or pencil. Regardless of where they work—whether with students, with the staff, or with parents and other family members—ask these helpers to follow these basic principles:

- Their main role is to be an empathetic listener. They should not try to impress their views, stories, or opinions on whomever they're working with. It's not their job to "fix" the people they are assisting but rather to simply be there for them, to be a caring presence.

- They should show sympathy for what the people they are working with are feeling through body language, but should not exhibit a great deal of emotion themselves.

- There are no magic words to say that will set things right. But there are some things helpers *shouldn't* say, including, "I understand" and "I know how you feel." In reality, they *don't* know exactly how the other people are feeling. Instead they could say, "I can't imagine how difficult this must be." Also, they should not offer: "I felt the same way when …." They must let each person's story be unique. This is not the time to share their own life experiences.

- In general, they should speak as little as possible themselves. They should be reflective listeners.

- Helpers should provide whomever they're speaking with permission to express a range of emotions (even nervous laughter or seeming indifference). Everyone deals with trauma differently and at different rates—there is no one correct way to feel at any one time.

- They should stress the commonality of the feelings of whomever they're assisting. They should emphasize that whatever these people may be feeling—anger, grief, disbelief, confusion, fear, like they're "going crazy"—others feel the same way, and these are all typical reactions to a crisis.

- They should help whomever they are speaking with predict what they will face in the immediate future and sources of strength and coping skills the people can draw upon.

- They should try to instill a sense of hope.

- Helpers should make note of every person they assist, and who among those they are particularly worried about.

Regrouping With Helpers

At the end of the day, don't let your helpers simply pack up and drive away. The Counseling Liaison and/or Campus Liaison should call a meeting of all the caregivers to: (1) systematically gather information to help your school community in the future, (2) formally thank these people for their assistance, and (3) provide the opportunity for these helpers to "vent."

At the caregiver meeting, ask the helpers what was working about the crisis response that day, what wasn't working, and what their recommendations are after being in the classrooms, on the school buses, and so forth. They can provide a great deal of important information for follow-up. In addition to the Counseling Liaison, it is helpful for the Crisis Coordinator/head administrator and a central office representative to attend this meeting, so they all have a sense of the needs for the following days. If any of the helpers will be coming back the next day to assist again, take the time at this meeting to plan their actions/assignments.

People who have given their time and energy to assist you during a crisis have provided a tremendous service and deserve recognition. Schools often forget to take the time for this, thinking about it only after the dust has settled and their helpers are long gone. But such a lack of organization or professionalism is really not acceptable. Pause for just a few minutes to thank your helpers. They will appreciate it and will be more likely to help you again if you need them.

Like you, most of these people have probably never been involved in a severe crisis. They will probably feel exhausted, emotionally drained, and a little shaken up from the day spent working in your school. Indeed, this may be the most difficult day many of them have ever spent in a professional capacity. All the helpers will benefit from taking a little bit of time to talk about what they experienced personally. At the caregiver meeting in Jonesboro, the caregivers said such things as, "I was so scared," and "I'm so sorry this happened, but I feel good about what I did." By allowing these people the opportunity to vent with one another about the day, you will help them to feel appreciated and proud of the assistance they provided.

References

Advice on managing the media after a tragedy. (1998, November). *Practical Strategies for Maintaining Safe Schools: School Violence Alert, 4*(11), 5.

Arkansas buries its dead. (1998, March 29). *ABCNEWS.com*. Available online: http://archive.abcnews.com/sections/us/DailyNews/jonesboro0327.html

Community crisis response. (1999, May 13). *OVC Fact Sheet*. Available online: http://www.ojp.usdoj.gov/ovc/help/ccr.htm

Counseling Jonesboro: The role of the school psychologists, the national crisis team, and the strength of the community. (1998, May). *Today's School Psychologist, 1*(10), 1, 6.

Crane, S. R. (1998, August 28). NASP creates a NEAT response team. *National Association of School Psychologists*. Available online: http://www.naspweb.org/CRANE.html

Fugate, L. (1999, March 23). "Kind of like having a nightmare." *Jonesboro Sun*, pp. 1A-2A.

Gamble, C. (1996, August 7). Pa. community mourns after losing 16 students, 5 adults in TWA crash. *Education Week, 15*(41), 10.

Grants and funding. (1999, April 14). *OVC Fact Sheet*. Available online: http://www.ojp.usdoj.gov/ovc/fund/nrd/intro.htm

Johnson, M. E. (1998). Responding to the shooting at Thurston High School in Springfield, Oregon. *NOVA Newsletter, 18*(5, 6), 2-5.

Johnston, R. C. (1998, May 27). Hope in the mourning. *Education Week, 17*(37), 26-31.

Kentucky community crisis response board. (1998, April). *Kentucky Teacher*, p. 12.

Lazarus, P. J. (1998, November). Florida school psychologists create state level crisis team. *NASP Communiqué, 27*(3), 10.

National Organization for Victim Assistance (NOVA). (1994). *A brief explanation of the Community Crisis Response Team: A project of the National Organization for Victim Assistance* [Handout]. Washington, DC: Author.

Paine, C. (1998, November). Tragedy response and healing: Springfield unites. *NASP Communiqué, 27*(3), 16-17.

Poland, S. (1997). School crisis teams. In A. P. Goldstein & J. C. Conoley (Eds.), *School violence intervention: A practical handbook* (pp. 127-159). New York: Guilford.

Riley, R. (1998, June 9). Speech at Safe and Drug Free Schools Conference, Washington, DC. Available online: http://www.ed.gov/Speeches/980609.html

Stockton, B. (1998, November). Back to school in Jonesboro. *NASP Communiqué, 27*(3), 12.

Trump, K. S. (1998, August 5). *Crisis in the classroom: Can your school's security pass the exam?* Available online: http://www.nsba.org/services/federation/nepn798.htm

When disaster strikes: Questions schools should consider when developing a crisis management plan. (1998, April). *Practical Strategies for Maintaining Safe Schools: School Violence Alert, 4*(4), 7.

chapter **five**

Processing the Crisis

A process is a systematic series of actions directed to some end (*Random House College Dictionary*, 1980). In terms of crisis response, to process is to systematically assist those affected in examining their feelings in order to help them minimize trauma and begin healing. Processing is not a complex therapeutic device; rather, it is simply talking. But it is a *way* of talking that facilitates discussion about a crisis by those affected by it.

Why Process?

As explained by the Pasco County (Florida) Crisis Intervention Team, when a crisis occurs, the emotions experienced are generally very strong and often difficult to resolve. When school personnel and students are involved, the impact of a death or crisis can be significantly debilitating, both to the individuals and to the normal school routine. Schools must accept the responsibility for alleviating some of the grief, pain, and fears that are often present following a crisis involving students or staff members (District School Board, 1994).

Research (e.g., Tuckman, 1973) has consistently shown that reaching out immediately to victims and their families during a crisis can help to prevent the development of posttraumatic symptoms. Two school crisis incidents clearly contrast the effects of providing and not providing prompt intervention to crisis victims. The first incident occurred in Chowchilla, California, in the early 1970s. In this horrific incident, a bus filled with children, grades K-12, was kidnapped and literally buried in the desert. The kidnappers had dug a large hole, drove the bus into it, and then covered it. After three days, the children managed to dig their way out and escape. They were physically unhurt but were hungry, exhausted, and traumatized. They were told by well-meaning adults to go home and forget about the incident

(Sandall, 1986). Terr (1983) found that five years later every single one of those Chowchilla children had clinical symptoms of depression, anxiety, or fears about the world. Some later appeared on television programs as adults to discuss their experience. They reported problems in their adult lives as a result of it (Pitcher & Poland, 1992).

In the second incident, a couple took 160 children and adults hostage in a Cokeville, Wyoming elementary school in May 1986. They had a bomb and demanded ransom money to finance a revolution. During the standoff, the bomb accidentally discharged, killing both terrorists and injuring 80 of the hostages. Sandall (1986) was the school psychologist for the district and was designated the crisis coordinator. He and the school's principal agreed that an immediate and active response was warranted. The following are a few of the actions taken (Pitcher & Poland, 1992):

- A town meeting was held the next day, in which crisis responders assisted the students, their families, and the community to cope with the crisis.
- The students were encouraged to visit the school as soon as possible (in order to nip "school phobia" in the bud).
- Faculty meetings were held to discuss the incident and ways to assist the students.
- The students were encouraged to discuss the incident and their feelings fully. Feelings were expressed through discussions, artwork, and writing.
- School was resumed as soon as possible with numerous opportunities provided for discussion of the crisis.

Sandall (cited in Pitcher & Poland, 1992) later found that the children who verbalized the most and the children who attended school most often after the crisis recovered the best. As Dr. Marilyn Gootman (1998) explained, "Denying pain and submerging it within can only cause greater psychological and physical pain with the passing of time."

Further, the benefits of processing are apparent in the *short term*. When you give people the time and permission to express their feelings after a crisis, those feelings become validated, leading to a return to normalcy more quickly. Things won't go back to normal just because you pretend the crisis didn't happen or didn't affect people.

An additional concern is that if you do not provide your school community members opportunities to process their reactions to the crisis, they will more likely talk with the media covering the crisis. School community members will satisfy their need to tell their "crisis stories" one way or another, but doing so with the media is not in their best interest. Media representatives have neither the mental health training nor, in many cases, the desire to truly assist school community members in processing their crisis reactions. The media's priority is to get a good story.

The National Institute of Mental Health (cited in Pitcher & Poland, 1992) has made three key recommendations for school personnel working with children during a crisis:

1. Remember that children are resilient.

2. Work with the children and their parents if possible.

3. Mental health personnel should seek out those who need their help rather than waiting for victims of crises to seek them out. Mental health personnel should be highly visible in the school following a crisis.

Parental support is critical to the recovery of children and teens after a crisis. By assisting your students' parents, you are indirectly assisting the students themselves. You might compare this aspect of the crisis response to the emergency procedures on an airplane: If the cabin becomes depressurized mid-flight, parents are instructed to put on their own oxygen mask first and then assist any young children flying with them. Only when parents are working from a position of strength can they fully assist their children in a crisis.

> "They're all victims—any little kid [who] has to watch something like this—in my eyes."
>
> —Sheriff Dale Haas, Jonesboro, Arkansas (Egerton, 1998)

In addition to addressing the needs of your students, don't overlook the needs of affected adults. Many adults in your school and community will require assistance in processing the traumatic effects of the crisis. For example, your school's staff—particularly teachers—must have the opportunity to work through their own issues about death and loss, as well as their shock and grief, if they are to be able to assist your students. Others who may need help include:

- Any people who have recently experienced the death of someone close to them or a significant loss.

- First responders on the scene (e.g., medical staff/hospital staff, firefighters, and police officers).

- Witnesses to the incident.

- Friends and family members of victims or suspected student perpetrator(s).

- Parents and other family members of your students.

- Family members of the school staff. (Although this group may be just as affected by the crisis as are students' parents, they are often given far less attention after a crisis than the parents of students).

- Local caregivers (e.g., your crisis response team members, clergy members, counselors, victims' advocates).

- Media personnel, who may be affected by a severe school crisis (particularly a crisis occurring in their own community). Commenting on the effect of the school shooting near Jonesboro, Arkansas, on the media, Grover Cooper, the now retired Superintendent of the Westside

School District, said, "We didn't have any problems with the local media. I know [they] were hurting, just like us" (Fugate, 1999, p. 1A).

Explained one reporter after covering the nation's worst school shooting to date (in Littleton, Colorado, on April 20, 1999): "Reporters are often thought of as uncaring, unfeeling exploiters of the grief and misery of others. But many of us who were assigned to cover the massacre at Columbine High have kids of our own.... I've been talking with my colleagues about how hard it is to take notes when your eyes are filled with tears, and how hard it is to broadcast when there's a lump in your throat. And they tell similar stories about how the story got to them. The invisible shield [the reporter used to protect himself emotionally from the stories he had covered for almost three decades] failed me on this one, and it will probably never be the same" (Lewis, 1999).

> "As the days passed [after our school shooting] many members of the media themselves became traumatized by the tragic events."
>
> —Cathy Paine, Crisis Response Team Leader, Springfield, Oregon, Public Schools (Paine, 1998, p. 16)

As explained by the National Organization for Victim Assistance (NOVA), "Many people live through a trauma and are able to reconstruct their lives without outside help. [However,] most people find some type of benign outside intervention useful in dealing with trauma. Recovery from immediate trauma is often affected by ... [a] supportive environment [and] validation of the experience" (NOVA, 1994). You can be instrumental in providing such assistance to your school and community.

Barriers to Processing

In a school crisis, the administrators set the tone and pace of the crisis response. Unfortunately, many administrators reject the need for themselves, or anyone else, to take the time to process the crisis. Many people (particularly men) in such leadership roles are more comfortable focusing on *actions* rather than *feelings*. Thus, many administrators have a tendency to discuss only logistics when they meet with their faculties and support staff after a crisis. They generally come in and say, for example: "Here's the plan—we're going to do 'x,' we're going to do 'y,' and we're going to do 'z.' The kids come back at such-and-such time tomorrow."

Communicating such practical information is important, of course, but the emotionality of the situation must be dealt with. Otherwise, your school staff may receive the message that they are simply expected to do their jobs (i.e., assist the students) and maintain "a stiff upper lip," so to speak. The problem with this expectation is that school staff members are human beings who have feelings, and most care a great deal about their students and their schools. When a crisis occurs and they are not provided the time and assistance they need to process its effects, their work with students will

156 *Coping With Crisis*

be negatively impacted in the short term, and their overall performance may be affected in the long term. If you believe that processing and counseling are appropriate only for the students, for the good of your school and community, rethink your position.

Some administrators may resist processing a crisis because they are uncomfortable with the mental health profession itself. In many communities, receiving counseling carries a stigma. As one principal bluntly explained after a crisis at his school: "I don't like counselors." What is important for administrators to keep in mind is that there is a distinction between short-term counseling for otherwise healthy people after a traumatic event and long-term therapy used to treat any number of mental conditions and disorders. While you may have a negative opinion of the latter, short-term assistance is appropriate for all those affected by a crisis, regardless of age, gender, or professional position. If you are uncomfortable talking about "feelings," focus instead on "reactions to the crisis" (NOVA, 1997). Everyone involved in your school's crisis has had a reaction to it, and their reactions are what need to be discussed.

> "Give Sorrow words; the grief that does not speak knits up the o'er wrought heart and bids it break."
>
> —From *Macbeth*, by William Shakespeare

Clarified clinical psychologist Judy Lyons: "At a time of trauma, people need to be reassured that their reactions are normal. They need to talk, they generally don't need formal therapy or medication. They should be told that changes in sleeping, eating, concentration, irritability, and social withdrawal or dependence are normal responses that will go away in the next month or so" ("School Officials in Pearl," 1997).

A third reason school personnel may not process a crisis is that they feel their crisis is less severe than some highly publicized, catastrophic events, such as those that occurred near Jonesboro, Arkansas, in West Paducah, Kentucky, in Littleton, Colorado, and elsewhere in the country. However, every single crisis is important to the individuals who were involved in the incident. Even if only one person was injured in your situation, if the incident was traumatic in any way, it's important for your school and community members to talk about their reactions to the crisis. Never underestimate the effects of a crisis.

Crises caused by violence are not the only situations necessitating processing. If one of your students drowns, for example, or if one of your teachers is killed in a car accident on the way to school, processing will be necessary. And, if a crisis incident occurs off school grounds but affects your school community in any way, this situation should be processed at school as well. For example, in July 1997 three school-age girls were abducted, molested, and brutally murdered in Spotsylvania, Virginia. There were "… no viable leads as to who had committed these horrific crimes, leaving the people of this beautiful, tranquil suburban community in a state of agitation and continued fear that similar events could happen again" (Feinberg, 1998). As the leader of the national crisis team invited into the community a few months later to support the residents explained: "Clearly the tension felt in the community had a strong ripple effect in the schools, and the school personnel at our sessions were showing many of the telltale signs of post traumatic stress" (Feinberg, 1998).

Finally, some school personnel may have good intentions and recognize the need for processing the effects of a crisis, and even try to do so. However, many may not know how to process effectively. For example, if you gather the faculty together after a crisis and simply ask them, "Who would like to talk about how you feel after this crisis?", they may not have much to say. They may feel put on the spot or fear they will be perceived as weak or ineffective if they speak up. Or they might not know where to begin to express their emotions. To make processing the effects of the crisis most helpful for your school and community, a proven counseling model should be employed. (*The next section, "How Do You Process?", outlines such a tool for your use.*)

How Do You Process?

This section outlines a simple yet powerful counseling model that has been used by the National Organization for Victim Assistance (NOVA, 1997) for two decades and has proven helpful for people of all ages after natural disasters and crises of many kinds, including those caused by violence. It works extremely well one-to-one, with small to mid-size groups of people (e.g., 50), and even with several hundred participants at once (although the seating arrangement would need to be modified and it may be more difficult for participants to hear the speakers well).

The National Organization for Victim Assistance (NOVA) trains members of its Community Crisis Response Teams (CCRTs) and other interested caregivers (e.g., school psychologists, social workers, members of the clergy, and victims' advocates) on this technique in an intensive five-day course. Obviously, there won't be time for this training in the midst of a crisis. During a crisis, your school and community need help *now*. If a NOVA team—or anyone else trained in this model—is not assisting your school (*see "Help to Request" in Chapter Four for more information*), you can still benefit from fundamentals of the model even without formal training. The Counseling Liaison and other mental health caregivers in your school and community can use the following guidelines to implement the basics of the model. While not a substitute for NOVA training, these guidelines can help those affected to more effectively process their reactions to the crisis. (*NOTE*: In a crisis situation, the NOVA model has several advantages over other commonly used counseling models. Even if your school's counseling staff are trained in another model, you may find it helpful to supplement with principles of the NOVA model.)

To Contact NOVA:

- For assistance with the model, or to inquire about training for the future, call (202) 232-6682 (232-NOVA). This number is staffed by NOVA 24 hours per day to assist those requesting help or information.

- Additional contact methods for NOVA include FAX and online:
  - (202) 462-2255 (FAX)
  - nova@access.digex.net (e-mail)
  - www.access.digex.net/~nova (Web site)

General Processing Guidelines

First, a few general points about processing a crisis:

- During processing sessions, *enlist the involvement of any outside crisis response team members* assisting your school. However, *processing sessions should always involve caregivers from within your school* (i.e., do not simply turn the meeting[s] over to a local psychiatrist or psychology professor from a nearby local college; this person will not know better than you how to help your school community).

- All members of your school community (and many in the surrounding community as well) will need the opportunity to process the crisis. *Hold separate processing sessions for the students and staff.* However, the adults and children can process together during family/community meetings (*see "The Family/Community Meeting" in Chapter Two*).

- *Provide the time for your students to discuss the incident and their feelings fully* and encourage them to do so. (*NOTE*: Prior parental permission is not required for this type of counseling/discussion.) This discussion should take place within the students' classroom groups and with the assistance of the teacher and at least one counseling staff member (three, if you plan to follow the full NOVA model) or administrator in each affected class. (*NOTE*: Very young students, such as kindergartners, should be reunited with their primary caretakers as soon as possible after a traumatic event.)

> "She fell right beside me ... I saw the blood ... They screamed, 'Run' ... I just wish I could have gone back ... Maybe I could have saved her."
>
> —A few sensory perceptions of students at Westside Middle School (Jonesboro, Arkansas), recounted by school psychologist Betty Stockton (Zenere, 1998, p. 38)

- The *Counseling Liaison can lead the staff in processing the crisis* either during the day of the crisis if school has been canceled or right after school if your school remains open for the rest of the day.

- *The staff session should be mandatory for all.* Attendance is important for the short-term functioning and the long-term recovery of your school and everyone in it. Yet practical experience has found that when school staff are given a choice about attending an after-school processing session they often do not attend (Lieberman, 1999). Note that if the meeting is held after school, the bus drivers serving your school would need to maintain their regular schedule and would not be able to attend. (They should be assisted in processing their crisis reactions at another time.)

- *Process the crisis as close as possible to the crisis scene* (i.e., at your school).

- *Choose a location that is conducive to discussion and ensures the privacy of those participating* (i.e., it is quiet, has a door that closes, has permanent walls without a great number of viewing windows).

- *Bar the media (even the local media) from attending* any processing sessions (*see "The Family/Community Meeting" in Chapter Two for additional information*).

- *Have drinking water and tissues available.* You might also want to provide some healthful snacks.

- *Allot enough time for the session.* A processing session may become quite emotional, and people should not be interrupted by outside demands mid-discussion. Allowing the discussion to come to a natural conclusion must be a priority. Everyone who wishes to speak must be allowed the time he or she needs, and problem solving and the identification of coping skills should not be rushed. (In the West Paducah, Kentucky, case study, remember the resourceful school administrator who took the entire student body to the school's gym and played Simon Says to allow the faculty time to finish their processing.) Find a way to provide the time the staff and students need for this important aspect of healing. If you must limit the time of a processing session, indicate those time limits before the discussion begins.

- *Communicate the importance of processing.* The best way to convey this message is for the Crisis Coordinator/head administrator to participate in the processing session with his or her staff. A strong leader can model and openly express emotions and still be respected and admired. Although administrators need to maintain their composure during the crisis response, at the end of the day they are no less affected (and sometimes more so) by the trauma than anyone else at the school. During the processing session, all members of the school community should feel welcome to relate to one another simply as human beings with feelings, setting aside the school's everyday hierarchy. Another benefit of the administrator participating in the processing session is that he or she will hear the comments made by the staff and be able to identify those staff members who are severely affected by the crisis. The administrator can then provide some extra support to those individuals in the future.

- *Remember that everyone's story is valid.* The story of the teacher down the hall is every bit as important as your story, for example. It doesn't matter if you were standing next to the victim, or if you almost got hurt, or if that teacher was at the other end of the building when the crisis occurred—his or her story is still important. Sometimes people deny this fact and argue the point or attempt to shut others out. Sometimes there's an attitude of, "Only I get to talk because I was closer to the scene or because I knew the victim better than you did." Everyone in your school community has been affected by the crisis, and the severity of trauma experienced by individuals is influenced by each person's unique history of crisis and loss. You must insist upon an accepting forum in which everyone may speak, regardless of the role they played in the crisis event.

> "Whoever survives a test, whatever it may be, must tell the story. That is his duty."
>
> —Elie Wiesel, Holocaust Survivor

- *Provide permission for a range of emotions, particularly in the student discussions.* Teachers often ask after such discussions, "Why aren't all the kids crying?" Many students won't cry. And some may exhibit behaviors that you don't consider appropriate, such as letting out a little nervous laugh when they hear the bad news. (Laughter relieves tension.) Another student may say, for example, "I don't care. I didn't like her anyway." Bear in mind that a student may say "I don't care" in an attempt to push the incident away and an hour later may be crying. The point is that people process crises in different ways at different rates—there is no one correct way to feel at any given time.

- *Begin to identify those who may need more in-depth assistance* to recover from the crisis (*see "Providing Counseling Services" in Chapter Seven for more information*). Those who need more assistance may be the obvious people you'd think of: close friends or family members of victims or suspected student perpetrator(s), injured survivors, and witnesses to the event. However, other individuals who have no direct involvement in the crisis may experience a great deal of trauma due to their own history of crisis and loss or due to a general lack of coping skills.

- *Not all participants need to speak during a processing session.* (For example, only about 20 of the approximately 50 staff members spoke during a Heath High School processing session after the school shooting in West Paducah, Kentucky.) Participants who do not wish to discuss their sensory perceptions will benefit from hearing others' feelings. They will likely realize that there is commonality between what they've heard and what they've felt themselves.

- The participants may wish to pray during and/or after a processing session. If so, *allow time for prayer.* (Prayer is not a required aspect of the model, however.)

- *Read through and become comfortable and familiar with all the steps of the model* (listed in the next section) before implementing it with a group.

The NOVA Model

Goals

- To guide the release of emotional "steam"
- To address/counsel a large number of individuals after a community tragedy
- To provide peer validation for emotions felt
- To help establish social support, rebuild community bonds, and promote hope for the future

Advantages

- It works with one individual, a few individuals, or a group of individuals.

- It provides a consistent method for processing and instills confidence in your school's caregivers for facilitating such sessions. (If you stick to the script/procedures outlined following, the task of facilitating processing sessions is a lot less scary. You may be working with the most traumatized group of people you've ever encountered, but using the model outline will give you the confidence you need to lead the discussion appropriately.)

"… [C]ounselors and administrators (in the Cypress-Fairbanks I.S.D., Houston, Texas) are in awe about how well the [NOVA] model works and how much processing they have seen students do. Many counselors have commented that they will not be so anxious and scared about what to do when future tragedies occur."

(Poland, 1998, p. 14)

- It provides participants the opportunity to process the crisis themselves, which is more therapeutic than just hearing about the need to process it. (Too often in schools well-meaning counselors and/or school psychologists go into a classroom and stand up in front of the students to tell them how important it is to process and that all of their emotions are okay. The problem is that the caregivers spend all their time talking to the students about the importance of processing, but the students are just listening rather than actually *doing* the processing themselves. Thus, the individual participants are not really helped, and no one realizes the commonality of their feelings, which is comforting to survivors of trauma.)

- It complements traditional school approaches but places more emphasis on the survivors talking than the counselors talking. (Many counselors talk more than is helpful during such sessions and have a tendency to discuss their own personal experiences—such as when a friend/relative died—which shifts the focus from the survivors' situation and is not relevant or therapeutic.)

- All members of the school community—even young children—can understand this approach and participate, due to its emphasis on sensory perceptions (i.e., that which is seen, heard, tasted, felt, and smelled).

- The model helps participants to explore their memories of and feelings about an event because, unlike other counseling models, it emphasizes sensory perceptions. The theory is that since we encode our memories by our sensory perceptions, focusing on those perceptions brings our memories and experiences into sharp focus so that we can talk about them. (The sense of smell, for example, is most closely associated with memory, as it is controlled by the most primitive part of the brain.) If you simply ask a participant, "How do you feel about this?" he or she may not have much to say. Asking instead, "What did you see, what did you hear, what did you smell?" provides some concrete and powerful information to explore.

- It helps those traumatized to anticipate and plan for their immediate future, as the model includes a "problem-solving" component that is often overlooked by other counseling models.

What you'll need

- Three mental health caregivers per session (e.g., the Counseling Liaison and other members of your school's mental health staff and/or members of any outside crisis response team assisting your school).

- Several large sheets of paper and an easel (or tape to attach the papers to a wall).

- Markers (three different colors are preferable).

- A chair for each participant (including the Facilitator) arranged in a circle or horseshoe. The circle should be as small as possible, with no extra chairs. All participants should be able to hear and see one another. (*NOTE*: You may need to remain flexible on this point. If you have hundreds of people in a session, you won't have room for that many chairs in a circle, and even if you did the people wouldn't be able to hear one another speaking.)

Roles of the session leaders

The tasks of the three people leading the processing sessions are as follows:

Facilitator
- Know the factual details of the trauma.
- Explain the roles of the Scribe and Caregiver(s).

- Clarify the ground rules and security issues.
- Give permission to the group to say whatever they like.
- Lead the processing session.
- Maintain emotional control of yourself. (If you start to cry or otherwise emote, the Scribe will need to take over the role of Facilitator for the remainder of the session. If you feel capable, you could become the Scribe for the remainder of the session.)
- Focus completely on the one person who is speaking. Maintain eye contact and an open, accepting body posture. Do not turn your attention from the speaker to any other member of the group, even if someone else is sobbing uncontrollably. (*NOTE*: The exception to this rule is if someone interrupts the speaker and you must ask that person to be quiet.)

Scribe

- Provide emotional and practical support to the Facilitator.
- Record each participant's comments:
  - Record at least one comment per participant.
  - Write down words and phrases rather than complete sentences, but do not paraphrase.
  - Underline key words/phrases, or use different colors of marker to denote sensory perceptions, problems/challenges, and coping skills.
  - Record selectively. (You won't be able to record everything and keep up with the discussion.)
  - Stand to the side of the paper so the participants can see what you've written.
  - Denote changes in speaker with a mark or symbol.
- Speak only when called on by the Facilitator or if the Facilitator becomes emotionally overwhelmed.

Caregiver(s)

- Circulate throughout the room (outside the circle) and quietly assist participants who become distraught.
- Follow any participants who leave the circle and offer them assistance. (If possible, begin and end the session with everyone together.) However, do not ask anyone to leave the circle if they've not chosen to do so on their own. Crying—even sobbing—is a natural part of the process and should not be treated as a disruption.
- Address the group as a whole only if the Facilitator asks you to do so.

Steps for the Facilitator to follow

1. Introduce yourself, the Scribe, and the Caregiver(s), and explain all of your roles.

2. Clarify security issues. Emphasize that the participants are free to say anything they need to say and that anything they choose to express will be kept confidential by everyone participating. Explain that the Scribe will be recording some of the comments but that the group will choose what they would like to do with the papers at the end of the session—including destroying them if they wish.

3. Clarify the ground rules of the session:

   - Everyone must respect the privacy of the speakers by keeping their statements confidential.

   - Only one person may speak at a time. When one person begins to speak, all of the other participants must listen to that person. (If others are conversing while a participant is speaking, say to the speaker, "Can I come right back to you?" and then address the others by saying, "You will have the chance to talk about [the topic] later, but right now we all need to listen because some very important and very personal things are being expressed." Then turn your full attention back to the speaker.)

   - If anybody leaves the circle, one of the Caregiver(s) will check with him or her and offer assistance.

4. Review the facts of the crisis sequentially. Be sure to list all the names of the injured and/or deceased and the suspected perpetrator(s) if they are known. (Do not speculate or philosophize. Just briefly summarize the known facts.) End the review of facts with the current status.

5. Then say, "I am so sorry that this has happened to you."

6. Begin to involve the participants by asking them to take a deep breath and to close their eyes if they wish. Ask them to focus on their sensory perceptions at the time the crisis occurred: what they saw, heard, touched, smelled, and/or tasted. (Focusing on their sensory perceptions will take the participants back to the exact moment of the crisis.)

7. Ask the participants, "Who will tell me where they were and what they were doing when they heard about (the crisis)?" or "… when they saw (the event) happen?" *Wait through the silence.* If no one responds, wait for a full minute or so and then continue to ask the group similar questions (e.g., "Who will tell me who they were with?" "… what they saw?" "… what they smelled at the time?" while looking around the circle until someone begins to speak. Eventually someone will begin to describe his or her sensory perceptions.

   For example, a teacher who missed a severe crisis at her school had this to say about the incident: "I'll tell you where I was, I was home sick that day. It was like the television was screaming at me and I could smell my soup boiling on the stove, and I couldn't believe it. I felt so guilty because I wasn't here with all of you and I wasn't here to help, but yet I was so relieved because I wasn't here."

Another teacher who'd had first aid training and helped save lives after a school shooting later said, "I smell the blood, I taste the blood. It's all over me." The processing session helped her to understand that these sorts of perceptions are normal after trauma and that they take a while to go away.

8. Respond minimally to the speaker. Say, for example (as appropriate):
   - "I can't imagine what that would have been like."
   - "I can't imagine how difficult that must have been for you."
   - "This wasn't your fault."
   - "It's understandable that you feel that way."
   - "It must have been upsetting to (hear, feel, smell, see, taste) that."
   - "You are not going crazy."
   - "You are not the first person to feel this way."
   - "That is not uncommon after a tragedy."
   - "Others have reported similar perceptions and thoughts."

9. Do not prompt the speaker by asking probing questions such as, "Did you see the blood (or other gory/traumatic details)?" or "Didn't you feel guilty?"

10. After the speaker finishes talking about his or her sensory perceptions, lead the speaker in exploring the thoughts and emotions he or she has been having in the aftermath of the crisis—the time since the incident occurred to the present. Ask questions such as, "How have you reacted since that time?"

11. Respond to the emotions expressed by saying, "It's not uncommon for survivors of crises to feel (whatever the speaker said)." This gives the group permission for a range of emotions and validates what the speaker has expressed. It's not necessary for you to say a great deal, because the powerful aspect of this process is for everybody else in the room to recognize that the speaker's thoughts and feeling are almost exactly like theirs and that they're not the only ones feeling such things.

12. Speakers may dwell on feelings of guilt/regret, helplessness, anger, and fear. For example, it is common for people to wonder, "Did I do the right thing?" A teacher may ask, for example, "Did I clamp down (on an artery) and give first aid to the right kid?" Simply respond: "After a tragedy, people often second-guess themselves, and they are not sure they did everything perfectly. But it sounds like you did a very good job" or "… it sounds like you did everything that you could" or "… you did the right thing by keeping yourself and your students safe."

13. Let the speaker talk for as long as he or she wants. When there is a pause, validate what the speaker talked about using reflective listening.

14. Don't assume anything. Let the participants tell you what happened and how they reacted.

15. Next address the "prediction" component of the model, which identifies the immediate future for the survivor. To pinpoint what the speaker thinks he or she will face in the near future, ask, "What are you worried about right now?" Speakers may express some very practical concerns (e.g., how to help an injured student when he or she returns to school) and/or they might revisit some of the uncomfortable feelings they expressed previously (e.g., guilt, fear). For example, after a school shooting, one teacher asked: "I feel afraid every morning when I get up, and I don't want to come to school. How long is that going to last?"

    If you can predict problems that the speaker doesn't anticipate (e.g., media pressures, involvement in the criminal justice system), give as much concrete information about such issues as you can.

16. Help to predict possible emotional reactions to the crisis. Discuss typical mental and physical responses to crisis and grief (*see "Crisis Effects and Grief" in Chapter Seven for examples*) and long-term stress reactions (*see "Long-Term Effects" in Chapter Twelve for information*).

17. Next focus on coping techniques and sources of strength for the speaker. This addresses the "preparation" component of the model. Ask, "What have been your sources of strength? What helps you to cope?" (Let the speaker think of his or her own coping mechanisms. Neither you nor the other participants should intervene here.) Typical responses include God/church/spiritual beliefs, parents, a spouse, other family members, colleagues/administrators at the school, friends, and diet/exercise/rest.

18. When the speaker has finished talking, ask, "Is there anything else you would like to say?"

19. Then tell the speaker sincerely, "I am so sorry this happened to you." (It may sound hokey to say that same phrase 30 times—or however many speakers there are—but it isn't hokey during a processing session. Hearing these words brings closure and helps each speaker to feel heard and validated.)

20. If possible, stay with one individual through his or her sensory perceptions, emotions, prediction, and preparation, and then repeat the entire sequence with the next speaker.

21. Continue by asking, "Who else would like to talk?" Say, "It's not necessary that everybody talk, but if you would like to, I'm listening. Please begin your comments with your sensory perceptions." Then wait through the silence until someone else begins to speak. You may need

to periodically repeat the question until someone volunteers. (The waiting can be awkward and cause you anxiety. But do not let this anxiety get the best of you and start throwing out verbal "stuff" that is irrelevant. The model will work if you have the strength to patiently wait through the silences and gently repeat the questions while maintaining eye contact with the group.)

22. Do not emote, and do not discuss your own experiences.

23. Show sympathy through your body language (e.g., lean forward in your chair or incline your head to indicate attentiveness) and with eye contact. Keep your facial expressions generally neutral, but reflect concern or sadness when appropriate.

24. After every person who wishes to speak has talked, stand and review the session using the notes taken by the Scribe. Discuss the listed sensory perceptions, the emotions, the predictions, and the coping (preparation) skills identified by the group. Emphasize the commonality of the group's reactions to the crisis, and then address those who only listened: "Those of you who did not talk, I know you were listening. I know you had many of the same feelings."

25. Compliment the group on their resources, strength, resiliency, and community spirit, and then build on the coping strategies identified. You will not be able to solve all of their problems and heal the entire trauma during this time, but you can emphasize hope for the future and should strive to do so.

26. Thank the group for talking about their experiences and emotions.

27. Specify the additional support that is available in the community and/or school, including outside agencies and any other processing sessions and family/community meetings scheduled (*see "The Family/Community Meeting" in Chapter Two for additional information*).

28. Discuss with the group what they want to do with the notes taken during the session.

29. Invite any individuals who would like additional assistance to stay in the room following the session. Explain that you, the Scribe, the Caregiver(s), and the other members of your crisis response team (or outside crisis response team assisting your school) who are present will be available to talk with any participants who have questions or would like comforting.

References

District School Board of Pasco County. (1994). *Crisis intervention team program rationale and structure*. Land O'Lakes, FL: Author.

Egerton, B. (1998, March 25). "It's the worst thing I've ever seen," sheriff says: Rampage leaves community in shock, tears. *Dallas Morning News*, p. 1A.

Feinberg, T. (1998, March 22). NASP/NEAT & NOVA: A crisis partnership that really works. *National Association of School Psychologists*. Available online: http://www.naspweb.org/office/cq/CQ265NASPNEAT.htm

Fugate, L. (1999, March 23). "Kind of like having a nightmare." *Jonesboro Sun*, pp. 1A-2A.

Gootman, M. (1998, December 3). Helping our teens heal when a friend dies. *Jewish Family & Life*. Available online: http://www.jewishfamily.com/Features/996/helping10.htm

Lewis, G. (1999, May 3). When a professional shield cracks: Covering Colorado rampage took toll on reporter. *MSNBC*. Available online: http://www.msnbc.com/news/265324.asp

Lieberman, R. (1999, January 22-23). *Crisis Intervention Workshop*, Walnut Creek, California.

National Organization for Victim Assistance (NOVA). (1994). *Recovery from immediate trauma* [Handout]. Washington, DC: Author.

National Organization for Victim Assistance (NOVA). (1997). *Community crisis response team training manual: Second edition*. Washington, DC: Author.

Paine, C. (1998, November). Tragedy response and healing: Springfield unites. *NASP Communiqué, 27*(3), 16-17.

Pitcher, G. D., & Poland, S. (1992). *Crisis intervention in the schools*. New York: Guilford.

Poland, S. (1998, May). NEAT chairman leads NOVA team in Paducah. *NASP Communiqué, 26*(7), 14.

Random House college dictionary (rev. ed.). (1980). New York: Random House.

Sandall, N. (1986). Early intervention in a disaster: The Cokeville hostage/bombing crisis. *NASP Communiqué, 15*(2), 1-2.

School officials in Pearl, Miss., help community cope with tragedy. (1997, November 11). *School Board News*, p. 4.

Terr, L. C. (1983). Chowchilla revisited: The effects of a psychic trauma four years after a school bus kidnapping. *The American Journal of Psychiatry, 12*, 140.

Tuckman, A. (1973). Disaster and mental health intervention. *Community Mental Health Journal, 9*(2), 151-157.

Zenere, F. (1998, November). NASP/NEAT community crisis response. *NASP Communiqué, 27*(3), 38-39.

chapter **six**

Immediate Aftermath of the Crisis

The Mornings After

When Will Things Return to Normal?

After something bad happens at a school, it is natural for the school community members to yearn for things to return to the way they were before the crisis. Because that can't happen, they yearn for things at least to return to "normal" so that they can stop thinking about the event and feeling their

Photo by David Zawalski

anger or grief. However, if your school's crisis was severe, things will never be exactly the same. Your expectations of education will have been violated forever, and a return to normalcy is not as easy as simply driving home from school the day of the crisis and "putting it behind you." It will take time, and it will take effort.

Imagine that your school is the one pictured in the snow globe. A way to visualize a crisis occurring there is to imagine the globe being shaken upside down until all the snowflakes inside it are churning. After a little time, all of those individual snowflakes will settle again, but they will never go back to exactly the same place. Likewise, your school will never be quite the same. That's not to say that the activities of your school will never return to normal—they will, and sooner than you may think.

The important point is that you must allow this process to unfold naturally, at its own pace. The healing of your school community members cannot be controlled or rushed, nor will your school environment return to normal sooner if you behave as if the crisis did not occur. On the contrary, you must continue to systematically address the crisis effects in the days and weeks following the incident to facilitate the return to normalcy. The following are suggested steps to take in the aftermath of a school crisis:

- Reopen your school as soon as possible.

  If you closed your school early the day of the crisis (*see "Task List" in Chapter Two for guidelines on making this decision*), for the benefit of your students it is important to reopen the school as soon afterward as you can—the next day if possible. Members of the crisis response team (e.g., the Crisis Coordinator, Counseling Liaison, and/or Campus Liaison) should have met with the faculty and support staff after school the first day of the crisis to provide them with the opportunity to process their own reactions to the crisis (*see Chapter Five, "Processing the Crisis"*) and to formulate a plan for assisting the students. Although a lot will be happening the first day and evening of the crisis (*see Chapter Two, "Continuing the Crisis Response"*), it's preferable, if time allows, to work longer with the staff members the first day so that the students can return to school the next day for assistance and emotional support.

  The crisis literature (e.g., Poland, Pitcher, & Lazarus, 1995) clearly shows that the sooner a crisis intervention is provided to survivors, and the more survivors have the opportunity to talk about their reactions to the incident, the better their chances are for a full and expedient recovery from the crisis effects. Emotional support must be provided to your students as soon as possible, and some of the best support for children after a crisis comes from trained school personnel. The love and attention of their parents is, of course, critical to children's recovery, but trained school personnel are more knowledgeable than most parents about typical childhood reactions to crisis and how to resolve them.

Additionally, in many families today both parents work outside the home, so if the students are at home rather than in school they may be left without the assistance of attentive adults sensitive to crisis effects.

- Do not significantly alter the school environment before the students arrive back at school.

After the police finish their work, the custodial staff should clean up the worst of the damage (e.g., blood and broken glass) and generally make things orderly. However, the Crisis Coordinator/head administrator should not delay the reopening of school for major repairs such as filling bullet holes (*see the discussion later in this section of an appropriate time and method for taking such actions*). Nor should you try to remove such evidence of the crisis such as impromptu memorials (e.g., flowers, ribbons, cards, stuffed animals, religious symbols, etc.) created by school community members.

Before the beginning of the 1998 school year, multiple members of a North Carolina high school band were killed in a tragic car accident. When a member of the National Emergency Assistance Team (*see "National Crisis Response Teams/Organizations" in Chapter Four*) called the school's principal to offer him assistance, the well-meaning but misguided principal mentioned: "Well, we've got all these flowers. All these flowers just keep arriving—they're everywhere! They're down the hallway, they're out in front, and school starts tomorrow, and I just told the custodians to get rid of them all."

Perhaps this administrator was not comfortable with emotionality and expressions of grief, perhaps he did not realize the extent of the emotional effects such a crisis would have on his students and staff, or perhaps he just wanted to forget the tragedy had occurred. But by removing the bouquets, he did not erase the crisis. Instead, he denied his entire school community a meaningful remembrance of the deceased students. The surviving students were not provided the opportunity to see the flowers—many of which they probably sent themselves—when they returned to school. (*See the discussion later in this section of a more appropriate way to manage such spontaneous memorials.*)

Even more important than maintaining such impromptu memorials after a crisis, do not attempt to erase the presence of the victims of the crisis at school. Some misguided teachers and administrators remove the victims' personal things right away. Others

"The school was closed the next day. I went to another school because I wanted to have someone to talk to."

—Student in Springfield, Oregon, speaking to the media after the 1998 school shooting there

"The most impromptu of the memorials became one of the most powerful for a community looking for solace in this tragedy. Within hours of the shooting, community members of all ages placed flowers, posters, balloons, plants, teddy bears, candles, photos, poems, crosses, and other mementos on the chain link fence in front of Thurston High [in Springfield, Oregon]. Ultimately, this memorial stretched the entire length of the campus, some 150 yards, and represented the community's outpouring of grief in a sea of flowers. For several days, vehicle and pedestrian traffic was nonstop as thousands passed by to pay their respects."

(Paine, 1998b, p. 16)

try to help surviving students by scrambling up the desks in victims' classes. They might think, "Now that will help. Nobody will realize where (the victim) would have been." But these actions do not help. In fact, they anger people and rob them of the opportunity to feel natural emotions by remembering the deceased when they reenter the room, looking at the empty desk, and thinking, "This is where (the victim) would have been seated."

Just such a situation occurred in the Kansas classroom of a second grade student we will call Mary, who was murdered in 1992. The little girl's teacher was told about her death before school the next day and went to school early to prepare herself for the other students' arrival. Only one person beat her to the school: the building principal. When the teacher arrived, he had just finished moving Mary's desk and personal possessions out of the room and had taken down all of her artwork. He told the teacher, "Keep their mind on the 'three R's' today. They are not to talk about Mary." Of course, these actions did not cause the students to forget about their murdered classmate. Instead, the actions created an atmosphere in which the students did not feel allowed to discuss their emotions about Mary and her death, which helped no one. (*See the discussion later in this section of how to assist students in coping with their crisis reactions when they return to school.*)

"It's important that the staff knows what should be said, what shouldn't be said, and how it should be said."

—Superintendent David P. Black, Montoursville, Pennsylvania, speaking about a staff inservice held before students returned to school after 21 school community members were killed in the 1996 explosion of TWA Flight 800 bound for France (Gamble, 1996)

• Prepare the faculty for the students' reentry to school.

The Crisis Coordinator and/or Campus Liaison should hold a mandatory faculty meeting before school on the first and second days that the students return to school. Provide time for the staff to express any fears or concerns they have about the day, and review the plans made for assisting the students. Be sure to tell the faculty that they have permission to temporarily modify and/or set aside the regular curriculum to address the emotionality of the crisis or loss (*see "Modifying the Curriculum" later in this chapter for additional information*).

• Carefully plan the students' return to school.

If your school was closed after the crisis (*see "Task List" in Chapter Two for guidelines on making this decision*), the Crisis Coordinator/head administrator should provide an opportunity for the school community members to visit the campus before classes resume. After the May 1998 school shooting in Springfield, Oregon, for example, "students, their families, and staff were given the opportunity to visit the Thurston campus on Memorial Day, allowing them to enter the campus supported by family, friends, counselors, NOVA volunteers, and 'comfort dogs.' Although many of the 2,000 visitors sat or stood in the repaired cafeteria, not all were able to do so. There were many tears that day ..." (Paine, 1998b, p. 16).

While most parents will bring their children to school on the first school day after a severe crisis, a number will still arrive by bus. Pay particular attention to the needs of any such students. If you have enough mental health workers from within your school or district, or volunteer counselors assisting your school (*see "Local Caregivers/Agencies" in Chapter Four*), arrange to have a counselor ride each school bus that morning. That way, there will be an extra adult to assist the bus driver, and if any students become visibly upset on the way to school the counselors on their buses can sit and talk with them.

On the day students return to school, have all the adults in the school (e.g., teachers, administrators, central office/school board representatives, your crisis response team, and any outside crisis response team members assisting your school) greet the students and their families as they arrive. Post these adults outside, at the doors of the school, at the bus bays, and in the hallways. The intent is to reach out to the students and reassure them about their return, saying, for example: "We're glad you're here today"; "I know this is hard, but we're going to get through this together"; or "I'm really sorry about what happened to your friend (name) and I'd like to help you."

You might also plan a special assembly or event at the beginning of the day to help ease the students back into the school routine. For example, after the 1998 school shooting in Springfield, Oregon, the school administrators began the first day of classes following the shooting with a free breakfast for the entire school. After the breakfast, the students reported to their classes to meet with counselors (Paine, 1998b).

It is also important, prior to the students' return, for the Crisis Coordinator/head administrator to decide on the schedule for the day (i.e., whether your students will be expected to move with a normal bell schedule or whether that schedule will need to be modified to address the emotionality surrounding the crisis). Factors to consider include: Will you need more time than one class period to discuss the crisis with the students and help them to process their reactions to the crisis? Will the students be afraid to go outside (or to the cafeteria, or wherever the crisis occurred)? Any after-school extracurricular activities should be held as scheduled unless carrying out an activity is not possible because of damage to the area needed for the activity, extreme fear associated with the area, or some other factor. However, any field trips planned for the day should be canceled.

• Work to nip "school phobia" in the bud.

The key recommendation for reducing "school phobia" is to return your students to school as quickly as possible. Do everything you can to discourage parents from allowing their children to stay at home after a school crisis. Even having students sit in their parents' car in the school parking lot is preferable to them remaining at home!

The Parent/Family Liaison, Counseling Liaison, members of your school's counseling staff, and/or other crisis response team members should contact the family of each student not in attendance the first day of classes after the crisis and arrange a home visit. During the visit, talk with the student about his or her fears and emphasize to the student that nearly all the other students are at school, that they are upset as well, and that they are receiving assistance together. Then, make a suggestion such as, "Let's try a few hours at school. Your mom can come too, and then if you are still uncomfortable you may go home."

When students wish to stay home—or their parents choose to keep them home—after a severe school crisis, it is generally because of a lack of information about what they can expect at school that day. Ask whether or not the student and his or her family attended the family/community meeting (*see Chapter Two*) the night before. Acknowledge the fearful student's feelings and reassure the student by emphasizing the safety measures being taken and the counseling services being offered at school.

"School reopened on Thursday, two days after the killings. All the kids and teachers were nervous and upset…. One of my classes was especially hard because both Britthney (Varner, killed in the shooting) and Drew (Golden, a suspected student perpetrator) had been in it."

—Sara Short, 12, student at Westside Middle School near Jonesboro, Arkansas (Casey, 1999)

See "Verifying Information/Crisis Fact Sheet" in Chapter One for guidelines on sharing the facts of the crisis with students in an appropriate format.

If the crisis involved the suicide of a school community member, see Chapter Eleven, "Special Considerations for Suicide."

See "Why Process?" and "How Do You Process?" in Chapter Five for information about the important processing sessions that should be held at the classroom level.

- Continue to provide emotional assistance to students.

Following any special assembly or activity planned for the beginning of the first school day after a severe crisis, the day should continue with a discussion of the updated crisis facts and a processing session for the students in every class. If the crisis was less severe, the processing sessions would occur only in the affected class(es). (*NOTE*: If processing sessions already occurred the day of the crisis—*see "Task List" in Chapter Two*—they can be shortened or skipped the next morning, depending upon the severity of the crisis.) There should be no time limits put on the classroom discussions or the time devoted to processing students' reactions to the crisis; there is no higher priority for this first day back at school.

The Counseling Liaison and other members of your school's mental health staff (as well as members of any outside crisis response team assisting your school) should follow the schedule of all injured and/or deceased students and staff throughout the first day, as there will likely be extreme emotionality in their classes. After the school shooting near Jonesboro, Arkansas, the NOVA team (*see "National Crisis Response Teams/Organizations" in Chapter Four*) focused on slain teacher Shannon Wright's classes. When a crisis results in the death of school community members, an important component of the discussions in their classes will be deciding what to do with the victims' chairs, desks, and other items such as displayed artwork. Student input should be sought.

If the crisis was severe, all the students would probably benefit from a modification of the curriculum for a limited time in order to continue to address the emotionality of the situation. (*See "Modifying the Curriculum" later in this chapter for suggestions on ways to assist the students with their crisis reactions throughout the day.*)

Any students who have been significantly affected by the crisis should be provided individual counseling services at your school at any time during the day, either at their request or on the recommendation of their teachers. (*See "Providing Counseling Services" in Chapter Seven for guidelines on working with upset students—and staff—one-to-one at school.*)

- Stay in contact with parents.

If the crisis was severe, it is important to provide parents with ongoing information about the status of the crisis response and their children's recovery from the crisis effects. On the first day back to school after the crisis, the Parent/Family Liaison should send home a note to parents reviewing what was done to assist their children, the resources available to them both at school and in the community, and steps they can take to assist their children at home (*see "Helping Your Child Cope" in Chapter Eight*).

Each day that your team provides a crisis response, the Counseling Liaison or the Parent/Family Liaison should make personal contact by phone with the parents of those students who have been most affected by the crisis and/or those who needed individual counseling assistance that day.

- Provide structure at school in the days following the crisis.

The schedule on the first day back to school after a crisis will likely need to be modified somewhat so that faculty and the crisis team can spend time assisting the students to cope with their crisis reactions. However, in the days that follow it will be important to emphasize a return to everyday school routines. Even if some change in routine had been planned before the crisis, return to the previous schedule and maintain it for a time "… in order to provide a sense of security and comfort" (Lieberman, 1998, p. 15).

On the second day back after the crisis, your school should be on a normal bell schedule, and almost all of

"I think our students are doing extremely well. We're real pleased with the way they have tried to get back on track. We were all shaken and upset, and we went through a grieving process. But now attendance is back to normal, and we're trying to put this behind us and move forward. It's something you can never forget."

—Pearl (Mississippi) High School Principal Roy Balentine, two weeks after classes resumed following a school shooting in which two people were killed and seven wounded ("School Officials," 1997)

the students will likely be back in school. Begin the day by providing any updated crisis information to the students. The Crisis Coordinator should choose whether to read a statement to the entire school via the intercom or to have teachers share a prepared statement with their classes. A sample statement follows.

Sample Statement to Be Read to a First Period Class

On Tuesday, March 9, Amber Smith, a seventh grade student at Maintown Middle School, suffered a gunshot wound to the leg at the end of the school day as students were preparing to leave their seventh period class. The weapon, which discharged from inside another student's backpack, was taken into police custody. Amber was transported to a local hospital and today is listed in stable condition.

The suspect, seventh grade student Alex Nagy, was suspended pending a disciplinary hearing. In addition, the police have filed criminal charges against him. The school system has been investigating this incident internally, and after the completion of a preliminary investigation the shooting appears to have been purely accidental.

Several unreliable reports were given to the media during the past 24 hours in which our middle school was portrayed in a negative manner. We believe this information to be false. The administration is proud of our students and their excellent academic and social record. We truly believe that our students are a family. Nevertheless, as in any family, an individual may sometimes behave inappropriately.

The Maintown Middle School family needs your support. Therefore, if any of you have information regarding possession of a weapon on campus or any other type of serious infraction, please notify a faculty member such as a teacher, counselor, or your principal. Anonymous tips can also be left with Crime Stoppers at 444-TIPS. Our school administration values you, and we express, as always, our belief that it is an honor to be a Knight and to be part of this school community.

Continue to provide opportunities within the classrooms for your students to ask questions and process their crisis reactions. Gradually reintroduce the regular curriculum, taking your cue from the students. The second day back to school after the crisis will feel much more like a regular school day unless a new and tragic development occurs (e.g., an injured victim dies). Depending upon the circumstances and severity of the crisis, a few or many students (e.g., those who were close to the victim or who have their own set of problematic circumstances) will need to be seen by counselors individually over the following days, weeks, or possibly months.

See "Providing Counseling Services" in Chapter Seven and "Long-Term Effects" in Chapter Twelve for more information.

- Meet with your crisis response team members.

  Meet with your entire team at the end of every day during which the team provides crisis intervention. These meetings need not be lengthy, but it is important for all of your team members to have the opportunity to compare notes about their respective tasks throughout each day, to make plans for the next day, and to process their ongoing reactions to the crisis and crisis response (*see "Why Caring for Caregivers Is Necessary" in Chapter Ten*). It also is important for the Crisis Coordinator/head administrator to keep your central office and/or school board apprised of the crisis response status.

- Reevaluate your school's need for outside assistance.

See "Help to Request" in Chapter Four for additional information about the local, state, and national resources available to your school after a crisis.

  Even if you did not request additional help during the initial response to a severe crisis, it is not too late to benefit from such assistance now. The Campus Liaison and Crisis Coordinator should reevaluate whether the school, at this point, requires additional outside assistance to recover from the crisis. In West Paducah, Kentucky, community leaders requested the assistance of a NOVA team almost a week after the school shooting that occurred there, when they determined that there were gaps in their ongoing crisis response. And in Spotsylvania, Virginia, a NEAT team was called in to assist the community months after three school-age girls were abducted, molested, and brutally murdered in 1997 (Feinberg, 1998). The school leaders in Spotsylvania were concerned about the long-term effects of these unsolved crimes on their school staff, and the team provided much assistance to these people, many of whom showed "… the telltale signs of post-traumatic stress" (Feinberg, 1998).

- Return personal possessions to the families of deceased victims.

  It is important to determine the most sensitive manner to return the personal effects of deceased school community members to their families (District School Board, 1994a). The Parent/Family Liaison and/or Crisis Coordinator should call or visit the families to discuss this issue. Ask the families if they are ready to receive the belongings of their deceased loved ones, and if they would like to make an appointment to collect them at the school. (After school or during class time would be less hectic.) Or the families may prefer that the personal belongings be delivered to their homes.

  The names of the deceased must also be removed from your school's mailing list, automatic call machine/computer, guidance/school newsletter list, and any other "automatic contact" locations (District School Board, 1994a).

- Address the physical effects of the crisis.

Visiting the crime scene is important to many survivors of a school crisis. For this reason, the school should not rush to erase the physical traces of the crisis—such as bullet holes in a wall—or do so without the input of your school community members.

After the police have finished their work at the crime scene and okay your entrance, and after any blood and/or broken glass have been cleaned up, allow school community members to visit the scene. A member of your school's counseling staff (or a volunteer counselor assisting your school) should monitor the area and be willing and able to provide emotional support to those who visit there. This person should offer (but not force) help if needed but should otherwise leave the survivors to their thoughts.

After the school shooting near Jonesboro, Arkansas, many teachers, parents, and students felt the need to walk around the grounds where the shooting occurred at all hours of the day and night, examining the bullet holes in the wall of the building. Doing so was healthy for them, because it helped them to understand the reality of what had happened there. When someone is having difficulty accepting or understanding how a terrible event has occurred, seeing a physical manifestation of the event is helpful. Walking up to a wall and putting a finger in a bullet hole, for example, will help the person grasp that yes, a shooting really did happen. It will also help the person process his or her reactions to the crisis and move on.

Your next step is to determine an appropriate time to make repairs or improvements (e.g., filling in bullet holes or repainting the cafeteria) associated with the crisis. You might want to delay these activities for at least three to seven days, and sometimes up to several weeks. These changes should not take place without the awareness and approval of the school community; the decision should not be just one person's (e.g., the principal's). Take your cue from the students and staff in timing these repairs. Perhaps even form a small "committee" of representative staff members and student leaders to discuss when and how such physical remains of the crisis will be removed.

- Address informal memorials to the crisis victims.

After a severe crisis, you can expect that members of your school and surrounding community will spontaneously create some type of memorial to its victims. Whether school administrators like it or not, people may do such things as hold candlelight vigils outside the school, send or leave flowers, and place symbolic items (e.g., ribbons, wreaths, photos, bouquets, stuffed toys, candles, religious symbols, and cards and notes) in front of your school or along its fence. These actions fulfill a human need to express sorrow and community unity after a tragedy and should not be discouraged. In fact, the sensitive administrator will establish a certain area at the school for such "offerings," perhaps even hanging block paper on which people can write their memories and messages of condolence. (*NOTE*: Closely monitor the inclusion of candles in such impromptu memorials, since candles are a fire hazard if left lit and unattended.)

Like the physical remains of the crisis, the decision about when to remove such items should be made with sensitivity and regard for the emotional needs of survivors. Involving a few students and staff in this decision will help ensure that the needs of the entire school community are served.

> "The lobby of Heath High School [in West Paducah, Kentucky] has been filled with flowers, balloons, and notes since Tuesday morning, tributes to the students who were killed and those still hospitalized."
>
> (Holliman, 1997b)

When the time is right to remove such "offerings," the savable items from any impromptu memorials should be placed in storage boxes at the school so that victims' family members can have the opportunity to look through them and determine if there is anything they wish to keep. The Parent/Family Liaison should carefully review the contents and discuss with the Crisis Coordinator/head administrator anything that might be hurtful prior to the family members' viewing of the materials. It may be necessary to store the materials until the families are ready and able to make a decision about when to look at them and what to keep.

After the massacre at Columbine High School in Littleton, Colorado, Denver firefighter Fred Turner devised an innovative way to salvage the small mountain of flowers left at an impromptu memorial near the school that would otherwise have been thrown away. As he described on the "Oprah Winfrey" show (May 21, 1999), he emptied 14 wheelbarrow loads of flowers into the bed of his pick-up truck and later picked the petals from the stems. He then dried the petals, and, with the assistance of approximately 60 other volunteers, preserved the dried petals in small pieces of tulle tied with ribbons in the school's colors—blue and silver. Each petal bundle had the inscription "We are Columbine, April 30, '99" and, explained Turner, contained the "tears, love, and thoughts" of the community.

And, as reported in a Denver newscast (Channel 7, May 21, 1999), a local business called Professional Restoration donated the labor to clean savable items from the impromptu memorial for the Columbine victims, such as stuffed animals and sympathy cards. The items had been damaged by exposure to the elements and a fire that was sparked by a candle left burning at the memorial by a mourner. Some of the restored items will be used in a permanent memorial to the victims that is planned for the future.

See "Memorializing Victims" later in this chapter for guidelines on more permanent, planned memorials.

- Continue with any preplanned special events, if possible.

  If a preplanned special event falls shortly after the crisis, it is important that it not be canceled because of, or entirely clouded by, the crisis effects. While you do need to acknowledge the continued pain and grief occurring after a severe crisis, it is equally important to emphasize that life does go on and that the survivors have the right to feel happiness and other emotions besides sorrow in the wake of the crisis. In Springfield, Oregon, Thurston High School's graduation ceremony was held just two weeks after a 15-year old student of the school killed two classmates and wounded more than 20 others. At the "upbeat" graduation ceremony, classmates cheered two of the students wounded in the shooting as they accepted their diplomas ("Springfield Graduation," 1998, p. A5). Teacher Paul Halupa, who delivered the commencement address, acknowledged the effects of the shooting on the school, saying, "In a patched cafeteria and a flowered fence we learned things. In our crisis we learned to love" ("Springfield Graduation," 1998, p. A5). And while "… the bloody images remained in the minds of many of the 2,400 relatives and friends who attended the ceremony … , [it was] … 'a happy occasion,'" said one graduate ("Springfield Graduation," 1998, p. A5).

- Be alert for additional causes of trauma.

  A severe crisis threatens people's sense of security, and in the days and weeks that follow a severe crisis the survivors will likely be hypervigilant and fearful. Thus, anything even slightly disturbing that happens shortly after a severe crisis will provoke a strong reaction from its survivors and others in the surrounding community. In Pearl, Mississippi, two weeks after the 1997 shooting at a high school there, the town's junior high school had a bomb scare. Said school attorney "Skip" Jernigan, "We were criticized for having a fire drill to evacuate. But if we had mentioned a bomb, we would have had mass hysteria and a stampede because of the terror that still exists" ("School Officials," 1997). Unfortunately, bomb threats and other scares are common shortly after many school crises, and you should be alert for "copycat" threats or actions (*see "'Copycat' Incidents" in Chapter Twelve for more information*). The best policy is to tell the truth about any such incident and follow the appropriate emergency procedures.

Modifying the Curriculum

According to prominent psychologist Abraham Maslow's (1943) hierarchy of needs, safety and security needs (e.g., to be safe from crimes and disasters) are preceded in importance to human beings only by physiological needs (e.g., for food, water, and shelter). According to Maslow and other psychologists, all of these needs must be met before higher order needs (i.e., belongingness/love needs, esteem needs, and self-actualization needs—and, one can assume, the need to learn) can be addressed. Thus, if your students' security has been threatened—which will most likely be the case if your school experiences a severe crisis—they will not be able to pay much attention to academics until their sense of security is somewhat restored. Rather than try to fight this natural human response to crisis, it is best to either modify or set aside the regular curriculum (e.g., shorten assignments or provide alternate activities that focus on the crisis, postpone quizzes/tests) for a short time so that you can address your students' emotional issues.

Teachers must understand—and be clearly told—that the normal school-day activities should not be the top priority after a severe crisis. Otherwise, they may be hesitant to modify or set aside the curriculum in order to take care of their students. For example, on the morning following the suicide of a Texas student, a teacher asked the school psychologist who was in her classroom to lead a processing session with the girl's classmates, "Do you want to talk to them before or after I give the test scheduled for the day?" When the school psychologist pointed out that her students were openly weeping and were in no condition to be tested, the teacher responded that she "team taught" and that her class would fall behind that of the other teacher if she did not administer the test.

> "'After the shooting (at Bethel Regional High in Bethel, Alaska, in 1997), said Pat Martin, a social studies specialist with the district, 'it was more like a support group than a school.' But the rituals of public education have picked up where they left off, routines once again falling into place."
>
> (Fainaru, 1998, p. A21)

The school psychologist helped her see that her response was one of denial and discomfort because her student had committed suicide. He led her to understand that a tragedy had occurred and that her students would not be helped by taking a test that they could not possibly perform well on that day. Focusing on academics rather than the crisis would also have resulted in the loss of an opportunity to teach about the warning signs of suicide and prevention steps. Thus, the Crisis Coordinator/head administrator must tell the faculty, verbally and in writing, that they have permission to modify or set aside the regular curriculum to address the emotionality of a severe crisis or loss.

> "We are not doing academics. We are in classrooms with counselors and answering questions."
>
> —Principal Karen Curtner, Westside Middle School, near Jonesboro, Arkansas, on the first day back to school after the school shooting there (Skiba, 1998)

The regular curriculum should be set aside at the beginning of the first day students return to school after a severe crisis (or the first period after a more minor crisis if the school remains open). During this time the students should be given the updated facts of the crisis and be guided in processing their reactions to the crisis (see "Why Process?" and "How Do You Process?" in Chapter Five). However, students may need more time than this to focus on the emotionality of the situation before they are ready to turn their attention back to academics.

Bear in mind that while teachers should not force a "regular day" on grieving students, their classes should not be completely unstructured either (District School Board, 1994b). To strike the appropriate balance, you, as teachers, might incorporate into your class appropriate artwork, writing and reading activities, the use of music, drama, and/or memorializing activities if the crisis involved the death of a school community member. In this way, processing the trauma temporarily becomes the curriculum. (*NOTE*: Although this section is directed to teachers, members of your school's counseling staff and/or parents might also wish to use some of the techniques suggested.)

Many psychologists believe that "… children can effectively process their trauma if they express their emotions through writing or drawing" (Sleek, 1998, p. 12). These types of alternate activities can be especially helpful when many of your students do not feel like talking about their feelings. Suggestions for different types of helpful activities follow, and you are encouraged to use your own creativity and ideas, as you know your own students best. (*NOTE*: Be sure to provide a "standard" assignment as an alternate for any student who does *not* wish to focus on the crisis and its effects.)

Artwork

Drawing, painting, and the like, because they are "right brain" creative activities, are particularly helpful ways of connecting with one's feelings and expressing strong emotions such as grief and fear. Explained art therapist and psychologist Robin Goodman, "Drawing a picture can feel safer (than talking) to a child because it's slightly removed" (Levine, 1998, p. 137). The products your students create will help you to understand how they perceive what happened during the crisis and can facilitate conversation about how they are coping. "[You] can ask questions about the picture rather than asking the child directly, 'Are you sad?'" explained Dr. Goodman (Levine, 1998, p. 137).

The artwork also "… becomes something tangible that the children can touch and put their feelings into," according to staff at the Children's Bereavement Art Group, a community service project of Sutter Hospice in Sacramento, California (Sutter Cancer Center, 1998). You should not judge what your students produce. Simply let them express themselves in their own way. (Remember that children tend to be less inhibited, and thus are sometimes more graphic or literal, than adults. However, if one of your students produces an image you find particularly gruesome or disturbing, or a suicidal image, you should show it to your school's psychologist or counselor.)

"Only recently [a year after the school shooting at Westside Middle School], has Mandy [Paige's younger sister] … talk[ed] about what happened to her sister [Paige Ann Herring]…. I asked her if she wanted to talk to a teacher or a counselor," said her mother, "and she said, 'You can take me, but I won't talk.' … Mandy draws and writes a lot. When she first heard about [the tragedy] she said, 'I've got to have a piece of paper.' I was scrambling to get her one …. The first thing she did was draw an angel, with Paige's name."

—Pam Herring, Jonesboro, Arkansas (Ashcraft, 1999, p. 14A)

If your students ask you to interpret their artwork, say as little as possible. Instead, according to therapist Darin Pyatt, who leads art therapy groups with at-risk teens in Nederland, Colorado (personal communication, March 1, 1999), "get the kids to tell you what they think their drawings mean." When students ask you to interpret their work, she explained, they're trying to find out about themselves, but "they're the authority on their own experience." An explanation she offers to students is that "any interpretation I would give would be as much about me as it would you." (And, if that interpretation is coming from a teacher who also has been affected by the crisis, rather than a more objective therapist, it might have a great deal to do with the teacher's own experience.) If the students press you for an interpretation, ask "very open-ended, facilitative questions" advised Pyatt, such as, "How did you feel when you made this?" You might also make leading comments, such as, "I'm curious about this part of your drawing" or "I like your use of color; can you tell me about that?" Pyatt continued: "The most interpretative statement I would make is, 'If this were my painting, I would feel ....'" Remember that the point of the artwork is not psychoanalysis; it is merely a means for your students to express their emotions and crisis reactions.

> "The creative drive is perhaps the most familiar domain for nourishing the spirit of children in secular schools. In opportunities for acts of creation, people often encounter their participation as a process infused with depth, meaning, and mystery."
>
> (Kessler, 1998/1999)

Finally, regardless of what your students create in what medium, you might wish to display their creations in your room for a while to validate what they've expressed. You might even borrow a suggestion from the Children's Bereavement Art Group, which is to have a "Family Night" soon after the crisis to show the students' family and friends how they have expressed their feelings about the crisis through their artwork (Sutter Cancer Center, 1998). In addition to validating the students' emotions, this event might help the family members better understand how the crisis has affected their children and facilitate a healthy dialogue between the students and their families.

- *Having Student Draw the Victims*

  Artwork does not have to be complex to be therapeutic. For example, you might have your students simply draw a picture of an injured or deceased victim ("Fernside Online," 1998).

- *Having Students Draw Themselves*

  Self-portraits made by students who have survived a crisis are often very illustrative of their fears and sense of loss. A few days after the 1995 bombing of the Alfred P. Murrah Federal Building in Oklahoma City, for example, many students there drew themselves as small, weak, and puny (e.g., with no muscles). Later, after their spirits had been restored, these same children saw (and drew) themselves as strong and capable again.

Students, both those who actually experienced a crisis and others who learned about the crisis, may make drawings of themselves as the crisis victims to help them process their fears. For example, after the shooting at Westside Middle School near Jonesboro, Arkansas, many students at the adjacent elementary school expressed their fears, explained Mary Savage, a therapist from Arkansas State University, by drawing themselves "… like they were the ones and their teachers were the ones [who] got killed" (Associated Press, 1998).

- *Drawing Something for Your Students*

On a spring afternoon in 1995, in New Haven, Connecticut, a school bus carrying eight five- and six-year old children was caught in the crossfire of rival drug dealers. One six-year old boy was shot in the head (the boy later survived surgery, suffering some neurological impairment). The bus went to a nearby middle school, where the children were met by police officers and emergency medical personnel. Their parents were contacted, and the police did *not* interview the children. When the middle school staff attempted to engage the children in conversation about what they had seen, the children were uncommunicative, "… clutching their knees and staring into the distance" (Marans & Schaefer, 1998, p. 330). When trained clinicians arrived on the scene ten minutes later, they sat down with the children and asked them if they would like to draw a picture. Each child refused to draw, but when asked if they would like the clinician to draw something, "the response was unanimously positive, as was the requested content of the pictures: 'Draw my mommy'" (Marans & Schaefer, 1998, p. 330). The clinicians asked the children what the "speech bubbles" that went along with each drawing should say, and after discussing these pictures the children became more verbal.

As described in Marans and Schaefer (1998):

> [One of the children then asked a clinician to] draw a picture of a head. "Whose head?" the clinician asked. "Um, a boy's head … that just got shot with a bullet." The rest of the children overheard this request and immediately turned their attention to the picture. The clinician requested details in order to complete the picture and asked if any of the children wished to add something themselves. Three children scribbled the same ingredient with a red marker—blood from the head wound that soon covered much of the page (p. 330).

The children then asked questions about what was happening to their classmate who had been shot, and about bodily functions (e.g., about how much blood the human body contains). By the time their parents arrived they were engaged in "… a more spirited group discussion about various physical feats each could perform" (Marans & Schaefer, 1998, p. 330).

If your students refuse your suggestion to draw after a crisis, they might be interested in having you draw something for them, either individually or as a group. The elements that they ask you to incorporate into the drawing, and the comments they make during the process, will provide you with insight about their reactions to the crisis and their coping skills. Employing the technique of asking them to fill "conversation bubbles" or "thought bubbles" for characters in the picture, as the clinicians did with the children in the New Haven example, would also provide you with valuable information about your students' thoughts and emotions.

- *Abstract Art*

Rather than drawing a specific person or scene, your students might benefit from using color in abstract patterns to express themselves. They might, for example, illustrate their emotions with paints in colors of their choosing (gray and violet swirls may represent grief, orange and red zigzags may represent anger, etc.). You could introduce this activity to young students by showing them the Dr. Seuss book *My Many Colored Days* (1996, with paintings by Steve Johnson and Lou Fancher).

- *Collage*

You might have your students create a collage, either individually or as a class, about the crisis and/or their feelings about what has occurred. (You could collect magazines from the recycling bins at your local supermarket or your town's recycling center, as well as newspapers, to provide them with materials from which they can select words and images.)

- *Clay*

Even students who do not like to draw or paint (those who "can't draw") may enjoy working with clay (e.g., modeling clay). They could mold a shape or symbol to represent the crisis. The students can keep the shapes, destroy them, or even symbolically "transform" (i.e., remold) them into a more positive symbol to represent healing and recovery. (For some students, pounding on their clay rather than molding it could be a way to release some strong emotions and/or tension after a crisis!)

"There is something that happens to me in pottery class—I lose myself in the feeling of wet clay rolling smoothly under my hands as the wheel spins. I have it last period, so no matter how difficult the day was, pottery makes every day a good day. It's almost magical—to feel so good, so serene."

—Student quoted in Kessler (1998/1999)

- *Safe Sanctuary*

  This teacher-guided activity, suggested by therapist Darin Pyatt (personal communication, March 1, 1999) and described in the book *Spinning Inward* by educator and therapist Maureen Murdock (1987), could be used to address the safety/security needs of older students and provide them with a creative outlet. (*NOTE*: This activity could also be used with younger students, although you will need to adapt the vocabulary for age-appropriateness.) After quieting the students, and before they begin their artwork, you would read to them the following:

  > *Close your eyes and begin to focus your attention on your breath, [noticing] the air [moving] in and out of your nostrils. Give yourself the suggestion that with each exhalation your body becomes more and more relaxed.* (Pause) *Good. Now imagine that you are moving through time and space to a place that is a sanctuary for you. The sanctuary is safe, simple, and beautiful. It may be located in nature, in the hills or near the sea, it may be in your room at home, or any place of your own choosing where you feel safe and secure. Go there now and experience the colors, textures, smells, sounds, tastes, and how your body feels in this place. You'll have several minutes of clock time equal to all the time you need to relax in this sanctuary.* (Pause for three minutes.)

  > *Now it is time to return here, bringing with you the sense of safety and security that you have experienced in your own sanctuary, ready to draw it or write about it. In a moment, I will count to five. Open your eyes at the count of five, feeling relaxed and alert. One ... two ... three ... four ... five* (p. 142).

  The students' drawings of their "safe sanctuaries" will symbolize for them the feeling of security they experienced during the exercise. It is important to remind the students that they can return to these safe "places" in their mind's eye anytime they feel the need to do so simply by focusing their attention in this manner; they will carry these sanctuaries with them when they leave your classroom. You should also explain that each time they "visit" their sanctuaries, the sanctuaries will become more vivid and life-like, and thus, more secure and protective.

- *Sympathy Cards*

  Your students might like to draw, color, or paint handmade sympathy cards for a student or parents who have suffered a loss. You could provide envelopes and an address for mailing or offer to deliver the cards (District School Board, 1994b). Either way, you should review every card for appropriateness of content before sending or delivering them.

- *Free Expression*

  Instead of, or in addition to, the previous artwork suggestions, you might let your students come up with their own ideas for what they would like to create, providing them with a variety of media and offering help or suggestions only when requested.

Language arts activities

- *Reading Passages*

  You might read to older students appropriate passages from some "self-help" books about death or loss (such as the classic *When Bad Things Happen to Good People*, by Harold S. Kushner) or whatever the appropriate subject is (natural disasters, etc.). Regardless of whether your students identify with the specific excerpts you read, they might be surprised and reassured to know that people of all ages struggle with strong emotions after a loss—so much so that hundreds of books have been written on the subject. Or you could share poems that allude to death, the appropriate crisis topic, or even the expression of strong feelings in general. You would then follow the reading passages with a classroom discussion.

  For young students, you could read aloud children's literature (and/or poetry) that incorporates the appropriate theme. Your school's psychologist or counselor, school librarian, or public library's children's literature specialist can provide suggestions.

  As age-appropriate, you might also guide your students in locating and exploring content about the crisis topic on the World Wide Web (e.g., news accounts of similar crises). The online possibilities are almost endless (which is why you must carefully monitor the content the students review, perhaps even doing the initial "searching" yourself and "bookmarking" only appropriate Web sites for your students to see). Some organizations are developing online forums about disasters for children. For example, a psychology professor at a Virginia university has created a disaster intervention Web site called "Disaster Stuff for Kids" (http://www.jmu.edu/psychologydept/4kids.htm) that contains reading material, links to other relevant sites, and a "My Story" page to allow children to post online their own experiences and thoughts about crises (Sleek, 1998).

- *Quotations*

  You might share and discuss with your students famous quotations about the type of crisis they experienced and related topics (e.g., death, grief, catastrophe, fear, friendship, healing, hope, community). You could also ask them to suggest their own "key words" that represent their emotions or concerns and then find quotations focused on those words. Or you could have them select one from among a list of quotations you provide as the basis for a brief essay.

- *Poetry*

  You might encourage your students to write poems or sonnets to express their emotions. Then, you could bind their compositions as a class book (perhaps placing it in the school library for a short time for others to read).

- *Letters*

  Your students might wish to write personal sympathy notes to a student or parents who have suffered a loss. You could provide an address for mailing or offer to deliver their letters yourself (District School Board, 1994b). Either way, you should review every letter for appropriateness of content before sending or delivering them.

  When a crisis results in a death, students may gain some comfort by writing to the deceased, saying things that they feel had been left unsaid. Writing these thoughts as if the deceased would read them is a helpful way to bring closure to these unresolved issues. For example, a student might want to apologize for teasing the victim in the past. A friend of the victim might want to say something that he or she never did in person, such as that the friendship meant a great deal to him or her. Discuss with the students what they would like to do with the letters. The students could keep the letters; leave them at the gravesite; send them to the victim's family (if appropriate); or even take a symbolic action such as burning them, letting them float away in a river or creek, or simply tearing them up (envisioning themselves being freed from any guilt about the unexpressed words as their letters disappear).

  If your students hear news of a crisis similar to the one they experienced happening elsewhere (either soon after your school's crisis or in the months or years to come), they might wish to send condolence letters to the affected school. Through their words, your students can give those in the affected school hope for the future, as they write about how—although it was difficult—they survived their crisis and how they know those at the other school will as well. For example, the students at Pearl High School (in Pearl, Mississippi) created a posterboard of sympathy notes and cards for the students at Heath High (in West Paducah, Kentucky) after the school shooting there. This posterboard was placed exactly where the shooter stood in the lobby of Heath High. Later, Heath High students wrote "messages of hope on oversized cards" and mailed them to students at Westside Middle School (near Jonesboro, Arkansas) after their shooting (Williams, 1998).

"It's been nine years since our tragedy, and we still remember it with horror. But now we also see the good things that surround us every day of our lives. We hope that these feelings of comfort come to you soon."

—Text from a letter written to Westside Middle School near Jonesboro, Arkansas, by a high school class in Stockton, California, who lived through a school shooting as elementary students (Johnston, 1998, p. 28)

- *Journals*

  You might encourage your students to keep personal journals throughout the crisis aftermath. Pouring their emotions onto the pages of a journal is a nonthreatening way for students to identify and express their feelings. Reviewing their journal entries also provides you with an opportunity to monitor their coping skills. It is important to watch for any hints about or references to suicide (*contact your school's psychologist or counselor immediately*), feelings of irrational guilt about the crisis, and/or extreme or persistent grief that may require individual counseling intervention.

  You might also introduce your students to the technique of "free writing" (or "stream of consciousness" writing) in which they do not consciously think about what to write and the best way to express it but rather "turn off" their critical mind. In free writing the writer allows his or her hand to write as quickly as possible—without editing or punctuation—whatever comes, for as long as the words keep coming. This creative writing technique is particularly helpful whenever people are feeling overwhelmed by strong emotions (e.g., when emotions are preventing them from sleeping, eating, or concentrating on a necessary task).

See "Providing Counseling Services" and "Crisis Effects and Grief" in Chapter Seven.

Music

Music is a potent force for recovery after a trauma. In fact:

> "[S]ound therapy" … dates back thousands of years. "The use of sound and music is the most ancient healing modality," says Jonathan Goldman, founder and director of the Sound Healers Association in Boulder, Colorado, and author of Healing Sounds…. "It was practiced in the ancient mystery schools of Egypt, Tibet, India, Athens, and Rome for tens of thousands of years." … Pythagoras, who discovered that all music could be expressed in numbers and mathematical formulas, founded a school that, among other things, trained students to release worry, fear, anger, and sorrow through singing and playing musical instruments (Gerber, 1998).

People in our society today naturally use music in many ways as well. As described in Gerber (1998), "Most of us, at one time or another, practice our own version of music therapy. We instinctually make—or seek out—sound to express our emotions. A mother naturally sings to soothe her baby. When we're depressed, we play or make our favorite music, either to lift us out of our gloom or to intensify it; when happy, we play joyous music to enhance the mood."

Why does music affect us? A French researcher, Dr. Alfred Tomatis, discovered that "… all cranial nerves lead to the ear, which explains why soothing musical harmonics not only induce states of deep relaxation but directly affect breathing, the voice, the heart rate, and digestion" (Gerber, 1998). Jonathan Goldman, of Boulder's Sound Healers Association, elaborated, "External energy sources, particularly sounds, are especially powerful in affecting our internal rhythms" (quoted in Gerber, 1998). Of course, use of music with your students does not need to be as complicated as the methods of Pythagoras to be effective! You don't even need to know *why* it works—you just need to know that young people *like* music and that incorporating it in the classroom after a crisis may be helpful.

- *Relaxation Exercise*

  Don Campbell, composer, music researcher, teacher, healer, and author of *The Mozart Effect*, suggested this simple relaxation exercise: Intone a long "o" (as in "ocean") or "ah" (as in "aha") sound for three minutes. "You may feel silly for the first minute, he warns, but after the second you'll get into it, and after the third, you'll feel the effects" (Gerber, 1998).

- *"Entrainment" Tape*

  "Psycho-musicologist" Dr. John Ortiz, author of the *Tao of Music*, recommended the following exercise to one of his former clients. Make an "entrainment" audiotape by finding "… three songs that sound like your depression, three that feel like you want to feel, and three in between." Then fill in the rest of the tape with some of your favorite music (Gerber, 1998). You might have your students try this technique, thinking about the music they'd use during class and completing the actual audio taping at home.

- *Humming Relaxation*

  With this activity, you would instruct your students to sit somewhere where it is quiet and softly hum or chant different vowel sounds imagining that they are "directing" the sounds to various parts of their body (wherever they are holding their tension or anxiety). "When we create and focus on sound," sound therapists have explained, "we begin to stop the constant chatter in our minds, which is the first step to … deep relaxation" (Gerber, 1998).

- *Anger Release*

  If your students are angry or tense, you might play an energetic piece of music (e.g., a march). As the music plays, ask your students to, as described in Gerber (1998), "Move your body for five to seven minutes, letting the music release your emotions. Then your mind can look at the situation with a more objective, and compassionate, attitude."

- *Composing a Song*

  If you are musically inclined, you might assist your class in writing a song about the crisis and/or their reactions to the crisis. The words could be set to a familiar melody, or the students could even compose their own music. If their song turned out well, and the lyrics were appropriate, you might have them perform it for other members of your school community.

- *Singing*

A less complicated activity is to have your class sing uplifting or otherwise appropriate songs. You could audiotape these songs for your students to play back at later times when they feel the need for some emotional support.

- *Discussing Song Lyrics*

Every group of students will have a few songs that are particularly meaningful to them. For example, for the middle school survivors of the Jonesboro, Arkansas, shooting in 1998, the most popular song was "My Heart Will Go On," the theme from the blockbuster movie *Titanic* (performed by Celine Dion).* When students listen to the same song over and over again, obviously they hear an important message in that song's lyrics.

Whereas the ballad "My Heart Will Go On" provides a positive message, young people don't always choose the most wholesome, helpful songs as their favorites. While you likely cannot keep in touch with the songs en vogue at the moment with your students, you can expose your students to songs that they may not think to listen to or may never have heard (e.g., older songs and those by artists favored by their parents' generation). The following are just a few suggestions of such selections that might be appropriate for playing for and discussing with your students. Add to or replace this list with your own favorites:

- "What's Going On" (Marvin Gaye). This song's plea for non-violence becomes more poignant if the students are told that Marvin Gaye's own father later fatally shot him.
- "Imagine" (John Lennon). This song asks listeners to image "a brotherhood of man" and "all the people living lives of peace," among other ideals.
- "Candle in the Wind" (Elton John).
- "Tears in Heaven" (Eric Clapton). Eric Clapton wrote this song after the death of his son.
- "Let it Be" (Paul McCartney).
- "Bridge Over Troubled Water" (Simon & Garfunkel).
- "Everybody Hurts" (REM). This song's message to "hang on" when "your day is night ... [and] ... it seems like everything is wrong"

* "My Heart Will Go On" was written by James Horner and Will Jennings; distributed by Famous Music Corp. (ASCAP), Blue Sky Rider Songs (BMI).

would be particularly helpful if the crisis involved the suicide of a school community member.

- "Greatest Love of All" (Whitney Houston). This song would also be helpful after a suicide. Its lyrics, such as, "The greatest love of all is easy to achieve, learning to love yourself, it is the greatest love of all," impart a message of the worth of every person.
- "Hands" (Jewel). The lyrics of this more recent song discuss healing and affirm that everyone is okay.

• *Relaxing Background Music*

You don't even have to ask your students to focus on the music for it to be beneficial. You might simply play soft, relaxing background music in your classroom after a crisis. Select any instrumental piece that appeals to and relaxes you personally, or use one of the following suggestions from therapist Maureen Murdock (1987) and music researcher Don Campbell (cited in Gerber, 1998):

- "Concertos for Violin, Harp, and Flute," Georg Philipp Telemann (any version)
- "Handel: The Complete Sonatas for Recorder," Ton Koopman (Harmonia Mundi)
- "Music for the Mozart Effect: Volume I," Don Campbell (Spring Hill Music)
- "Canon in D," Pachelbel (RCA Victrola)
- "The Four Seasons," Antonio Lucio Vivaldi (Angel)
- "Passages," William Ackerman (Windham Hill Records)
- "Songs of Sanctuary," Adiemus (Virgin Records)
- "Sonic Stress Reduction Rosa Mystica," Therese Schroeder-Sheker (Celestial Harmonies)
- "Renaissance of the Celtic Harp," Alan Stivell (Applause by Phillips)
- "Pianoscapes," Michael Jones (Narada Music, BMI)
- "Environment Series" (Atlanta, Syntonic Research Series): nature sounds such as birds, seashore, and rain
- "Chariots of Fire," Vangelis (Polydor)

Drama

In May 1998, a 15-year old student shot and killed his parents and then two of his classmates (wounding 22 others) at his Springfield, Oregon, high school. This tragedy inspired award-winning playwright William Mastrosimone to write the play *Bang, Bang, You're Dead*, which includes plot elements from the Springfield, Oregon, school shooting (which occurred at Thurston High) as well as elements from the shootings near

Jonesboro, Arkansas, and in West Paducah, Kentucky. "I wrote this from the pit of my stomach," said Mastrosimone (Barnard, 1999, p. 5A). Mastrosimone then donated the play "… to schools across the nation in hopes its in-your-face message will force young people to confront their culture of violence and do something about it" (Barnard, 1999, p. 5A). When he sent it to Thurston High, drama teacher Mike Fisher discussed it with his students, and "… they overwhelmingly wanted to do the play" (Barnard, 1999, p. 5A).

The one-act play was performed in Bend, Oregon, to an audience of approximately 350 teens, teachers, and parents who "… hugged and wiped away tears, then gave the cast a standing ovation" (Barnard, 1999, p. 5A). "… [I]ts raw power," noted Barnard (1999) "comes from the cast—13 students who actually lived through the shooting at Springfield's Thurston High School" (p. 5A). Cast member Betsy Reinhart explained, "A lot of people think we're trying to put our tragedy on stage. That's not what we're doing. We're trying to spread a message" (p. 5A).

The script of *Bang, Bang, You're Dead* is posted at no fee on the Internet (http://bangbangyouredead.com/home.html) for use by other schools. You may wish to use this play with your students, or encourage them to perform their own improvisations. Expressing their emotions through acting, from the safe standpoint of a character they play, may assist some students to identify and verbalize their crisis reactions.

Memorializing activities

If the crisis at your school involved the death of a school community member, your students may wish to memorialize the victim. Major or permanent memorials would require the approval of your school's administration (*see "Memorializing Victims" later in this chapter for guidelines*), but there are some simple activities your students can do as a class to fulfill their need to remember the deceased. If, however, the death was a suicide, the suicide victim should not be memorialized because of the danger of suicide "contagion" (*see Chapter Eleven, "Special Considerations for Suicide"*).

- *Listing Attributes*

  When someone they know is killed, your students will want to reminisce about the person after they get past the initial horror and trauma resulting from the crisis. You might list on butcher paper or the chalkboard positive characteristics your students relate about the deceased (e.g., you could make a chart entitled "The 20 Best Things About [Name]"). You could also have students relate favorite memories of the person. Your students will probably enjoy retelling their memories because doing so makes the person "come alive" again and seem meaningful, to have had an impact. (Later you might deliver these lists to the deceased's family.)

- *Memory Books*

  You could have the class create a "memory book" of the deceased ("Safe Crossings," 1998). You might, for example, bind your students' poetry, drawings, photographs, collages, pressed flowers, fondest memories of the person, wishes of condolence to the family, and any other suitable contents into a scrapbook, and deliver this finished work to the deceased's family.

- *Balloon Ceremony*

  After the 1992 murder of a second grade student in a small town in Kansas, some of her classmates approached their teacher before lunchtime and said, "We know we're not supposed to talk about Mary [on the instructions of their school principal] but can we let some balloons go for her?" The teacher did not ask the principal what he thought of the idea; instead, she bought the balloons over lunch and allowed her students to have this brief memorial to their classmate that they so desperately needed. Each child held a balloon, and as they let go of their balloons (outdoors) they imagined that they were letting go of their friend Mary, that she was ascending to heaven or whatever they happened to personally believe in.

- *Memory Ribbons and Other Decorations*

  Your students might wish to wear a symbol of their grief. If so, you could assist them in making "memory ribbons" to pin to their shirts as a sign of unity and mourning. After the school shooting near Jonesboro, Arkansas, for example, "white ribbons, a silent tribute to the slain, appeared on nearly everyone in town, on nearly every vehicle, and on hundreds of front lawns" (McLemore, 1998). Mourners in West Paducah, Kentucky, also wore white ribbons after the school shooting there ("Girls Killed," 1997).

"Students [in Jonesboro, Arkansas] wore white ribbons as they filed past red and white bouquets that lined the walkway where the victims were gunned down .... A flowered cross hung from the flagpole, and the flag flew at half-staff. No lessons were taught, and all outdoor activities were canceled, including recess. Students made cards for the 11 people who were wounded, including the five who remained hospitalized ...."

(Associated Press, 1998)

Your students might also want to "decorate" their classroom, the scene of the crisis, and/or locations that were significant to the victims. At Heath High, for example, the locker of slain student Jessica James was decorated with red roses (Holliman, 1997a). And in the lobby of the West Paducah, Kentucky, school, community members hung tiny paper butterflies over the spot where each slain student fell (Williams, 1998). Note, however, that such decorations should not be permanent. And if the decorations are to be made in common areas of the school (as opposed to your classroom), you should first discuss the changes with your school's administration and/or crisis response team to be sure that they won't upset other members of your school community.

- *Web Sites*

  If your school has a World Wide Web site, you might ask your administration and/or crisis response team for permission to post some text and images related to the crisis or victims. (Ask the site's "Webmaster" or computer skills instructor at your school for assistance.) After 21 school community members from Montoursville High School (Montoursville, Pennsylvania) were killed in the 1996 TWA Flight 800 crash, for example, the school established a Web site containing "… information on the town's crash victims and offer[ing] people around the world an opportunity to send condolences to people [there]" (Gamble, 1996, p. 10). Your students could contribute materials for the Web site.

  After the school shooting in West Paducah, Kentucky, the school set up a Web site entitled "We Believe in Heath! In Memory …" that contained photographs of a memorial garden dedication ceremony and the Paducah holiday parade. The site also provided a forum for both students and staff to express their condolences and share their thoughts on the crisis and memories of the slain victims. Among the e-mail messages posted from students were these:

  — "This is a very tough time for all of us. I think it is great how our school has come together. I hope we can get back to normal soon and the media will leave us alone …." (Justin Lewis)

  — "I know that in a time like this you can't think of one positive thing but look at how we have all come together. From now on I am going to try my best to really get to know and appreciate everyone I come in contact with because you don't realize what you have until it's no longer there. I have faith that I'll see my friends again some day." (Courtney Taylor)

  — "In Loving Memory of Nicole, Kayce, and Jessica. We will always remember the good times we had with each of you. You will be in our hearts forever and always. We will remember the incident that happened on the morning of December 1st, 1997. We will not let one person tear this community apart, for the sake of you and all others who were injured both physically and emotionally …." (Rachel Cownie and Molly Tilford)

- *Spontaneous Memorials*

  Your students may not need you to suggest any memorializing activity to them; they may already have their own ideas about what they would like to do to remember the deceased or they may, through unplanned actions, create a simple, spontaneous memorial. After a Houston eighth grader drowned in

"… Melissa ['Missy' Jenkins, paralyzed in the Heath High shooting] [was] spending her days [in the hospital] reading through stacks of letters and cards from around the world and looking over what [her father] indicated was a three-inch stack of printouts of e-mail letters sent to her through the school."

(Associated Press, 1997)

1998, for example, the students in his PE class created their own moving ceremony on the spur of the moment. Their coach had taken them outside and had given them a choice about what they could do (i.e., they could play a game, sit quietly, or do whatever they felt comfortable doing). The coach then walked to the end of the field, where he intended to sit by himself for a little while to remember his student, but behind him followed most of the others. Without any prompting from him, the students removed the "memory ribbons" they were wearing and placed them at the foot of the goalpost. On their own they then formed a circle and did what they wanted to do—they said a little prayer.

Revisiting the regular curriculum

With all the focus within your classroom on the trauma caused by the school crisis, it is important not to lose sight of the fact that students' reactions to the crisis will come and go throughout the day. As Vicki Beckerman, who runs a bereavement group for children in Glen Ridge, New Jersey, explained: "Kids don't grieve nonstop. They grieve, and then they play. They shoot a few baskets, and then they cry. They watch a sitcom and laugh until they cry. The ability to strike a balance is the key to their emotional survival" (Levine, 1998, p. 137).

You should give your students permission to express a range of emotions (even nervous laughter or seeming indifference) in your classroom. Everyone deals with trauma differently and at different rates—there is no one correct way to feel at any one time. Thus, it is important to tell children and adolescents that it is okay not to be sad every minute of the day.

In fact, you should explain that humor is important after a crisis. Laughter is a tension release for the body, and it's helpful for survivors of a crisis to be able to find something that's positive and/or to make light of some (tasteful) situation during the day.

> "Life does not cease to be funny when people die any more than it ceases to be serious when people laugh."
>
> —George Bernard Shaw

As for when you should return to the regular curriculum, take your cue from your students. After a period of time (which will vary depending upon the severity and nature of the crisis), they will have worked through much of the emotionality of the situation and they will be ready to pay attention to academics again. After doing nothing but talking (and/or drawing, writing, or singing) about the crisis for the first period, the second period, the third period, they will eventually be ready for the curriculum. You'll know because they will have tired of dwelling on their sorrow and anger. You may not want to give them a quiz or a test at this time, but they will be ready to do some work.

Funerals

Funeral Planning

If your school's crisis resulted in the death of a school community member, the family of the deceased will handle the funeral arrangements with the assistance of a funeral director (and possibly their clergy member). However, it may be helpful for a school representative (e.g., the Parent/Family Liaison or Crisis Coordinator) to talk with the family member who is handling the funeral arrangements, because that person will not likely be in tune with the needs of the hundreds of students and school staff who have been affected by the death. While the school must ultimately respect the wishes of the family, you can make some recommendations about the funeral service that will address the school's concerns. Experience has shown that most parents of deceased students are generally receptive to such input.

For example, you might recommend that the funeral be held after school, in the evening, or on a Saturday so that more parents can attend with their children. A strong presence of involved adults is necessary to help the students better cope with both the death and the funeral ritual itself. If hundreds of students attend a funeral with only a few caretaking adults (e.g., the school counselors) present, they will likely be incredibly emotional, and simply because they outnumber the adults, they will not receive the support they need.

The timing of the funeral is of particular importance if the death was a suicide. Because of the danger of suicide "contagion," it is crucial to avoid any sensationalism of the death. Hundreds of students leaving school at 11:00 in the morning to attend the funeral of someone who committed suicide whom they hardly knew, for example, would glorify the death.

See Chapter Eleven, "Special Considerations for Suicide."

While the family may be receptive to your suggestions, they may not have the desire or authority to coordinate the logistics involved. In such cases, if the family gives you their permission, you could call the funeral home and/or clergy member to discuss your recommendations. For example, after the father of a Houston student who committed suicide heard the school psychologist's recommendations, he told the psychologist that he appreciated what he had to say but that the funeral home had already arranged an early afternoon funeral. However, the father thought that if the school psychologist called the funeral home, the funeral director might be willing to change the arrangements. The funeral director was concerned that the funeral procession reach the cemetery before dark but was in fact willing to change the time of the service to 4:00 PM at the request of the school psychologist. That way, the needs of the family, school community members, and funeral coordinators were all served.

Other recommendations you might make to the family of the deceased and those assisting them with funeral arrangements (i.e., funeral director and clergy member) include the following:

- If more than one student was killed, the family members might consider a joint funeral.

  After the school shooting in West Paducah, Kentucky, for example, the families of Kayce Steger, Nicole Hadley, and Jessica James held a joint public visitation and funeral for the three girls at Paducah's largest church (Mead, 1997). This cooperative arrangement served to unite the community in their mourning and support of one another after the tragedy (thousands of people paid their respects to the three girls and their families). It also allowed the students who attended to experience and cope with this painful ritual just once, rather than prolonging the agony throughout three services over multiple days.

- If the service is to be private, or if separate funerals are to be held (in the event of multiple deaths), consider a community-wide memorial service.

See "Role of the Clergy" in Chapter Nine.

  To foster a sense of community support after a tragedy, your local clergy might consider collaborating on a city-wide memorial service for the victims. Such a service was held in Jonesboro, Arkansas, after the school shooting there because there were five separate funerals and because many in the community had been affected by the tragedy. Prior to the service Reverend Fred Hoffstein, one of the clergy members who helped with the planning, explained, "It will be an effort that crosses denominational and faith lines. It will be a service seeking hope and healing. It is essentially to help the community deal with its pain, but we've opened it to everyone who wants to come. We know that the pain from this tragedy extends well past our city limits… (McLemore, 1998). An estimated 10,000 people attended this memorial service held at Arkansas State University.

- If it was a student who died, the parents might consider purchasing a special type of unfinished casket upon which his or her friends and classmates can write good-bye messages.

  Allowing the students to express their affection for the victim, as well as their pain, in this manner is a healthy activity. Seeing these messages of friendship and love might also be comforting for the family of the deceased. The three girls shot in West Paducah, Kentucky, for example, were buried in identical white caskets. Before their joint funeral, their caskets, banked by flowers and letter jackets, were covered with messages from friends written in felt-tip pen, such as "Jessica—I'll miss you sitting next to me in English" and a simple "I loved you" (Mead, 1997; Pedersen & Van Boven, 1997).

- If music is to be played at the service, songs could be selected that emphasize hope for the future and the ongoing stream of life.

  While you might recommend songs, the final choice will be a very personal decision for the family of the victim. A favorite song of the deceased, or a song significant to the family, may be played. Or the music may be limited to spiritual hymns. If other songs are considered, the family should carefully consider the messages contained in the lyrics, particularly in the case of a suicide. For example, the ballad "My Heart Will Go On" (from the soundtrack of the movie *Titanic*, performed by Celine Dion),* played at the funeral of Jonesboro school shooting victim Natalie Brooks, has a positive message for grieving students. Lyrics such as "There is some love that will not go away, You're here, there's nothing I fear, And I know that my heart will go on …" emphasize that the survivors will live through the pain of losing someone they love, holding his or her memory close in their hearts.

Funeral Etiquette

A funeral is an important ritual for saying good-bye to and remembering the life of someone who has died. The ceremony also serves another purpose for survivors, providing those who are mourning the loss with a sense of mutual support. Further, as stated in "Funeral Etiquette" (1998), "[A funeral] permits facing openly and realistically the crisis the death presents. Through the funeral the bereaved take that first step toward emotional adjustment to their loss."

Children, at a very early age, "… have an awareness of and a response to death" ("Funeral Etiquette," 1998), and your students will likely wish to attend the funeral of a school community member. However, they should have a choice about attending and should not be made to feel badly if they are uncomfortable with or frightened of the ceremonial aspects of death. If the students are preadolescent, their parents will have the final say about whether they attend the funeral. The parents' decision will depend in part on the circumstances surrounding the death, the child's temperament, the attitude of the child's family, and the wishes of the child (Levine, 1998).

If the students are to attend the funeral and/or a community memorial service, their teachers can help to prepare them for what will happen through classroom discussions about funeral terminology and etiquette. Explained Dr. Alan Wolfelt (1998), "Children are naturally curious about everything, including death. But death is a taboo subject in many families. A parent or family member who would gladly help a child with his [or her]

---

* "My Heart Will Go On" was written by James Horner and Will Jennings; distributed by Famous Music Corp. (ASCAP), Blue Sky Rider Songs (BMI).

science homework may be uncomfortable answering the same child's questions about death, funerals, and cremation. You can help by being someone [students] can turn to with [their] questions. Encourage [the students] to ask you anything [that they] want to about the death and the funeral. Give [them] honest answers in words [they] will understand." Points teachers can cover (from "Ceremonies," 1998; "Consumer Tips," 1998; "Funeral Etiquette," 1998; Leimer, 1996; Wolfelt, 1998) in your discussion follow.

Terminology

- Ashes—What is left of a dead body after cremation. (Because the remains don't really look like ashes, a more accurate description is "cremated remains.")
- Burial—The act of placing a dead body (which is inside either a casket or, if cremated, an urn) to rest in the ground. After a body is buried, it "breaks down" (decomposes) over the years until just a skeleton is left.
- Burial Plot (or Gravesite)—The place in a cemetery where a person who has died is buried.
- Casket—A box in which a dead body is buried.
- Cemetery—An open space set aside for the burial of dead bodies and cremated remains.
- Columbarium—A building at a cemetery where cremated remains are kept.
- Condolences—Personal notes (or sympathy cards) and/or flowers sent to the family of the person who has died to express one's sorrow about the death and support for the family members in their time of grief.
- Cremation—The process of burning a dead body until all that is left are small pieces of bone. Cremation has been performed for thousands of years (e.g., it was used by the ancient Greeks and Romans) and is becoming a more frequent method of disposing of dead bodies in our society today. A body to be cremated is handled with as much respect and dignity by those who perform cremations as is a body to be buried.
- Crematorium (or Crematory)—A place where a body is cremated. (The dead body is placed into a container and put into the cremation chamber. The chamber door is tightly sealed and a gas jet creates a searing heat that ignites the body and burns it for a few hours until only bone fragments remain. There is no smoke and no smell during cremation. After the cremation the small

"Think twice before withholding all information about cremation from children. Some would say that cremation is too violent a process to explain to children, yet children can cope with what they know. They cannot cope with what they don't know or have never been told. Often their imaginations can conjure up explanations much scarier than reality.... [And] if a child is told that God took the person to heaven yet the adults around [him or her] are all talking about something called cremation or ashes, [the child] may well become more confused and upset than ... if a compassionate adult gently told [him or her] the truth."

(Wolfelt, 1998)

pieces of bone are collected and processed down to the consistency of sand—what people often refer to as the "ashes.")

- Dead—When a person's body is no longer working. The heart does not beat and the brain does not think. The body does not breathe, feel, see, hear, taste, or move any more.

- Embalming—The process of preserving a dead body for viewing.

- Eulogy—A brief speech given at a funeral to recount the life of a person who has died and to offer praise and respect to him or her. A family member, close friend, business associate, or clergy member generally delivers a eulogy.

- Funeral (or Funeral Service)—A ceremony in which the family and friends of a person who has died gather to remember that person and express their love, respect, and grief for the person. This ceremony provides the opportunity to say good-bye to the person who has died and is generally held in a funeral home or church.

- Funeral Director—A person who runs a funeral home and assists the family of a person who has died to plan a funeral.

- Funeral Home—A place where dead bodies are brought to prepare them for burial or cremation.

- Funeral Procession (or Cortege)—The act of driving the body (or cremated remains) of a person who has died from the funeral home or church to the cemetery. The procession of cars carrying the body and the family and friends of the person who has died moves slowly in a line with all the cars' headlights turned on.

- Grave—The hole in the ground at a cemetery where a dead body or cremated remains are buried.

- Headstone—An upright monument, inscribed with the person's name, date of birth, and date of death, that marks the gravesite of a person who has died. (An alternative is a "ground marker," which achieves the same purpose but is set flat into the ground.)

- Honorary Pallbearers—Close associates of the deceased whom the family wishes to acknowledge, but who do not actually carry the casket. These individuals are generally associated with the person who has died through political, church, or civic activities.

- Mass Cards—Cards notifying mourners that a Catholic mass is to be held for the person who has died.

- Mausoleum—A building in a cemetery in which dead bodies (within caskets) and/or cremated remains are entombed (rather than buried).

- Memorial Donation—A contribution made to a specific cause or charity in memory of the person who has died (in lieu of flowers).

- Memorial Service—A ceremony in which the family and friends of a person who has died gather to remember that person and express their love, respect, and grief for the person. Like a funeral, except that the body of the person who has died is not present.
- Mourners (or Bereaved)—Survivors of the person who has died who are grieving his or her death.
- Obituary—A newspaper article that is written about the life of a person who has died and provides visitation and funeral information.
- Pallbearers—Family members, friends, church members, or business colleagues selected to carry the casket during a funeral.
- Private Service—A service by invitation only, generally attended only by the family and close friends of the person who has died. (Before a private service there is often a public visitation.)
- Scattering—When a dead person's cremated remains are scattered into the air, water, or ground rather than being buried. (Cremated remains are usually scattered in a place significant to and previously requested by the person who has died.)
- Urn—A container (often resembling a large vase) in which cremated remains are stored.
- Urn Garden—An area of a cemetery reserved for the burial of urns.
- Viewing—A time when family and friends of the person who has died gather (usually at the funeral home) to see the body of the person who has died and say good-bye. Viewing the body also is important in coming to terms with the finality of death. Children should be made to understand that the body will look different in death than in life. Because there is no more life in the body, if touched (which is discouraged unless by a family member or close friend) it will feel stiff, hard, and cold. The color of the skin may look different as well, as the body has been embalmed.
- Visitation—A gathering (held sometime before the funeral) of the relatives and friends of the person who has died so that they can offer support to the family of the deceased. The body is generally present, either with a closed casket or an open casket for viewing.

Etiquette

- Mourners do not have to wear black to a funeral, but they should dress semi-formally and in good taste in order to demonstrate dignity and respect for the person who has died and his or her family. Dark colors (e.g., black, navy, gray, brown) are still the accepted norm for those attending a funeral, although brighter colors are now considered appropriate for the deceased's family members (Leimer, 1996).

- Mourners should sign the register book with their full name when they attend a service or visitation (and include their relationship to the deceased if the family does not know them).

- If the service is not held in a church or funeral home and is more informal (e.g., the scattering of cremated remains in an outdoor setting), "street clothes" are generally appropriate.

- Visitation times are listed in the obituary or can be obtained by calling the funeral home. Mourners' presence at a visitation is a message to the deceased's family that they care. At a visitation, mourners are not required to approach the casket (if open) to view the body.

- Mourners may also go to the funeral home at any time during the funeral home's suggested hours to pay their respects to the person who has died, even when the deceased's family is not there.

- When sending condolences, mourners should clearly identify themselves and their relationship to the deceased in their notes or cards.

- A floral tribute is an appropriate way to express sympathy to the family of the person who has died, as flowers represent life and beauty. Flowers can be sent to either the funeral home (often preferred) or the home of the deceased or his or her family. If a floral tribute is to be sent to the residence, a planter with a note indicating the mourner's continued sympathy for the family generally is suggested.

- If mourners make a memorial donation, they should make it according to the wishes expressed by the family. An "In Memoriam" card (supplied by the funeral director) can be given to the family.

- Sympathy cards and personal notes are always appreciated, even if mourners were just acquaintances of the person who has died. Mourners should express themselves sincerely and include a statement such as, "I'm sorry about your loss."

- If mourners knew the deceased and his or her family well, a telephone call is very thoughtful. Mourners should offer their assistance during the call, and allow the family member to discuss the person who has died if he or she wishes to do so. Be a good listener.

- If mourners give a mass card to a Catholic family, they should be sure their name, address, and zip code are legible on the envelope.

- If there is an unstructured time reserved during the service in which people are invited to share a special memory of or thought about the person who has died, mourners are welcome to make a brief comment if they knew the person well and they are comfortable speaking out. (However, not saying anything during this time does not indicate that mourners cared about the person any less than those who do speak.)

- When talking with a family member of the person who has died, mourners should offer a simple condolence, such as:
  - "I'm very sorry."
  - "My sympathy to you and your family."
  - "I enjoyed knowing (name) and will miss (him or her)."
  - "(Name) was a wonderful person."

  It is not necessary for mourners to come up with a profound statement about life and death; a simple heartfelt expression of sorrow will be meaningful to and appreciated by the family. Mourners might also clasp the family member's hand in theirs, or, if they know the family member, embrace him or her. Mourners can encourage the bereaved to express his or her feelings about the person who has died if he or she wishes to do so, but should not pry or overwhelm the family member with too much conversation.

- Mourners should not say:
  - "I know how you feel," because they can't know exactly how the bereaved feels. Each and every relationship is unique.
  - "I felt the same way when (someone the mourner loved died)," because this shifts the focus from the person who has just died and the pain of his or her family.
  - (If the person who died was a child) "Luckily you have another son/daughter," as this negates the significance and unique qualities of the child who has died.
  - (If the person who died was a child) "You can always have another son/daughter," as one child cannot replace another.

- If school community members are saddened by the death of a school community member they are allowed to and encouraged to attend the funeral (unless it is a private service), even if they were just acquaintances of the deceased. The presence of many well-wishers will mean a great deal to the family, even if the family does not know some of the mourners well enough to approach them and express their appreciation for their attendance.

The etiquette suggestions just presented are appropriate for most traditional funeral services of most religious denominations. However, if the deceased was a member of a religious denomination with practices that are unfamiliar to you and/or your students, you may need to educate yourself about those customs in order to discuss them with your class. Alternatively, your school might ask a member of the deceased's religion, a person who helped with translation during the crisis (if any), or a bilingual parent from within the same religious community to explain the traditional ceremonies of the deceased's native culture so that school community members can be respectful of these customs. After the 1989 school shooting in Stockton, California, in which five children from the city's large Southeast Asian immigrant community were killed, for example, "... local leaders had to learn the religious and cultural customs of the largely Buddhist community to organize funerals and religious ceremonies" (Johnston, 1998, p. 31).

Finally, encourage students who plan to attend the funeral to attend with their parents or another adult family member. Then end your classroom discussion with the opportunity for the students to ask any and all questions they may have about death and the funeral ritual, as well as to express any fears they have surrounding these issues. If appropriate, you might also suggest that a student or students leave a special gift (e.g., a note, a flower, a meaningful symbol) near, on, or in the casket (as appropriate) as a way of saying good-bye ("Ceremonies," 1998).

School Procedures

Before and after the funeral of a school community member, your school should take the following steps, recommended by the District School Board of Pasco County, Florida (1994a):

- The Crisis Coordinator/head administrator should send a letter to all parents of students affected by the death or crisis. This letter should discuss the facts of the crisis and the grieving process. It should also encourage parents to talk with their children about the funeral and any other memorial services and urge the parents to accompany their children to those services if the children wish to attend. (*See "When Will Things Return to Normal?" previously in this chapter and "Verifying Information/Crisis Fact Sheet" in Chapter One for additional pointers on communicating with parents throughout the crisis.*)

- If the death was a suicide, this letter also should contain information about suicide "contagion" and suicide warning signs and urge parents to seek immediate help if their children give any indication of suicidal ideation (*see "Suicide Postvention" and "Suicide Statistics, Causes, and Myths" in Chapter Eleven for additional information*).

- The Crisis Coordinator/head administrator should release students from school who wish to attend the memorial or funeral service. The students and their families should provide their own transportation to the service.

"Reflecting our society's complex relationships ... some of our ceremonies and memorials are more inclusive today than they were a few decades ago. They transcend the boundaries of who has traditionally been expected to grieve.... In some cases such as national tragedies or tragedies that tap into our collective values and fears ... people who are grieving may not even know the victims but feel the need to participate in ritual. These are ... people for whom no established mourning roles exist.... [N]ew and modified traditional rites and memorials incorporate the realities of the new world in which we live. Our era is filled with new situations and dilemmas ... e.g., random violence .... Our rites and memorials reflect the flavor of our contemporary society ... [and] give meaning to death, help us heal, and give us the strength to continue life in an increasingly complex and rapidly changing world."

(Leimer, 1996)

- Members of your crisis response team, the administration, and counseling staff should attend the funeral, both to pay their respects and to provide support to any students needing assistance.
- The school might provide a gathering space at the school and refreshments for staff, students, and their families immediately following the service. Students who attend the funeral may need time afterward to process the experience, but they are often not invited back to the family's home and often have no other supportive place to gather. Before offering this service to the students and staff, the Parent/Family Liaison or Crisis Coordinator should check with the family of the deceased to avoid conflicts with any arrangements they have made.

Memorializing Victims

"Rituals have existed throughout time—they seem to be a part of what it means to be human," explained family therapists Evan Imber-Black and Janine Roberts (1992, p. xvii). Rituals and ceremonies that mark life changes, such as death, are particularly important. "Significant loss, such as in death," noted Imber-Black and Roberts, "… requires a period of mourning in order to fully grieve and reengage in life … [and] rituals to initiate healing following a death are found in every culture and religion" (1992, p. 36). But less common, they explained, are "… rituals to heal the trauma of violence and abuse, although many people are beginning to invent these out of a profound need for healing" (1992, p. 36).

After a severe school crisis, attending the funeral and sending a bouquet of flowers may not seem like enough to members of your school community. Particularly if the crisis involved violence, the students, staff, their families, and community members will need and want ceremony and rituals to express their sorrow, outrage, and shock. Often such activities involve memorializing the victims of the crisis in some way. Explained school psychologist Cathy Paine (1998a, p. 25), "School memorials or memory activities serve an important function in the grief process for students and staff. A memorial promotes the healing process by providing an opportunity for students to join together and participate in a ritual…. [A] school memorial brings closure to a period of grieving and serves as a clear statement that it is time to move on with regular school activities."

The school should not try to prevent such memorial activities. Rather, by *guiding* these memorial efforts, the school's administrators can both facilitate the healing of the school community and help to ensure that the long-term needs of the school are met. Unfortunately, there have been few recommendations available to school administrators about what is appropriate concerning memorializing victims and what is not. As a result, some administrators have made some poor decisions about the way in which students are memorialized. The difficulty is that their schools are affected by these decisions for years to come, and sometimes permanently. Thus, this section provides many guidelines and examples you can follow to ensure that any memorials created by your school will be appropriate immediately after your school's crisis and in the future.

Cautions Regarding Memorializing

One of the most important, and most difficult, rules about memorializing is that *the victim should not be memorialized in any way if the death was a suicide*. Even if the victim's family is very "invested" in memorializing him or her, and even if the other students want a memorial as well, the ban on memorializing is crucial to help prevent suicide "contagion" (*see Chapter Eleven, "Special Considerations for Suicide"*). Statistics show that suicide is on the minds of a lot of students at any given time, and they can be influenced by any glorification of a suicide (whether intended that way or not). Explained school psychologist Richard Lieberman, "When children think about suicide they are not thinking clearly. It is not a far stretch for a child who sees a beautiful tree, a yearbook dedication, or a memorial plaque to imagine he or she [would] receive such attention in death" (California Association of School Psychologists [CASP], 1998, p. 14).

This memorializing ban after a suicide should be absolute: There should be no plaques, no trees planted, no yearbook dedication, no school dances held in the victim's honor, nothing permanent. (The same policy should be in effect after any death of a school community member resulting from a high-risk behavior, such as driving drunk or an accidental drug overdose.) If funds are donated to the school, they should go to a worthy cause such as a scholarship fund or a suicide prevention organization rather than a physical, permanent memorial.

If the deceased died of a disease or was the victim of violence, for example, the policy would be different, although you still need to exercise caution. When planning a memorial, first consider the cause of death and then think about what your school has done historically to memorialize students and staff who have died. In general, a "consumable" gesture (such as a scholarship) is preferred to any sort of permanent memorial such as a statue or plaque in a prominent location. Sadly, if your school erected a memorial for every school community member who died, after some time the school would begin to assume the appearance of a cemetery, because over the years a lot of bad things happen to students and staff.

Further, you should not rename your school in honor of a deceased school community member. After the school shooting near Jonesboro, Arkansas, Mitchell Wright, the husband of slain teacher Shannon Wright, asked the district to rename the Westside Middle School building in her honor. A

See "Suicide Postvention" in Chapter Eleven for more information on this topic, including guidelines by the American Association of Suicidology that administrators can use to justify such decisions to family and friends of the victim.

much-loved teacher, Mrs. Wright died saving the life of one of her students. "It didn't surprise me when I learned that my wife had sacrificed her own life to shield one of her students from the bullets," said Wright. "In all the world there were two things she loved most—our son, and teaching at Westside Middle School" (Casey, 1999, p. 13). While there is no question that Shannon Wright was deserving of such a commemoration, renaming the school in her honor would have permanently linked the school with the tragedy. It already will be difficult for the middle school to live down its notoriety following the school shooting, yet it does share the "Westside" name with the elementary and high schools in its complex, and after many years people will no longer automatically link the middle school with tragedy. An alternate suggestion might be to name any new school built in the area in Shannon Wright's honor (as the tragedy would not have occurred there), but the best course of action would likely remain a more traditional, low-key memorial. An example sometimes used in such situations is a garden bench with a memorial plaque.

When emotions are running high immediately after a crisis it is sometimes difficult to keep the "big picture" in mind. And although you do want to serve the needs of those grieving a loss, you must be careful not to overshadow for years to come the focus on what goes on inside your building, which is learning in what should be a cheerful, hopeful school environment. (*See "Gift of the Tragedy" later in this chapter for examples of some permanent memorials to victims that have been created in an appropriate manner.*)

Finally, you should be cautious about accepting gifts from the families of victims without first discussing with them your policies on memorializing. The counselors at one Austin, Texas, high school learned this lesson the hard way. In 1997 a student there committed suicide, and her mother wanted to donate a glass cabinet to put outside the counselors' offices. The school didn't have much in the way of furniture, so the counselors thought, "Well, okay. A glass cabinet couldn't hurt. That would be a nice remembrance." Unfortunately, the cabinet was delivered with a very large plaque memorializing the suicide victim at its center (which the counselors probably should have anticipated, given that the cabinet was coming from the victim's mother). It is much easier to have an open dialogue with the family and friends of victims before any memorializing plans are made than to address such awkward situations after the fact.

Gift of the Tragedy

A phrase coined by the National Organization for Victim Assistance (NOVA) is "gift of the tragedy." At some point after the initial trauma is addressed, a community that has suffered a crisis will need to ask themselves, "What will be the gift from this tragedy?" Neither we nor NOVA mean to imply that the crisis event was a good thing, or that it is better that it happened. What this statement means is that the tragedy cannot be undone, the death cannot be changed. Given that reality, this question asks survivors to consider what can be done now to both honor and remember the deceased *and* to focus on the ongoing lives and needs of those who survived them.

Sometimes the gift of the tragedy is intangible. Perhaps it is a stark reminder to survivors of the preciousness of life and how quickly it can be snatched away. In the case of Nicole Hadley, one of three girls murdered in the West Paducah, Kentucky, school shooting, the gift of the tragedy was a gift of life to Thomas Hereford IV of Jeffersonville, Indiana, who received Nicole's lungs after her parents donated her organs (Hewitt, 1997). "The gift, as … Hereford knew that it must, came out of someone else's sorrow and tragedy…. 'They're very courageous and caring people to be willing to do something like that,' said Hereford" (Hewitt, 1997). In addition to her lungs being transplanted, Nicole Hadley's heart was successfully transplanted into a fortunate recipient in Louisville, Kentucky (Bridis, 1997; Cabell, 1997). After Nicole's death her mother said that "… only recently Nicole had expressed a desire to donate her organs if she were to die" (Hewitt, 1997).

> "… [W]hatever this town has learned from its tragedy, the lesson came at too high a price. 'This community has shown that it's wholesome, caring, compassionate, forgiving, and reconciling,' (Fred) Paxton (publisher of the Paducah Sun) [said]. 'But we didn't need an event like this to prove it.'"
>
> (Hewitt, 1997)

Often, however, the gift of the tragedy is more concrete. For example, the best soccer facility in the state of Montana is at a Butte elementary school. In 1994 a fifth grade boy there was fatally shot by another fifth grader he had had a previous argument with on the playground. Because the slain student (as well as his twin brother) was a soccer player, and his father the soccer coach, the donated funds were used to build this facility in which the state soccer playoffs are now held. This type of memorial to a deceased student is ideal, because it is something that can be used by the entire community indefinitely. The tragic death of this fifth grade boy was acknowledged in a way that continues to enhance the lives of survivors. Other schools should strive to strike this balance when considering memorials to school community members.

Another example of a memorial that benefits the community and surrounding region is the Stockton Children's Museum. In 1989 a shooter on the Cleveland Elementary School playground murdered five of the school's students. A year after the shooting, Janet Geng, a teacher who was shot and injured at the school, conceptualized the children's museum, and by 1995 the 22,000 square foot facility—one of the largest children's museums in the country—became a regional attraction drawing 38,000 visitors per year (Johnston, 1998). What is particularly interesting about this memorial effort is that it was driven more by the city of Stockton than by Cleveland Elementary. The city leased the museum's board its space for $1.00 per year, and today "the city's commitment has grown to include staffing and paying the museum's utility bills" (Johnston, 1998, p. 29).

The story of how the museum came about is told in a museum brochure, but nowhere in the museum itself is a mention of the school shooting. As reported in Johnston (1998), "Geng says the museum is not the right place for a formal reminder.... 'This was not so much of a memorial, but a living thing that other parents and children who were injured could come to and see smiles on the other children,' she says. 'They've seen enough sadness.' As for herself, Geng credits the museum with helping her reclaim much of what she had lost" (p. 29).

"One of the ways to make sense of [the tragedy] is to make good out of evil, and that's what we did."

—Patricia Busher, Principal, Cleveland Elementary, Stockton, California (Johnston, 1998, p. 28).

Not every memorial to a deceased school community member must be as subtle, however. Particularly after a catastrophic crisis there may be overwhelming community support for some type of memorial that directly honors the lives lost. In these cases of extreme need, providing such a memorial is appropriate. For example, in May 1998, Heath High School in West Paducah, Kentucky, dedicated a memorial garden at the school in honor of the victims of the school shooting that occurred there. "Originally school officials were just going to plant some flowers in a small area of the school's courtyard and put out some benches. But the community wanted more and backed it up with money [approximately $100,000 in actual funds and materials from corporate and private donations] and time" (Williams, 1998).

The finished memorial forms a large circle in the school's courtyard, enclosed by a wall with three entrances—one to honor each girl killed in the tragedy. Set within the circle is a smaller semicircular garden containing a stone memorial set upright in the ground. Engraved upon it are the victims' names and the Biblical passage St. John 14:1, which reads: "Let not your heart be troubled; believe in God, and believe in me also." According to Principal Bill Bond, "During the planning, some wanted to make it even bigger. We almost had to start building to keep it from growing." Commenting that the project was therapeutic for the community, Bond added: "A lot of people wanted to help but they felt kind of helpless [before this project]. They were looking for some kind of vehicle to show their support" (Williams, 1998).

At Westside Middle School near Jonesboro, Arkansas, the school library now contains a "... massive stained glass window ... with five roses" to commemorate the five lives lost in the school shooting that occurred there (Stockton, 1998, p. 12). Elsewhere in the school, there are "... pen and ink composite drawings in the halls and poems displayed in needlepoint" honoring the victims (Stockton, 1998, p. 12). Fifteen trees (one for each of the Westside victims) were planted near the front of the Westside campus (Childress, 1999), and, as in West Paducah, the school community members have planned a memorial garden for the area where the victims fell. Explained school psychologist Betty Stockton, this area is hoped to be a "… lasting memorial with spaces for academic enrichment such as natural science experiments, as well as an appropriate living memorial to the victims" (Stockton, 1998, p. 12). According to Westside superintendent Dick Young, the Westside Memorial Garden will have "… a pavilion, amphitheater, assorted greenery, and [a] ribbon-shaped sundial inscribed with the names of those slain" (Hinkle, 1999a, p. 15A). It is expected to be completed the summer or fall of 1999.

Bear in mind that whatever your school decides to do concerning memorializing victims, you likely won't be able to please everyone involved. For example, while the majority of the school community and surrounding community wanted a memorial garden at Westside Middle School near Jonesboro, the husband of slain teacher Shannon Wright took issue with the plan. "I can't see [how] you can take an area where a bloodbath happened and make it pretty," he said. " [The school and community spent a large sum of money] for a memorial garden," he continued, "and the kids don't even have a playground. I think they should sow some grass and put up five shade trees and be done with it" (Ashcraft, 1999, p. 14A). In light of the differing opinions that are bound to occur, the best any school can do is include in the decision-making process the school community members and family members most affected by the crisis and encourage everyone to strive to reach consensus on any memorializing plans made.

Another kind of "memorial" does not honor the victims as much as address the pressing needs of survivors. Making a dramatic change in the school environment after a severe crisis can be a way to facilitate feelings of safety and security for survivors. After the school shooting near Jonesboro, Arkansas, for example, school officials built a wooden fence behind Westside Middle School to shield the grounds from the hill from which the shooters fired. They also cleared out the brush and shrubs that had provided the shooters cover, leaving only a few trees. "Well, that's what the students and staff wanted," said a school official. When you look at the fence—which does not run behind the adjacent elementary and high schools in the Westside complex—you realize that if anyone ever wanted to fire from there again he or she could shoot over the fence. But the point is that this structure provides a boundary, which gives those who survived this tragedy a sense of security.

Student Activities

In the aftermath of a school crisis, older students (i.e., middle/junior high and high schoolers) often feel a need to take some positive action. When something bad has happened in their school or community, they want to be involved in some meaningful way, to contribute to making the world a better place. For example, if flooding caused the crisis, they may wish to fill sandbags or to collect blankets and food for survivors. If the school crisis involved the death of a school community member, students might collect funds for the burial of the victim or to pay the family's medical bills. These types of activities help students to process the crisis by enabling them to assume some control over the circumstances. Assisting in the crisis response helps students to feel more like survivors than victims and allows them to contribute to the betterment of their school and/or community.

It is important to encourage students in, and even direct them toward, these efforts. Explained Dr. Marilyn Gootman, "Just when teens are trying to establish their own power and identity, the death of a friend can render them powerless. As a result, rage and guilt overwhelm them and their immaturity might lead them to express these feelings in actions that are destructive to themselves or others. That's why they need us to redirect them, to restore their sense of power by steering them towards constructive things they can do" (Gootman, 1998).

Indeed, students often do a lot of good through such actions. For example, in 1996, when a Houston, Texas, high school student named Robbie needed a kidney transplant, many of the students at his school (at which Robbie's father taught, as well) decided they wanted to publicize the need for organ donation. They worked hard at this effort, fund-raising, printing cards, appearing on television and in the newspapers to raise awareness. During this campaign by his classmates, Robbie did get the organ transplant that he needed. But the story does not have a happy ending: Robbie's body rejected the kidney, and he died the day before a benefit dance was to be held at the school.

Although they lost their classmate, these students didn't abandon their effort. They held the dance and continued to raise money because they realized there were many other individuals also needing organs. By sticking with their project they contributed to a valid need in our society as well as provided concrete assistance to Robbie's family (i.e., thousands of dollars to assist with the high medical bills incurred). Perhaps more important, the students' work on this worthy cause helped them to deal with the untimely death of their friend Robbie.

Another ambitious effort was the formation of temporary suicide hotlines in Houston's Cypress-Fairbanks Independent School District to address the aftermath of student suicides in some of the high schools there. School psychologists trained the student volunteers who staffed the phones at their school from 4:00 to 10:00 PM (with adult assistance). Although they will never know if they actually prevented a suicide (there were none at the school during that time period), the students received some beneficial training in preventative skills and learned about giving of themselves by making this commitment to be there to listen to their peers.

(*NOTE*: A suicide helpline/hotline is really the only acceptable type of "memorial" after the suicide of a school community member, as it focuses on survivors and on preventing additional deaths. If students in your school undertake such a project, the staff in charge might be criticized by teachers saying, for example, "I can't believe you're putting these kids in a position where they're answering the phone and somebody might be calling who is suicidal." The school psychologists' response in Houston was that the students are actually in that position every day, and it's better to put them in that position with a trained counselor sitting next to them than in the isolation of their peer relationships.)

School administrators and/or your school's counseling staff can encourage students to channel their energy into such positive actions and guide them in undertaking appropriate activities to achieve their goals. Such activities could include raising money for a scholarship fund, for medical research, or for a worthy cause that is particularly significant to the deceased's family and/or is relevant to the nature of the crisis. To raise such funds students can hold any number of functions, such as car washes, dances, or basketball games (District School Board, 1994b). When students approach you with the idea for a project (or asking for ideas), try to make sure they are really committed to seeing it through before promising too much support. You might want to wait to see if they return after your initial conversation. If they do, you'll know that the commemorative effort is truly important to them. By the same token, the students, rather than the faculty member or administrator assigned to assist them with the activities, should do the actual work.

Students can also act to effect change in the broader sphere, even nationally. After the shooting at Westside Middle School near Jonesboro, a Harrisburg (Arkansas) high school student wrote to U.S. Senator Tim Hutchinson urging Congress to recognize teacher Shannon Wright's heroism with a "... nationally recognized day when people could reflect on the tragedy and the courageous actions of those involved in the Westside shooting," said Hutchinson (1999, p. 1B). Senator Hutchinson introduced Resolution 53, the National School Violence Victims Memorial Day, which was approved by the Senate in March 1999 with strong bipartisan support. The senator also wrote to all the Arkansas school superintendents and encouraged them to develop school violence awareness activities in their districts (Hutchinson, 1999).

For Concerned People Elsewhere ...

Memorializing Victims of Another School's Crisis

After learning of a severe school crisis elsewhere, your students may wish to memorialize the victims of that crisis. Should that be the case, your school's mental health staff and/or administrators should guide the students in deciding what to do. The following are a few suggestions:

- Hold a fund-raiser to raise money for the school in crisis (or for the United Way or other agency managing the school's donations), to help fund counseling services, a scholarship, or the like.

- Collect and donate supplies needed by the school or the people assisting the school community.

- Send flowers, a plant, a banner, a poster, poetry, sympathy cards, and/or e-mails to the affected school community members.

- Implement a relevant program at your own school (e.g., an anonymous "tip line" for reporting threats/weapons, an anger management program, mediation, a prom night program to discourage drunk driving, peer support groups, a suicide hotline, bully-proofing and violence prevention programs, etc.) to help improve the school environment and decrease the odds that a similar crisis might happen at your school.

- Work to effect change in the larger community and/or society (e.g., help to organize an awareness workshop about factors that contributed to the crisis, write to elected representatives about causal problems in our society, etc.).

It is best to avoid permanent memorials to the victims of another school's crisis. Should your school decide to erect any sort of permanent memorial, it should be more about an overriding societal concern than about the specific victims of the crisis. (For example, rather than planting a tree for each victim—as the affected school might do—your school community members might plant a "peace tree.") (*See the entire section "Memorializing Victims" in this chapter for other suggestions and cautions.*)

Raising and Dispersing Funds

After a severe school crisis, government funds may be available to your school. These grants will likely be earmarked for important services, such as funding intensive and/or long-term counseling for your school community members. (*See "Financial Support" in Chapter Four for suggestions about requesting and making use of such financial assistance.*)

In addition to the fund-raising efforts of your students (*see "Student Activities" previously in this section*), others in your school and community will also likely gather funds after a tragedy. After the school shooting in West Paducah, Kentucky, for example, the PTA printed and sold T-shirts and sweatshirts commemorating the victims of the crisis (the design contained three large ribbons representing the three girls killed in the attack and five smaller ribbons representing those injured). Proceeds from these sales went into funds for the victims and their families.

A former graduate of Heath High in West Paducah, Steven Curtis Chapman, a prominent Christian singer, performed benefit concerts after the school shooting to raise funds for his alma mater. His efforts brought in approximately $20,000, which was administered by a private trust and used for the memorial, counseling services at the school, and donated to victims' families. Additionally, Heath High School received approximately $71,000 in donations sent directly to the school. These funds were distributed among the victims' families (e.g., offset medical and burial expenses).

In Jonesboro, Arkansas, a local radio station sponsored two benefit concerts after the shooting at Westside Middle School. The money raised through these events was given to the local university for the establishment of scholarships for Westside students.

Local corporations may make donations and businesses may set out "collection buckets" around your town. If your school's crisis has been well publicized, donations may also pour in from around the country and the world, as they did after the school shootings in West Paducah, Kentucky, and near Jonesboro, Arkansas. Your school will need to determine a plan for distributing such funds, as these are generally not used for counseling services and the like. In West Paducah, many of these funds were donated as a contribution to the school's memorial garden. In Jonesboro, Arkansas, the approximately $362,000 in donations was given to a community fund (other monies were donated to a school fund) and divided among the injured victims and families of the deceased, including the formation of a scholarship for Zane Wright, son of slain teacher Shannon Wright.

The decision about how to disperse donated funds should be a joint one. In Jonesboro, the "Westside Crisis Fund Committee," made up of school and community members, was formed to manage and disperse the donations in partnership with the United Way of Jonesboro. As a general rule, assisting victims' families with medical and/or burial expenses should be considered first. Any remaining funds might be devoted to scholarships, an excellent way to memorialize the victims and focus on survivors. In Stockton, California, for example, after the 1989 school shooting at Cleveland Elementary, the Cleveland Children's Scholarship fund was created from contributions received by the school. This fund has awarded monies to survivors of the crisis, including Sovanna Koeurt, the mother who assisted the school with translation during the crisis and became a community leader afterwards. Koeurt was awarded "… one of five full-tuition scholarships offered by the nearby University of the Pacific [and funded by the Cleveland Children's Scholarship] in honor of the children who died" (Johnston, 1998, p. 31). The fund continues even today: In 1998 the fund "… awarded $30,000 … to about 30 applicants. And a fund-raising concert that was held after the incident has grown into an annual, five-concert children's series" (Johnston, 1998, p. 29).

Memorializing by Parents/Other Community Members

After a severe school crisis, other concerned adults in your community (e.g., family members of victims, emergency responders, politicians, etc.) may find creative ways to memorialize the victims and effect change in the community, state, or even the nation. If invited to participate in these efforts, your school should support them in whatever ways are appropriate (e.g., collaborating on and/or publicizing them).

For one memorializing activity, after the May 1998 school shooting in Springfield, Oregon, people in seven Northwest states stitched 700 pieces for a quilt. According to organizers, "the quilt began as a way of stitching the emotional wounds of all those devastated by the horror of children killing children" (Hinkle, 1999b, p. 7A). Some of the quilt squares are hand-painted by children, some are embroidered with words of sympathy, and all are "… connected with a central square imprinted with the words, 'Join hands against violence'" (Hinkle, 1999b, p. 7A). The traveling Thurston Healing Quilt was displayed in churches in Jonesboro, Arkansas, before the year anniversary of the school shooting there and inspired local people, such as Little Rock elementary school classes, to add quilt pieces. Said a Jonesboro quilting organizer, "It will become not only a Thurston quilt but our healing quilt" (Hinkle, 1999b, p. 7A).

Additionally, the parents of victims may be particularly motivated to positively impact our society and alter societal conditions that contributed to the school crisis. Suzann Wilson, mother of student Britthney Varner (who was killed in the Jonesboro, Arkansas, school shooting), for example, formed a lobbying group called "People Against Violence Everywhere" in an effort to change the nation's gun laws. In 1998 she testified before Congress in support of a bill that would "… force firearm manufacturers to make new guns childproof and hold parents responsible if their weapons are used by minors" (Casey, 1999, p. 11). The parents of the three girls murdered in the school shooting in West Paducah, Kentucky, together formed the KNJ Foundation, Inc. ("K" for Kayce, "N" for Nicole, and "J" for Jessica). The mission of this national foundation is to end school violence and support its victims (The KNJ Foundation, 1999).

After the 1998 school shooting in Springfield, Oregon, Springfield Fire and Life Safety Chief Dennis Murphy met with various congressional representatives—as well as with the National Education Association, the Center to Prevent Handgun Violence, and the National Rifle Association—to discuss cooperative ways to eliminate violence in schools ("Ribbon of Promise," 1998).

Murphy and the president of the Springfield Firefighters Association, Paul Esselstyn, also began a campaign called "Ribbon of Promise" to increase awareness of the problem of school violence. They distributed sky blue (representing both sorrow and hope for the future) memory ribbons in their community with a theme of "Let it End" ("Ribbon of Promise," 1998). "The problem is bigger than Springfield and the other cities where [school violence] has happened," they said, "but not bigger than the nation. We need to get out of denial and into action" ("Ribbon of Promise," 1998, p. 7).

> "If people want to mark [the anniversary of the Westside Middle School shooting] they can have a prayer and create an awareness throughout the year that it can happen, and will continue to happen, until people say, 'We are tired of it. We are tired of burying our kids.' You can have all the little memorial services you want to, but until you do something positive, it won't mean a thing."
>
> —Pam Herring, mother of slain student Paige Ann Herring (Ashcraft, 1999, p. 14A)

Specific Guidelines for Schools

The following guidelines, recommended by the National Organization for Victim Assistance (NOVA) (cited in Paine, 1998a) and the District School Board of Pasco County, Florida (1994a), represent best practice in memorializing deceased school community members following a crisis:

- Remember that *if the death was a suicide, no school memorial* is advised (*see Chapter Eleven, "Special Considerations for Suicide"*).

- If possible, conduct the memorializing activity within a week of the death.

- Involve your students and/or staff in the memorial planning, particularly those who were emotionally close to the deceased.

- Keep the memorial service short (e.g., 15-20 minutes for elementary students and 30-40 minutes for secondary students).

- Carefully select any musical pieces to be played or performed (*see "Funeral Planning" previously in this chapter and "Music" in the "Modifying the Curriculum" section of this chapter for guidelines*). A focus on soft, soothing pieces will help to maintain a calm atmosphere (which is particularly important with students of middle school age). Consider including student musical performances as part of the memorial service.

- Include several appropriate speakers (e.g., school, district, and/or city and state representatives) during the brief memorial service. Exercise caution in focusing on religion and including religious speakers if yours is a public school. Also be sure that all members of your school community and the surrounding community are adequately represented and addressed by the speakers selected. The televised memorial service attended by residents from across the state of Colorado after the April 1999 school shooting at Columbine High School in Littleton, for example, was criticized by some as "too Christian" and "too white."

- If it is age-appropriate to do so, include student representatives among the speakers. They can read a speech, a poem, or another tribute, or sing a song. A school staff member should preapprove student selections, and talk to the students beforehand about the high level of emotionality they may experience while participating in the memorial. Practicing their contributions will help the students alleviate some of the anxiety associated with this public performance.

- Strive to involve all of the students, not just those who will speak during the service, in some aspect of the memorial. Classes, for example, can contribute banners, signs, or other decorations for the gathering space. Students might also wish to create memory ribbons to distribute to audience members.

- You may wish to also include physical symbols of life and hope for the future, such as flowers, balloons, and/or candles. The state-wide memorial service after the Columbine High School massacre in Littleton, Colorado, was touchingly concluded with the release of a white dove as each of the 13 victims' names were read by the governor.

- Notify the families of the deceased about the special service and/or memorializing activities planned by your school so they may attend if they wish, and do not be offended if they do not attend. Attendance at such memorial services may be too painful for mourning family members.

  - The National Organization for Victim Assistance recommends that direct involvement by the parents and/or other family members of the deceased in *planning* school presentations not be sought during the early crisis response. However, because each crisis situation is unique, we recommend that the Parent/Family Liaison and Crisis Coordinator/head administrator make this decision on a case-by-case basis in order to balance the wishes of victims' families and the guidelines for appropriate school memorials.

- Prepare your students for the memorial service, explaining what will happen during the service and your expectations for respectful behavior. During the memorial service itself, teachers should remove any students who behave inappropriately. Note, however, that sincere expressions of emotion (e.g., weeping) are not "inappropriate" and should not be censored.

- Encourage all of the students (and staff members) to attend the memorial service at the school. Such services are generally a "... powerfully unifying experience for a school, and ... send a message to students that each person is important in the school and deserves to be honored" (Paine, 1998a, p. 25). However, attendance should not be mandatory.

- When a memorial service or related activity is held at your school, be sure to give students the option of taking part in a different activity if they do not wish to attend the memorial, or dismiss those students. Note, also, that some parents may object to their children attending the memorial service.

- Reconvene classes for at least a short time after the school's memorial service so that teachers (and peers) can provide emotional support to students. Teachers should accompany (or have another student accompany) any students who are experiencing intense grief to a counseling room for a one-to-one discussion with a member of your school's mental health staff.

See "Providing Counseling Services" in Chapter Seven for additional information.

- Take your time when planning any type of permanent memorial to the crisis victims, and be sure to observe best practice guidelines for such memorials (*see "Cautions Regarding Memorializing" previously in this chapter*).

- Involve all appropriate school community members (e.g., staff, students, and family members) in the planning, design, and (if possible) construction of any permanent memorial. Note, however, that it is important to establish at the outset who will make the final decisions about design, location, budget, and so forth.

- On the advice of Dr. Robert Pynoos, director of Trauma Psychiatry Services at UCLA, "carefully consider the location of any permanent memorial. It should be placed in a location where students can choose to look at it, but it should not confront the students every time they enter the school" (Paine, 1998a, p. 25).

References

Ashcraft, H. (1999, March 21). Pam Herring's world fell apart in March of '98. *Jonesboro Sun*, pp. 1A, 14A.

Associated Press. (1997, December 12). Carneal indicted for shootings. *ABCNEWS.com*. Available online: http://www.abcnews.com/sections/us/shootings1212/index.html

Associated Press. (1998, March 27). Arkansas students face fears as they return to deadly site. *Idahonews.com*. Available online: http://www.idahonews.com/032798/NATION_/16024.htm

Barnard, J. (1999, February 9). Youths who survived shooting in Oregon act it out in stage play. *Houston Chronicle*, p. 5A.

Bridis, T. (1997, December 4). Shooting suspect may have had help. *Detroit News*. Available online: http://detnews.com/1997/nation/9712/04/12040078.htm

Cabell, B. (1997, December 3). Who is Michael Carneal? *CNNinteractive*. Available online: http://www.cnn.com/US/9712/03/school.shooting.pm/

California Association of School Psychologists (CASP). (1998, November). Teen suicides: Life, after death. *NASP Communiqué, 27*(3), 14-15.

Campbell, D. (1997). *The Mozart effect: Tapping the power of music to heal the body, strengthen the mind and unlock the creative spirit*. New York: Avon.

Casey, K. (1999, March). When the shooting stopped. *Ladies' Home Journal*, pp. 10-13.

Ceremonies, rituals, and children: Part 1. (1998, December 3). *Safe Crossings*. Available online: http://www.providence.org/safecrossings/documents/activ2.htm

Childress, A. (1999, March 23). "Terrible Tuesday" reminders, images are part of reality. *Jonesboro Sun*, pp. 1A-2A.

Consumer tips—Funeral homes. (1998, November 30). Available online: http://www.yellowpages.ca/ctips/Funtip.html

District School Board of Pasco County. (1994a). *Crisis intervention team program: Administrator's checklist for dealing with a schoolwide loss/crisis*. Land O'Lakes, FL: Author.

District School Board of Pasco County. (1994b). *Handling a class after a student dies* [Handout]. Land O'Lakes, FL: Author.

Dr. Seuss. (1996). *My many colored days*. New York: Random House.

Fainaru, S. (1998, October 20). Killing in the classroom: Many struggle to put their world together. *Boston Globe*, pp. A1, A20-21.

Feinberg, T. (1998, March 22). NASP/NEAT & NOVA: A crisis partnership that really works. *National Association of School Psychologists (NASP)*. Available online: http://www.naspweb.org/office/cq/CQ265NASPNEAT.htm

Fernside online. (1998, December 3). *Activities page*. Available online: http://www.fernside.org/kids/active.html

Funeral etiquette. (1998, November 30). *Ontario Funeral Service Association*. Available online: http://www.turnerporter.ca/etiquet.htm

Gamble, C. (1996, August 7). Pa. community mourns after losing 16 students, 5 adults in TWA crash. *Education Week, 15*(41), 10.

Gerber, S. (1998, March). The sound of healing: Every culture in the world has used sound and music to heal. Finally we're catching up. *Vegetarian Times*, p. 68.

Girls killed in Kentucky school remembered. (1997, December 5). *Excite News*. Available online: http://nt.excite.com/News/971205/16.NEWS-SCHOOL.html

Gootman, M. (1998, December 3). Helping our teens heal when a friend dies. *Jewishfamily.com*. Available online: http://www.jewishfamily.com/Features/996/helping10.htm

Hewitt, B. (1997, December 22). Marching on: Stunned by tragedy, the people of Paducah search their hearts and find the healing grace of compassion. *People Weekly*, p. 42.

Hinkle, B. (1999a, March 21). Memorial services are scheduled Wednesday. *Jonesboro Sun*, pp. 1A, 15A.

Hinkle, B. (1999b, March 21). "Thurston Healing Quilt" to be on display at Jonesboro area churches. *Jonesboro Sun*, p. 7A.

Holliman, J. (1997a, December 3). Kentucky County's schools increase security. *CNNinteractive*. Available online: http://www.cnn.com/US/9712/03/school.shooting.folo/

Holliman, J. (1997b, December 4). Investigators: Suspect may have told others of shooting plan. *CNNinteractive*. Available online: http://www.cnn.com/US/9712/04/school.shooting.folo/

Hutchinson, T. (1999, March 24). Senate passes motion to honor school violence victims. *Jonesboro Sun*, pp. 1B, 19B.

Imber-Black, E., & Roberts, J. (1992). *Rituals for our times: Celebrating, healing, and changing our lives and our relationships*. New York: HarperCollins.

Johnston, R. C. (1998, May 27). Hope in the mourning. *Education Week, 17*(37), 26-31.

Kessler, R. (1998, December/1999, January). Nourishing students in secular schools. *Educational Leadership (ASCD), 5*(4).

The KNJ Foundation. (1999, March 10). Available online: http://www.knj.org/main/html

Kushner, H. S. (1997). *When bad things happen to good people* (rev. ed.). New York: Avon.

Leimer, C. (1996, November 12). Death rites and memorials in a new era. *Tombstone Traveller's Guide*. Available online: http://www.uh.edu/~cleimer/new.html

Levine, K. (1998, June). How children grieve. *Parents*, pp. 133-137.

Lieberman, R. (1998, Fall). Schoolyard tragedies: Coping with the aftermath. *School Safety*, pp. 14-16.

Marans, S., & Schaefer, M. (1998). Community policing, schools, and mental health: The challenge of collaboration. In D. S. Elliott, B. A. Hamburg, & K. R. Williams (Eds.), *Violence in American schools* (pp. 312-347). New York: Cambridge University Press.

Maslow, A. H. (1943). A theory of human motivation. *Psychological Review, 50*, 370-396.

McLemore, D. (1998, March 28). Two victims of attack are laid to rest. *Dallas Morning News*, p. 1A.

McRee, L., & Bergeron, T. (1997, December 3). Paducah reflects on tragedy. *ABC Good Morning America*.

Mead, A. (1997, December 4). Caskets bear written farewells; funeral will take place Friday. *Knight-Ridder/Tribune News Service*. Available online: http://web2.searchbank.com/infotrac/session/7/649/305300w7/5!xrn_1

Murdock, M. (1987). *Spinning inward: Using guided imagery with children for learning, creativity & relaxation*. Boston: Shambhala.

Ortiz, J. (1997). *The Tao of music: Sound psychology*. New York: Samuel Weiser.

Paine, C. (1998a, November). Memorials: Guidelines for educators and communities. *NASP Communiqué, 27*(3), 25.

Paine, C. (1998b, November). Tragedy response and healing: Springfield unites. *NASP Communiqué, 27*(3), 16-17.

Pedersen, D., & Van Boven, S. (1997, December 15). Tragedy in a small place. *Newsweek*, pp. 30-31.

Poland, S., Pitcher, G., & Lazarus, P. (1995). Crisis intervention. In A. Thomas & J. Grimes (Eds.), *Best practices in school psychology—III* (pp. 445-459). Washington, DC: National Association of School Psychologists.

Ribbon of promise. (1998, September). *School Safety Update*, p. 7.

Safe Crossings. (1998, December 3). *Activities/exercises*. Available online: http://www.providence.org/safecrossings/documents/ac

School officials in Pearl, Miss., help community cope with tragedy. (1997, November 11). *School Board News, 17*(21), 4.

Skiba, K. M. (1998, March 27). Arkansas students get lesson in healing. *Milwaukee Journal Sentinel*. Available online: http://onwis.com/forums/shoot/0327ark.stm

Sleek, S. (1998, June). After the storm, children play out fears. *American Psychological Association's Monitor, 29*(6), 12.

Springfield graduation remains upbeat. (1998, June 7). *Longmont Daily Times-Call*, p. A5.

Stockton, B. (1998, November). Back to school in Jonesboro. *NASP Communiqué, 27*(3), 12.

Sutter Cancer Center. (1998, December 3). *The Children's Bereavement Art Group*. Available online: http://www.suttercancer.org/support/support/children/children.html

Williams, L. (1998, March 28). West Paducah relives horror of high school shootings: Jonesboro killings upset fragile healing. *St. Louis Post-Dispatch*, p. 22.

Wolfelt, A. (1998, November 30). Helping children understand cremation. *The Mourner's Corner*. Available online: http://www.centerforloss.com/mourners.htm

chapter **seven**

Addressing the Trauma

Crisis Effects and Grief

Determining the Degree of Trauma

The nature and severity of a school crisis will in part determine the effects of that crisis on the survivors and the community. Violence, for example, often has a more profound effect on people than other forms of crisis. As noted in Pitcher & Poland (1992, pp. 111-112), "... [C]rises or disasters associated with the actions of humans are more traumatic and difficult to recover from than those generated by natural events ... [and] aggression and deliberate maliciousness seem to strike the hardest into our psyche." And studies have shown that post-traumatic stress disorder (PTSD) is "... apparently more severe and longer lasting when the stressor is of 'human design' especially in cases of human individual violence" (Lazarus, 1996, p. 23). Obviously, crisis effects will be more widespread in your school community if an assailant fires upon your school and many are injured and killed than if one student is killed in a car accident.

The number and severity of injuries are not the only factors that will determine the degree of crisis effects for both individuals and your school community, however. Crises tend to bring up unresolved issues from the past, particularly those related to trauma and loss. In 1983 a bus carrying Jonesboro, Arkansas, students and teachers to a competition for vocational-technical students overturned en route, killing five teachers and four students, and injuring 29 others (Egerton, 1998). Any surviving school staff who were still in the Jonesboro school system in 1998 when five people were killed in the shooting at Westside Middle School likely had a heightened reaction to the crisis. Additional crises can cause people to remember previous crisis incidents. A crisis reaction can also be exacerbated by previous losses (whether similar in nature to the crisis event or not) and/or lack of support experienced after the earlier loss.

For Concerned People Elsewhere ...

Remembered Crisis Reactions

If a severe crisis has occurred at your school in the past, affected school community members may experience a stress reaction when they learn of a similar crisis elsewhere. They may find that vivid memories of your school's incident come flooding back even a decade later. When a severe school crisis elsewhere is publicized, be alert for long-term stress reactions at your school and take any steps necessary to provide emotional support to affected school community members (*see "Providing Counseling Services" later in this chapter*).

It is important to bear in mind, as well, that people who weren't directly involved in a crisis or were not close to the victim(s) can also be severely affected by the crisis. For example, if one of your students—who for the sake of this example we'll call Paul—commits suicide, you naturally would be concerned about Paul's best friend, who we'll call Ray. Let's say that Ray has everything else besides the loss of his friend going right in his life; he's a good athlete, has a supportive family, and excels in school. But another student, who we'll call Sarah, does not. Sarah might have hardly known Paul, but nothing is working well for her. She is depressed, struggling both academically and socially, and has made suicide threats in the past. While the first days after Paul's death will be rocky for Ray, in the long term Sarah, not Ray, might be the one who is going to experience the most difficulty (and who should be assessed for suicide risk).

Members of your school community may be more vulnerable to a severe crisis reaction than others if they have experienced any of the following in the past:

- Relocation
- Death of a family member or close friend
- A significant loss (e.g., loss of a job, loss of a cherished pet, a divorce, etc.)
- Poverty
- Being the victim of a crime
- Serious illness
- Suicidal ideation

The following questions can help you anticipate the degree of emotional trauma for your school community following a school crisis or the death of a school community member:

- Who was the person killed or injured? Was he or she a long-time member of the school community? Well known? Well liked?
- What happened to the person? If he or she died, was the death unexpected (e.g., murder, suicide, accident)? An unexpected and/or violent death will be more difficult to deal with than a death due to a serious illness, for example.
- Where did the death occur? A death that occurs on school grounds will be more traumatic.
- What other tragedies have impacted your school, district, or community recently? The current crisis will cause other unresolved issues and emotions to resurface.
- Who was the suspected perpetrator (if an act of violence occurred)? If the person believed to be responsible for the injury or death is also a member of your school community, the degree of emotionality will be much higher.

In addition to physical injury or death, crisis outcomes may include psychological debilitation for many. Yet crises, although terrible events, also present opportunities for personal growth and making changes. Because crises bring unresolved issues to light, dealing with crisis effects sometimes allows people to work on problems that were previously hidden. Confirmed Marlene Wong, head of District Crisis Teams for the Los Angeles Unified School District (personal communication, February 1998), "After the (catastrophic 1994) earthquake (in the Bay Area of California), it was like everything that was in these families' closets fell out," whether anger, child abuse, or substance abuse. (In fact, the American Red Cross estimates that child abuse, spousal abuse, and/or substance abuse increase 50-200% after a disaster or trauma.) The aftermath of a crisis is a good time for your school community members to get help for these problems; if they do not, coupled with the crisis effects, the problems will only intensify.

"What does not destroy me makes me stronger."

—Friedrich Nietzsche

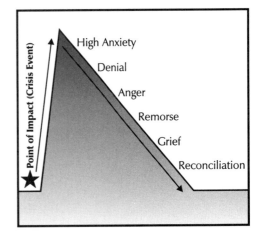

While each person has his or her own unique history of crisis and loss, a typical reaction to a crisis is illustrated by the figure following. The "road to reconciliation" may be a long one, doubling back on itself from time to time as you are flooded with emotions ranging through these stages and back and forth among them. The length of time it takes each person to navigate these stages will depend upon the severity of the crisis, the person's role in the crisis, his or her coping skills and support system, and his or her life experiences. There is no prescribed time after which an individual should "recover," nor is there one correct way to feel at any given time or stage. There are some emotions and behaviors common to many people after a crisis, however, and the following sections present such typical crisis reactions for both adults and youth as well as some information about the grieving process.

Adult Crisis Reactions

Adult reactions to a crisis often fall into the categories of panic and defeat. It is normal to have a lot of anxiety and to want to flee the scene. It is also common to feel that the world is a very unsafe place. Unresolved issues based on your life history may resurface at this time and add to the emotionality. Waves of emotion may flood your thoughts. According to the American Red Cross (1993), the following are typical signs of stress in adults after a crisis event.

Feelings

- Sadness
- Anger
- Guilt/self-reproach
- Anxiety
- Loneliness
- Fatigue
- Helplessness
- Shock
- Yearning

- Emancipation
- Relief
- Numbness
- Hopelessness
- Fear/panic
- Deprivation
- Diminishment
- Embarrassment/humiliation

Cognitions

- Disbelief
- Confusion
- Preoccupation

- Sense of presence
- Hallucinations (visual, auditory)

Physical sensations

- Hollowness in stomach
- Tightness in chest
- Tightness in throat
- Oversensitivity to noise
- Depersonalization

- Breathlessness/shortness of breath
- Weakness in muscles
- Lack of energy
- Dry mouth

Behaviors

- Sleep disturbances
- Appetite disturbances
- Absent-minded behavior
- Social withdrawal
- Dreams about the incident
- Avoidance of reminders of the incident

- Sighing
- Restless overactivity
- Crying
- Treasuring objects

According to the National Organization for Victim Assistance (NOVA), individuals usually "… exist in a normal state of equilibrium, or balance" that involves "everyday stress, both positive and negative…. [But] trauma throws people so far out of their range of equilibrium that it is difficult for them to restore a sense of balance in their life" (1994c).

Trauma is generally caused by "acute" stress, that is, stress caused by a "… sudden, arbitrary, often random event" (NOVA, 1994c). Examples include crime, violence, natural disasters, accidents, and acts of war. And as stated in NOVA (1994a), "The normal human response to trauma follows a … pattern called the crisis reaction. It occurs in all of us." Explained trauma therapist Dr. Peter Levine (1994, p. 50), "At the root of a traumatic reaction is the 280-million year old heritage that we share with nearly every crawling creature on earth—a heritage that resides in the area of the nervous system known as the reptilian brain. Primitive responses that originate in this portion of the brain help the organism protect itself against circumstances that are potentially damaging or dangerous to survival." During the crisis reaction, our physical response is based on our instincts and our emotional responses are heightened by our physical response, as detailed following (NOVA, 1994a):

Physical

1. Physical shock, disorientation, and numbness: "frozen fright"
2. "Fight or flight" reaction:
   - Adrenaline pumps through the body.
   - Body may relieve itself of excess materials, like ingested food.
   - One or more physical senses may become more acute while others "shut down."
   - Heart rate increases.
   - Hyperventilation, sweating, and so forth occur.
3. Exhaustion following the physical arousal of "fight or flight"

Emotional

- *Stage One:* Shock, disbelief, denial
- *Stage Two:* Cataclysm of emotions (anger/rage, fear/terror, sorrow/grief, confusion/frustration, self-blame/guilt)
- *Stage Three:* Reconstruction of equilibrium (an emotional roller-coaster that eventually becomes level (balanced)

Trauma is accompanied by many types of losses for survivors, including (NOVA, 1994d):

- Loss of control over their own life
- Loss of faith in their God and/or in other people
- Loss of a sense of fairness or justice
- Loss of personally significant property
- Loss of loved ones
- Loss of a sense of immortality or invulnerability
- Loss of a perceived future

"In their private hours, your parents will imagine you as a wife, a mother, an actress in the movies or at the village playhouse. For myself, I see you married—as my own daughter was married a year ago—in a church ceremony the antipode of the one you were the center of last week."

—Journalist Roger Rosenblatt (1999, p. 120), in an open letter to Rachel Scott, killed in the April 1999 school shooting at Columbine High School in Littleton, Colorado

---

Regressive behaviors are quite common in young people after a crisis. But children are not the only ones who may regress after a crisis. When experiencing trauma adults may find themselves regressing to "childhood," mentally and/or behaviorally (NOVA, 1994d), in such ways as:

- Singing/humming childhood songs
- Assuming a fetal position
- Calling a police officer or other authority figure "daddy" or "mommy" (or at least thinking of the person in that way)
- Feeling "little" and/or "weak"
- Wanting "mommy" or "daddy" to come take care of them
- Feeling like they did as a child when something went terribly wrong

Childhood/Adolescent Crisis Reactions

Children's responses to a crisis or tragedy will vary some by child and by the age of the child but typically will fall into four main areas:

1. Fear of the future
2. Academic regression
3. Behavioral regression
4. Nightmares, night terrors, and sleep disturbances

The typical crisis reactions can be broken down by age of the child, as follows (Pitcher & Poland, 1992, pp. 194-196):

Preschool (Ages 1-5)

- Thumb-sucking
- Bed-wetting
- Fear of the darkness
- Fear of animals
- Clinging to parents/caregivers
- Night terrors
- Loss of bladder/bowel control
- Constipation
- Speech difficulties (e.g., stammering)
- Loss or increase of appetite

Early Childhood (Ages 5-11)

- Irritability
- Whining
- Clinging
- Aggressive behavior at home or school
- Overt competition with younger siblings for parents' attention
- Night terrors, nightmares, fear of darkness
- School avoidance
- Withdrawal from peers
- Loss of interest and poor concentration in school

Preadolescence (Ages 11-14)

- Sleep disturbance
- Appetite disturbance
- Rebellion in the home
- Refusal to do chores
- School problems (e.g., fighting, withdrawal, loss of interest, attention-seeking behavior)
- Physical problems (e.g., headaches, vague aches and pains, skin eruptions, bowel problems, psychosomatic complaints)
- Loss of interest in peer social activities

Adolescence (Ages 14-18)

- Psychosomatic symptoms (e.g., rashes, bowel problems, headaches, asthma)
- Appetite and sleep disturbance
- Hypochondriasis (i.e., obsessive preoccupation with one's health, usually focusing on a particular symptom)
- Amenorrhea or dysmenorrhea (i.e., absence of or disrupted/painful menstruation, respectively)
- Agitation or decrease in energy level, apathy
- Decline in interest in the opposite sex

continued—

See "Anticipate Typical Childhood Responses to Crisis" in Chapter Eight for suggestions on how parents can help their children cope with these crisis effects.

See "Providing Counseling Services" later in this chapter for suggestions about how school mental health workers can help address these childhood reactions.

- Irresponsible and/or delinquent behavior
- Decline in emancipatory struggles over parental control
- Poor concentration

Young people sometimes express their emotions through "acting-out" behaviors (e.g., temper outbursts, being argumentative). If the crisis involved a death, for example, some youths may "… act out noisily and physically as a way of affirming that they are still alive" (District School Board, 1994b). Or they may behave in a clingy, dependent, and "immature" manner, including experiencing developmental setbacks. According to the American Red Cross (1993), the following are the most common signs of stress in a child or teen after a crisis:

- Crying
- Hyperactive or silly behavior
- Lack of emotional display
- Irritability
- Temper outbursts/tantrums
- Restlessness
- Misbehavior/acting-out behaviors
- Clinging to adults
- Unusual lack of maturity or overmaturity
- Being demanding
- Getting lost
- Changes in sleep/being afraid to go to bed by himself or herself
- Rambunctiousness
- Inactivity/lethargy
- Fear/worry
- Guilt
- Changes in appetite
- Changing his or her physical appearance

After a violent homicide, a child or teen may exhibit some or all of the following crisis effects (Zenere, 1998, p. 39):

- Concern that the person suffered
- Horror from repeatedly visualizing the crime in his or her mind
- Constant need to tell and retell the story of the crime
- Need to reenact the crime through play
- Desire to seek revenge against the murderer
- Yearning to join the loved one
- Questioning his or her belief in a God and an afterlife
- Desire to plan his or her own funeral (especially with teens) (*NOTE*: This is a strong warning sign of suicidal ideation, and the student should be followed up with.)
- Fear about dying
- Fear of a loved one dying
- Fear of being left alone
- School phobia
- Nightmares
- Behavioral regression
- Inability to concentrate
- Exhibiting very aggressive behaviors

After the school shooting near Jonesboro, Arkansas, for example, both parents and teachers saw these crisis effects in the children. As described in Lieberman (1998):

> *Many students suffered from post-traumatic stress symptoms. Children reported intrusive thoughts, recollections, and nightmares. Parents observed regressive behaviors, eating and sleeping irregularities, and myriad complaints of aches and pains. Responses varied from child to child; one child cowered on the arm of a friend, another cried for her lost friend and a recently deceased grandmother, while other children appeared to be angry, and some simply relieved their tensions in silliness. Their initial responses of fear and anger evolved across a complex range of emotions that often resulted in expressions of guilt, shame, or grief* (p. 14).

A sign that a young child has been traumatized is "repetitive play." Explained trauma therapist Dr. Peter Levine (1994), "Compulsive, repetitive mannerisms—such as repeatedly zooming a toy car into a doll—are an almost sure sign of an unresolved reaction to a traumatic event. (The activity may or may not be a literal replay of the trauma)" (pp. 50-51). This type of play can help children to make sense of what has happened, but it also "… illustrate[s] the ongoing and often unrecognized emotional struggles children experience after witnessing … death and destruction" (Sleek, 1998, p. 12).

Childhood Post-Traumatic Stress Disorder

A severe crisis reaction, and/or one that appears weeks, months, or even years after the crisis, might be an indication of childhood post-traumatic stress disorder (PTSD). In discussing childhood trauma, therapist Dr. Peter Levine commented, "After working for more than 20 years with people suffering from trauma, I can safely say that at least 75% of my clients have traumatic symptoms that remained dormant for a significant period of time before surfacing. For most people, the interval between the event and the onset of symptoms is between six and 18 months; for others, the latency period lasts for years or even decades" (Levine, 1994, p. 49).

According to the American Psychological Association (cited in Lazarus, 1996), a diagnosis of PTSD in children requires that:

> *… [T]he child has been exposed to a traumatic event in which both of the following were present: (1) the person experienced, witnessed, or was confronted with an event or events that involved actual or threatened death or serious injury or a threat to the physical integrity of self or others; (2) the person's response involved intense fear, helplessness, or horror. In children this may be expressed instead by disorganized or agitated behavior* (p. 23).

The main symptoms of childhood PTSD are as follows (La Greca, Vernberg, Silverman, Vogel, & Prinstein, cited in Lazarus, 1996, p. 23):

- Reexperiencing the trauma during play, dreams, or flashbacks. For example, a child may:
  - Repeatedly act out what happened during the trauma when playing with toys.
  - Have distressing dreams about the trauma.
  - Be distressed when exposed to events that resemble the trauma or at the anniversary of the trauma.
  - Act or feel as if the trauma is happening again.
- Avoidance of reminders of the trauma or general numbness to all emotional topics. For example, a child may:
  - Avoid all activities that remind him or her of the trauma.
  - Be unable to remember parts of the trauma.
  - Withdraw from other people.
  - Have difficulty feeling positive emotions.
- Increased "arousal" symptoms. For example, a child may:
  - Have difficulty falling or staying asleep.
  - Be irritable.
  - Have difficulty concentrating.
  - Startle more easily.

According to researchers (Davidson & Foa; Van der Kolt, cited in Lazarus, 1996, p. 23), the most critical determinants in developing PTSD are: "(1) perceived life threat, (2) the potential for violence, (3) the experience of extreme fear, and (4) a sense of helplessness." One researcher (Pynoos, cited in Lazarus, 1996) found that sex, age, and ethnicity were not important in determining who would develop PTSD. Rather, Pynoos stated, "... the development of PTSD has been most related to degree of exposure" (p. 23).

There are, however, some psychological predictors that put children at risk for PTSD (La Greca et al., cited in Lazarus, 1996, p. 24). These include:

- Ineffective ways of coping with stress (e.g., denial, passivity, avoidance)
- Insufficient or diminished social support (i.e., from family, friends, and teachers)
- Other stressful events happening after the crisis (e.g., parents separating or divorcing, parent losing a business or job)

Immediate Trauma Recovery

According to the National Organization for Victim Assistance (NOVA, 1994b), "Many people live through a trauma and are able to reconstruct their lives without outside help. [However] most people find some type of benign outside intervention useful in dealing with trauma" (*see "Providing Counseling Services" later in this chapter*).

A number of factors can affect recovery from immediate trauma. As listed in NOVA (1994b), these include:

- The severity of the immediate crisis reaction
- The victim/survivor's ability to understand what has happened
- The stability of victim/survivor's equilibrium after the crisis event
- A supportive environment
- Validation of the experience

According to NOVA (1994b), recovery issues for survivors include:

- Assuming some control of the event in one's mind.
- Coming to an understanding of the crisis event and, as necessary, redefining values (e.g., redefining one's life's priorities).
- Reestablishing a new equilibrium/life.
- Reestablishing trust.
- Reestablishing a future/new life.
- Reestablishing meaning (e.g., investing in new routines, redefining one's life purpose).

> "Not all children who have experienced a traumatic event are in immediate need of therapy."
>
> (Lazarus, 1996, p. 25)

The Grieving Process

Grief is the state of "keen mental suffering over affliction or loss" and of "sharp sorrow," also described as anguish, woe, and misery (*Webster's*, 1996, p. 840). It is most commonly associated with loss due to death. According to Dr. Elisabeth Kübler-Ross (1997), there are five classic stages of grief:

- *First Stage*—Denial
- *Second Stage*—Bargaining
- *Third Stage*—Anger
- *Fourth Stage*—Depression
- *Fifth Stage*—Acceptance

Although in various cultures and periods of history a "mourning period" (often of a year) was prescribed following the death of a loved one, people take different amounts of time to work through the grief stages. Additionally, some people might work through the first few stages relatively quickly but then revisit an earlier stage and/or get "stuck" in one of the stages. Others might achieve acceptance but then become angry or depressed once again after a "triggering" event (e.g., the year anniversary

> "I thought that after a year we'd find some kind of magical cure, and that life would be like it was before Britthney died," said the mother of one of the girls killed in the school shooting near Jonesboro, Arkansas. "But that is not happening. There is no magical cure. Sometimes I get angry.... I just get angry. I look at people with their children and I think, 'They have their children. Why don't I have mine?'"
>
> (Ashcraft, 1999, p. 15A)

of the crisis event or death). Explained Dr. Kübler-Ross (1997), "People in mourning have to come to grips with death before they can live again. Mourning can go on for years and years. It doesn't end after a year: that's a false fantasy. It usually ends when people realize that they can live again, that they can concentrate their energies on their lives as a whole, and not on their hurt, and guilt, and pain."

Like crisis reactions, the length and severity of a grieving period will be different for different people. Factors influencing the intensity of a person's grief include the relationship to the deceased; the age of the deceased; whether the death was anticipated (i.e., after a long illness) or unexpected; whether the death was violent; previous trauma or losses experienced by the survivor; the extent of his or her support system (e.g., caring family, wholesome relationships); his or her religious beliefs; and his or her overall equilibrium and coping skills ("Grief," 1998).

Children also grieve, although they may do so differently than adults, depending upon their age and maturity. As noted in "Children and Death" (1998), "... children can and do handle death well—often better than the adults around them. Like adults, children need to come to terms with death and the grief that accompanies it." Children's understanding of death (or lack thereof) is determined in large part by their age and corresponding cognitive development. In general, their understanding of death has been found to be as follows ("Children and Death," 1998; Flatter, Herzog, Tyson, & Ross, 1998; Levine, 1998):

> "Pain is the most individualized thing on earth. It is true that it is the great common bond as well, but that realization only comes when it is over. To suffer is to be alone. To watch another suffer is to know the barrier that shuts each of us away by himself. Only individuals can suffer."
>
> —Edith Hamilton ("Journey of Hearts," 1998)

Approximate Age	Understanding
1 to 3 Years	Most concerned with how a death will affect their daily routine and needs.
	Use "magical thinking," believing something they did caused the death or that they can bring the deceased back.
	Cannot differentiate between death and long-term absence.
4 to 5/6 Years	Do not view death as permanent (confusion compounded by cartoons, movies, fairy tales, video games, etc., in which characters die and later are revived).

Cannot grieve as adults do, as children of this age do not understand permanence (concepts of past, present, and future do not begin to make sense until around age 5).

Have verbal ability, but take things very literally. Hence, parents should avoid using death analogies such as "going on a trip" or "going to sleep," since they could make children afraid to go on a trip or to sleep by themselves.

6/7 to 8 Years   Begin to understand that death is permanent but believe it can happen only to the elderly.

If a young person dies, may demand to know why.

8 to 10 Years   Begin to understand that death is part of the natural order and that people of all ages die for many reasons.

Understand that death could happen to them.

6/7 to 11 Years   Children's growing cognitive abilities help them to think more realistically and understand the finality of death.

May seek comfort in religious/spiritual beliefs and/or explore the scientific aspects of death.

Capable of grief (as defined by adults).

11 and Older   Capable of understanding that death results when internal biological processes shut down.

Adolescents   Should fully understand the finality of death by about age 13, but many do not (again perhaps a result of media in which characters die and are miraculously revived). Adults should help to ground teenagers in the facts.

The way in which adults at the school discuss a death that affects the school community with and around the students is very important. No matter the students' age, you must answer their questions honestly. However, provide as few details as are necessary to satisfy their curiosity, and provide no gory ones that may frighten them. With young students, carefully consider how they may interpret your words. For example, saying someone died because "God loved him or her so much and wanted him or her in heaven" may make young students fearful of

"[Returning to school after a shooting had occurred there] was unlike anything I've ever felt before. I've been around death before in my life but nothing like this ... nothing that's really gotten down to the very core of me and made me want to break down and cry right there."

—Student at Thurston High School, Springfield, Oregon (Paine, 1998, p. 16)

being loved by God. Saying that someone is "happier in heaven" may make a young child think the deceased is happier in heaven because of something the child did here on earth (i.e., "magical thinking"). As explained in Levine (1998), "It's just a short leap [for a young child] to feelings of guilt and responsibility ..." (p. 134). Be aware that children of many ages (as well as adults, for that matter) might also experience a fear of "spirits" and "ghosts" associated with the death (NOVA, 1997).

For Concerned People Elsewhere ...

Grieving

Bear in mind that one does not need to love or even know another person to grieve his or her death. Many people experience an element of grief after the death of a favorite celebrity (e.g., Princess Diana). The nation may grieve as a whole after the death of a respected leader, such as Dr. Martin Luther King, Jr. Often, in such cases, people feel a loss that transcends the characteristics of the person who has died. Dr. King's death, for example, highlighted the ongoing injustice of racial inequity and prejudice. And a student who is gunned down at school may become symbolic of "any child" for communities across the country, with his or her death representing a loss of innocence, a violation of the sense of security felt about our nation's schools, and the pervasiveness of senseless violence. Students may grieve the death because they relate to the victim as a peer. Parents and school staff may react emotionally to the news because they can imagine such an incident happening to their child or student.

Such "grief from a distance" is sometimes difficult for those who are not so affected to understand and accept. Family members, colleagues, and peers may wonder what is "wrong with" someone who feels grief after the death of someone he or she didn't know and, until the crisis incident, had not heard of. Even the person who is experiencing the crisis reaction may not entirely understand his or her response; he or she may just feel depressed or hopeless for a time.

If such is the case for you and/or others in your school or community, provide permission for a range of emotions. Be gentle with yourself and others. Depending upon the intensity of the crisis reaction and on how many people are experiencing it, it may be necessary to formally address the crisis effects. For example, counseling services may be needed within the school (*see "Providing Counseling Services" later in this chapter*). You may want to hold some sort of community memorial service (*see "The Family/Community Meeting" in Chapter Two*) or to take some action individually to make yourself feel better, such as speaking with your clergy member, sending a sympathy card, or contributing to a memorial fund. (*See "Memorializing Victims" in Chapter Six for additional ideas.*) Most important, do not belittle yourself or others for feeling such grief: These feelings are a reflection of our shared humanity.

Family Members of the Deceased

As noted in "Grief: A Time to Heal" (1998), published by the National Funeral Directors Association, when someone close to you has died and "… you struggle to accept this difficult loss, you may find yourself consumed by pain, fear, and grief. Grief is a natural response to losing someone who was important to you. Grief hurts, but it is necessary. When a death tears your world apart, grieving is the process that helps put it back together." If it is your child who has died, "… you will likely experience several common reactions of bereavement [*see "Adult Crisis Reactions" and "The Grieving Process" previously in this chapter*], but to a greater degree than normal" ("Will I Ever Stop Hurting?" 1998).

There may be no greater pain in this world than losing your child, no matter what his or her age is. Wrote Dr. Marilyn Gootman (1998), "Kids are not supposed to die. It's against all the rules of nature. It's not right. It's not fair. It shouldn't ever happen." Psychologists say this is just "… one of many reasons why the death of a child is possibly the most difficult loss of them all to accept" ("Will I Ever Stop Hurting?" 1998).

> "I always believed that if one of my children died, I'd go crazy. But I've since learned that the pain is so great the mind absorbs it in little pieces. Maybe that's God's way of helping us cope."
>
> —Suzann Wilson, mother of Britthney Varner, 11 (killed at Westside Middle School near Jonesboro, Arkansas) (Casey, 1999, p. 11)

If your loved one has died in a school crisis, it is important that you recognize that the powerful emotions you are feeling and the "crazy" thoughts you may be having are indeed normal. You also need to know what you can do to help yourself and your family members survive this tragedy and where you can turn for assistance. The following are suggestions in each of these areas ("Grief," 1998; Overbeck & Overbeck, 1995; "Will I Ever Stop Hurting?" 1998; Wolfelt, 1998).

What you may be feeling/experiencing

Grief is a very individual process, just as each relationship between any two people is unique. There is no set time for grieving to end, and there is no one correct way to feel at any given time. No one will grieve exactly like you do, but there are some reactions that are common for many. You may feel or experience:

- Shock and denial. You may not accept at first that your loved one is actually dead.

- Depressed. Even if you are usually a caring person, you may find that right now you don't care about anything or anyone—including yourself and your other family members.

- Obsessive thoughts about the circumstances of your loved one's death. You may torture yourself by recreating the scene over and over in your mind.

- Dreams and/or nightmares about your loved one.
- Thinking you see your loved one or hear his or her voice.
- Weight loss, hair loss (or graying).
- Shortness of breath.
- Difficulty getting to sleep or staying asleep.
- Irritability.
- Extreme emotionality.
- Listlessness/lack of motivation to function in your daily life.
- Numbness. "You may feel like a spectator watching what's going on," said Dr. Earl Grollman, noted author of books on death and grief. "This response is nature's way of protecting you, of insulating you from what is happening" ("Grief," 1998).
- Overwhelmed or out of control.
- Lonely.
- Obsessive "if only" thoughts (e.g., "If only I hadn't sent him or her to school that day," "If only I had been there," "If only I had said good-bye.").
- Altered feelings toward your spouse (if it was your child who has died). Men and women often grieve differently, causing communication problems.
- Sexual dysfunction (if it was your child who has died). As noted in "Will I Ever Stop Hurting?" (1998), "One spouse may want to feel intimacy, but the other may not want the closeness, because letting down the emotional barrier means feeling the pain. Sexual problems can last up to two years or longer after a child's death."
- Helpless and childlike.
- Confused and panicky or frightened.
- Preoccupation with your loved one. You may think of him or her constantly.
- "Secondary losses" (e.g., no longer being a parent or a spouse).
- Stigmatized (if the death was a suicide).
- Anger. You may feel extreme amounts of anger, at, for example:
  - The suspected perpetrator (if the death resulted from an act of violence).
  - The school for not protecting your loved one and/or not being able to prevent the crisis.
  - The doctors, nurses, paramedics, and/or police who couldn't save your loved one.
  - The funeral director.

- God.
- Your deceased loved one for leaving you.
- Your deceased loved one for doing something to cause his or her death (if the death was the result of an accident).
- Yourself.
- The media (for the way in which they covered the story of your loved one's death).

- Guilt. You may feel extreme amounts of guilt about, for example:
  - Being alive when your loved one is not.
  - Feeling anger toward your loved one who has died.
  - Not being present when your loved one died.
  - Not saying good-bye to your loved one.
  - An argument you had with your loved one, either recently or in the past.
  - Disciplining your child (if it was your child who died). As noted in "Will I Ever Stop Hurting?" (1998), "You may feel guilty for not [having been] 'better' to your child."
  - Not having been able to prevent your loved one's death.
  - Not being responsive to or capable for your other family members during your time of grieving.

Ways to help yourself/your family members cope

- Attend the funeral. Doing so will help you accept the reality of the death.

- Express your grief openly. As noted in Wolfelt (1998), "Ignoring your grief won't make it go away; talking about it often makes you feel better."

> "We are healed of a suffering only by experiencing it to the full."
>
> —Marcel Proust

- Take time to cry, and don't be afraid to show your tears to other mourners and/or your family members.

- "Don't try to 'protect' other family members by hiding your sadness …" ("Grief," 1998).

- Express any anger you may be feeling.

- Find caring friends or family members who will listen to your pain without judging you.

- Help your family members and friends to help you by telling them what you need and that it is all right for them to talk to you about your deceased loved one.

- "Avoid people who are critical or who try to steal your grief from you. You have a right to express your grief; no one has the right to take it away" (Wolfelt, 1998).

- Don't be afraid to lean on others right now and to ask for professional help if you need it.

- Avoid making any major decisions or big changes in your life.

- Lighten your schedule and workload while grieving.

- Try to eat, and rest as much as possible.

- Exercise. Even brief walks will help alleviate your depression and "… provide an outlet for your emotional energy" ("Grief," 1998).

- Pray, if you are a religious person.

- Write in a journal, draw, or find other ways to express your sad feelings.

- Give yourself and others permission for a range of emotions. Everyone grieves differently, and there is no one correct way to feel at any given time.

- Be gentle with yourself and others.

- Allow yourself to laugh if you find something positive to laugh about. Laughter is a natural tension reliever for the body. Remember, you are not expected to be sad every minute of every day.

- Anticipate a long-term grieving process. Your grief reaction may be heightened, for example, on anniversaries of the death, during the trial (if applicable), on the birthday of your deceased loved one, and on any other family holidays. (*See "Long-Term Effects" in Chapter Twelve for more information.*)

- Recognize that your grief will not last forever. Although your love for your deceased family member will always continue, you will not always grieve the loss this intensely.

"The mind has a dumb sense of vast loss—that is all. It will take mind and memory months and probably years to gather the details and thus learn and know the whole extent of the loss."

—Mark Twain

Where to turn for assistance

- A trusted friend or family member.

- Your clergy member (if applicable).

- The school's mental health workers.

- A private counselor, particularly one specializing in grief and loss. (Family counseling might also be helpful.)

- The funeral director.

- Your county's victims' advocate (generally reached through the prosecutor's office). He or she can help you navigate the legal process and provide other services as well.

- Any local bereavement support group.

- A local chapter of a national self-help group, such as:
  - Parents of Murdered Children (POMC)—(513) 721-5683
  - Families and Friends of Missing Persons and Violent Crime Victims—(206) 362-1081 or (800) 346-7555
  - The Compassionate Friend, Inc.—(630) 990-0010 (supports parents who have lost a child to any type of death)
  - They Help Each Other Spiritually (THEOS)—(412) 471-7779 (for individuals whose spouse has died by any cause)
  - Mothers Against Drunk Driving (MADD)—(214) 744-6233 (for survivors of people killed in vehicular accidents caused by drunk driving)
  - Violence Project of the National Gay Task Force—(212) 714-1141 (for survivors of gay or lesbian victims of murder)

After the loss of a loved one, it is natural to feel so sad that you wonder how you will survive the anguish. It is normal to wish you would die as well, in order to escape the pain. It is normal to feel guilty that you are alive when your loved one has died. However, it is not okay to be thinking about harming yourself in any way. *If you are having any concrete thoughts about, or making plans for, your own death, please get help immediately.* Call—at any time of the day or night—a trusted family member or friend, your clergy member (if applicable), your counselor (if applicable), your local hospital, 911 (or 0, if that is the emergency number in your area), any local crisis hotline, or even the National Adolescent Runaway and Suicide Hot-Line toll-free at 1-800-621-4000. (It doesn't matter if you're an adult—call anyway.) This number is staffed 24 hours per day, and the crisis responders will be able to refer you to a helping agency in your state.

> "Grief comes in unexpected surges.… Mysterious cues that set off a reminder of grief. It comes crashing like a wave, sweeping me in its crest, twisting me inside and out. Then recedes, leaving me broken. Oh, Mama, I don't want to eat, to walk, to get out of bed. Reading, working, cooking, listening, mothering … nothing matters. I do not want to be distracted from my grief. I wouldn't mind dying. I wouldn't mind at all."
>
> —Toby Talbert ("Journey of Hearts," 1998)

Assisting surviving children

As noted in Overbeck and Overbeck (1995), "It is said that when a child's brother or sister dies, actually three people are lost: the sibling and both parents. The sibling also loses a friend, playmate, confidant, role model, and lifelong companion. For the parents, the loss of a child is often so traumatic that they have little left to give the surviving children." The following are some suggestions for helping your surviving children cope with the death in your family, whether the deceased was a sibling, parent, or other family member:

- Allow them to attend the visitation or funeral, but don't force them to go. (See "Assist Your Child in Understanding Death and Funerals" in Chapter Eight for guidelines on age-appropriate attendance.)

- Prepare them for what will happen at the visitation or funeral beforehand. You might also designate a trusted family friend to accompany them if they feel the need to leave the service.
- Answer their questions about the death honestly. (*See "Assist Your Child in Understanding Death and Funerals" in Chapter Eight for information about children's developmental understanding of death.*)
- Give them permission to grieve by letting them see you grieve.
- Do not become angry with them if they do not grieve in ways you consider appropriate. For example, they may greet the news of a loved one's death with nervous laughter. Or they may feign indifference (which is a way of distancing themselves from the painful event) and then express their grief later by "acting out" or regressing behaviorally.
- Allow them to play and laugh. Make sure they understand that they are not expected to be sad every minute of every day and that they have the right to have their needs (e.g., for attention) met, even after a death.
- Encourage them to resume their normal activities when they feel ready to do so.

"Weeping is the most human and universal of all relief measures."

—Dr. Karl Menninger ("Journey of Hearts," 1998)

- Do not hide your tears from your children, and allow them to cry. Don't tell them to "be brave" and "not cry" ("Children and Death," 1998).
- Talk to them about the death, and encourage them to talk about their grief.
- As noted in "Children and Death" (1998), "Even if your child is too young to talk about the death, you can still communicate your emotions. Hugging and touching will comfort young children who can sense the anguish in the family, even if they don't understand what has happened. Children surrounded by sadness need to be assured that they are loved."
- Reassure them that they will not die from the same cause or in the same way.
- Reassure them that you will not die (in the immediate future).
- Reassure them that they had nothing to do with the death. Young children often use "magical thinking," and they believe that their thoughts/actions caused the death or that the death is a punishment for or rejection of them.
- Reassure them that you love and want them. Make sure they know that they will not be expected to replace a deceased sibling.
- Reassure your children that their "… relationship to the deceased hasn't ended—only changed" ("Children and Death," 1998). Allow them to talk about the deceased family member, keep photos of him or her displayed, and so forth.

- Give them extra physical reassurance (e.g., hugs and kisses, hand holding).
- Maintain regular family routines to the extent possible.

Issues for surviving grandparents

- As expressed in "Will I Ever Stop Hurting?" (1998), "Grandparents have the double burden of grieving for their grandchild and seeing their son or daughter suffer pain."
- Grandparents can help their son or daughter by helping in his or her household (e.g., babysitting, preparing meals).
- Grandparents can listen empathetically to their son or daughter.
- Grandparents should not take over the funeral arrangements. As noted in "Will I Ever Stop Hurting?" (1998), "… that is something [their] child, as the bereaved parent, must undertake as one step in working through his or her own grief."
- Grandparents should not deny their own grief even though they are supporting their son or daughter ("Will I Ever Stop Hurting?" 1998).

Feelings of Guilt

Feelings of guilt are quite common for people of all ages after a crisis or death. Often these feelings are irrational (i.e., the survivors had nothing to do with the crisis or could have done nothing better or differently than they did, but they believe otherwise). At other times, crisis survivors do have valid reasons to feel guilty (e.g., they had forewarning of the crisis event but didn't take it seriously or didn't act). In either case, guilt is not a productive emotion in which to become entrenched. Guilt does nothing to change the outcome of the tragedy and interferes with the healing of survivors. Counseling assistance from a trained mental health worker is generally needed to resolve such debilitating feelings.

Feelings of guilt after a crisis or death assume many forms, including the following:

- "Survivor's guilt"

  Sometimes survivors feel guilty that they are alive when the deceased is not. "Many survivors feel they should have died instead of the person(s) who did," explained the National Organization for Victim Assistance (NOVA, 1997, p. 4-3). NOVA continued, "Often survivors feel their survival was a mistake and that the other people who died should have lived. Some survivors feel that there is a certain amount of suffering and loss allocated to any particular

"Survivor's guilt," said Westside Middle School teacher Lynette Thetford, who was shot in the abdomen during the attack on the school near Jonesboro, Arkansas, "still causes her to question why she got to live and others did not. 'I had always heard of survivor's guilt' [Thetford said,] 'but I didn't know it was as strong as it is.'"

(Watkins, 1999, p. 20A)

community and that if they had died or been injured, someone else could have been spared."

- Confusion about causality

  Young students often think that their thoughts or behavior caused the event (e.g., "I was mad at my brother so he was killed," "If I had been good, Mommy wouldn't have died," "I dreamed the shuttle was going to blow up; it's my fault!" etc.).

- Feeling you should have done more

  After the 1992 suicide of a Houston high school student, another student told a school psychologist there, "You know, I should have called her (the suicide victim) last night. I feel so guilty that I didn't call her. I could have prevented her death." The school psychologist assumed the boy knew something about the student's suicidal plans and asked, "Did you call her a lot?" The boy replied, "No. I've never called her in my life." The school psychologist then asked, "Did you have her phone number?" "No, but I still should have called her," asserted the student.

  Following a 1985 school shooting at a Houston, Texas, high school, during which "students dove under tables and fled from every exit," many students "... later expressed remorse that they had behaved in what they subsequently viewed as a cowardly manner. Some students felt they should have grabbed the gun and prevented the shootings. A few students felt they should have somehow read [the student perpetrator's] mind and known what he was planning" (Pitcher & Poland, 1992, p. 128).

  After the school shooting at Heath High School in West Paducah, Kentucky, teachers at the elementary school the student perpetrator had previously attended expressed feelings of dismay that they somehow should have known, that they could have somehow discovered the student's violent potential when he was a student there.

  After the same school shooting, student Ben Strong, who stood his ground to the shooter and convinced him to eventually put down the gun, told his father, "I just feel guilty. I didn't respond soon enough" (McRee & Bergeron, 1997). (Strong had not taken seriously the shooter's earlier warning to him.)

  Dr. Warren Skaug, the pediatrician of one of the student perpetrators of the school shooting near Jonesboro, Arkansas, said: "I don't feel like I am totally absolved of guilt. With regard to ferreting out trouble in the family, there may have been more ... that we could have known. Yes, we looked that chart over with care, but if you look in retrospect, you wished you'd asked more questions sometimes" (Associated Press, 1998b).

A few minutes before the shooting began on the grounds of Westside Middle School near Jonesboro, Arkansas, one of teacher Lynette Thetford's students reported that she had seen Drew Golden, one of the student perpetrators, pull the fire alarm that lured students and staff outside. As Thetford walked out of the school building, she looked to see if Golden had gone between her classroom wing and another wing that was under construction. Thetford blames herself for not looking toward the trees—where the two snipers lay in wait—as she exited. "I was the first one out," she said. "I took my little grade book and walked right out there. In a way, I have felt like I led them all to their death" (Watkins, 1999, p. 20A). In hindsight, looking into the trees seems to Thetford like a prudent action, but no reasonable person would expect shots to be fired during a school's fire drill evacuation procedure.

After a 1997 school shooting in Bethel, Alaska, a friend of the shooter, "overcome with guilt," tried to commit suicide. "I felt betrayed by Evan (the student perpetrator) and I felt some guilt that I should have stopped it," he said. "I felt as if I had been shot myself when I talked about Evan. It was like he was dead. I felt like I had lost a brother" (Fainaru, 1998, p. A1).

- Guilt that you were less traumatized

After the school shooting in West Paducah, Kentucky, some of the staff members expressed feeling badly because they had not experienced as much of the trauma as their colleagues. "I should have done more. I just stayed with my class," said a few teachers who were in other parts of the building at the time. (They felt badly even though they did the correct thing by keeping their students safe in their classrooms.)

After the school shooting near Jonesboro, Arkansas, the mother of a third grade boy told reporters, "He was afraid to go to sleep. He felt guilty 'cause he was able to go to sleep" (Associated Press, 1998a).

- Guilt about going on with life

When students' friends die, the students may feel that they are being disloyal if they still have fun or when they make new friends. Adults, explained Dr. Marilyn Gootman (1998), "… can explain that being friendly with others is the ultimate tribute to their friend—because the deceased friend taught them how important friends are. We also can let them know they have a right and a responsibility to enjoy life, that being sad all the time will not help them or their friend."

- Guilt about previous conflicts with, and negative thoughts about, the deceased (Overbeck & Overbeck, 1995).

- Guilt for feeling some relief if the death came after a long illness or extreme suffering (Overbeck & Overbeck, 1995).

After a Suicide

When the death is a suicide, survivors will experience all of the expected grief reactions as well as some troubling mixed feelings. As explained in NOVA (1997):

> ... [S]uicide causes particularly complex reactions in the surviving loved ones. Grief is often accompanied by a sense of betrayal, guilt, and misunderstandings. For some survivors the following way of viewing death by suicide is helpful. Suicide may be thought of as a homicide in which the perpetrator is also the victim. The survivors can then grieve and remember with love the victim while at the same time feel outrage and anger at the perpetrator (p. 4-24).

Providing Counseling Services

See "Injury/Death Notification" in Chapter One for guidelines and some scripted phrases for delivering injury/death notifications on the telephone, in person at school, and at the hospital.

It is beyond the scope of this book to detail exactly how to work with students, their families, and the school staff after a school crisis. Nor do we need to provide this comprehensive information, as your school and/or district's mental health staff (i.e., school psychologists, counselors, and perhaps crisis response team members) have specialized training in the pertinent issues. We recommend that school administrators follow their advice about providing counseling services after a school crisis. (*NOTE*: If for some reason the mental health staff supporting your school do not have this training and/or are spread too thin to address your school's needs after a severe school crisis, we encourage you to request outside assistance as soon as possible. *See "Help to Request" in Chapter Four.*) Having said that, the following are some of the most important points regarding counseling after a school crisis for review by the Counseling Liaison and other members of your school's mental health staff:

- Assist in getting everyone back to their classrooms—where they will be safe and accounted for—as soon as you can after the crisis incident.

- After a severe crisis, cancel all scheduled appointments and counseling activities not related to the crisis to devote all your resources to the crisis response (District School Board, 1994a).

- Target the following five groups for counseling assistance first: (1) those who were injured in the crisis event, (2) those who witnessed the event in close proximity, (3) those emotionally close to the victims of the crisis (e.g., siblings, close friends), (4) those known to be at risk or to have suffered a recent loss, and (5) those known to have had a previous suicide attempt.

- These at-risk students might request counseling services of their own accord, or their teachers may refer them. However, list and locate these students and ensure that they receive counseling support. This support may include pulling them out of class shortly after the crisis so that counselors can speak with them individually.

- Most of these students will welcome the opportunity to talk about their crisis reactions. However, you might utilize artwork, language arts activities, and/or music with those who do not open up to you (*see "Modifying the Curriculum" in Chapter Six for specific suggestions*). The day after your first attempt, ask them again if they would like to talk, and continue to stress your availability for discussion and emotional support.

- Dispense with the requirement for parental permission prior to providing counseling services in the midst of a crisis and in its aftermath. Parents will be grateful that you provided "emotional first aid" to their children during the crisis.

- Communicate closely by phone with the parents of affected students as soon after the crisis as is possible. Review with them the most common childhood reactions to crisis (*see "Childhood/Adolescent Crisis Reactions" previously in this chapter*) and what parents can do at home to assist their children (*see "Helping Your Child Cope" in Chapter Eight for suggestions*). Ask the parents how they think their children are recovering from their crisis effects and about any specific concerns they have.

- Lead processing sessions for both your students and the school staff. The entire staff can meet together; student discussions should take place at the classroom level. (*See "How Do You Process?" in Chapter Five for instructions.*)

See "Suicide Postvention" in Chapter Eleven for guidelines to follow if the death was a suicide.

- During processing sessions, be alert for any individuals who are experiencing a severe crisis response and might benefit from individualized assistance. Do not make such recommendations in the group setting; rather, speak with those individuals after the processing sessions. Refer such individuals to your school's mental health staff, your crisis response team, or any outside crisis response team assisting your school, or make an outside referral.

- Follow the schedule of the deceased, as there will likely be extreme emotionality in these classes. Lead processing sessions (*see Chapter Five, "Processing the Crisis"*) in these classes, and provide emotional support to grieving school community members.

- Review the daily absentee lists to identify all the students who are absent, particularly those at-risk (District School Board, 1994a). Follow up with these students and, if necessary, their families.

- Proactively reach out to all those who may need your assistance after a crisis. Counselors should be in classrooms (as needed), the hallways and common areas, and on the school buses.
- After a crisis keep your school building open into the evening and during other times when it would normally be closed (i.e., over the weekend, on holidays) with counseling staff available to speak with those who come to the school seeking assistance.
- Communicate with the counselors at other area schools so that they can provide assistance to the siblings of victims and suspected student perpetrator(s). Also contact the guidance staff at "feeder" schools that victims or suspected student perpetrator(s) recently attended (District School Board, 1994a).
- Pair a counselor with each clergy member (if any) assisting your school during the crisis response.
- Provide all volunteers with guidelines for assisting students, their families, and staff (*see "General Points When Using Outside Help" in Chapter Four*). Ask volunteers to record the names of all those they work with and their general impressions and concerns.
- Have a counselor available to assist those visiting the crime scene/crisis location.
- Have counseling staff available to assist families after the family/community meeting(s) (*see Chapter Two*).
- After a minor or moderately severe crisis, your school's teaching staff will likely be able to assist up to 95% of the students in the classroom setting. Ask them to refer any students in obvious distress for school-based counseling services.
- Another student should escort these distressed students to the counseling area (District School Board, 1994a).
- Teachers should sign out students leaving class for counseling support and utilize special counseling passes for this purpose (District School Board, 1994a).
- Set up areas for both individual and group counseling, and clearly mark these areas with signs (District School Board, 1994a).
- Track the names (and total number) of students utilizing the counseling services at school. Review these student contacts during your staff and/or crisis team meetings (District School Board, 1994a).
- Designate a "friend's room" where students can go to talk to and support one another. A counselor should be available in this room for assistance if requested (District School Board, 1994a).

- Be available to consult with and counsel staff regarding their own crisis reactions as well as any concerns they may have about their role in the crisis response or their students' recovery (District School Board, 1994a).

- Members of your school's counseling staff should attend any funerals to offer assistance to any students not accompanied by their parents.

- Counseling services should be provided at school the day of and the day after any memorial service, since there is usually a heightened crisis reaction at these times (District School Board, 1994a).

- Assist students with appropriate memorializing activities (*see "Memorializing Victims" in Chapter Six for guidelines*). Note, however, that activities that are permanent, costly, highly ambitious (e.g., a suicide hotline), and/or that may upset or otherwise affect other bereaved school community members should have the prior approval of the Crisis Coordinator/head administrator and/or your school's crisis response team. *If the death was a suicide (or the result of another high-risk activity), no memorializing of any kind should occur.*

See "Suicide Postvention" in Chapter Eleven for guidelines to follow if the death was a suicide.

- In the weeks that follow the crisis, as well as near the anniversary date of the crisis the following year, follow up with all students who were referred for counseling services at school. Assign a school counselor or psychologist who regularly serves your school to keep track of which students require follow-up and whether or not this contact has been made.

- Provide permission for a range of emotions.

- Avoid religious symbolism and platitudes.

- Provide bilingual services, if necessary, and counselors who speak the primary languages (and understand the native cultures) of affected students and their families.

> "Death gashes the emotions just like a knife gashes skin. With time and proper care, both kinds of wounds heal. They leave scars, but they do heal. Reassurance, reasoning, and redirection are the salves we adults can provide to expedite the healing process for our teens."
>
> —Dr. Marilyn E. Gootman (1998)

> "Needless to say, Pollyannaish optimism or banal platitudes should be avoided."
>
> (Schniedman, cited in "Suicide in Children and Adolescents," 1998, p. 9)

- Make a mental health referral for any student or staff member you believe needs individualized assistance from a private counselor. Then follow up with the family or staff member within the next few days to ask if the appointment has been made. You can't force a parent to make the appointment for a student, but you can have a discussion about the importance of seeking mental health assistance you believe is needed. If the parent says something like, "No, I didn't make the appointment because I think she's doing okay now," you might say, for example, "This was a severe incident. What has really changed about (the student's) coping skills, problem-solving abilities, and/or self-esteem in the past two or three days?" Stand by your recommendation. (*See "Get Additional Assistance When Necessary" in Chapter Eight for helpful responses to parents' most common reasons for neglecting to obtain needed mental health assistance for their children.*)

- Do not hesitate to recommend private therapy if you believe that a student desperately needs it. Some schools' mental health workers don't make such recommendations out of fear that their district will then have to pay for the treatment, but that hardly ever happens. In addition, this stance detracts from the professionalism of your school's mental health personnel. If you know what a student or family needs, tell them. Otherwise you are not using the skills and knowledge you've been trained (and hired) to utilize. (For a student who has an Individualized Education Plan [IEP], responsibility for providing needed services would likely be an issue. In such cases, consult with your school's special education supervisor before recommending private therapy.)

- Follow your school's/district's policies for making outside referrals (e.g., providing "x" number of names; at least two). However, if you're convinced that a specific agency, facility, program, or private practitioner would be the best place for the family to obtain the help they need, encourage them to go there. Unless there is an obvious conflict of interest (i.e., you're somehow profiting from the referral), making such a recommendation would not be problematic for your school and would help the school community member(s).

- Know your professional ethics; avoid overinvolvement with clients (particularly students).

- Provide counseling services for as long as any of your school community members will benefit from them. Depending upon the severity of the school crisis, that may be for a week or a month, until the end of the school year, throughout the summer and into the next school year, or even for several years following the crisis (e.g., on the anniversary date)! Many schools stop providing these services too quickly; be conservative and continue to provide emotional support until it is obvious that these services are no longer needed by your school community.

> "Trauma work is multifaceted and takes a while—from several months to the end of life, but certainly more than 90 minutes."
>
> (Schniedman, cited in "Suicide in Children," 1998, p. 9)

- After a certain point, you may want to move the counseling services related to the crisis to a less central or intrusive location so that you can place the focus of your school back on academics and hope for the future. There is no hard-and-fast rule regarding when this move should occur; take the cue from your school community and make this a group decision. (Your school's and/or district's mental health workers, administrators, and crisis response team should jointly make such a decision.)

- Bear in mind that everyone on your school's mental health staff "... can be of assistance even if they are not providing direct counseling services to students. Staff will be needed to answer phones, escort students, maintain ... counseling/contact cards/records, check at-risk student schedules, provide breaks for counseling staff, etc." (District School Board, 1994a).

- Provide regularly scheduled breaks for all staff and volunteers involved in providing counseling services after a crisis. Establish a written break schedule and a break room to ensure that this occurs. Provide healthful snack foods and beverages in the break room (District School Board, 1994a).

- After a severe school crisis, make plans to provide counseling services to staff, students, and their families during the summer and to carefully orchestrate the beginning of the next school year. (Because federal grants to fund such services are sometimes not received for months after the tragedy, the services may need to be funded locally and/or counselors' contracts extended. *See "Financial Support" in Chapter Four for more information.*)

- Help ease the transition of victims and/or suspected student perpetrator(s) back to school (*see Chapter Twelve*).

- Process your reactions frequently with your colleagues/school's crisis response team. Meet briefly with such people at the end of every day your school provides a crisis response. Don't forget to "take care of the caregiver" (*see Chapter Ten, "Who Cares for the Caregiver?"*).

The following are some general responses that could be given by school staff and parents to typical childhood reactions to a crisis. The reactions are broken down by age (Pitcher & Poland, 1992, pp. 195-196):

Preschool (Ages 1-5)

Children in this age group are particularly affected by disruption of their previously secure world and routines. They look to family members for comfort and are profoundly affected by the crisis reactions of their parents and other elders. Abandonment is a major fear.

- Encourage expression through play reenactment.

- Provide verbal reassurance and physical comforting.

- Give frequent attention to affected children.

- Encourage expression regarding earlier losses of pets or toys.

- Provide comforting naptime and bedtime routines.

- Allow the children to sleep in the same room with their parents for a short time after the crisis.

See "Modifying the Curriculum" in Chapter Six for specific ideas in the areas of art, language arts activities, music, and memorializing activities that counselors may wish to employ with individuals or groups of students after a crisis.

Early Childhood (Ages 5-11)

Regressive behavior is the most typical crisis response of this age group, and loss of pets and/or prized objects following a crisis is very difficult for children this age to deal with.

- Respond to regressive behaviors with patience and tolerance.
- Conduct play sessions with adults and peers.
- Hold discussions with adults and peers.
- Relax expectations in school and at home (with a clear understanding that this change is temporary and that the normal routine will resume when the children are feeling better).
- Provide opportunities for structured, but not demanding, chores and responsibilities at home and at school.
- Rehearse any safety measures to be taken in the event of a future crisis.

Preadolescence (Ages 11-14)

Peer reactions to the crisis are quite significant to this age group; preadolescents want to feel that their crisis reactions are similar to others'. Adult responses should focus on lessening anxiety and any feelings of guilt.

- Provide group activities geared toward the resumption of routines.
- Provide opportunities for involvement in same age group activities.
- Conduct group discussions geared toward "reliving" the crisis and rehearsing appropriate behaviors in the event of a future crisis.
- Provide structured yet undemanding responsibilities.
- Temporarily relax expectations for performance at home and at school.
- Provide additional individual attention and consideration to affected students.

Adolescence (Ages 14-18)

The majority of activities and interests of this age group are focused on same-age peers, and teens are especially distressed by any disruption of their peer group activities.

- Encourage participation in any community rehabilitation and reclamation work (*see "Memorializing Victims" and "Modifying the Curriculum" in Chapter Six for ideas*).
- Encourage the resumption of social activities (e.g., athletics, clubs, etc.) when the students are ready.
- Encourage discussion of the crisis event and reactions with peers, extended family members, and significant others.
- Temporarily reduce the expectations for school and general performance.

- Encourage, but do not force, discussion of the crisis and its effects within the immediate family.

The following guidelines (many adapted from Monahon, cited in Lazarus, 1996) are provided to assist counseling staff in determining when an *immediate* referral should be made for private counseling. Make such a referral for a child:

- Who experienced a trauma that was severe enough to provoke post-traumatic stress disorder (PTSD) symptoms in almost everyone.

- Whose post-traumatic behavior is endangering himself or herself or others.

- Whose reaction to the trauma includes threatening suicide, talking wistfully about being dead, or dwelling on issues related to death or dying.

- Whose reaction to the trauma is so severe that his or her ability to differentiate between fantasy and reality is compromised.

- Whose reaction to the trauma is so severe and overwhelming that his or her daily functioning is greatly disrupted and age-appropriate activities cannot be pursued.

- Whose parents' depression or anxiety is so severe and debilitating that the parents prevent the family from reaching a sense of equilibrium and well-being, no matter how well the child is recovering.

The following guidelines (many adapted from Monahon, cited in Lazarus, 1996) are provided to assist counseling staff in determining when a referral should be made for private counseling *after six weeks*. Make such a referral for a child:

- Whose primary focus of conversation and play is the crisis/trauma.

- Who is easily overcome by extreme fear.

- Who has regressed to the behavior one would expect of a much younger child and shows no signs of regaining his or her former skills and/or abilities.

- Who continues to have severe sleep disturbances caused by the trauma.

- Who exhibits a lack of pleasure in most routine activities or continues to be withdrawn and apathetic.

- Who complains of illnesses or physical pains for which no medical explanation can be found.

- Who continues to experience vivid terror in response to trauma-related sensory "triggers" with no decrease in intensity, frequency, or both.

- Whose behavior continues to have a negative impact on others.

- Whose continued distractibility and lack of focus are inhibiting learning at school.

- Who continues to blame himself or herself for the crisis or misperceives himself or herself as "bad."
- Whose overall changes in personality are dramatic and anxiety provoking to parents and/or teachers.
- Who exhibits reactions or behaviors following the crisis that are particularly upsetting to the child.
- Whose parents' reactions to the crisis continue to be so upsetting that they interfere with the parents' ability to take charge of the family and establish a sense of normality.

References

American Red Cross. (1993, February). Normal grief reactions. *Disaster mental health services I: Participant's attachments* (Attachment 14, ARC 3077-1A). Washington, DC: Author.

Ashcraft, H. (1999, March 21). Pam Herring's world fell apart in March of '98. *Jonesboro Sun*, pp. 1A, 14A-15A.

Associated Press. (1998a, March 27). Arkansas students face fears as they return to deadly site. *Idahonews.com*. Available online: http://www.idahonews.com/032798/NATION_/16024.htm

Associated Press. (1998b, April 5). Doctor recounts treating Jonesboro victims: He says many of the injured will need counseling. *Dallas Morning News*, p. 29A.

Casey, K. (1999, March). When the shooting stopped. *Ladies' Home Journal*, pp. 10-13.

Children and death. (1998). *National Funeral Directors Association (NFDA)*. Available online: http://www.nfda.org/resources/marketplace/brochures/children.html

District School Board of Pasco County. (1994a). *Crisis intervention team program: Administrator's checklist for dealing with a schoolwide loss/crisis*. Land O'Lakes, FL: Author.

District School Board of Pasco County. (1994b). Handling a class after a student dies [Handout]. Land O'Lakes, FL: Author.

Egan, T. (1998, June 14). From adolescent angst to school killings. *The New York Times*, pp. 1, 20.

Egerton, B. (1998, March 25). "We had children lying everywhere," paramedic says: Rampage leaves community in shock, tears. *Dallas Morning News*, p. 1A.

Fainaru, S. (1998, October 20). Many struggle to put their world together. *Boston Globe*, pp. A1, A20-21.

Flatter, C., Herzog, J. M., Tyson, P., & Ross, K. (1988, November 30). *Grief*. Available online: http://www.ctw.org/parents/article/0,1175,NzE2LDIxMQ==,00.html

Gootman, M. (1998, December 3). Helping our teens heal when a friend dies. *Jewish Family & Life!*. Available online: http://www.jewishfamily.com/Features/996/helping10.htm

Grief: A time to heal. (1998). *National Funeral Directors Association (NFDA)*. Available online: http://www.nfda.org/resources/marketplace/brochures/grief.html

Journey of hearts: A healing place in cyberspace. (1998, January 12). Available online: http://www.kirstimd.com/grief1.htm

Kübler-Ross, E. (1997). *On death and dying*. New York: Collier Books.

Lazarus, P. (1996). Identification, diagnosis and referral of children with post-traumatic stress disorder. *FASP Newsletter*, (3), 23-27.

Levine, K. (1998, June). How children grieve. *Parents*, pp. 133-137.

Levine, P. (1994, Summer). Understanding childhood trauma. *Mothering*, pp. 49-54.

Lieberman, R. (1998, Fall). Schoolyard tragedies: Coping with the aftermath. *School Safety*, pp. 14-16.

McRee, L., & Bergeron, T. (1997, December 3). Paducah reflects on tragedy. *ABC Good Morning America*.

National Organization for Victim Assistance (NOVA). (1994a). *The crisis reaction* [Handout]. Washington, DC: Author.

National Organization for Victim Assistance (NOVA). (1994b). *Recovery from immediate trauma* [Handout]. Washington, DC: Author.

National Organization for Victim Assistance (NOVA). (1994c). *Stress and trauma* [Handout]. Washington, DC: Author.

National Organization for Victim Assistance (NOVA). (1994d). *Trauma and loss* [Handout]. Washington, DC: Author.

National Organization for Victim Assistance (NOVA). (1997). *Community crisis response team training manual* (2nd ed.). Washington, DC: Author.

Overbeck, B., & Overbeck, J. (1995). Concerning siblings. *TLC Group*. Available online: http://www.counselingforloss.com/cllc/article3.htm

Paine, C. (1998, November). Tragedy response and healing: Springfield unites. *NASP Communiqué, 27*(3), 16-17.

Pitcher, G. D., & Poland, S. (1992). *Crisis intervention in the schools*. New York: Guilford.

Rosenblatt, R. (1999, May 10). A note for Rachel Scott. *TIME*, p. 102.

Sleek, S. (1998, June). After the storm, children play out fears. *American Psychological Association's Monitor, 29*(6), 12.

Suicide in children and adolescents. (1998). *Child Therapy News, 6*(1), 1-10, 24.

Watkins, A. (1999, March 24). Teacher's life no longer same after fatal day. *Jonesboro Sun*, pp. 1A, 20A.

Webster's encyclopedic unabridged dictionary of the English language. (1996). New York: Gramercy Books.

Will I ever stop hurting? A parent's grief. (1998). *National Funeral Directors Association (NFDA)*. Available online: http://www.nfda.org/resources/marketplace/brochures/stop.html

Wolfelt, A. (1998). *Helping yourself with grief*. Available online: http://www.batesville.com/html/body_5b.htm

Zenere, F. (1998, November). NASP/NEAT community crisis response. *NASP Communiqué, 27*(3), 38-39.

chapter eight

Points for Parents

Assisting the School

When a crisis occurs at your child's school, you have the right to expect the school to provide a competent and timely response to the crisis. The school has obligations to you, as a parent, that include:

- Keeping your child as safe as is possible under the circumstances;
- Communicating the facts of the incident to you and the other parents; and
- Providing services (e.g., classroom discussion and counseling sessions) to your child to assist him or her in processing the effects of the crisis.

However, you may not have considered *your role* in the crisis response. While the school bears the primary responsibility for addressing the situation, there are a few simple things you can do that will greatly assist the school in doing so:

- *Try to remain calm.*

  When you send your child to school in the morning, you naturally expect to see him or her return home in the afternoon unharmed and untraumatized. When you hear that something bad has happened at the school—especially a catastrophic crisis such as a shooting—it is difficult not to think the worst and panic. Of course you will want to go to the school to determine the well-being of your child. However, give the school representatives the chance to tell you about the situation. Don't go running through the halls screaming your child's name or otherwise become hysterical. Your doing so would only add to the chaos and hinder the school representatives from regaining calm and order in the school.

When you arrive at the school, there will likely be a school representative to meet you and other family members. If such a person is not readily available, report to the front office of the school. Give your name and your child's name, grade, and classroom teacher. Be patient. It may take a few minutes for the school representative to tell you the facts of the situation (sometimes the rumors that have spread about a school crisis are much worse than the actual incident), the steps the school is taking, and the status of your child. If you are asked to go to another room in the school building (e.g., the library where other parents are gathering) to receive this information, be sure to go there immediately. It will be important for you to hear the complete facts from an adult in the school so that you understand what your child has experienced and the assistance available to your child.

If the crisis is catastrophic and the school is closing for the rest of the day, go to your child's classroom to collect him or her only after you've been given the facts of the crisis and the okay of a school representative. The school representative may wish to accompany you to the classroom, or you may be asked to wait while he or she brings your child to you. Respecting the school's procedure will help the school to maintain order after the crisis.

If your child was injured, allow a school representative or other caregiver to drive you to the hospital. You will be frightened and shaken, and driving in such a condition might jeopardize your own safety. Also be sure to call another family member or close friend for support.

- *Leave your child at school if it is remaining open.*

  You have the right to take your child home with you after a school crisis. However, if the school is remaining open, we strongly encourage you to leave your child there with his or her classmates. (*NOTE*: The exception would be if your child were very young, such as a kindergartner. The school will want to reunite very young children with their primary caretakers as soon as possible after a crisis, which research shows is most helpful for their recovery [Pitcher & Poland, 1992].)

  Leaving your child at school will allow him or her to participate in the valuable classroom discussion that will be taking place and give him or her the opportunity to ask questions and receive the guidance of educators trained in crisis response (e.g., counselors and school psychologists). Your child will also have the support of his or her peers and will be able to see that his or her feelings about the tragedy are similar to many of theirs, a concept that is comforting to most people after a trauma.

  If you are unsure about whether to bring your child home with you or to leave him or her at school, go with a school representative to see what is happening in your child's classroom before making your decision. You will be able to see for yourself whether your child is indeed safe. If you see an orderly crisis response happening—if you see the children with their teacher, a supportive environment, and safety and security—you will feel more comfortable leaving your child in school for the rest of the day. You might also ask your child if he or she feels comfortable remaining at school with his or her teacher and classmates.

- *Leave the intervention to the professionals.*

  As a parent, you are the most important person in your child's life, and obviously you will be a critical factor in his or her recovery after a traumatic event. Your support and care of your child at home will be essential after a crisis. However, you should not attempt to provide a crisis intervention to a group of children or teenagers. People trained in crisis response and mental health will deliver counseling services at the school.

  Some well-meaning parents try to become too involved after a tragedy at school, to the point that they interfere with what the school is trying to do to assist the students. For example, after a student suicide in Houston, Texas, in 1994, a parent told a group of very upset students to come to her house. She had good rapport with her child and child's friends and felt certain that she could help them deal with the effects of the crisis. What actually happened is not what she had expected. The mother soon called the school to report that all of the kids were in the family room, they had shut her out of the room, and she didn't know what was going on with them. She was very worried because they would not make her a part of the intervention. She wanted a school counselor to come to her house to assist with the situation. She was advised to bring the students back to the school where they could obtain the assistance of trained educators.

- *Avoid the media.*

  A school crisis will almost always draw some media attention. Depending upon the severity of the crisis, literally hundreds of media representatives could be gathered outside the school. They will all be attempting to get a story on the air or in print as quickly as possible and they may aggressively approach you for information or a quote.

  You have the right to speak with the media if you choose. However, we encourage you not to do so. It is more helpful to allow a *school representative* to talk with the media, since he or she can provide complete and clear information about the status of the crisis and what the school is doing to resolve the situation. A school representative will be holding a press conference as soon as school personnel have finished addressing the immediate needs of the students and their families. Simply repeat

"No comment" or "You need to speak with someone from the school" and avoid making eye contact with the media. If you feel intimidated or need assistance, return to the school building. The school's security staff and/or the police will direct you to another exit or escort you past the media.

If you do choose to speak to a reporter, be sure to respect the privacy of other families. Do not provide the names of victims or suspected student perpetrator(s) to the media. (Consider how you would feel hearing this information for the first time on the news.) Also, do not speculate about the crisis or spread rumors. Your statements could be broadcast or reprinted many times, which could be detrimental to your child's school and your community.

- *Attend the family/community meeting to be held that evening.*

Whether the school remains open or closes for the rest of the day, there will likely be a family/community meeting held later in the evening. At this meeting school representatives (and any other appropriate officials, such as the police and district attorney) will outline for you the plan for the following day(s) and provide an updated report of the crisis. They also will discuss the counseling services available to your child and steps you can take at home to help your child cope. You will have the opportunity to ask questions and vent some of the strong emotions you are likely feeling. You might also receive some comfort from being in the presence of other concerned family and community members.

You are strongly encouraged to attend this meeting and to bring your child and any other affected family members with you. Be sure to read the Crisis Fact Sheet provided to you by the school and the parent/family information packet distributed at the meeting. Speak with a school representative after the meeting if you do not understand something on these sheets or if you need some additional assistance for your family.

- *Help with translation, if necessary.*

Some communities have a large immigrant population, with multiple languages spoken within the community. Stockton, California, is one such place. In 1989, when a gunman shot and killed five elementary school students and wounded 29 others in that community, about two thirds of the victims were members of Southeast Asian immigrant families. Four of the deceased children were from Cambodian families, one was from a Vietnamese family (Johnston, 1998). In such communities, language and cultural differences can often become barriers in times of crisis. If yours is a diverse community, and you have knowledge of the language(s) and/or religious and cultural customs of a minority population, you may be able to help the school clearly communicate the facts of the crisis to panicked family members.

Helping Your Child Cope

Even the most loving and supportive parents might not know exactly what to do or say to help their children after a crisis. Children who have experienced a school crisis will likely be overly sensitive and quite emotional. The rules of everyday parenting simply don't apply in these special situations. All too often well-meaning parents begin to talk about what happened by saying, "I understand what you're going through." But their children will likely reject that statement, because the parents *don't* entirely understand. The children might throw back at them, for example, "Was *your* best friend ever killed?" and turn away from their parents. This type of common exchange is unfortunate, because children need their parents' help to fully recover from the effects of a traumatic event. The following are some tips for better helping your child to cope after a crisis.

"Reach, Don't Preach"

Parents have a tendency to want to "fix" things when their children are upset. They want to say, for example, "Do this, do that, and you'll feel better." This type of directive approach is not very helpful after a crisis, however, because what children need most is simply to have their feelings recognized and validated. There are no magic words you can say to erase the hurt and fear. The best thing you can do to help your child is to *listen* to him or her. Children are resilient, but they still need opportunities to discuss their emotions.

You may be willing to listen, but how do you encourage your child to talk about a traumatic event if he or she isn't opening up? Don't say that much. Simply be with your child. Be in the same room, sit down with him or her, perhaps share an activity (e.g., drying the dinner dishes or putting together a jigsaw puzzle). Don't say, "I understand." Instead, tell your child, "I can't imagine how difficult this must be. I'd like to understand how you're feeling." Stay close by your child, remain open and supportive, and he or she will eventually talk.

When your child expresses his or her feelings, be careful not to talk too much in response. Sometimes little more than a grunt or an acknowledging "Hmmm" is all that is needed to keep your child talking! If you say too much in an emotional situation, you risk having your child "shut down." Show sympathy through your body language (i.e., assuming an open, attentive posture, leaning forward or inclining your head in an interested manner) and by maintaining eye contact with your child as he or she speaks.

Remain nonjudgmental about the feelings your child expresses. There is no one correct way to feel at any given time after a tragedy. Provide permission for a range of emotions, even those you may feel are inappropriate. For example, your child may laugh nervously when he or she hears of a death. This does not mean you've raised an insensitive child. Laughter is a natural tension release for the body. Your child may say "I don't care" in an attempt to distance himself or herself from the traumatic event. Then he or she may cry an hour later.

Some children (particularly older adolescents) simply won't cry in front of you. Some children will be very fearful, others angry. Some may be truly shut off from their emotions and will not feel much of anything in the early stages.

Anticipate Typical Childhood Responses to Crisis

Children's responses to a crisis or tragedy will vary some by child and by the age of the child, but they typically fall into four main areas:

1. Fear of the future
2. Academic regression
3. Behavioral regression
4. Nightmares, night terrors, and sleep disturbances

Expecting and accepting such reactions by your child will help you to respond with patience, tolerance, and love. Keep in mind that these reactions are completely normal and are only temporary. The following guidelines (many recommended by the American Red Cross Disaster Services and the National Organization for Victim Assistance) will help you in responding to these four typical childhood reactions to crisis.

Fear of the future

Feeling fear after a crisis is natural for children as well as adults. You can help to allay much of your child's fear by providing verbal reassurance (e.g., saying such things as, "You're safe now" and "I'm glad you're here with me now"). Repeat such assurances as often as necessary. Also reassure your child that the unpleasant feelings he or she may be experiencing after the crisis are normal responses to stress and/or grief and won't last forever.

While you want to reassure your child, the bottom line is that parents cannot absolutely guarantee their children's safety, which is scary even to them. In age-appropriate terms, you need to tell your child that you are doing everything possible to assist him or her and ask your child what else you can do to help him or her to feel safer.

Allow your child to discuss his or her own theories about the crisis and provide factual information in age-appropriate language. (Note, however, that while you want to be honest with your child, you should share as few details—and no gory ones—as necessary.) Encourage your child to talk about the event, describing what he or she saw, heard, thought, smelled, tasted, and felt at the time of the crisis (i.e., his or her sensory perceptions).

Talk in hopeful terms about the future to assist your child in rebuilding trust and faith in his or her own future. Physical comforting (i.e., giving extra hugs and kisses, hand holding, and a close physical presence) and extra time spent with your child (especially at bedtime) are also very healing.

Help your child to identify his or her specific fears, and problem solve about those fears with your child in an age-appropriate manner. For example, your child may be afraid to walk past the media surrounding his or her school after a severe crisis. In that case, you could help think of solutions, such as driving your child to school rather than having him or her walk for the next couple of days or escorting your child to the door of the building.

> "… [A]ccept [your] child's fears as being very real to him or to her, even if they sound unrealistic or unwarranted to you."
>
> (Pitcher & Poland, 1992, p. 182)

Your child may be uncertain about how to behave toward an injured class-mate when he or she returns to school. You could discuss with your child appropriate ways to behave and to express sympathy.

Assist your child in identifying the coping skills and resources available to help him or her during this difficult time, including yourself and other family members, spiritual faith/church, his or her classroom teacher, the school counselor, a youth group leader/mentor, friends, resting, eating well, exercising, and engaging in enjoyable activities for distraction.

You could also encourage your child to engage in some therapeutic activities such as drawing or writing about the crisis and his or her reactions to it. Artwork, poetry, letter writing (even when the letter is not, or cannot, be sent), composing songs and music, and the like, are all healthy ways for a child to connect with his or her feelings and to express grief and fear. Explained art therapist and psychologist Robin Goodman, "Drawing a picture can feel safer to a child because it's slightly removed" (Levine, 1998, p. 137). These products will help you to understand how your child perceives what happened and can facilitate conversation with your child. "Parents can ask questions about the picture rather than asking the child directly, 'Are you sad?'" explained Dr. Goodman (Levine, 1998, p. 137). Don't judge what is produced: Let your child express himself or herself in his or her own way.

Finally, with younger children, pay close attention to the nature of their play. After the 1995 bombing in Oklahoma City, children who survived the explosion played "hospital" with toy figures missing limbs. Children who survived 1989's Hurricane Hugo represented trees with broccoli during dinner and then flooded the "trees" with gravy (Sleek, 1998). Child victims who escaped from a 1976 kidnapping of a school bus in Chowchilla, California, later "… coped with the trauma by playing 'kidnap' on the school playground" (Lieberman, 1998, p. 14). After seeing television coverage of the bombing of Iraq during Operation Desert Storm, American children reenacted the war in a sandbox using toy trucks and airplanes. This type of play helps children to make sense of what has happened. As noted in Sleek (1998), "These forms of post-traumatic play [also] illustrate the ongoing and often unrecognized emotional struggles children experience after witnessing … death and destruction" (p. 12).

Academic regression

Immediately after the crisis, your child's school will likely modify or set aside the regular curriculum for a short period so that school personnel can address the emotionality of the situation (i.e., the crisis essentially becomes the curriculum). For example, tests and quizzes will likely be canceled and time will be spent in the classroom processing the effects of the crisis. However, even after this time frame, if your child is grieving he or she may lose interest in schoolwork and regress academically. One Houston, Texas, student, for example, failed all of his subjects after the suicide of his sister.

It is important to encourage your child to return to school as soon as it reopens (even if this is the day following the crisis). Children need to return to school immediately after a school crisis to receive appropriate assistance from the trained educators.

Returning to school immediately also nips "school phobia" in the bud. As school psychologists have explained:

> Following a major shock children often fear leaving their families and loved ones. Going to school, especially if there have been anxieties about school in the past, may become a problem. It is important to communicate to your child that, no matter what, he or she must go to school. [Explain to your child in age-appropriate terms that school] is an important part of his or her life with peers and necessary toward the development of independence. Often children will point out aspects of the school … they fear; however, in almost every case [even after a school crisis], it is the fear of leaving home that is really behind the school phobia. It may be necessary to confer with [your] child's teacher and counselor to develop a supportive plan with which to ease [your] child's adjustment to or continuing [attendance of] school (Pitcher & Poland, 1992, p. 183).

When your child returns to school, encourage him or her to complete all schoolwork, and provide assistance if necessary. Reestablishing this normal routine and responsibility soon after the crisis will help your child to regain his or her equilibrium.

If your child continues to experience problems with school attendance and/or performance after several weeks (e.g., two to three), discuss the situation with the classroom teacher and/or school counselor. Some sort of individual intervention may be necessary to help your child get back on track. Your child may also need private counseling to assist in his or her recovery, and school personnel can make a referral for you.

Behavioral regression

Even more common than academic regression is behavioral regression. Behavioral regression often takes one of two forms: (1) clinginess, dependency, and "immature" behavior, including developmental setbacks (e.g., toileting problems); or (2) aggression, anger, and "acting-out" behaviors (e.g., fighting with a sibling, temper tantrums, being argumentative). The following are typical signs of stress in a child after a crisis. It is perfectly normal for your child to exhibit any of these behaviors or feelings after a traumatic event:

See "Crisis Effects and Grief" in Chapter Seven for a more in-depth discussion of childhood crisis reactions, including typical reactions broken down by age group.

- Crying
- Hyperactive or silly behavior
- Lack of emotional display
- Irritability
- Temper outbursts/tantrums
- Restlessness
- Misbehavior/acting-out behaviors
- Clinging to adults
- Unusual lack of maturity or overmaturity
- Being demanding
- Getting lost
- Changes in sleep/being afraid to go to bed by himself or herself
- Rambunctiousness
- Inactivity/lethargy
- Fear/worry
- Guilt
- Changes in appetite
- Changing his or her physical appearance

Be prepared to tolerate for a while any regressive behaviors exhibited by your child. These behaviors help children to process the emotionality of the incident and express their fears, and they will eventually pass. In the meantime, modify your behavioral expectations somewhat. Maintain your family structure, main responsibilities, and crucial standards for your child, but relax rules and be flexible about chores and less important expectations. Focus on recognizing and praising any responsible behavior exhibited, and be more tolerant overall. Give your child some "space." Also educate babysitters, daycare providers, other family members, and any others who interact with your child and may not understand how the crisis has affected him or her and his or her behavior.

Also recognize that your child will respond to your own reactions to the crisis. If you are distracted, fearful, or upset by what has happened, you may be behaving differently and/or may not be giving your child as much positive attention as normal. Or, if you are glued to the television after a crisis—as many adults were during Operation Desert Storm, for example—you will likely be temporarily out of touch with your child's needs. Of course, when children do not receive their usual amount of attention (for whatever reason) from their parents, they change their behavior—often negatively—to get their parents' attention one way or another. (*NOTE*: Avoid excessively viewing television coverage of a traumatic event. Consider the television to be a source of information, but once you have the facts, turn it off!)

Nightmares, night terrors, and sleep disturbances

All parents have probably answered a call in the night from their young child's room at one time or another. Nightmares are common for young children, and they will likely experience them more frequently in the wake of a crisis. Provide your child with a nightlight, or better yet, allow your young child to sleep with you or another family member (such as an older sibling) for a time after the traumatic event.

You may not expect your older child or adolescent to experience trouble sleeping or fear of the dark, but such behaviors are quite natural after a trauma. For example, a 17-year old Texas boy who found his sister after she had hung herself asked his mother for a nightlight. She expressed surprise. "I told him that was silly," the mother told a school psychologist. Do not belittle your older child for needing some nighttime comfort after a crisis. Supply the nightlight, and don't worry. Your child won't be using it three years (or likely even three months) from now.

Take Care of Yourself

When a severe crisis occurs at your child's school, you will likely be affected as well. You may experience strong emotions, such as fear for your child's safety, anger about what happened or anger at being fearful, and vulnerability because your sense of security was violated. You may also feel sadness or grief if your child or another member of the school community was harmed in some way. The following are typical signs of stress in adults after a crisis has occurred:

- Poor concentration/forgetfulness
- Confused thinking/indecision
- Unclear communication
- Excessive fatigue
- Tearfulness
- Upset stomach
- Headaches
- Irritability
- Anger
- Being argumentative
- Hopelessness
- Inactivity or overactivity
- Sleeplessness
- Loss of or increase in appetite
- Depression

See "Crisis Effects and Grief" in Chapter Seven for a more in-depth discussion of crisis reactions.

Sometimes people are severely affected by a crisis even when they weren't directly involved in the event, because crises tend to bring up unresolved issues from the past, particularly those related to trauma and loss. You may be more vulnerable than others if you have experienced any of the following in the past:

- Relocation
- Death in the family
- A loss (e.g., loss of a job or a pet, a divorce, etc.)
- Poverty
- Being the victim of a crime
- Serious illness

Crises and disasters have also been shown to have dramatic effects on entire families. Some typical effects on family units include:

- Disrupted belief in personal security
- Increased vulnerability
- Increased irritability, arguments, family discord
- Clinginess, acting-out behavior, and regression
- Illness and psychosomatic (i.e., a physical disorder caused by emotional factors) problems

- Exhaustion
- Decreased intimacy between family members
- Survivor's guilt
- Substance and drug abuse
- Domestic violence

(In fact, the American Red Cross has estimated that child abuse, spousal abuse, and/or substance abuse increase 50-200% after a disaster or trauma.)

While these are all typical reactions to a crisis, experiencing one or more of these for any length of time will not be helpful to yourself or your family. Not only does parental despair often interfere with a child's ability to recover from a trauma, but children are sometimes forced to become "parents" to adults who are scared or worried. For your own sake, and for the benefit of your child, you must find a way to cope with your feelings of helplessness, fear, and/or anger. Until you do so, you won't be much help to your child, and he or she needs you after experiencing a crisis.

"... [C]hildren are often reluctant to talk about their own feelings following a [crisis], particularly because they're well aware of the emotional struggles their parents and other adults are going through."

(Sleek, 1998, p. 12)

Additionally, unless you address your own reactions to the crisis, you will have difficulty tolerating your child's regressive behaviors. Just when you need to be more structured, more patient, more tolerant, and really loving, your own stress reactions may cause you to "fly off the handle" quickly or yell at your child. Thus, your own reactions to the crisis can interfere with your ability to handle your child's stress, which will exacerbate the situation.

What can you do to take care of yourself and process your reactions to the crisis? The following are a few suggestions:

- Recognize your feelings. Examine your behavior and think about whether you might be having a reaction to the crisis.
- Talk to others about your feelings. Doing so relieves stress and helps you realize that others affected by the crisis share similar feelings.
- Attend the family/community meeting held by the school. Learn the facts of the crisis and ask questions.
- Accept help from others in the spirit in which it is given.
- Get enough rest.
- Get as much physical activity as possible, such as walking.
- Eat balanced meals regularly.
- Give someone (such as your child) a hug; touching is very important to healing.
- Communicate an "I'm not hopeless" attitude.

- Whenever possible, take time to do something you enjoy.
- Be gentle and tolerant with yourself and with others in your family and community.
- If you are a religious or spiritual person, take time for prayer (and encourage your child to pray as well). A study conducted by one social psychologist (Pennebaker, cited in Johnson, 1998) actually found that prayer is effective in promoting health and that it works in the same way as talking to friends about the crisis.

- Do not hesitate to speak with a counselor or someone else trained in crisis reactions and/or with your clergy member (if applicable).

> "If any of your [crisis] responses are severe, or they continue to persist for an extended period, we encourage you to seek help for yourself, your child, or your family member. Sometimes we all need someone to lean on for a short while."
>
> —American Red Cross Disaster Services

Shield Your Child From the Media

After a severe school crisis, media representatives like to speak with eyewitnesses to the event—often the students. Personnel at your child's school will do their best to protect your child from intrusive media contact on the school grounds. However, once your child leaves school, he or she will be susceptible to approaches from the media unless you step in to help. If your child is frightened or sad because of the crisis, probing questions from the media may exacerbate his or her stress reaction. And if many media representatives—including the national media—are assembled, the sheer number of people, the volume of questioning voices, and the bright lights focused upon the children can be intimidating for them.

The day of the shooting at Columbine High School in Littleton, Colorado, in April 1999, a local television reporter, with a camera crew in tow, ran down a sidewalk alongside terrified students asking the traumatized teens to tell him what they had seen and experienced inside the school. The students had just left a home near the school where they had taken refuge after escaping the bombs and the gunfire. They were running toward comfort, to safety. They were looking for their parents—not their "15 minutes of fame."

A national news broadcaster related about the Columbine shooting, "Four hours after the first shots rang out, I was on the scene, interviewing the kids who had survived the massacre. We didn't just stick cameras and microphones in their faces. We asked first if they wanted to talk to us. If they didn't, that was fine. But most of the high schoolers seemed to have a desire to tell their stories—to share them with someone else…. These kids had just been through hell…. The dad part of me wanted to reach out and hug [them] for dear life. But the journalist part of me held back …" (Lewis, 1999).

Although this national broadcaster did his best to respect the feelings of his young interview subjects, it is not in the best interest of young people to relate their crisis reactions to the media. The need to tell one's "crisis story" is a healthy one that will promote healing (*see Chapter Five, "Processing the Crisis"*), but with students such "processing" should occur with their parents and with school personnel trained in crisis response and trauma. Media representatives have neither the mental health training nor, in many cases, the desire to truly assist students in processing their crisis reactions. The media's priority is to get a good story.

Even those respectful reporters who sincerely care about the effects their questions may have on the people they interview are not an appropriate audience for relating traumatic experiences immediately following a crisis. As the reporter quoted previously pointed out, the "journalist side of him" held back from offering comfort. After all, these professionals are on the scene to gather and disseminate information, not as caregivers. And they won't be there to support their interview subjects seconds after they get the quote they need. They're on to the next witness, the next story angle, leaving the traumatized person who has just expressed his or her emotions without support.

One of the best ways to help shield your child from unwelcome media contact is to escort him or her to and from school (rather than having your child walk, ride the bus, or drive as usual) as long as the media are covering the crisis. (The media will also likely be present outside any family/community meeting held at the school and around any impromptu memorial site. Sticking close to your child at these times and locations is also wise.) Avoid making eye contact with the media, and if media representatives approach you firmly tell the reporters that your son or daughter is not giving interviews. Most media representatives will respect your position. However, if you feel threatened or need assistance, seek refuge in the school building. The school's security staff and/or the police can direct you to another exit or escort you past the media.

If you or your child is caught off guard by a media representative and taped or photographed against your wishes, ask the reporter to respect your privacy and not use the material. Some, though admittedly not all, reporters will honor your request. Refusing to state (or spell!) your name will also make the reporter less likely to print or air your statement or photograph.

It is also important that you talk with your child about the media and explain why, although the media play an important role in our society, it is often not a good idea to talk with reporters after a crisis. Make sure your child understands that he or she does not *have* to talk to a reporter just because he or she is asked a question. Provide your child with a verbal line of defense, such as: "I don't want to talk to you," "Please leave me alone," "Don't take my picture," or, for older children, "No comment."

Of course, you or your child may *want* to speak with the media, and you have every right to do so. If you or your child decide to give an interview, be sure you stick to the facts and your personal experiences. It is extremely important that you avoid spreading rumors and speculating about the crisis, respect the privacy of other families, and not provide the names of victims or suspected student perpetrator(s) to the media. (Consider how you would feel hearing this information for the first time on the news if you were a family member of someone involved in the crisis.) We recommend that you insist on being present during any formal or informal interviews your child gives and closely monitor the emotional effects the questions seem to be having on your child. Do not hesitate to intervene if your child becomes distraught. Finally, keep in mind that relating traumatic experiences to the media does not have the same healing effect as processing crisis reactions with a trained mental health practitioner. Don't let the excitement of talking with media representatives interfere with your child's immediate or long-term recovery from the crisis.

Maintain Family Routines

After a crisis, psychologists advise parents to "make sure children get back to their daily routine, such as school, sports, and playtime with friends, so they can better see that life can continue as it did before ..." (Sleek, 1998, p. 12). Routines are an important coping mechanism for children, who thrive on structure, and should be reestablished as soon as possible after a crisis.

Maintaining family routines also illustrates for children that life continues even after a severe crisis or a death. Children and adolescents need to be given permission not to be sad every minute of every day. As Vicki Beckerman, who runs a bereavement group for children in Glen Ridge, New Jersey, explained: "Kids don't grieve nonstop. They grieve, and then they play. They shoot a few baskets, and then they cry. They watch a sitcom and laugh until they cry. The ability to strike a balance is the key to their emotional survival" (Levine, 1998, p. 137). Children must feel they have a right to have their day-to-day needs (e.g., for attention, for play, etc.) met, even after a crisis.

Assist Your Child in Understanding Death and Funerals

If a crisis involves the death of a school community member, it will be important for you to discuss the process and meaning of death with your child. As noted in "Children and Death" (1998), "... children can and do handle death well—often better than the adults around them. Like adults, children need to come to terms with death and the grief that accompanies it." Children's understanding of death (or lack thereof) is determined in large part by their age and corresponding cognitive development. In general, children's understanding of death is typically as follows ("Children and Death," 1998; Flatter, Herzog, Tyson, & Ross, 1998; Levine, 1998):

Approximate Age	Understanding
1 to 3 Years	Most concerned with how a death will affect their daily routine and needs.
	Use "magical thinking," believing something they did caused the death or that they can bring the deceased back.
	Cannot differentiate between death and long-term absence.
4 to 5/6 Years	Do not view death as permanent (confusion compounded by cartoons, movies, fairy tales, video games, etc., in which characters die and later are revived).
	Cannot grieve as adults do, as children of this age do not understand permanence (concepts of past, present, and future do not begin to make sense until around age 5).
	Have verbal ability, but take things very literally. Hence, parents should avoid using death analogies such as "going on a trip" or "going to sleep," since they could make children afraid to go on a trip or to sleep by themselves.
6/7 to 8 Years	Begin to understand that death is permanent but believe it can happen only to the elderly.
	If a young person dies, may demand to know why.
8 to 10 Years	Begin to understand that death is part of the natural order and that people of all ages die for many reasons.
	Understand that death could happen to them.
6/7 to 11 Years	Children's growing cognitive abilities help them to think more realistically and understand the finality of death.
	May seek comfort in religious/spiritual beliefs and/or explore the scientific aspects of death.
	Capable of grief (as defined by adults).

| **11 and Older** | Capable of understanding that death results when internal biological processes shut down. |
| **Adolescents** | Should fully understand the finality of death by about age 13, but many do not (again perhaps a result of media in which characters die and are miraculously revived). Parents should help to ground teenagers in the facts. |

You know your child best and can explain the process of death in terms you believe he or she will understand. Whatever age your child is, answer his or her questions honestly. However, provide as few details as are necessary to satisfy your child, and provide no gory ones that may frighten him or her. (According to the National Organization for Victim Assistance [1997], your child may also be afraid of "spirits" or "ghosts" associated with death.)

If your child is young, carefully consider how he or she may interpret your words. For example, dismissing your child's fears about death by "… saying that death happens mainly to very old people [may inadvertently cause] an aversion to, or even fear of, being around the aged …" (Katz, 1998). Saying someone died because "God loved him or her so much and wanted him or her in heaven" may make your child fearful of being loved by God. Saying someone is "happier in heaven" may make your young child think the deceased is happier in heaven because of something your child did here on earth (i.e., "magical thinking"). As stated in Levine (1998), "It's just a short leap [for a young child] to feelings of guilt and responsibility …" (p. 134).

Sharing age-appropriate children's books that deal with loss and death (*see the Appendix*) may help you to explain the situation to your child. Ask a librarian at the school or local public library for other recommendations. The counselor or psychologist at your child's school would also have appropriate books to either lend or recommend to you.

> "In some cases a child may feel a vague sense of guilt for having recently or frequently displeased the deceased or for having [had] unkind thoughts about that person. The child may then see the [death] as abandonment or punishment. Other young children react to the death of someone they have known directly with fear that their own parents will die and abandon them in the same way."
>
> (Katz, 1998)

If someone in the school community commits suicide, your conversation about death with your child assumes even more importance. If your child is mature enough to understand that suicide is a death by choice of, and at the hand of, the deceased, then you should strongly emphasize that suicide is a very poor solution to life's problems. Such a discussion is critical, since "there is mounting evidence that [children and teens] follow the suicidal actions of their peers, a trend known as suicide clusters or contagion" (Nemours Foundation, cited in California Association of School Psychologists [CASP], 1998, p. 14). Discuss with your child what positive options are available, and where he or she can turn for help (e.g., discussing these thoughts with you or another family member) in the event that he or

See "Suicide Statistics, Causes, and Myths" in Chapter Eleven for a more detailed discussion of the prevalence and precipitators of suicide.

See "Suicide Postvention" in Chapter Eleven for other tips on discussing suicide appropriately with children and teens.

she should ever contemplate suicide. Some people are afraid to mention the word "suicide" to young people, believing that discussing the issue will give children the idea to commit the act. However, according to the California Association of School Psychologists, "Asking a child or adolescent whether he or she is depressed or thinking about suicide can be helpful. Rather than 'putting thoughts in the child's head,' such a question will provide assurance that somebody cares and will give the young person the chance to talk about problems ..." (CASP, 1998, p. 14).

Besides wanting to know about the process of death, your child may have questions and concerns about the *meaning* of death. Share your personal religious beliefs with your child as you see fit. If you attend a church, your clergy member will also be able to assist you in comforting your child. If you believe in an afterlife and in God, Rabbi Marc Gelman has recommended explaining "... directly and convincingly that the person who has died is still all right, that it's their body who has died, but their soul is with God." He added, "This is one of the greatest religious promises, that death is not the end of us" ("Regrouping After Tragedy," 1998).

Your child may wish to attend the funeral of the deceased school community member and/or a memorial or community service honoring the deceased. Funerals and memorials are an important ceremony for remembering the person who has died and for saying good-bye. However, children have often been discouraged from attending such ceremonies in our society. When determining whether your child is old enough to attend a funeral or memorial, Claudia Jewett Jarratt, a child and family therapist in Massachusetts, has advised that "the circumstances surrounding the death, [your] child's temperament, the attitude of [your] family, and the wishes of [your] child are more significant than the child's age ...." However, she went on to say that, "going to the cemetery and seeing the coffin lowered into the ground can be traumatic for children under seven" (Levine, 1998, p. 134).

"Remember that any child who is old enough to love is old enough to mourn."
(Wolfelt, 1998)

Many psychologists today encourage funeral and memorial attendance by children, particularly if they are older than seven years of age. Explained Dr. Alan Wolfelt (1998), "Children who are included in funeral planning, are encouraged to view the body (if culturally appropriate) and attend the funeral, and are compassionately guided through all these steps are best prepared to begin their journeys toward healing."

See "Funerals" in Chapter Six for a list of terminology related to funerals and funeral etiquette.

If you allow your child to attend a funeral or memorial service, be sure to prepare him or her for what will happen there. It also would be best if you (or another adult family member) attend the service with your child to provide support and assistance if necessary. If you skip the ceremony, you will miss sharing that emotional experience with your child and will miss an excellent opportunity to have a heartfelt talk with your child about his or her reactions to the tragedy. Finally, during your discussion with your child about the death and the funeral, "… don't tell your child to 'be brave, don't cry.' This is a sad situation, and [your] child needs to express his or her sadness" ("Children and Death," 1998).

Encourage Positive Actions

While young children have a need to reenact a crisis through their play to make sense of the event, older children (such as middle/junior high students and high schoolers) often need to take action. When something bad has happened in their school or community, they want to be involved in some meaningful way, to contribute to making the world a better place. For example, if flooding caused the crisis, your older child may wish to fill sandbags or to collect blankets and food for survivors. If the school crisis involved the death of a school community member, he or she may want to collect funds for the burial of the victim. If the death was a suicide, he or she may want to begin a suicide prevention hotline at the school. Your child may also be comforted by focusing on the emergency preparedness activities and safety procedures (e.g., increased security at the school) implemented after the crisis.

These types of positive actions will help your child to process the crisis by allowing him or her to assume some control over the circumstances. Contributing to the crisis response in some way helps a child to feel more like a survivor than a victim. Encourage and provide opportunities for your child to undertake any such projects that he or she may wish to be involved with.

Get Additional Assistance When Necessary

It is natural for children to exhibit some of the typical reactions to crisis detailed previously in this chapter (*see "Anticipate Typical Childhood Responses to Crisis"*). However, if these stress reactions seem particularly severe (i.e., to the point that they are greatly interfering with your child's enjoyment of life and/or ability to function in his or her normal capacity), or if they last for a long time (i.e., several weeks), be sure to ask for additional assistance. The best place to turn would be the counselor or psychologist at your child's school. Someone trained in crisis reactions and mental health can help set your mind at ease and help you determine what additional steps, if any, should be taken to assist your child.

"If there is one rule of thumb to keep in mind as you guide [your] child through the funeral experience it is this: Follow the child's lead. If you listen to [him or] her and pay attention to [his or] her behaviors, the child will teach you what [he or] she is curious about, what doesn't interest [him or] her, what makes [him or] her scared."

(Wolfelt, 1998)

See "Modifying the Curriculum" and "Memorializing Victims" in Chapter Six for other appropriate activities you may wish to suggest to your child.

"If the behaviors—and usually it's avoidance or anxiety—persist even after parents talk with their child and do all the other caring things they know how to do, then they probably need to contact a school psychologist or counselor."

—Dinah Graham, Assistant Professor of Psychology, Texas Woman's University in Denton (Thomas, 1998)

Be sure to get help immediately if your child expresses any suicidal thoughts. (You could contact the school counselor/psychologist, a crisis/suicide prevention hotline, your local hospital, or private mental health practitioners for assistance.) According to the Centers for Disease Control and Prevention (CDC), "Suicide is now the third leading cause of death nationwide for 15- to 24-year olds and the second leading cause of death for children ages 11-19" (cited in CASP, 1998, p. 14). Parents must take suicidal talk seriously: Do not dismiss it as innocent melodrama or attention-seeking behavior. If you believe your child's suicidal talk to be manipulative, then allow yourself to be manipulated! That's better than the potentially tragic result if you ignore your child's cry for help.

Be sure to get help immediately if your child expresses any suicidal thoughts.

Also ask for additional assistance if your child is experiencing emotions or expressing thoughts that you don't understand or don't know how to respond to. For example, many children experience feelings of guilt after a crisis. These feelings may be rational (i.e., your child perhaps could have done something to prevent the crisis but didn't) or irrational (the crisis had nothing whatsoever to do with your child but he or she believes otherwise). Either way, the assistance of a trained mental health worker will likely be necessary to help your child understand and resolve these types of strong and—if left untreated—debilitating feelings. Remember that you are not alone. The school is a valuable resource available to assist your child, and it should always be your first step in requesting additional assistance. Stay in close communication with your child's school if you have any reason to be concerned about your child's recovery after a crisis.

Likewise, if a school representative contacts you about your child and makes a referral for private counseling, heed that person's advice. Make the appointment for your child the very same day! Don't wait a few days hoping that your child's condition will improve. If you think about it, you'll realize that very little will significantly change about your child's coping skills, problem-solving abilities, or self-esteem in two or three days. The school will not make a referral for private counseling lightly. But if the trained mental health workers at your child's school believe your child is at risk and needs more individual or long-term assistance to recover from the trauma than they can provide, they will work in the best interests of your child and recommend private counseling.

Surprisingly, many parents do not follow up on these referrals. Given that almost all parents want what is best for their children and care about their health, this lack of follow-up doesn't seem to make sense. But there are some common reasons many parents fail to obtain the additional assistance necessary for their children:

- Counseling carries a stigma in some communities. You may have a dislike of counselors and the counseling profession.
- Financial concerns may hold you back.
- You may feel that you are too busy to make or keep the appointment or just "don't get around to it."
- You might fear the counseling process, worrying that the counselor may not just focus on your child but instead delve into your family's mental health issues and perhaps discover family secrets.

If you are hesitant to obtain counseling services for your child because you dislike counseling in general, keep in mind the difference between short-term counseling for otherwise healthy people after a traumatic event and long-term therapy to treat any number of mental conditions and disorders. Take the time to talk to the school counselor or psychologist and make sure you understand exactly why he or she is concerned about your child, what type of assistance he or she believes your child needs, and how long it might be expected to take. Ask what the short-term and long-term effects might be if your child does *not* receive private counseling.

If finances are your main concern, discuss this issue with the school counselor or psychologist. He or she will likely be able to help you find a way to afford the services. For example, your private health insurance plan might cover mental health treatment. Low-cost county and state sponsored services are also available in many communities. And, after a severe school crisis or natural disaster, government funds will likely be available to provide counseling services for survivors.

If you feel you are too busy to obtain the private counseling needed for your child, then reassess your priorities and make the time! Treat your child's "injured psyche" with as much care as you would a broken arm. If your child needed a visit to the emergency room, you would find the time to bring him or her. Counseling after a traumatic event can be just as vital. If you have work conflicts, explain the gravity of the situation to your supervisor, or ask the school counselor or psychologist to do so for you. Or have another family member, your child's babysitter/caretaker, or a trusted family friend bring your child to his or her appointments. Remember, your child will likely need only a few appointments: Be creative and find a way to get him or her there.

Finally, it's important to understand that counseling services recommended for a child who has experienced trauma will focus primarily on the child. If issues do for some reason arise that revolve around the family, the mental health professional is trained to address these issues in a supportive and confidential manner. It is important to put your child first after a crisis and not be concerned about protecting any family secrets.

Be Aware of Long-Term Effects

See "Long-Term Effects" in Chapter Twelve for information about pathological stress reactions—such as post-traumatic stress disorder—if you are concerned about your child's recovery.

Depending upon the severity of the crisis your child experiences, it may take quite a while for him or her to fully recover. Grief, in particular, will take a long time—sometimes even years—to heal. As noted in Levine (1998), "Children, like adults, grieve for a long time and reexperience loss from different perspectives as they move along the developmental spectrum" (p. 137). Remain supportive and open to listening to your child's feelings about the trauma or loss. Again, if your child's reaction to the crisis seems particularly severe, or if you are concerned about how long it persists, speak with a mental health worker (e.g., the school psychologist) and/or your clergy member (if applicable).

Some specific events or time frames, called "triggering events," will likely bring the trauma back into sharp focus for your child. Triggering events occur when a person senses something similar to something he or she was aware of during a crisis. If the crisis occurred, for example, after a fire alarm sounded at school, the next time the school's fire alarm (or any other fire alarm) rings will probably be frightening for your child. Hearing a news report about a similar event elsewhere is another "trigger" (NOVA, 1994). In some cases, significant family events such as birthdays and holidays can also trigger an emotional reaction (CASP, 1998). The school will be sensitive to such triggers, but you can also help your child by providing additional understanding, comfort, and attention at these times.

Another trigger that will cause survivors of a crisis to remember the event is referred to as the "anniversary" effect. According to the National Organization for Victim Assistance (NOVA, 1994), first-, second-, and third-month anniversaries of the crisis remind many people of their losses. The crisis reaction may continue on the crisis date each month and be particularly strong on the year anniversary of the event. Such trigger events can "... bring back the intense emotion that occurred with the original trauma, ... [although] the intensity of the long-term reactions usually decreases over time, as does the frequency of the reexperienced crisis" (NOVA, 1994).

A Final Note ...

> The mental health workers at your child's school, private counselors (if necessary), and your clergy member (if you attend a church) will be able to greatly assist your child in recovering from a crisis. However, the importance of your role as a parent cannot be overstated. The best thing you can do for your child after a crisis is to simply respond with patience, love, tolerance, support, and structure. You just need to be yourself, to care, and to listen.

If Your Child Learns of a
School Crisis Elsewhere

When a severe crisis happens at a school, the local—and often the national—media will likely cover the story. Because children watch TV, listen to the radio, see newspapers and newsmagazines, and access the World Wide Web, chances are your child will be exposed to coverage of school crises, possibly violent ones. After the school shootings during the 1997-98 and 1998-99 school years in West Paducah, Kentucky, near Jonesboro, Arkansas, in Littleton, Colorado, and elsewhere, for example, there was a bombardment of media coverage that likely scared most school-age children in America.

Making the events even more frightening is the fact that, as stated in Thomas (1998), "the enemy isn't some unknown bogeyman or army. It's fellow students, firing guns and slashing knives, leaving behind dead classmates and teachers while psychologically and physically wounding many others." Your child will likely ask you questions after media exposure of these types of events. "Your kids see the headlines. They watch the evening news. Their school friends talk about it. And sooner or later, they're going to ask: 'Why?' and 'Will this happen to me?'" (Thomas, 1998).

If your child asks these types of questions after learning of a school crisis, or if you know your child has been exposed to media coverage of such a traumatic event, have a frank conversation with your child about what has occurred. Said Dinah Graham, assistant professor of psychology at Texas Woman's University (TWU) in Denton, Texas: "I think we tend to not want to upset children, so we might avoid talking about [the crisis]. But what that does is it often creates more fears. What kids conjure up in their minds is perhaps worse than what happen[ed]. So be straightforward and give answers, if you know them. And if you don't, say, 'We don't know'" (Thomas, 1998).

See "Suicide Postvention" in Chapter Eleven for tips on discussing suicide appropriately with children and teens.

While honesty is the best policy, when talking about a school crisis provide as few details as will satisfy your child's curiosity. Also, don't promise your child that violence or a severe crisis will never happen at his or her school. Said Dan Miller, director of the school psychology training program at TWU, "You can't necessarily diminish it and say it only happens once in a blue moon" (Thomas, 1998). The key is to provide verbal reassurance, emphasizing that schools for the most part are very safe.

In addition to providing reassurance, discuss with your child actions he or she can take to help ensure a safe environment at his or her own school. For example, encourage your child to tell an adult if a fellow student threatens violence or suicide or brings a weapon to school. Also emphasize the safety procedures in place at your child's school that are designed to keep him or her safe.

See "Helping Your Child Cope" previously in this chapter for a more detailed discussion of typical childhood reactions to crisis, long-term crisis effects, and suggestions about how to assist your traumatized child.

If your child seems to be significantly affected by coverage of a school crisis elsewhere—for example, if he or she becomes afraid to go to bed or if his or her schoolwork or behavior are affected—discuss the situation with your child's teacher and the school counselor or psychologist. Because crises tend to bring up unresolved issues from the past, particularly those related to trauma and loss, people can be affected by a crisis even when they weren't directly involved in the event. Your child may be vulnerable to a stress reaction if he or she has experienced the following in the past:

- Relocation
- Death of a family member or friend
- A loss (e.g., of a pet, a parent through divorce)
- Poverty
- Violence at home or in the neighborhood
- Suicide threat or attempt

References

California Association of School Psychologists (CASP). (1998, November). Teen suicides: Life, after death. *NASP Communiqué, 27*(3), 14-15.

Children and death. (1998). *National Funeral Directors Association (NFDA)*. Available online: http://www.nfda.org/resources/marketplace/brochures/children.html

Flatter, C., Herzog, J. M., Tyson, P., & Ross, K. (1988, November 30). *Grief.* Available online: http://www.ctw.org/parents/article/0,1175,NzE2LDIxMQ==,00.html

Johnson, T. B. (1998, November). [Review of the book Opening up: The healing power of expressing emotions]. *NASP Communiqué, 27*(3), 21.

Johnston, R. C. (1998, May 27). Hope in the mourning. *Education Week, 17*(37), 26-31.

Katz, L. G. (1998, December 3). Discussing death with preschoolers. *ERIC Clearinghouse on Elementary and Early Childhood Education, Parent Library.* Available online: http://ericps.ed.uiuc.edu/npin/respar/texts

Levine, K. (1998, June). How children grieve. *Parents*, pp. 133-137.

Lewis, G. (1999, May 3). When a professional shield cracks: Covering Colorado rampage took toll on reporter. *MSNBC.* Available online: http://www.msnbc.com/news/265324.asp

Lieberman, R. (1998, Fall). Schoolyard tragedies: Coping with the aftermath. *School Safety*, pp. 14-16.

National Organization for Victim Assistance (NOVA). (1994). *Long-term crisis reactions* [Handout]. Washington, DC: Author.

National Organization for Victim Assistance (NOVA). (1997). *Community crisis response team training manual* (2nd ed.). Washington, DC: Author.

Pitcher, G. D., & Poland, S. (1992). *Crisis intervention in the schools.* New York: Guilford.

Regrouping after tragedy. (1998, March 25). *ABCNEWS.com.* Available online: http://archive.abcnews.com/sections/us/DailyNews/gma_coping.html

Sleek, S. (1998, June). After the storm, children play out fears. *American Psychological Association's Monito*r, *29*(6), 12.

Thomas, K. M. (1998, March 26). When tragedy strikes, kids will want answers. *Dallas Morning News,* p. 1C.

Wolfelt, A. D. (1998). The mourner's corner. *The Center for Loss and Life Transition.* Available online: http://www.centerforloss.com/mourners.html

chapter **nine**

Community Concerns

Leadership Role of Your School

During any crisis that impacts your school and surrounding community (e.g., a natural disaster, an act of violence), it is crucial for the school to assume a leadership role within the community for the crisis response. Specifically, your school representatives should reach out to other appropriate agencies to open the lines of communication and facilitate interagency collaboration during the crisis response. Further, your school building should be kept open and viewed as a source of support both for your school community and the surrounding community as a whole.

Sometimes this open, collaborative role does not come naturally to schools. School personnel may not view these types of actions as appropriate, if they think about them at all. For example, schools are often reluctant to involve the central office and even the police in a crisis (even when it's apparent that a crime has been committed), preferring to handle the situation internally. Some schools are reluctant to hold meetings for parents and community members after a school crisis. Often, this reluctance is the result of uncertainty; many schools lack confidence in conveying information about mental health and crisis resolution to parents and other family members.

It makes sense, however, for your school to assume a leadership role in many ways, because the school is a focus of the surrounding community. It's natural and easy for parents to come to your school when they need information and/or support. Your school, also, can provide helpful information in a timely manner to people assisting with the effects of the crisis elsewhere in the community.

The key actions schools should take are detailed in the crisis response instructions provided in the previous chapters of this book. The following is a review of the points specifically pertaining to *community/interagency collaboration*:

- Involve the police (and other emergency responders) when appropriate.

  Historically, schools have tended not to report crimes committed at school for various reasons, such as:

  – An attempt to avoid negative publicity.
  – The fear of being blamed.
  – The fear of retaliation (particularly targeted toward teachers).
  – An attempt to avoid litigation.
  – A preference for their internal system of providing disciplinary consequences.
  – A desire to avoid stigmatizing the offender.
  – Confusion about which incidents are serious enough to report.

See "Summoning Help" in Chapter One for quick tips on information to provide to, and ways to work with, emergency responders during a crisis.

  Any time a weapon (or the threat of a weapon, such as a bomb threat) is involved in a school incident, or any time illegal drugs are involved, it is essential that the school notify the police. If an action would be considered a crime if it occurred on the street rather than on your school grounds (e.g., a sexual assault, a physical fight resulting in injuries, etc.), then you must contact the police. It is essential that schools, law enforcement agencies, and juvenile authorities work together to provide appropriate legal consequences and interventions when a crime occurs on campus. Traditional disciplinary consequences administered by schools are not appropriate in these cases. This interagency involvement also ensures that victims receive the services they need. And, contrary to the fears some administrators have, involving the appropriate authorities will help to vindicate the school in the event of litigation, as this action demonstrates that the school took the incident seriously and did everything possible to address it appropriately. (*See "Liability and Litigation" in Chapter Twelve for more information.*)

- Communicate closely with your central office.

  Besides having an aversion to involving the police, some school administrators even think it is wise to keep news of serious incidents that occur at their school from their central office. For example, in November 1998 an assistant principal in a Florida elementary school intervened with and calmed a student who was lunging at another student with a switchblade. But the school's principal would not let her treat this as a serious offense, punishable by suspension or expulsion, because he did not want the paperwork sent to the central administration. (Needless to say, the police were not contacted either!) The principal insisted that the paperwork state only that the student brought a "nuisance item" to school.

Unfortunately, this mentality likely will not change until school principals begin to be evaluated not on whether or not such an incident occurred at their school but on whether they had an effective crisis plan and organized discipline policies in place when it occurred. Administrators who neglect to report (and thus address appropriately) serious school incidents may live to regret their decision, however. Such incidents are difficult to keep under wraps and have a way of "snowballing." There are few events in the careers of administrators that can positively or negatively shape their success and the public's perception of them like their response to a crisis. As the National School Public Relations Association (NSPRA) warned, "… you don't want to be placed in a position of covering up an incident. Once you lose your credibility, you have lost any chance of bringing everyone together to solve the problem" (Bagin, 1998).

- Collaborate with community leaders.

Immediately after the school shooting at Westside Middle School near Jonesboro, Arkansas, all appropriate authorities and agencies—from the school leaders to mental health organizations, the police, the Red Cross, the local clergy, the county prosecutor's office and judges, and the mayor—mobilized to collaboratively address the crisis. Everyone worked well together in the face of the tragedy to sort out all of the issues and required actions. The school was intimately involved in planning the crisis response with the local leadership. Westside Middle School also quickly realized that they needed some additional assistance. Just six hours after the shooting, the county prosecutor's office and the state's attorney general called in a national crisis response team to assist the local caregivers with the crisis intervention (*see "Help to Request" in Chapter Four for more information*). These decisive and collaborative actions did much to help everyone effectively cope with the crisis and promote healing within the community.

After a high school student sprayed 50 rounds of ammunition into his Springfield, Oregon, school's cafeteria in May 1998, wounding 22 people and killing two students, the response was coordinated at the district and city level. According to Cathy Paine, a crisis response team leader there:

> *School administrators and city officials had previously collaborated in drafting the district's* Emergency Procedures Manual. *They formed a joint 'command center' at City Hall, which was a clearinghouse for inquiries from both the press and the public. Additional phone lines set up by 10:00 AM [the shooting occurred at*

See "Summoning Help" in Chapter One for guidelines on involving your central office during a crisis.

7:55] the day of the tragedy were staffed 24 hours a day through the four-day holiday weekend by city and school district employees (Paine, 1998, p. 16).

Your school's central office should notify the appropriate city and community leaders when a severe school crisis occurs. These leaders should include emergency management personnel, the mayor, and/or the county judge, if the crisis is of a severe enough magnitude (i.e., a crime scene, with multiple deaths) to warrant their involvement in the crisis response.

- Communicate with other area schools.

See "Summoning Help" in Chapter One for tips on quickly alerting area schools.

As soon as possible after you secure the safety of those involved in your school crisis and summon help from both the police and your central office, alert all the other schools in the area about the crisis. Such notification is necessary so that they can take safety precautions to protect their own students and staff and so that they can notify any family members and close friends of victims (and potential victims) and suspected student perpetrator(s) within their school communities.

In the event of a catastrophic, city-wide crisis—such as the Oklahoma City bombing in 1995—all of the city's school principals should meet and communicate about the crisis as quickly as possible. The goal would be to coordinate their crisis response efforts on a district-wide basis. Such a group effort will be helpful any time a crisis directly impacts more than one school, whether or not the schools are in the same district.

- Hold a family/community meeting on the evening of a severe crisis.

See "The Family/ Community Meeting" in Chapter Two for details about the meeting's format and content.

This meeting has two main purposes:

1. To give everybody the facts so that there is no confusion, and to explain the school's crisis response plans.
2. To provide a forum for members of the school community to process the crisis, and to communicate to parents and other family members ways in which they can assist their children and themselves in coping with the effects of the crisis.

- Contact the families of victims and suspected student perpetrator(s).

See "Verifying Information/Crisis Fact Sheet" in Chapter One for information about verifying facts with family members when a crisis occurs outside school hours and/or off-campus.

Many school administrators put off making such contacts. But as uncomfortable as these contacts may be (particularly for large schools, when administrators do not know the parents), school officials must reach out to surviving victims and their families and to the families of deceased victims during a school crisis. Your school can be of assistance to these families in many ways, and an open dialogue with them can help the school obtain the facts necessary to provide an appropriate crisis response. By visiting the families, you also can provide a much-needed intervention with surviving school-age siblings of victims (i.e., helping them to cope with their grief and process their reactions to the tragedy and working with their teachers to gently transition them back to school).

Communicating with the family members is particularly important when the death is a suicide, as there are some particularly sensitive issues in these cases. (*See "Suicide Postvention" in Chapter Eleven for more information.*)

While perhaps not as immediate a priority for schools as supporting the families of victims, if the suspected perpetrator(s) in a crisis are students in your school, school representatives should communicate with their families as well. (*See "Families of Suspected Student Perpetrators" later in this chapter for guidelines.*)

Other Area Schools

If a crisis occurs at another school in your district and/or town, you will likely need to provide some sort of crisis response within *your* school. Depending upon the severity and nature of the crisis, you, as a school administrator, may or may not need to stop what you are doing to immediately respond to what happened. However, you will need to know the facts so that you will be able to respond appropriately should something related to the crisis come up within your school.

Schools in close proximity to a school experiencing a severe crisis tend to underestimate the effects on their own school communities. However, an over-response to a crisis is preferable to an under-response. The response required of you will depend in large part upon the severity of the crisis that has occurred elsewhere and on how close your school's connection is with the affected school(s). For example, a rapid and sensitive response will be called for if your school community includes family members of victims, potential victims, and/or family members of suspected student perpetrator(s). "Feeder schools"—those with logical connections to the school at which the crisis occurred, such as a victim's last-year school or one from which a victim or suspected student perpetrator recently transferred—will also be affected.

When a crisis occurs at another area school, your school's administration and counseling staff should both participate in the crisis response at your school. The following are some of the things you will need to do:

- Secure the safety of your students and staff.

  When you are notified of the crisis—whether that notification comes from your central office, the school in crisis, or the media—take any and all necessary measures to protect the safety of your school community members. Particularly if the crisis is a violent one, err on the side

See "Injury/Death Notification" in Chapter One for guidelines on the sensitive task of alerting family members of the injury/death of their loved ones.

See "Task List" in Chapter Two for guidelines on paying condolence visits to family members.

See "Containing the Media" in Chapter Three for information about "running interference" with the media for the families of victims and suspected student perpetrator(s).

of caution, as perpetrators sometimes target more than one school for violence. In the fall of 1984 in Houston, Texas, for example, an 11-year old boy was shot while raising the American flag in front of his school. The gunman had already fired on another school down the street, shooting at and missing some kids walking into that school. After shooting the 11-year old, he went to a third school and was firing against the side of the building. This case highlights the need to take precautions immediately when violence is occurring at a neighboring school.

Recommended safety measures include getting everybody inside—and keeping everybody inside—until you're sure about what's really happening. Evacuate the playground and bring students and staff in portable classrooms inside the main building if it is safe to do so. Lock your school's doors and post staff at the entrances to let in any parents who arrive (which they may do if the crisis has been publicized by the media). Then, if the perpetrator(s) have not been apprehended, cancel every extracurricular event involving schoolchildren that has been scheduled for that day. Supervise the students closely when they leave school at the end of the day. In such crisis situations, it is prudent to advise parents to pick up their children after school.

In Jonesboro, Arkansas, when the staff of University Heights Elementary School (12 miles away from the Westside school complex) heard there had been a school shooting, they wisely locked their school's outside doors and kept the students in their classrooms. Said school librarian Robin Nichols, "At the time, we just knew it was a shooting. We didn't know if there were going to be other happenings in the city." The school kept all doors locked for about 40 minutes, until it was clear that the shooting at Westside was an isolated incident (Egerton, 1998).

- Immediately notify affected family members within your school community.

Specific people within your school community, both students and staff, may have an urgent need to know what is happening at the school experiencing a crisis. Siblings of student victims and suspected student perpetrator(s), as well as family members on the staff, should be notified of the situation at once.

Have your school counselors or psychologists call the affected family members individually from their classes to explain what has happened. Then keep them updated on the status of the crisis as information becomes available.

In Jonesboro, Arkansas, Joy Rapert, a second grade teacher at the University Heights school, was just one such person with a great need

See "Threatening Person Outside the Building" and "Armed Intruder Inside the Building" in Chapter One for more information.

See "Injury/Death Notification" in Chapter One for guidelines on the sensitive task of alerting family members of the injury/death of their loved ones.

to know the facts. As described in Egerton (1998), she "… spent a harrowing 40 minutes waiting for word about her two grandchildren who attend[ed] Westside, and daughter, a speech therapist there." Every minute counts when providing such information to worried family members and friends.

- Give the facts to the entire school community.

  In addition to family members and close friends, there may be more subtle ripples of effect within your school. A victim's best friend might attend your school, or one of your teachers might have coached a team on which injured students played, for example. To ensure that all affected individuals receive timely and accurate notification of the crisis, share the facts of the situation with your entire school community, including the students (even young students). Doing so will also help to control the spread of rumors within your building about the crisis.

  Encourage all affected members of your school community to attend the family/community meeting that will be hosted that evening by the school experiencing the crisis. (*See "The Family/Community Meeting" in Chapter Two for information about the meeting's format and content.*)

See "Verifying Information/Crisis Fact Sheet" in Chapter One for information about obtaining/verifying crisis facts and how to share those facts with your school community appropriately and in age-appropriate language.

- Communicate the facts to any parents who call or arrive at your school.

  If a severe crisis that is occurring within your district or town is publicized by the media, parents of your students (and perhaps family members of the staff) will likely call or arrive at your school seeking news about the crisis and the well-being of their loved ones. Share with these family members all of the verified facts—but *only* the verified facts—as you learn them. (*See "Communicating With Parents/Family Members" in Chapter One for tips on reassuring family members both on the telephone and at person at school.*)

If the crisis involved the suicide of a school community member, see "Suicide Postvention" in Chapter Eleven for guidelines on what, and what not, to say.

- Decide whether to close your school early or keep it open for the rest of the day.

  If your school is directly affected by the crisis, you will need to decide whether to dismiss your students early or keep school in session for the rest of the day. Even if your school was not directly affected, if the crisis was catastrophic, some shaken parents may wish to take their children home with them. If you are keeping school open for the rest of the day (*see "Task List" in Chapter Two for guidelines*), encourage the parents to leave their children at school where they can be told the facts of the crisis and have the opportunity to "process" their reactions to the crisis (*see the next bullet for an explanation*) with the assistance of your school staff.

  Encourage concerned parents to attend, with their children, the family/community meeting that will be hosted that evening by the school experiencing the crisis. (*See "The Family/Community Meeting" in Chapter Two for information about the meeting's format and content.*)

- Process the crisis with your students and staff, as necessary.

To "process" a crisis is to systematically assist those affected by the crisis in examining their feelings about it. The purpose is to minimize trauma and begin healing. Processing, therefore, is a way of talking that facilitates discussion about a crisis by those affected by it. If processing is necessary, separate processing sessions should be held for your students and staff. These sessions should be led by the mental health workers at your school and/or any outside crisis response team assisting the school(s) in crisis (see "Help to Request" in Chapter Four for more information).

As explained by the Pasco County (Florida) Crisis Intervention Team, when a crisis occurs the emotions experienced are generally very strong and often difficult to resolve. School personnel and students are no exception: The impact of a death or crisis on a school can be significantly debilitating to the normal school process. Schools must accept the responsibility for alleviating some of the grief, pain, and fears often present following a crisis involving students or staff members (District School Board, 1994).

See "How Do You Process?" in Chapter Five for a proven method of processing the effects of a crisis with people of all ages.

If only a few of your school community members (e.g., family members and close friends or associates) are directly affected by the crisis, processing should occur on a one-to-one basis with these individuals. If many in your school are affected by the crisis, or if the nature of the crisis is such that news of the incident will cause your students anxiety or fear for their own future safety (e.g., a serious act of violence, a kidnapping, etc.), discussion about the crisis should occur on a classroom-by-classroom basis. The faculty can process their reactions to the crisis together as a group, perhaps after school.

If yours is a "feeder school" of one of the key individuals in the school crisis (e.g., the school that a suspected student perpetrator attended in the past), processing should definitely occur with the staff (and perhaps students). For example, after the school shooting in West Paducah, Kentucky, members of the national crisis response team led a processing session for the staff of the elementary school that all the victims and the perpetrator had attended. At this before-school processing session many staff members expressed feeling dismay that they had not done something differently when the shooter had attended their school, that they somehow should have known. Having the opportunity to express these uncomfortable feelings and receive reassurance was very helpful for these educators.

- Address media concerns.

Advised a school public relations specialist, "Even though your district or school may not be directly involved in a crisis incident, you may get numerous [media] requests to react to an incident, or share information about what your [school or] district is doing to prevent similar situations. Avoid commenting on the response actions taken by the [school or] district involved in an incident since you cannot know all the details of what occurred. Instead, make a positive, generic statement about education and your own prevention programs" ("Crisis Communication," 1998, p. 4).

It is very important that you do not publicly speculate about the facts of the crisis, what could have prevented it from occurring, or the competence of the school personnel involved in the crisis response. Such statements could come back to haunt your school and/or district, particularly if someone involved in the event later files a lawsuit. (*See "Liability and Litigation" in Chapter Twelve for more information.*) Further, you should encourage your students, staff, and their family members to not speak with the press, allowing appropriate representatives from the school(s) involved to provide the media with accurate information. No one who speaks with the media should provide personal information about victims, suspected student perpetrator(s), or their family members. If family members of key individuals involved in the crisis are members of your school community, your school staff should help to shield them from the media. (*See "Containing the Media" in Chapter Three for guidelines.*)

- Send a note for parents home with your students.

If the crisis was severe enough to be publicized within your town and/or district, send a note home for parents to proactively provide them with information about the incident. In your letter, detail the verified facts of the crisis incident to help control rumors. Discuss the crisis effects their children may experience (*see "Anticipate Typical Childhood Responses to Crisis" in Chapter Eight for this information*), and encourage concerned parents to attend, with their children, the family/community meeting that will be hosted that evening by the school experiencing the crisis (*see "The Family/Community Meeting" in Chapter Two*). Also mention the steps your school has taken (e.g., "processing" discussions) to address the effects of the crisis, if any, and mention your school's safety and prevention programs, if appropriate.

See "Task List" in Chapter Two for other tips on composing this letter and a sample letter.

- Collaborate on the crisis response.

In a major, city-wide crisis, all the city's school principals should meet as quickly as possible to coordinate their crisis response efforts on a district-wide basis. Your central office should organize the collaboration, which would likely include a mandatory meeting either after school the day of the crisis or before school the following day. Communications during the day (i.e., by phone, FAX, e-mail, etc.) on the days following the crisis also are advisable. In large school systems divided into regions (such as the Houston Independent School District of 200,000 students, which has four regions), a meeting of the principals of all the regions would be necessary.

Such a collaborative effort will be helpful whenever a crisis directly impacts more than one school, even if the schools are not in the same school district. Coordination of efforts can be accomplished as simply as through a joint meeting of the schools' administrators and crisis response team members. For example, if the majority of the crisis reaction is occurring in another school in your area, but your school is impacted as well, then your school's leaders might find the input of that school's crisis responders valuable in planning your crisis response and determining the best way to share resources. Particularly when a community-wide focus is needed, cooperation between area schools will eliminate duplication of effort (e.g., all parents can be invited to one family/community meeting rather than schools holding separate meetings; one media specialist can field interview requests for all the affected schools, etc.). At the very least, school principals should share information via the telephone and FAX one another pertinent facts and documents relating to the crisis (*see "Verifying Information/Crisis Fact Sheet" in Chapter One for examples of pertinent information to share*).

Another important way to collaborate on the crisis response is to temporarily release appropriate members of your school staff to assist another area school coping with a severe crisis. The best local resources in the event of a school crisis are school personnel, because they understand the school climate and school operating procedures. Nationally certified school psychologists (NCSP), in particular, are invaluable after a school crisis, as they have specialized training in child development and trauma. Because school psychologists (and other human resources) are spread thin in many areas of the country, assigned to multiple small districts, it is critical for school systems to share these personnel among districts in the event of a severe crisis. Assess the situation, and quickly release any of your school counselors, psychologists, nursing staff, and crisis response team members who are willing to assist the other school. (Even scheduled special education meetings and testing should take a backseat to an emergency response for the affected school.) However, do not send members of your school's security staff unless you are certain that the incident is isolated to the other school and that your security staff will not be needed to contain the media at your school (*see "Containing the Media" in Chapter Three for more information*).

See "Funerals" in Chapter Six for a list of terms related to funerals and funeral etiquette.

• Address any issues related to funerals.

If the crisis resulted in the death of a school community member, some of your students and/or staff might wish to attend the funeral.

If so, prepare your students for what will happen as part of this ritual, and encourage them to attend with a parent or another adult family member.

For Concerned People Elsewhere …

Recommended Steps for All Schools After Another School's Publicized Crisis

Not only schools in close proximity to a school experiencing a severe crisis, but schools elsewhere in the country as well, may see crisis effects within their communities when a school crisis is publicized. At schools across the country, students and staff who learn of the crisis may be emotionally affected by the tragic news. There is also an ever-present danger of "copycat" crimes (*see "'Copycat' Incidents" in Chapter Twelve for more information*). The following is a list of critical steps every school in America should take whenever another school's severe crisis is nationally publicized:

- Review your school's crisis response plan. (If you don't have one, review the first four chapters of this book and then schedule a school and/or district meeting to begin addressing your need for a comprehensive crisis response plan.)
- Alert all of your school staff that in the few days after a publicized severe crisis your school may experience bomb threats; violent, attention-seeking actions by students; and imitations of the suspected student perpetrator(s)' dress and/or actions (e.g., students bringing toy—or real—guns to school or using threatening language).
- Rather than cancel school, provide extra security. Take every precaution necessary to protect human safety while at the same time maintaining the regular schedule and a calm atmosphere. You might, for example, check all backpacks as students enter the building and/or post security guards.
- Your school, the police (if necessary), and parents should work together to maximize the response to effects from the crisis that occurred elsewhere and to any threats your school receives. A sense of safety must be restored within your school.
- Make your school administration and security staff extra visible (e.g., positioning them in the hallways, common areas, and in classrooms, as appropriate) in the days following a publicized severe crisis.
- Instruct all of your school staff to immediately report any threats of violence or violent actions, both past and present. Follow up on all such threats.
- Have teachers increase their visibility as well—for example, by meeting and greeting students as they arrive at school.
- Encourage all the teachers to seize the teachable moment. Teachers can discuss, in age-appropriate language, any relevant prevention themes, such as the importance of students telling an adult about any threats or rumors of violence.

continued—

- Modify or set aside the regular curriculum for a short time to address the emotional effects resulting from news of the crisis.
- Provide counseling services within the school for any students and staff profoundly affected by the news of the crisis (e.g., those who have experienced a recent loss in their own lives).
- Communicate to parents any measures taken in the wake of a publicized severe crisis through a home letter. The purpose of the letter is to control rumors (e.g., about any threats your school may receive) and to reassure parents about the safety of their children at school. Encourage normal school attendance. Also detail the crisis effects their children may experience after learning of the severe crisis elsewhere and the steps they can take to assist their children.

See the relevant chapter sections in this book pertaining to each of these points for a full explanation and additional recommendations.

Families of Suspected Student Perpetrators

Imagine for a moment that your child has been involved in a violent school crisis. The telephone call that announced this frightening news has irrevocably changed your life in an instant. You are horrified and in disbelief that the precious child you sent to school that morning will not be coming home. You also are wracked with guilt, and so many powerful emotions are sweeping over you that you can hardly breathe and can barely stay upright.

Other parents are rushing to the school, desperate for the support of one another and for news of the crisis. But where can you turn for help? Everywhere in your community you could be perceived as the enemy— despised and harassed. Soon the media will descend upon you, imprisoning you in your own home, tearing into the fabric of your family's past, exposing your foibles and secrets, perhaps warping them out of context. You are frightened for yourself and terrified for your other children and family members. How can you protect them?

Police and judges will control your immediate future. You might face prosecution, you might be sued and lose everything you have worked so hard to establish. How will you survive this? How will you ever go on in your community? Why has this happened? And what could you have done to prevent it?

What you have just imagined is a moment in the life of a family member of a suspected student perpetrator. Yet unless one has lived through a tragedy such as the shootings that occurred at the schools in West Paducah, Kentucky, near Jonesboro, Arkansas, in Littleton, Colorado, and elsewhere in the country, one cannot truly comprehend the depths of the pain of the family members affected—both family members of victims *and* family members of suspected student perpetrator(s).

Pat Golden, the mother of Drew Golden (the younger of the two shooters in Jonesboro), was at work as postmaster in a nearby town the day of the shooting. She heard that there was a shooting at the school, and "… withdrew quietly to a back room, where a friend heard her crying softly, worried for Drew's safety. Her husband Dennis called to say authorities didn't know the whereabouts of their son. 'Then,' recalls … a friend and former colleague who had stopped by for stamps, 'the phone rang again. Pat let out a terrible, terrible scream, as though someone had died. I will never forget it as long as I live. By the time I ran back to see her, another employee said, 'She's already gone.' She just tore out of there" (Labi, 1998, p. 34).

After the tragedy the Goldens did not give any formal interviews, "… staying out of the media as much as possible" explained their attorney (Parks, 1998b, p. 26A). Pat and Dennis Golden did issue a statement, read by the public defender appointed as Drew's lawyer, saying that they "… would like to explain the situation and make it clear for everyone and to take away the pain for everyone, but they simply cannot. They, too, cannot understand, and they, too, are asking why Andrew, their 11-year old baby, is allegedly involved" (Labi, 1998, p. 34).

Gretchen Woodard, the mother of Mitchell Johnson, the other Jonesboro shooter, said of the anguish in her community caused by her son's actions, "I haven't been able to sleep. I close my eyes and that's all I see … and there [are] just no words from any of us or anything anyone can do that will ever make that right again." She told her son's spiritual advisor that she "… couldn't erase the images 'of the children hurting, of the parents trying to find their babies, the fact that these mothers will never get to hold their children again'" (Labi, 1998, p. 35).

William Howard, the public defender for Mitchell Johnson, said the family was "stunned" and looking for answers themselves. "All the pieces don't fit together in their mind," he said. "They believe Mitchell is a nice, polite boy and cannot conceive of him as a cold-blooded murderer" (Parks, 1998a).

Scott Johnson, Mitchell's father, told CBS News after the shooting, "As hard as it is for me to say that, my son is guilty" (Labi, 1998, p. 35). At his church the night after the shooting, when the congregation was asked to pray for "… those who were wounded and who died," Scott Johnson fell out of his chair and collapsed, "… breaking down and crying" (Labi, 1998, p. 35). After his son's sentencing hearing in August 1998, however, Scott Johnson "… criticized authorities … pointing out that the youth camp to which … Mitchell was headed had a poor reputation and (through his attorney) that school officials shared the blame for the shootings" (Shepherd, 1998). This was not a position likely to garner the family any support or sympathy within the Jonesboro community.

Ann and John Carneal, the parents of the shooter in West Paducah, Kentucky, also were shocked to learn that their son was the perpetrator of violence. When she first heard about the shooting, Ann Carneal began gathering blankets, water, and cups to bring to the school to help. Then she heard that Michael was the shooter. When John Carneal heard word of the crisis, he went straight to Heath to check on the safety of his two children. A guidance counselor told him that his daughter, Kelly, was okay but then said, "You need to come with me." John Carneal assumed he was going to be told that Michael was dead. Said Tammie Pierce, the wife of John Carneal's law partner, "John said he'd give anything if he himself could have been a victim, rather than being on the other side" (Pedersen & Van Boven, 1997).

The Carneals told their pastor that "... they had no idea what prompted the shootings" (Cabell, 1997) and the family was reported to be "... deeply distraught over the killings and determined to contact the families of the victims. 'They feel so helpless,' [said] Rev. Paul Donner, their pastor, 'and they want to do something'" (Hewitt, 1997).

The isolation most families of suspected student perpetrator(s) experience continues long after the actual tragedy, extending throughout the legal process, the sentencing, and beyond. At Michael Carneal's arraignment, his parents "... sat alone with a friend at the side of the courtroom. They left quickly after the hearing and declined to comment .... [In contrast,] many of [the families of victims and students crowding the courtroom] collected in a tight circle and tearfully embraced" (Bridis, 1998). At a hearing for Golden and Johnson in Jonesboro, "Mitchell's mother ... put her head on the table and Andrew's mother ... wept as prosecutors described the charges against their sons" (Associated Press, 1998c). "Those parents were utterly devastated," said the chaplain of the Arkansas State Police. "I pray we can find compassion for those parents because they're suffering as well. One of the mothers kept saying, 'Our life is ending. Our life is ending'" (Associated Press, 1998c). As noted in Stovall (1998), "If getting through the shock of a child's arrest is hard, getting through the next weeks, months, or years can be crushing. 'It is like being thrown up against a brick wall over and over again,' [said] Antonette (Tony) Dillingham," whose 19-year old son was convicted of murder in Texas in 1993.

The reactions of community members to families of suspected student perpetrator(s) derive from many factors, including:

- The community members' religious beliefs;
- The severity of the crime;

- The motivations of the suspected perpetrator(s) and the circumstances of the crisis incident;
- The culpability (or perceived negligence) of the parents/family;
- Any public statements made by the family members after the tragedy; and
- The outcome of any criminal trial and/or sentencing.

Blame of the families is more prevalent when the suspected perpetrator is a child, because parents tend to be held responsible for the actions of their children. Sometimes parents are even held accountable under the law. As of 1998, 42 states had enacted laws holding parents responsible for the crimes of their children. Of those, 17 make parents criminally liable (Faltermayer, 1998). Child access prevention (CAP) laws, for example, require adults (often parents and legal guardians) to keep all firearms, including hunting rifles, out of the reach of children. In three states, violation of these laws is a felony (Faltermayer, 1998). Unfortunately, these laws are rarely enforced. Until they are routinely prosecuted, and the parents of children who used their guns to murder are made examples for the rest of the country, children and teens will continue to use their families' firearms to perpetrate violence.

> "I also wonder about the boys' parents and Andrew's grandparents who helped raise him. Why didn't they know what their children were up to? I'm currently suing all of them to prevent them from ever selling their stories and profiting from Shannon's death."
>
> —Mitchell Wright, husband of teacher Shannon Wright, who was killed in the Jonesboro, Arkansas, school shooting (Casey, 1999, p. 12)

In locations where CAP laws are not in effect, or when laws holding parents responsible for the crimes of their children are not enforced, victims and their families may seek restitution from perpetrators' families through civil suits. After the shooting at Westside Middle School near Jonesboro, Arkansas, two such suits were filed on behalf of the victims' families naming shooter Drew Golden and shooter Mitchell Johnson, as well as their parents, Dennis and Pat Golden and Gretchen Woodard, respectively, as defendants. Drew Golden's grandfather, Doug Golden, was also named as a defendant, as were the manufacturers of the two rifles (Remington Arms and Universal Firearms) used by the boys in the slayings (Holmes, 1999b). The lawsuits, which seek an unspecified amount of compensatory damages and have been consolidated for trial purposes, claim, among other points, that "… the guns taken from Doug Golden's home were improperly stored, should have been equipped with trigger locks, and were negligently designed and manufactured" (Holmes, 1999b, p. 15A).

Even when there is nothing as concrete as irresponsible storage of guns or obvious warning signs of violence, families of suspected student perpetrator(s) are still targeted by community members for blame. As the father of a troubled son who brutally murdered his mother pointed out, "Most parents out there do everything they can for their children. But there are no guarantees, and that's probably the most frightening thing about parenting" (Stovall, 1998). Agreed the Texas father of another convicted murderer, "People don't understand that the next death-row inmate may be their niece or nephew—no matter how carefully they were raised.... People say, 'I'll never have to deal with anything like that.' ... I tell them, 'Before March of 1992, I was just as sure as you are'" (Stovall, 1998).

Parents of the perpetrators of violent crime report that some friends and relatives drop out of their lives. Said Dallas psychoanalyst and child psychiatrist Diane Fagelman Birk (cited in Stovall, 1998), "People don't want to identify with [crime-impacted families]. It scares them that it could happen to them, too, so they shun them as different."

Being shunned is bad enough, but some families also face harassment that can only be called venomous. Jackie Golden, grandmother of Drew Golden (one of the shooters in Jonesboro), for example, received an angry anonymous call that really shook her. "I hope your boy gets raped in jail and killed," said the caller. Trembling, Golden responded, "Andrew is still my grandson" (Faltermayer, 1998, p. 36).

Lloyd Brooks, the father of one of the girls injured in the Jonesboro shooting, expressed a more typical feeling about the suspected student perpetrators' families. "I don't want to punish the parents. I want to punish the kids," he said (Associated Press, 1998c). Many other community members were even more forgiving. A nurse in Jonesboro, for example, said, "I just really feel for the parents and families of the children. The (accused) boys' parents. I'm sure they're struggling, having a real hard time. My heart goes out to them" (Skiba, 1998). Agreed Reverend Richard Williams, executive director of City Team Ministries in Jonesboro, "Lots of people here are reaching out to all sides in this tragedy. They realize that the families of the two boys are suffering, too, that they have also lost their children" (McLemore, 1998).

In West Paducah, Kentucky, many community members supported the family of the student perpetrator, visiting them to offer them comfort. "This community will not turn its back on the Carneals. They have a home here," said one resident. Said another, "When you think about it, as terrible as it would be to lose a child, to have your child be the one responsible for killing those other children would be just unbearable. Just unbearable" (Hewitt, 1997).

After a school crisis in which members of the school community are injured and/or killed at the hand of a student, there will naturally be anger toward the suspected student perpetrator and perhaps his or her family. It may take a long time for those in a community to release their anger

> "I cannot even imagine what the boys' [who murdered my daughter] families are going through.... I am sure they loved their kids as much as we loved ours, and did the best they could."
>
> —Suzann Wilson, mother of Britthney Varner, who was killed at Westside Middle School near Jonesboro, Arkansas, reflecting on the long-term effects a year after the tragedy (Ashcraft, 1999, p. 15A)

and forgive, if they ever do, and we cannot tell affected community members how to feel about the person or people responsible for their pain. Community members, in their anger and grief, sometimes find it difficult to realize that the families of suspected student perpetrator(s) have been victimized in a sense as well. Plus all of the services available to community members after a severe crisis are geared to victims and their families, which means that the family members of suspected student perpetrator(s) must deal with their own painful issues with little support. We encourage anyone who does not choose to extend the suspected student perpetrator(s)' families compassion to leave them alone to struggle with their own demons.

The school in crisis can and should, however, take a more proactive position and make every effort to assist these families. These people do not cease to be members of your school community when their children are suspected of a crime (even such a heinous crime as shooting a classmate or teacher). In our society people are innocent until proven guilty, and the parents and siblings of suspected student perpetrator(s) have been victimized as well. Although perhaps a lower priority than providing immediate assistance to victims and their families, your school should do the following to reach out to families of suspected student perpetrator(s):

- The Crisis Coordinator/head administrator should contact the parents of suspected student perpetrator(s) to personally tell them about the crisis and the suspected involvement of their children—if possible, do not let them first hear this news on the television or radio.

  Tell them whether their children have been taken into custody and/or to the hospital, and offer to have a school representative (e.g., a member of the school's mental health staff) accompany them to the police station or hospital. Obviously these will be difficult calls to place. Use the Crisis Fact Sheet to remind you to stick to the facts, and avoid using emotional language/terms. As hearing this news will be quite traumatic for these families, you might follow the same guidelines for providing a death notification either on the telephone or in person, as applicable (see "Injury/Death Notification" in Chapter One for these guidelines).

- Visit the families of suspected student perpetrator(s).

  Sometime before the family/community meeting on the night of the crisis, the Crisis Coordinator, other available members of your school's crisis response team (particularly mental health workers), and members of any outside crisis response team assisting your school should visit with the family members of suspected student perpetrator(s). These visits should be made in person. State that you regret that the situation has occurred and you are sorry about their pain, and encourage them to seek comfort from their clergy member (if applicable). You could offer to relay any message from them to the families of victims.

- The school representatives visiting the families should make a mental health referral.

  Emphasized Dallas psychoanalyst and child psychiatrist Diane Fagelman Birk, professional counseling can help parents "… get through the pain and come out on the other side." Further, she recommends family counseling if there are other children in the family (Stovall, 1998). Because the families of suspected student perpetrator(s) will likely not utilize the counseling services available at school, and because their need for emotional support will likely surpass these services in any event, a private mental health practitioner will generally be the best source of assistance for these families. If private counseling is not feasible for these families, they might utilize the local mental health resources available through your city or county.

- "Run interference" with the media, if the families welcome your assistance.

  Often the families' attorneys will handle their public statements, but some families of suspected student perpetrators may wish to speak to the media directly to defend their families and/or correct misperceptions. If they do not wish to speak with the media, they may welcome the assistance of your Media Liaison or another staff member, including accompanying the family members from the school, if they've arrived there, to waive off the media. The school's assistance can also include communicating with the families later in the day as well as in the days following the crisis. During that time, you can lend support and even serve as a go-between with the media, if that would be helpful. Say, for example: "This incident is generating all this media attention. How can we help you? Perhaps we can share some information or a statement from you. We can take care of the media here at school, and then maybe they'll leave you alone."

- The Media Liaison and Crisis Coordinator should be discreet with the media.

  Have as much respect for the families of suspected student perpetrator(s) as you have for families of victims and survivors. Do not release the names of the suspected student perpetrator(s) prior to family member notification (*see "Injury/Death Notification" and "Communicating With Parents/Family Members" in Chapter One for more information*). Do not provide photos of or personal information about the suspected student perpetrator(s) without parental/family member permission. (The media will likely obtain photos and background information anyway with a little digging—such as scanning photos from a

"'… [A]ll the [media] craziness is starting back' as the first anniversary of what [Gretchen Woodard, the mother of one of the convicted student perpetrators in the March 1998 school shooting near Jonesboro, Arkansas] calls 'the day we all lost our innocence' approaches. 'I'm better prepared' for the media than [I] was a year ago [Woodard said]. 'I guess you learn a little.'"

(Holmes, 1999a, p. 1A)

copy of last year's yearbook—but they shouldn't come from the school.) Also, do not provide the names of close friends or family members of the suspected student perpetrator(s) or provide personal information about such individuals (e.g., what class they are in, where they work, where they live, etc.).

When speaking with the media, remember that it is important to avoid "glorifying" suspected student perpetrator(s) with excessive attention. Because children are attention seekers, a focus on the student perpetrator(s) could contribute to "copycat" incidents in the future (*see Chapter Twelve for more information about "copycat" crimes*). At some point you may need to do what Principal Bill Bond did in West Paducah, Kentucky: refuse to answer any more questions about the suspected student perpetrator. Instead discuss with the media what can be done to assist survivors and talk about positive prevention efforts.

- The Counseling Liaison and other crisis response team members should make every effort to assist the siblings of suspected student perpetrator(s) within the schools.

Perhaps the family members most at risk when the suspected perpetrator(s) are students are their siblings. These innocent children have not only lost a sibling and been traumatized themselves, but they may carry some of the weight of guilt and blame assigned to their family by the community and/or media. Without a great deal of support, the prognosis for these siblings is not good either socially or academically.

Kelly Carneal, the older sister of the West Paducah shooter, was fortunate in this regard. Embraced by her school community, she "… was not only welcomed back to school but encouraged to sing with the school choir at the slain students' funeral" (Pedersen & Van Boven, 1997). The year of the school shooting, Kelly Carneal held up well and was valedictorian of her graduating class. It is likely that this bright young woman will continue to thrive. Although one can only imagine how she has been affected by the tragedy, she was supported in pursuing her own excellence within the school.

Monte Woodard, the younger stepbrother of Mitchell Johnson, one of the Jonesboro shooters, was only 11 years old at the time of the murders. Monte likely expressed the feelings of many siblings of suspected student perpetrator(s) when he told friends that he "… was not going to live in a hole, not going to be denied the right to live his life" (Labi, 1998, p. 35). Yet despite this brave talk and his appeal for fairness, this little boy was afraid to return to school, "… worried that he would be punished for the sins of his brother" (Labi, 1998, p. 35). Monte's teacher "… came to his house with a letter from his classmates saying they still liked him and wanted him to return," his father said (Associated Press, 1998a).

Despite the letter, Terry Woodard said that "… he wasn't ready to send his son back. 'I've been around this town,' he said. 'These people don't forgive…. They don't see it that Monte didn't have [anything] to do with it. They just see him as Mitchell's brother'" (Associated Press, 1998a).

Not everyone would agree with Terry Woodard. Indeed, a great deal of discussion took place in the Westside school system about how best to provide services and support for Monte. An alternative school placement was briefly discussed, but all of the educators concerned decided that an alternative placement would be inappropriate. They were worried, however, that Monte would have difficulty in successfully returning to his own school. The NOVA team (*see Chapter Four*) responded by saying, "But that's our challenge [to assist in Monte's smooth transition back to school], and here's what we're going to do …." The team assisted the educators in talking with the school's teachers about the situation, and they, in turn, talked with their students. They emphasized that "Mitchell's brother didn't pull the trigger" and that he was not to blame for the tragedy. Fortunately, after implementing this plan, they found that Monte could indeed rejoin his class.

The school year following the tragedy, Monte began the sixth grade at Westside Middle School and is playing trumpet in the school band. Principal Karen Curtner told his mother, Gretchen Woodard, that Monte is "going forward" (Holmes, 1999a, p. 9A). Ironically, one of Monte's teachers his first year at Westside was Lynette Thetford, shot in the abdomen during the attack the year prior. "I was a little apprehensive about it at first," said Thetford, "but after that first day it was okay. He is just a normal kid" (Watkins, 1999, p. 20A).

"Monte has carried the weight of the world on his shoulders," said Woodard, and she is pleased that he has been treated well by both students and staff at Westside Middle School. "That's my blessing," Woodard said. "We're very, very grateful. That says a lot for the community" (Holmes, 1999a, p. 9A). With such support from the school community, there is no reason Monte Woodard should not continue to succeed both in school and as a productive community member in Jonesboro.

Families of suspected student perpetrator(s) may not have the desire or resources to move away from your community after a severe crisis, nor should they be expected to. Family members who remain in the community will have a very difficult time escaping the effects of the tragedy and will need your support. Noted a family friend of the Klebolds, whose son was one of the gunmen in the April 1999 massacre at Columbine High School in Littleton, Colorado, "[The Klebolds] don't see much of a future. They're trying to figure it out. Where do we go? … Who will like us? And they're kind people" (Abrams, 1999).

You have a responsibility to any of the siblings of suspected student perpetrator(s) attending your school to support them in making a fresh start and achieving to the best of their potential. In a high profile case, school administrators might discuss with the family whether the sibling of a suspected student perpetrator would prefer to transfer to another school within the same school system. Sometimes this option assists siblings in rejoining a school community with less stigma.

Role of the Clergy

God hath not promised sun without rain, joy without sorrow, peace without pain ... and God shall wipe away all tears ... (from the Holy Bible's book of Revelation).

When a severe crisis occurs at a school in your community—particularly a violent crisis—you, as a clergy member, can do much to assist others in coming to terms with the senseless act and to help ease the pain of victims and the grief of survivors. Religion can serve as a soothing balm for a community's burning anger and confusion. By the nature of your vocation you have an opportunity to plant the seeds of forgiveness and acceptance, to "... be advocates of peace and advocates of justice," as one Methodist chaplain in Jonesboro, Arkansas, explained the clergy's role after the school shooting there (Egerton, 1998).

"Close to 700 people packed the Heritage Fellowship Assembly of God Church [after the school shooting in West Paducah, Kentucky]. They danced in the aisles. They waved flags and streamers. They clapped and praised God at the tops of their lungs ...."

(Kreimer, 1998)

For Concerned People Elsewhere ...

Helping Role of the Clergy

One does not need to love or even know another person to grieve his or her death. And when a horrible tragedy anywhere in the nation or the world—and particularly a severe crisis involving schoolchildren—is publicized, many people may feel grief for the victims and anger if the crisis was a violent one. Through your sermons, you, as a clergy member, can assist members of your congregation in processing such emotions as well as reinforce any relevant life lessons. You might consider facilitating a memorial effort by your congregation (e.g., raising and donating funds or other needed supplies or sending sympathy cards) (*see "Memorializing Victims" in Chapter Six*). You might also organize and/or participate in a community-wide memorial service for your area (*see the rest of this chapter section for details*).

While there is much you can do to assist both your congregation and the school community after a school crisis, you need to keep in mind a few issues when offering your services to public schools. Primarily, the school in crisis may or may not accept your kind offer of assistance. Try not to take a refusal personally. It is more likely a reflection of the school or district having adequate resources available than a personal slight against you or your church. Schools generally prefer to utilize other school personnel to address their problems. So if the school in crisis is part of a large, well-staffed school district (such as the Cypress-Fairbanks Independent School District in Houston, Texas, which has approximately 150 counselors, 20 psychologists, and highly developed and rehearsed crisis response procedures), a crisis incident would have to be truly catastrophic for the district to need any extra assistance.

Naturally, public schools also are cautious about allowing "outsiders" to work with the students entrusted to their care. If you arrive at the school shortly after a crisis, you may be turned away unless you are already known to the school community and have a prior relationship with them. After a severe crisis, mental health workers and clergy members offering their services generally inundate schools, and someone on the school staff is charged with the task of screening these volunteers. Because this screening can take a great deal of time, it may not be a priority of the school in the immediate aftermath of a crisis. Volunteers approaching the school a little later in the crisis intervention may meet with a more positive response.

A school in a small community, however, might desperately need the assistance of local clergy members. Many small communities don't have a strong mental health cadre available for emergency assistance, and members of the clergy are crucially needed to help fill this role. For example, local clergy played a significant role in the crisis response of the town of Montoursville, Pennsylvania (population 5,000), in July 1996. When 16 members of the high school's French team and five adult chaperones were killed in the explosion of TWA Flight 800 bound for France, the community was devastated by their loss. David P. Black, the superintendent of the 2,450-student district, said: "We will be utilizing clergy, the high school student assistance teams, coaches, and teachers [for the crisis response]" (Gamble, 1996, p. 10).

Another issue to bear in mind is that there is simply no place for theological debate after a crisis at a public school. Members of the clergy of various denominations who wish to assist a school may not agree with one another's theological perspectives, and they likely will not know the religious beliefs of the students (unless they happen to be members of their own congregation). Thus, the theological aspect must be downplayed: As a clergy member, your primary function within a public school is to provide emotional support.

"All religions must be tolerated ... for ... every man must get to heaven his own way."

—Frederick the Great (1712-1786)

The need to deemphasize theology is particularly acute after the suicide of a school community member. Consider what happened in Houston, Texas. A counselor at a junior high school that had experienced a suicide called a district school psychologist to request help. He said, "I have four [clergy members] in my office. They're arguing about the afterlife. Will you come over here right away?" The school psychologist responded by saying, "I'm not coming because nobody has that answer." If those clergy members were given a classroom of children to work with, a problem would have arisen immediately. One might have said, for example, "I believe the spirit is wandering; he's going to be in hell forever," and another might have responded, "No, he has been embraced. He is in heaven. God is actually saddened that he didn't do God's work over his natural lifetime, but he has gone to heaven." Obviously this type of exchange is inappropriate and is not helpful to members of the school community.

These potential problems can be overcome, however, and there are many ways you *can* assist the school community members. The following are some ideas:

- If you are not allowed to assist within the school itself, focus your work within your own church.

  Members of your own congregation will be seeking you out for comfort and guidance after a severe school crisis, both on an individual basis and during your services. You can best support them in their time of need within your own house of worship. Ask the school to support your valuable work by announcing to the school community the various services and counseling and assistance efforts related to the crisis that will take place at your church.

  After the school shootings near Jonesboro, Arkansas, and in West Paducah, Kentucky, the clergy in those towns focused on a common theme: *forgiveness.* Forgiveness may be a difficult message for survivors of the crisis (particularly a victim's family members) to hear. Yet some level of forgiveness (or at least acceptance that the incident has occurred and cannot be undone) is required for healing. Obsessive anger—or even hatred—toward the suspected perpetrator(s) distracts survivors from focusing on their need to take care of one another, to grieve, and to look toward the future.

  Certainly forgiveness is an important theme in most major religions and denominations. Explained one Baptist minister in West Paducah, Kentucky: "… [W]e have to depend on [God]. And the main thrust of our message is that God is the most important thing in your life. And he demands forgiveness" (Goodwyn & Simon, 1997). In Jonesboro,

> "Among the busiest people in Jonesboro (Arkansas) last week were the pastors of its hundred or so churches, working on the sermons that would help their bewildered congregations make sense of the loss of four young girls and a teacher with a two-year old son at home."
>
> (Gegax, Adler, & Pedersen, 1998, p. 22)

many pastors urged forgiveness following the school shooting ("Arkansas Buries Its Dead," 1998), and Gary Cremeens, the minister at the funeral of Paige Ann Herring, the first victim to be buried, reminded those gathered that "the healing cannot begin until we forgive" (Labi, 1998, p. 36).

In West Paducah, Kentucky, the attitude of forgiveness expressed by the majority of community members was quite remarkable, due in large part to their strong religious faith. Said Reverend Bobby Strong, "At school they put up a big sign the second day that said, 'We forgive you, Mike.' And I know it's [because of] God that they can forgive him. It's definitely God, because we couldn't do it on our own" ("Paducah Students," 1997).

Ben Strong, the student who is credited with stopping Michael Carneal from killing even more people in the West Paducah school, met with the family of the shooter after the tragedy. He also asked permission to speak with the boy. As reported in "Paducah Students" (1997), "[Ben's] hope [was] to share God's forgiveness with the troubled teen. 'I guess I'd talk to him like a friend,' he [said], 'and I'd let him know we forgive him. Just let him know we're there for him.'"

Even Missy Jenkins, one of the surviving victims who will likely remain paralyzed from the shooting, urged her fellow students and community members to forgive the shooter from her hospital bed. She said, "I want people to know that I forgive Mike. And I want you to do the same" ("Paducah Students," 1997). Missy Jenkins addressed her attacker personally at his sentencing in December 1998, more than a year after she was shot. "I want [you] to look at me," she said. "I am paralyzed from the waist down. I spent five months in the hospital. I really feel helpless.... I just want you to know [this] because I have to live with this every day." Then she explained that she was "... prepared to accept whatever God wills for her future" and told Carneal, "I want you to know I have no hard feelings toward you. I am upset that this happened, but I can live this way" (Bartleman, 1998, pp. 1A, 3A).

Of course, not everyone involved was as magnanimous as Jenkins. Many were naturally very angry and expressed their feelings to Carneal. Kelly Hand, another student injured in the attack, spoke publicly for the first time at the sentencing when she told Carneal: "In my eyes, I would love to see you get the death penalty for what you did. You gave them the death penalty. They didn't do anything wrong or have a choice" (Bartleman, 1998, p. 3A).

After Michael Carneal's sentencing, Sabrina Steger, the mother of one of the murdered students, addressed the issue of forgiveness. Noting that "… the families [of the victims] have not been asked for forgiveness by either Carneal or his family," she said and, "… forgiving what happened will take time and the help of their ministers." She added that, "… there is a difference between forgiving someone for what he has done and punishing him for what he has done" (Oliver, 1998, p. 3A).

From a theological viewpoint (as well as from a mental health standpoint), some level of forgiveness after a severe school tragedy is vitally important. Determining how you might communicate the message of forgiveness to your own congregation will no doubt be a professional challenge.

- Counsel victims of the crisis within your congregation.

If victims of the school crisis and their families are members of your congregation, obviously you will want to spend a great deal of time with them. If necessary you will be called upon to deliver funeral and memorial services, and you can assist these grieving families in making appropriate funeral arrangements.

See "Funerals" in Chapter Six for suggestions.

Other survivors of the crisis will also need your support. Family members of the survivors, and other concerned citizens, will need help coping with their reactions to the crisis and any stress reactions they may experience. Your support can also help those suffering from severe or persistent crisis reactions from becoming self-destructive. (Bear in mind that the American Red Cross has estimated that child abuse, spousal abuse, and/or substance abuse increase 50-200% after a disaster or trauma.)

"I explored the Bible and it said, 'I am forced to restore what I did not steal'" (meaning that the community did nothing wrong, but still they lost many of their hopes and dreams, and sense of security).

—Minister in Jonesboro, Arkansas

After a random act of violence, the most compelling question is usually "Why?" Children (and adults, for that matter) will likely ask, "Why did it happen?" and "Why didn't God stop this from happening?" You can advise parents in your congregation about how to answer such questions. The answers you provide will, of course, depend upon your theological perspective. Among those given by the clergy (Van Campen, 1997) after the school shooting in West Paducah, Kentucky, were:

- "God gives us freedom to obey or disobey, and that freedom includes the ability to make really tragic choices…. Bad things happen to good people because evil is no respecter of persons."
- "Man makes wrong choices and pays for those wrong choices, but many times people pay for the wrong choices of others. We live in an imperfect world because it's populated with imperfect people."

- "God could have stopped the shootings. Why didn't he? I don't know.... God works through bad things to make good things happen. But we can't see that right now."
- "Sometimes God allows terrible things to happen to get our attention. Maybe we need to be a little more focused and give more attention to our children."
- "We can choose good, and we can choose bad. If God would come and interfere, he really would not be honoring the gift of free will he has given us."

See "Crisis Effects and Grief" in Chapter Seven for information about children's developmental understanding of death, age one to adolescence.

You also can advise parents about how to explain the meaning of death to their children and what you believe happens to the soul after death. Said religious leaders in Jonesboro, Arkansas, after the school shooting there, "Having parents work with their children will be critical to repairing [their] shattered lives." Explained Reverend Rodney Reeves, "What we're hoping to do is, parents at this point can be ministered unto and minister to [the children's] needs, and perhaps we [can] come around as a caring community of love and tell [the families] that God loves them. And that today is a new day" ("Regrouping After Tragedy," 1998).

If families of suspected student perpetrator(s) are members of your congregation, you may be the only person to whom they can turn right now for unconditional support and acceptance (see "Families of Suspected Student Perpetrators" previously in this chapter). Ministering to these family members may be one of your greatest challenges, as they may be tortured not only by grief but also by guilt and have many needs. After one school shooting, for example, a pastor told a national crisis response team member that the father of the shooter was "going to pieces" and "couldn't do anything without (the pastor's support)."

While you may willingly offer your assistance in counseling such family members, and not find such a level of dependence burdensome, another important aspect of your work will be to recommend mental health treatment to those you believe need more in-depth assistance. Some survivors will need the additional assistance of a mental health worker trained in trauma, in particular. A suggestion of mental health treatment from you would carry a great deal of influence and help to put such people on the road to recovery.

See "Long-Term Effects" in Chapter Twelve for signs of a pathological crisis reaction.

It is important to watch for the need for mental health treatment not just in the immediate aftermath of the crisis but over the long term as well. While you need to remain supportive and open to listening to your congregations' feelings about the trauma or loss, if someone's stress reaction seems particularly severe, or you are concerned about how long it persists, encourage that person to speak with a mental health worker.

- Go to the hospital to assist family members there.

    The school will have sent a Medical Liaison to the hospital with any injured or deceased school community members. That person will encounter parents and other family members who are seeking information about their loved ones and might appreciate your assistance. You can be a source of support for these survivors. Plus, you can assist in coordinating the injury/death notification efforts of the hospital personnel. After an injury or death notification has been given, you can help attend to the needs of the survivors, if they welcome your assistance during this time of tragedy. In Jonesboro, Arkansas, for example, "Hospital staff and clergy had to go to the holding area for desperate parents and call for wallet-sized photos of their children ... then go back and tell those parents whose children were dead" (Associated Press, 1998b).

    See the "Notification in Person at the Hospital" section of "Injury/Death Notification" in Chapter One for complete guidelines.

- Collaborate on a service for your entire community.

    The clergy members in Jonesboro, Arkansas, planned a city-wide memorial service for the victims of the school shooting that occurred there. Prior to the service, Reverend Fred Hoffstein, one of the clergy members who helped with the planning, explained, "It will be an effort that crosses denominational and faith lines. It will be a service seeking hope and healing. It is essentially to help the community deal with its pain, but we've opened it to everyone who wants to come. We know that the pain from this tragedy extends well past our city limits ... (McLemore, 1998).

    The memorial service, titled a "Service for Hope and Healing," was held at Arkansas State University one week after the shooting. An estimated 10,000 people attended. Attorney General Janet Reno spoke in person, and President Clinton—away on a goodwill trip to Africa—addressed the assembly via videotape.

    This service did much to bring the citizens of Jonesboro, and of the state of Arkansas, together and to set them on the path to healing. If the crisis in your community is catastrophic, you might work with other local clergy members to hold a similar open service for the members of your community and the surrounding areas.

- Attend all meetings held for caregivers.

    If an outside crisis response team is assisting the school in crisis, the team members will likely hold one or more sessions for local caregivers, which would include members of the clergy. (The school may hold these sessions independently if it is not receiving the assistance of an outside crisis team.) Such sessions were held after the school shootings in both West Paducah, Kentucky, and near Jonesboro, Arkansas. On the day after the shooting near Jonesboro, for example, the NOVA team (*see "National Crisis Response Teams/Organizations" in Chapter Four*) met with approximately 150 mental health professionals, clergy members, and medical staff who would be assisting the school the next day. During this meeting the NOVA team made some concrete suggestions about assisting victims of a severe crisis and dealing with the large-scale emotionality that accompanies such a tragedy.

The NOVA team also gave the local caregivers a refresher on crisis intervention principles. Specifically, they explained the NOVA model of "processing" reactions to a crisis, which has proven effective with all ages of people after a traumatic event. The NOVA counseling model emphasizes exploring the sensory perceptions of survivors to bring them back to the time of the crisis and encourage discussion of their crisis reactions. The clergy members assembled were quite impressed with the NOVA model, and many said, "I'm going to use this in my church," and "I'm going to build some of this into my service." (If you like the NOVA model, call NOVA at 1-800-TRY-NOVA to find out about future training opportunities in your state.)

In addition to learning the NOVA model of processing crisis reactions so that you can use it to help assist others, you might participate yourself. Clergy members and other caregivers are often personally affected by a crisis happening in their community, and sometimes they need just as much support as victims and survivors. You may experience a stress reaction at the time of the crisis, or you may experience such a reaction after listening to others express their pain and grief (*see "Why Caring for Caregivers Is Necessary" in Chapter Ten for more information*). You may also find that the crisis brings up some unresolved issues from the past, particularly those related to trauma and loss. One of the ministers assisting in West Paducah, Kentucky, for example, stated publicly after the crisis that he had been shot in the face while in the seminary. Not surprisingly, the violent shooting at the school had a profound effect on him. Even if you have no such serious incident in your own past, be sure to attend any sessions held for caregivers during which you can process your own reaction to the crisis.

If an outside crisis response team is not assisting the school or community, and no such sessions are offered, gather with other members of the local clergy and work through the model together. The session will provide you with the opportunity to receive support from others for your difficult work with survivors as well as provide an empathetic audience to whom you can vent some of the strong emotions you may be feeling.

- Offer your services to any outside crisis response team assisting the school or community.

See "The NOVA Model" section of "How Do You Process?" in Chapter Five for complete instructions on using this effective model, which you may wish to employ in your work in your own congregation and/or the school.

If an outside crisis response team is working in your community after the crisis, that team might include a clergy member whom you could assist. NOVA Community Crisis Response Teams, for example, typically include one or more clergy members. Such a team member might welcome your help in many capacities, such as planning a community memorial service, visiting with victims' families, and so forth.

See "National Crisis Response Teams/ Organizations" in Chapter Four for more information.

- Respond to direct requests for assistance at the school.

Even if the school does not involve you in its formal crisis response, if a student or staff member from within your congregation calls you for support, you are welcome to meet with him or her at the school. (Realize in speaking with your colleagues, however, that your presence at the school may upset other clergy members who were *not* specifically invited there.)

- Assist the school in handling injury and/or death notifications.

If you are invited to participate in the school's crisis response, one of the best ways you can help is to assist with the difficult task of notifying relatives of their loved ones' injury or death. Because school personnel are often uncomfortable providing this information, they too often send worried family members racing to the hospital in terrible suspense and jeopardizing their own safety on the road. The more humane course of action is for school personnel to tell family members what they know about their loved ones' medical condition, and school personnel may be more likely to do that if they have the assistance of a clergy member. If you assist in this manner, it's important that you limit your help to providing emotional support. Do not use religious symbolism unless the family members are members of your own congregation or ask you directly to pray with them.

See "Injury/Death Notification" in Chapter One for guidelines on delivering this news both in person and on the telephone and for addressing the immediate needs of survivors.

If you are not present when a death notification is delivered, or if the notification is done on the telephone, you might volunteer to go to the home of the survivor to attend to his or her immediate needs or to accompany him or her to the hospital. This assistance is particularly applicable if the person receiving the death notification is a member of your congregation.

- Be a comforting presence at the school.

If you are welcomed into the school after a crisis, a simple way to help is to be visible in the hallways and allow those who need your assistance to seek you out. After the school shooting in West Paducah, Kentucky, for example, "… school officials … opened the school doors to pastors and youth leaders" ("Paducah Students," 1997). Explained one clergy member who was there, "We just went … into the schools and walked through the halls and let the kids come up to us. Many of them did come up and say, 'Look, would you pray for me?' We just put our arms around them, embraced them, and prayed for them. Others just needed someone to embrace them and hold them and let them cry." ("Paducah Students," 1997).

- Assist the school in counseling students and staff.

If you are invited to participate in the school's formal crisis response, you will likely be paired with one or two mental health workers, generally from the school's counseling staff. You might work in classrooms helping students to process their reactions to the crisis (*see Chapter Five, "Processing the Crisis," for more information*).

You might also be asked to counsel and comfort those students, staff, and family members who desire additional assistance. After a severe school crisis, counseling services will likely be made available during the school day, after school and into the night, and even over weekends and/or holidays. After the school shooting at Westside Middle School near Jonesboro, for example, ministers participated in individual and group counseling sessions for community members, parents, students, and teachers that were held in the school's gym at all hours of the day and night for almost a week after the tragedy.

"[The families who came to the school to get counseling for their children] ... reminded me of pictures I've seen of soldiers after battle.... Today I did a lot of listening and let them talk."

—Leonard Higgins, Reserve Army Chaplain/ Campus Minister, Wellesley Foundation, Arkansas State University (Egerton, 1998)

As you participate in the school's crisis response, your role will be primarily that of *listener*. It will be important to minimize the theological aspect of your work. Remember that any class of students to whom you may be assigned will likely not be members of your church; therefore, you must use a more general humanitarian approach and refrain from imposing your religious beliefs upon them. (If the particular staff, students, or family members you are working with *are* members of your congregation, however, this caution might not apply.) Think of yourself as being in the school to mainly provide emotional support: a shoulder to cry on, someone to listen, a calming presence.

In your ministry work you may not have received any specific training in crisis and trauma. For you to be of maximum assistance, it will be helpful for you to follow some basic principles of crisis intervention. (*See "General Points When Using Outside Help" in Chapter Four for a list of helpful instructions for volunteers working in a school after a crisis.*)

References

Abrams, D. (1999, April 20). Gunman's parents ask: "How do we accept this?" *MSNBC*. Available online: http://www.msnbc.com/news/26356B.asp

Arkansas buries its dead. (1998, March 29). *ABCNEWS.com*. Available online: http://archive.abcnews.com/sections/us/DailyNews/jonesboro0327.html

Ashcraft, H. (1999, March 21). Pam Herring's world fell apart in March of '98. *Jonesboro Sun*, pp. 1A, 14A-15A.

Associated Press. (1998a, March 27). Arkansas students face fears as they return to deadly site. *Idahonews.com*. Available online: http://www.idahonews.com/032798/NATION_/16024.htm

Associated Press. (1998b, April 5). Doctor recounts treating Jonesboro victims: He says many of the injured will need counseling. *Dallas Morning News*, p. 29A.

Associated Press. (1998c, March 27). "My son is not a monster," father of one suspect says: Boys' parents also try to cope with killings. *Milwaukee Journal Sentinel*. Available online: http://www.onwis.com/forums/shoot/0327parent.stm

Bagin, R. (1998, June). Incidents of violence call for seasoned responses by school leaders. *NSPRA Bonus*, p. 5.

Bartleman, B. (1998, December 17). Heath: Fantasy gone too far? *Paducah Sun*, pp. 1A, 3A.

Bridis, T. (1998, January 15). Alleged shooter arraigned. *ABCNEWS.com*. Available online: http://archive.abcnews.com/sections/us/DailyNews/carneal0115.html

Cabell, B. (1997, December 3). Who is Michael Carneal? *CNNinteractive*. Available online: http://www.cnn.com/US/9712/03/school.shooting.pm/

Casey, K. (1999, March). When the shooting stopped. *Ladies' Home Journal*, pp. 10-13.

Crisis communication: Preparing an effective response. (1998, June). *NSPRA Bonus*, p. 4.

District School Board of Pasco County. (1994). *Crisis intervention team program rationale and structure*. Land O'Lakes, FL: Author.

Egerton, B. (1998, March 25). "We had children lying everywhere," paramedic says: Rampage leaves community in shock, tears. *Dallas Morning News*, p. 1A.

Faltermayer, C. (1998, April 6). What is justice for a sixth-grade killer? *TIME*, pp. 36-37.

Gamble, C. (1996, August 7). Pa. community mourns after losing 16 students, 5 adults in TWA crash. *Education Week, 15*(41), 10.

Gegax, T. T., Adler, J., & Pedersen, D. (1998, April 6). The boys behind the ambush. *Newsweek*, pp. 20-26.

Goodwyn, W., & Simon, S. (1997, December 6). Paducah murders. *Weekend Edition, National Public Radio (NPR)*.

Hewitt, B. (1997, December 22). Marching on: Stunned by tragedy, the people of Paducah search their hearts and find the healing grace of compassion. *People Weekly*, pp. 42-47.

Holmes, P. (1999a, March 22). "Craziness" returns for mother of Johnson. *Jonesboro Sun*, pp. 1A, 9A.

Holmes, P. (1999b, March 24). Mother says civil suit "hangs over head." *Jonesboro Sun*, p. 15A.

Kreimer, P. (1998, February 21). Move ahead, says young Paducah hero. *Cincinnati Post*. Available online: http://www.kypost.com/news/ben022198.html

Labi, N. (1998, April 6). The hunter and the choirboy. *TIME*, pp. 28-39.

McLemore, D. (1998, March 28). Two victims of attack are laid to rest. *Dallas Morning News*, p. 1A.

Oliver, J. (1998, December 17). Families comment after Carneal sentencing. *Paducah Sun*, p. 3A.

Paducah students learn forgiveness. (1997, December 18). *Maranatha Christian Journal*. Available online: http://www.mcjonline.com/news/news2333.htm

Paine, C. (1998, November). Tragedy response and healing: Springfield unites. *NASP Communiqué, 27*(3), 16-17.

Parks, S. (1998a, March 28). Investigators outline evidence in shootings. *Dallas Morning News*, p. 1A.

Parks, S. (1998b, April 8). Lawyer says he didn't know of abuse: Arkansas attorney for school shooting suspect heard allegation on TV. *Dallas Morning News*, p. 26A.

Pedersen, D., & Van Boven, S. (1997, December 15). Tragedy in a small place. *Newsweek*, p. 30.

Regrouping after tragedy. (1998, March 25). *ABCNEWS.com*. Available online: http://archive.abcnews.com/sections/us/DailyNews/gma_coping.html

Shepherd, C. (1998, September 13). News of the weird. *Boulder Sunday Camera*, p. 3F.

Skiba, K. M. (1998, March 27). Arkansas students get lesson in healing. *Milwaukee Journal Sentinel*. Available online: http://www.onwis.com/forums/shoot/0327ark.stm

Stovall, W. (1998, April 1). The parents' pain: Mothers and fathers of accused killers must deal with their own brand of grief and disbelief. *Dallas Morning News*, p. 1C.

Van Campen, T. (1997, December 2). Clergy, theologians offer answers to school shootings. *Knight-Ridder/Tribune News Service*. Available online: http://web2searchbank.com/infotrac/session/7/649/305300w7/9!xrn_3

Watkins, A. (1999, March 24). Teacher's life no longer same after fatal day. *Jonesboro Sun*, pp. 1A, 20A.

chapter **ten**

Who Cares for the Caregiver?

Why Caring for Caregivers Is Necessary

If you participate in the crisis response for a school in crisis within your own community, the state, or elsewhere in the nation, others may consider you a pillar of strength during this incident. However, school administrators, counselors, psychologists, and crisis response team members; police officers and other emergency responders; medical and hospital staff; clergy members; mental health workers; victims' advocates; state and national crisis response team members; and other "caregivers" are often affected themselves by a crisis and sometimes need just as much support as victims and survivors. The job you do doesn't make you less human, and you don't check your own feelings at the door, so to speak. (You may have had some training that enables you to control your emotional responses in times of crisis, and you may function at a high level in spite of them, but they are there, underneath, nevertheless.)

Nor can you entirely escape the effects of your own personal history of trauma and loss, which may resurface during a severe crisis. This process is known as "counter-transference," or "vicarious victimization" (Carroll, 1998, p. 28). Explained Servio Carroll, a school psychologist:

> *Counter-transference occurs when our own scars and injuries are revisited due to the sights, sounds, stories, or issues raised by victims or survivors. Post-traumatic stress reactions are more prevalent than most realize, and ... their presentation ranges from mild to severe. Given the*

range of events we have experienced since birth, ... it would be safe to say that all adults have unresolved issues to some degree (1998, p. 28).

These reactions can take you by surprise, as Carroll discovered when, after a shooting at his Wyoming school, he looked at a brick wall "peppered with bullet holes" and had memories of Havana, Cuba, in the 1960s. "... [I] thought I had dealt with the [Cuba] issue," explained Carroll. "And over the years I have been able to speak about it freely and without felt emotions. Obviously stronger memories of the past were still there, although I didn't know it" (1998, p. 28).

When you are called upon to respond to a school crisis, you will likely experience an immediate emotional reaction. If you are one of the key people responding, you might feel scared. You might also have a number of other unpleasant feelings, and that's to be expected. First will probably come denial: "This could not have happened." Next will come anger: "How could somebody do that?" And when it hits you that you're needed to help, you may feel anxiety or momentary panic. You might even feel completely unprepared to deal with this situation, but you are expected to deal with it nonetheless. You must move through these stages quickly, because you are one of the people who are supposed to *do something* during a school crisis.

Even after you move through these stages, the emotional effects on you will not stop. The American Red Cross (1993) characterized the emotional effects during trauma or disaster recovery into four stages: (1) the "heroic" phase, (2) the "honeymoon" phase, (3) the "disillusionment" phase, and (4) the "reconstruction" phase. The following are just a few of the reactions and activities associated with each phase that may be experienced by caregivers who assist with a school crisis as well as by the victims/survivors they assist.

Heroic Phase (Time of Crisis to Several Weeks After)

Emotional/Physical Reactions	*Activities*
Emotional numbness, uncertainty, fear, disbelief, denial, anger, self-blame, delusions of invulnerability, increased heart rate, senses more acute, overactivity	Search and rescue, assessment of damage, information gathering, mobilization of resources

Honeymoon Phase (1 Week to 3-6 Months After Event)

Emotional/Physical Reactions	*Activities*
Same as "Heroic," with addition of digestion problems, headaches, changes in appetite, inability to sleep	"Supervolunteers" emerge, community cleanup/relief efforts

continued—

Disillusionment Phase (2 Months to 1-2 Years After Event)

Emotional/Physical Reactions

Survivor's guilt, isolation, intrusive thoughts, depression, crying, anger, apathy, repression, sleep disturbances, post-traumatic stress disorder, increased injuries, psychosomatic illnesses, drug/alcohol use/abuse, social withdrawal

Activities

"Second disaster": assistance leaves, long hours at work, paperwork/documentation, lawsuits filed, rebuilding/restoring

Reconstruction Phase (Several Years After Event)

Emotional/Physical Reactions

Estrangement, role confusion, anger/frustration, moodiness, isolation/detachment, resolution, psychosomatic illnesses, allergies, shortness of breath/chest pains, ulcers

Activities

Long waits for additional assistance: federal program approval, insurance payoffs, lawsuit resolution

As you can see, the effects of a severe crisis are not alleviated within a short period of time. In fact, many effects do not set in for a while, and some even intensify and worsen over time if not addressed.

Among caregivers, the mental health workers who listen to victims and survivors of a crisis discuss their feelings are at special risk for experiencing a crisis reaction and "psychological burnout" (Johnson, 1998, p. 21). According to social psychologist James Pennebaker, it "… sometimes takes years of training for helping professionals to learn how to deal effectively with listening to a great deal of trauma, pain, and suffering …" (Johnson, 1998, p. 21). Listening to accounts of traumatic experiences can also pose health risks. According to the research of Christine Maslach, many helping professionals become "… emotionally exhausted, callous, and derive less satisfaction from their jobs as a result …" (Johnson, 1998, p. 21).

In addition to the caregivers, people who are not *trained* as caregivers but who assume a "caretaking" role during a crisis may need some additional support. After the school shooting in West Paducah, Kentucky, for example, high school senior Ben Strong, who had intervened with the shooter, convincing him to put down his weapon before shooting his school principal, was highly visible within the school assisting other students and speaking with the media. His mother, Doris Strong, was concerned that her son "… had not realized the magnitude of the tragedy in which he played a pivotal role. 'He's trying to help other kids,' she said. 'I don't think [he has] fully processed it all on his own at this point. [He has] just been reaching out to help others'" (Mead & Tagami, 1997). Even though "the central thing in [Strong's] life is religion" (Mead & Tagami, 1997), and his deep religious convictions and strong family support will greatly assist him in recovering from the trauma, this young man might benefit from some additional processing opportunities (see "Why Process?" in Chapter Five). Following a crisis in your community, watch for similar "heroes" who may need some extra support as well.

A Special Note to State and National Crisis Response Team Members ...

If "trickle-down economics" were applied to crisis response, and emotional support were equated with wealth, you would be the most impoverished caregivers in the nation. In a school crisis, the school counselor may assist the faculty and students. A school psychologist may assist the school counselor. Local mental health workers and clergy members may also assist the school. And one of your objectives is to assist all of these caregivers. Who, then, assists you? Doctor, heal thyself.

You may think that you don't need any help—after all, you've undergone rigorous training in crisis response and probably have witnessed the aftereffects of many traumas of varying severity. However, a violent school crisis, or one involving the senseless death of a child, may particularly affect you. After any severe school crisis, if you openly and honestly attend to your own feelings, you will likely find that you have been affected by your role in the crisis response. Said Dr. Poland after leading the NOVA team responding to the school shooting in West Paducah, Kentucky: "I maintained my composure while in Paducah, but after returning to Houston, I cried at the drop of a hat. I have had many opportunities to share my Paducah story and the retelling helps me to deal with the overwhelming emotionality" (Poland, 1998, p. 14).

You know what you need to do to cope with your own crisis effects: everything you advise those you counsel to do. Discuss your feelings with others. Take care of your physical needs. Be gentle with yourself and others. Provide permission for a range of emotions. And on and on. Don't forget to take your own sage advice to heart.

Positive Caretaking Actions

If you are to be of help to the school and community, you must acknowledge and begin to address your own issues concerning death, trauma and loss, and crisis. As one school psychologist noted, "... strong emotional feelings in a crisis situation [on the part of a trained crisis responder] signal the need to deal with unresolved issues" (Carroll, 1998, p. 29). You also must take care of your own physical and emotional needs throughout the crisis response and well beyond. In answer to the question "Who cares for the caregiver?" you should focus on three areas of support: yourself, your colleagues or fellow crisis response team members, and members of any outside crisis response team assisting the school.

"If you would lift me you must be on higher ground."

—Ralph Waldo Emerson

There are many actions you can take—many of which are detailed later in this section—to assist yourself in coping with a crisis and your stress reactions. Your fellow crisis response team members and/or coworkers also will be a positive source of support. Counselors, for example, can process their reactions to the crisis and their crisis response role together. School psychologists can also assist counselors within the school setting. If you are a member of the school community, your administrators should support your efforts, recognize your emotional needs, and encourage your recovery. Finally, if an outside crisis response team is assisting the school or community, attending their processing/intervention sessions for local caregivers can do much to validate your crisis reaction and provide much-needed emotional support.

The following are some suggested actions caregivers can take to help themselves and one another cope with the effects of a crisis in the immediate aftermath of the crisis and in the days and weeks that follow:

- Know yourself, and respect your limitations.

  Only you know your own history of trauma and loss and how those past events have affected you. Your innate personality and temperament will also be factors in your crisis response abilities. If you are expected to respond to the crisis, speak up about what you feel comfortable (and uncomfortable) doing. A crisis response is not effortless or stress-free for *anyone*. That having been said, if there is something you just can't handle (for whatever reason), respect your limitations and take on an alternate task.

  For example, in a typical large high school with six or seven counselors, there may be one or two who do not deal well with grief and intense emotionality. If you are such a person, do not let the Crisis Coordinator assign you to work with a classroom of traumatized students. Instead, you might work on the parent letter and Crisis Fact Sheet. If you are *not* true to you own needs, you may engage in avoidance behaviors to escape the actions expected of you, such as by staying home "sick" or arriving early only to stay shut in your office until the end of the day. Such avoidance behaviors are helpful to no one and will make you feel badly later. There is so much to be done during a crisis; work in areas where you will be comfortable with your contribution.

- Ask your family to support your crisis response work.

  Ideally, when you are neck-deep in a crisis response, your family and friends will be supportive and lessen other pressures on you. That is not always the case, unfortunately. During one catastrophic community crisis, the spouse of a victims' advocate who was assisting a national crisis response team from approximately 7:00 AM to 11:00 PM every night put a great deal of pressure on her. Instead of understanding the traumatic event and how her job was impacted, this man behaved in a jealous, nonsupportive manner during a difficult time for the victims' advocate both professionally and personally.

  If your family members don't naturally respond to your increased crisis response workload by saying, for example, "Sure, I'll take care of it. Don't worry," then explain what you are needed to do and ask them clearly for their support. Remind them that an intense crisis response generally lasts for no more than a few days and that others have a pressing need for you during this relatively short time. You might point out to your family members that although they may not be trained in crisis response, by supporting your work they are in a sense making a contribution to the crisis response and thus helping their community members. (*NOTE*: This suggestion assumes that you do not have a consistent pattern of putting professional tasks before your family's needs. If you do typically take care of others at your family's expense, then your family members probably have a valid complaint that you should address at a later time. We say "at a later time" because a crisis aftermath is not an opportune time to work on your personal relationships.)

- Take care of yourself physically.

  Don't forget to eat, even if you're not hungry. Try to swallow at least a few bites at what would usually be lunchtime and dinnertime. Also, stay hydrated by drinking lots of water. Be sure someone is put in charge of bringing all the team members and volunteer caregivers drinks and food that are easy and quick to eat on the run and healthful. Advised one crisis interventionist (Carroll, 1998, p. 29): "Avoid caffeine: coffee, chocolate, tea, sodas, etc." (Note, however, that if your body is used to running on sugar, caffeine, and/or nicotine, a crisis intervention is not the best time to go on a health kick or quit smoking!) Some vitamins, particularly the "Bs," are quickly depleted from the body in times of stress, and a daily B-complex supplement may be helpful.

  Rest as much as you can. Try to squeeze in a break for a few minutes at least every two to three hours. Deep, "cleansing" breaths during these breaks will help to calm and reenergize you. At home, try to get sleep. Gentle herbal supplements (such as Valerian capsules, the Bach flower essence "Rescue Remedy," or chamomile tea), if you have taken these in the past or if they are approved by your physician, may help you to fall asleep, as might warm milk. Avoid sleeping pills, if possible, since they may make you groggy and interfere with your mental sharpness the next day. Relaxing music, a warm bath, meditation and/or prayer, and spending a few minutes out of doors breathing fresh air may also help to sooth you. One crisis interventionist shared his coping method: "Keep a journal, [and] write through sleepless hours" (Carroll, 1998, p. 29).

Exercise, even if you can squeeze in only a brisk walk around the block, is a tremendous stress reliever. Physical activity will help to balance the effects of the stress hormones released in your body during a crisis and will likely improve your mood as well (even if only temporarily).

Do not stop doing all of the helpful things you usually do to cope with your life. During this time of stress, you need them more than ever. Also, avoid the use of alcohol and other drugs. Advised school psychologist Servio Carroll (1998, p. 28), "Don't complicate the problem with substance abuse."

- Stick together, and support one another.

When you are experiencing a crisis intervention, it is helpful to spend time in the presence of others who understand the stressors affecting you. Who better understands what you're going through than your colleagues or team members who are experiencing the crisis response with you? You might want to gather informally at the end of each day that you provide a crisis response. Have dinner together, for example, and discuss your reactions to the day. (If you must scatter and go your separate ways after dealing with a traumatic event, be sure to talk about your experiences with some other empathetic listener, such as your spouse or partner.) After the crisis is over (e.g., perhaps a month or so later), it may be comforting to process your reactions to the crisis again with these team members/colleagues (Lieberman, 1999).

- Use humor to relieve tension.

In Chapter Two we mentioned the importance of humor as a tremendous stress reliever for the body and mind. You may have to work at it, but at some point each day try to find something (not someone) to laugh about. Make some humorous, but tasteful, remark so that everybody can laugh and release tension. The importance of humor as a stress reliever is another good reason to gather with your crisis response team members/colleagues at the end of the day—they won't think "something is wrong with you" if you dare to laugh during a time of crisis. They will understand that you can care very deeply about the tragedy and still need to do something like laugh at a joke in order to cope.

- "Reassure yourself that you are normal and having normal [crisis] reactions. Don't label yourself crazy, weak, or ineffective" (Carroll, 1998, p. 29). Give yourself, as you give others, permission for a range of emotions.

- Recognize that trauma brings out feelings in you. As one crisis interventionist asserted, "Give yourself permission to feel rotten. It's normal" (Carroll, 1998, p. 29).

- Talk with others about your own feelings and reactions to the crisis.

  Explained school psychologist Servio Carroll (1998, p. 28), "… caregivers face burnout when their core needs are not addressed. As crisis workers, we become accustomed to trauma events and find it difficult to talk about our experiences to friends or relatives who may not understand. Although we have been trained in helping others, we often forget those skills when it comes to ourselves and our colleagues. Perhaps we are afraid to be seen as weak or unable to deal with our feelings or problems or unable to deal with our job."

  Reach out to your family members and close friends to explain what you are experiencing. They care about you and would like to understand what you are dealing with. Expressing your feelings to them will also help them to be understanding of any stress reactions you may exhibit at home.

  Process your reactions to the crisis often with your crisis response team members/colleagues. If an outside crisis response team assisting the school or community offers a processing session for local caregivers, be sure to attend. You might also gain some benefit from talking to a mental health worker one-to-one and/or to your clergy member if you belong to a church.

  No matter whom you talk to about the crisis and your crisis reaction, retelling the story of the trauma (and your involvement in the crisis intervention) from beginning to end, detailing how it unfolded, is a process that will likely be helpful to you.

- Remember that those around you have been affected by the crisis as well. Be gentle with others in your family, at the school, and in the community.

- Be kind to yourself. It's natural to second-guess yourself and your actions after a traumatic event, but think positively about your crisis response efforts and the future of the school and community.

- Don't panic if you have a flashback.

  Explained school psychologist Servio Carroll (1998, p. 29), "Flashbacks are normal; don't fight them. They'll decrease in time and become less painful." If flashbacks, illusions, or fantasies about the crisis persist for longer than one month, speak with a mental health professional (or another mental health professional if that is your vocation) about what you are experiencing.

- Ask for relief from your everyday responsibilities (in the short term).

  When you are working hard on a crisis response, and you're quite emotional, it can be very frustrating if your supervisor doesn't temporarily relieve you of the pressures of your everyday job. If you are a school psychologist, you might wish your administrator to say, "I know you're supposed to do this testing, but don't worry about it. Forget about it for the time being," or "I've got somebody else on that." If your administrator is also the Crisis Coordinator, however, he or she may not have had a moment to consider the ramifications of team members' everyday duties. If that is the case and you are feeling pressured, ask your head administrator (or another administrator, if he or she is tied up) for assistance in covering your usual responsibilities. That way you can focus on the crisis response with a clear mind.

- Over the long term, maintain as normal a schedule as possible. Make routine daily decisions in order to regain a sense of control and schedule your time to keep yourself busy, but don't make any big life changes for a while (Carroll, 1998).

- Do something you enjoy.

  You will not have a lot of time to yourself during the initial crisis response, but in the days and weeks that follow make an effort to engage in some activities you find pleasurable and relaxing. No matter how tragic the event, you are not expected to be sad every day. Seeing friends or engaging in hobbies or sports can provide a much-needed distraction.

- Remember your professional ethics and avoid overinvolvement.

  A fundamental element of caregiving during a crisis or traumatic situation is to remember and observe your professional ethics, whether you are a social worker, school counselor, psychologist, victims' advocate, clergy member, or other caregiver. One common problem with caregivers in schools is that they tend to go overboard and become overinvolved with the children they are assisting. There have even been cases in which school counselors have tried to "adopt" their clients, taking them home with them. That type of dual relationship is a clear violation of psychology principles (and one for which you could lose your license), yet people have difficulty seeing these problems when they are invested in helping a child who has survived a horrible situation.

  You must draw the line. Set appropriate limits on your involvement with those you counsel. Do not let the severity of the trauma, or your own stress reactions, cloud your judgment. Instead of taking a trauma-tized child home with you, for example, make an extra effort with the child's parents. If you have any doubts about the appropriateness of your actions, discuss your plans with a colleague, with a crisis response team member, or with your supervisor.

References

American Red Cross. (1993, February). Phases of disaster recovery. In *Disaster mental health services I: Participant's attachments* (Attachment 17, ARC 3077-1A). Washington, DC: Author.

Carroll, S. (1998, November). Crisis and counter-transference: Caretaking the care-taker. *NASP Communiqué, 27*(3), 28-29.

Johnson, T. B. (1998, November). [Review of the book Opening up: The healing power of expressing emotions]. *NASP Communiqué, 27*(3), 21.

Lieberman, R. (1999, January 22-23). *Crisis Intervention Workshop*, Walnut Creek, California.

Mead, A., & Tagami, T. (1997, December 2). Teen who intervened in shooting called hero. *Knight-Ridder/Tribune News Service*. Available online: http://web2.searchbank.com/infotrac/session/7/649/305300w7/7!xrn_2

Poland, S. (1998, May). NEAT chairman leads NOVA team in Paducah. *NASP Communiqué, 26*(7), 14.

chapter eleven

Special Considerations for Suicide

The suicide of a school community member is a violent act with many implications for schools. Especially if the suicide is of a young person, it is very disruptive to schools, and sadly it is quite common. According to the Centers for Disease Control and Prevention (CDC), suicide is the second leading cause of death for American children ages 11-19 (cited in California Association of School Psychologists [CASP], 1998). Yet few schools are prepared to deal with suicide effectively, or have any kind of comprehensive suicide prevention or postvention (i.e., intervention for survivors after the act) strategy. If a crisis involves the suicide of a school community member, all of the procedures for coping with crises presented in the rest of this book's chapters apply. However, there are some additional considerations and steps that should be taken after a suicide, which are detailed in this chapter.

It is crucial that the crisis response following a suicide be handled with delicacy and care. The need for sensitivity in suicide postvention is not due to the common belief that suicide is a sin or the embarrassment that may be caused to the suicide victim's family. Rather, the crisis response after a suicide must be handled appropriately to *protect other students*.

Simply stated, one of the primary goals of suicide postvention is to prevent further suicides. Compelling evidence indicates "… that [children and teens] follow the suicidal actions of their peers, a trend known as suicide clusters or contagion" (Nemours Foundation, cited in CASP, 1998, p. 14). In fact, one researcher has estimated that the suicide of a student increases the probability that a second suicide will occur within the deceased's school by 300% (Lamartine, cited in Poland, 1995). In a scenario typical of the suicide "contagion"/"cluster" phenomenon, by the end of June 1998, 30 children in the areas surrounding Victorville, California, had been hospitalized for suicide attempts following the double suicide of two 14-year old girls there in March (CASP, 1998).

This trend is not new: Ross (1985) pointed out that as early as the 1800s psychologists identified the "imitation factor" in suicide and that children and youth are more suggestible than adults. While the reasons for suicide "contagion"/"clusters" are not entirely understood, it is thought that children and teens—who are highly impressionable and may not fully comprehend the finality of death—may consider suicide a viable solution to life's problems when presented with an example of this behavior. Further, children and teens who might already be contemplating suicide can be influenced by the attention paid to a person who has taken his or her own life. And at any given time there are many youth who may be contemplating suicide. The 1997 national risk behavior survey of the Centers for Disease Control [cited in Fainaru, 1998b] revealed that 20.5% of high school students had seriously contemplated suicide and 15.7% had actually made a plan to commit suicide.

> "When a teenager dies of suicide, it presents suicide as an option to kids who are already vulnerable. They start to identify with the victim."
>
> (Nelson, cited in "Suicide in Children," 1998, p. 1)

If your school crisis involves a suicide, all members of your school community—including parents—need to understand the prevalence of youth suicide and to recognize the warning signs of suicidal ideation (*see "Suicide Statistics, Causes, and Myths" later in this chapter*). You should be aware of the potential for litigation (*see "Liability Issues Pertaining to Suicide" later in this chapter*). You should implement proven postvention procedures (*see "Suicide Postvention" later in this chapter*) and also work with the media to help ensure that coverage of the crisis (if any) is appropriate (*see "Media Coverage of Suicides" later in this chapter*).

Suicide Statistics, Causes, and Myths

Prevalence of Youth Suicide

Every four hours in America a child commits suicide (Children's Defense Fund, 1999). According to the Centers for Disease Control and Prevention, suicide is the third leading cause of death nationwide for 15- to 24-year olds and the second leading cause of death among children 11-19 years old (cited in CASP, 1998). An estimated ten to 25% of the students in any high school are at risk for suicide in any given school year (Hahn, cited in "Suicide in Children," 1998). In 1995, according to the CDC (cited in Fainaru, 1998a), 2,227 American children ages ten to 19 years old committed suicide, and it is estimated that for every completed suicide there are 100-120 suicide attempts ("Suicide Facts," 1998).

The United States has the highest suicide rate of 26 industrialized nations studied by the federal government, a rate that is double that of the other countries, according to CDC medical epidemiologist Dr. Etnienne Krug ("U.S. Tops in Child Murders," 1997). Currently, American suicide rates have leveled off near their all-time highs. According to the Centers for Disease Control and Prevention (1989-1994, 1995), the suicide rate among young teens (i.e., children ten to 14 years of age) increased 120% from 1980 to 1992. Noted Dr. Krug, "Since 1950, the rates of unintentional injury, disease, and congenital anomalies have decreased among children in the United States, but ... suicide rates have quadrupled" ("U.S. Tops in Child Murders," 1997).

As dire as these statistics are, they may in fact represent a gross underreporting of youth suicide. Many suicides are recorded as accidents, according to school psychologist Richard Lieberman, coordinator for the Los Angeles Unified School District's Suicide Prevention Unit. For example, the death of a teenage California boy who committed suicide on a school bus full of his peers by playing Russian roulette was listed as accidental (CASP, 1998). Researchers McGuire & Ely (cited in "Suicide in Children," 1998, p. 1) noted that "coroners are reluctant to label a child's death as suicide, and when there is no suicide note (which is usually the case), they are more likely to call it an accident."

Methods Used

- A suicide study in the state of Oregon (cited in CASP, 1998) found that ingestion of drugs (i.e., overdose) accounted for more than 75% of suicide attempts, but that less than 1% were fatal. Accordingly, the American Foundation for Suicide Prevention (1998c) reported that "ingestion accounts for very few male suicides."

- Of the 124 deaths among youth 17 years old or younger in the Oregon study (cited in CASP, 1998), 63.7% were caused by guns.

- According to the Center to Prevent Handgun Violence (cited in CASP, 1998), 92% of all suicides attempted with guns are completed.

- The California Association of School Psychologists (1998, p. 14) reported that "teens who have been drinking alcohol are five times more likely to use guns than any other suicide method" and that "every six hours, a youth aged ten to 19 commits suicide with a gun."

- According to the American Foundation for Suicide Prevention (1996a), 60% of all suicide victims (of all ages) nationwide use a gun to commit the act. In 1998, the Foundation reported that the use of firearms is now the most frequent method of suicide of children aged ten to 14 years (American Foundation for Suicide Prevention, 1998a).

- Data indicate that "hanging is more common in early adolescence than in later years" (American Foundation for Suicide Prevention, 1998c).
- According to the American Foundation for Suicide Prevention (1998c), the frequency of suicide method varies somewhat by geographic location, as follows:
  - Hanging: All locations
  - Firearms: Rural
  - Asphyxiation: Suburban
  - Jumping: Urban

Precipitators of Suicide

There are four completed male suicides for every completed female suicide; however, females are at least twice as likely to attempt suicide than males (American Foundation for Suicide Prevention, 1996a). According to the American Association of Suicidology, "Suicide cuts across all age, economic, social, and ethnic boundaries" ("Understanding and Helping," 1997).

Risk factors for suicide include (American Foundation for Suicide Prevention, 1996a, 1998c; CASP, 1998; Lieberman, 1999; Poland, 1995; "Suicide in Children," 1998):

- Previous suicide attempt. (Twenty-six to 33% of adolescent suicide victims have made a previous attempt.)
- History of substance abuse. (Alcoholism is a factor in approximately 30% of all completed suicides.)
- Mental illness. (Ninety percent of adolescent suicide victims have at least one diagnosable psychiatric illness at death—generally depression, substance abuse, or conduct disorders. And according to the National Institute of Mental Health [cited in Egan, 1998], more than 1.5 million children under the age of 15 are seriously depressed.)
- Exposure to suicide (i.e., suicide "contagion"). (Although this risk is commonly identified with regard to the suicide "clusters" of children and teens, it pertains to the family of suicide victims as well as to peers. Each year, between 7,000 and 12,000 children in the United States are exposed to suicide in the home when a parent commits suicide ["Suicide Facts," 1998], and data indicate that "individuals who attempt or complete suicide often have a significant family history of suicidal behaviors" [Bradshaw & Kaslow, 1996]. Additionally, according to the American Association of Suicidology [cited in "Understanding and Helping," 1997, p. 6], "Surviving family members not only suffer the trauma of losing a loved one to a suicide, but are themselves at higher risk for suicide and emotional problems.")

- Portrayal of suicide in the media, such as through motion pictures, news coverage, and/or song lyrics (Poland, 1995).

- Having a gun in the home. (Death by firearms is the fastest growing method of suicide. According to the American Foundation for Suicide Prevention [1998a], among people with no known mental disorders, those with a loaded gun in the house are 32 times more likely to commit suicide.)

- Exposure to violence.

- Sense of hopelessness (including confusion and self-doubt).

- Stressors, such as a recent disappointment/rejection or getting into trouble (e.g., at school, with the law).

- Pressures to succeed.

- Financial uncertainty/poverty.

- Divorce/formation of stepfamilies.

- Mobility of families/moving into a new community.

- Family dysfunction or changes (e.g., illness or death in the family, parental marital conflict).

- Lack of connection to religion.

- Loss (e.g., of a prized object, a person, a state of well-being, or social supports).

- Sexual orientation confusion.

- Fantasy concept/preoccupation with death.

- Cultural issues. (According to Hoberman [cited in "Suicide in Children," 1998, p. 9], "suicide rates tend to correlate with the degree of social acceptance of suicidal behavior in particular cultures and subcultures.")

- Anger and/or rage causing acting-out behavior toward self or others. (The American Foundation for Suicide Prevention [1998c] has reported, "Attempts to reconstruct the mental state of teen suicides from psychological autopsy research suggest that high levels of anxiety or anger are commonly present just prior to death.")

- Learning disabilities. (Per Jan-Tausch [cited in "Suicide in Children," 1998, p. 2], "Evidence increasingly suggests that adolescents with learning disabilities ... are at high risk for suicide.")

- "Loss of face" with peers (Shaffer, cited in Poland, 1995).

In one study of youth suicides (*Fatal and Nonfatal Suicide Attempts Among Adolescents—Oregon, 1988-1993*, cited in CASP, 1998), the following were the most frequent reasons survivors gave for attempting suicide:

- Family discord (59.4% of responses; most frequently cited reason by females and children 12 years old or younger)

- Argument with boyfriend/girlfriend (32.6%)
- School-related problems (23%)

In order of the potential effect on a suicidal youth, the following should be viewed as the "straw that can break the camel's back" and cause a young person to follow through with plans to commit suicide (Hawton, cited in "Suicide in Children," 1998):
- Argument with parent(s)
- Break-up of romantic relationship
- Peer/friendship problems
- School (e.g., grade/teacher) problems

Other precipitating factors that can bring a child or teen to the "crisis point" of committing suicide include a recent rejection or humiliation and discipline problems (Poland, 1989). (In fact, school officials should be alert to the increased risk of suicide that may accompany disciplinary actions and notify parents/guardians immediately if students who are being suspended or expelled hint about or threaten suicide.)

Warning Signs

According to the Academy of Child and Adolescent Psychiatry (cited in CASP, 1998), the following signs in youth have been correlated with attempted suicide and should be watched for by parents, physicians/pediatricians, and all school staff (i.e., teaching, administrative, counseling, and support staff):
- Previous suicide attempts or threats
- Plans made or attempts to secure the means for suicide
- Thinking or talking about suicide
- Scratching, cutting, or marking the body
- Risk-taking behavior (e.g., running away, jumping from heights)
- Withdrawal from activities, family, and/or friends
- Alcohol and other drug use
- Neglect of personal appearance
- Marked personality and/or behavior change
- Persistent boredom, inability to concentrate
- Decline in quality of schoolwork
- Physical symptoms associated with emotions (e.g., stomachache, fatigue)
- Loss of interest in pleasurable activities
- Not tolerating praise or rewards

- Verbal hints (e.g., "I won't be a problem for you much longer.")
- Putting affairs in order (e.g., giving away belongings)
- Becoming suddenly cheerful after a period of depression (which may indicate that a decision has been made to commit suicide)

Other suicide warning signs include (Lieberman, 1999; "Suicide in Children," 1998):

- Prolonged depression
- Preoccupation with death and/or suicidal themes
- Destructive play or repetitive unrealistic play

Common Suicide Myths

The following are a few of the more widely believed myths about suicide and the facts debunking them (Greene, cited in "Childhood Suicide," 1998; Poland, 1989; Shamoo & Patros, cited in "Childhood Suicide," 1998):

- *Myth*—People who talk about suicide don't commit it.

  Reality—Young people who talk or write about suicide are at risk. Those who talk of suicide are crying out for help, communicating that they want positive changes in their lives.

- *Myth*—Children are cognitively and physically incapable of implementing a suicide plan successfully.

  Reality—As reported in "Childhood Suicide" (1998, p. 4), "Children who contemplate, threaten, or attempt suicide in the six- to 12-year old group most frequently use jumping from heights, ingesting poison, hanging, stabbing, drowning, running into traffic, and burning. TV often provides the model, means, and methods. None of these methods requires any lengthy or complicated planning or specific physical attainment."

- *Myth*—Suicidal youth really want to die.

  Reality—There is often ambivalence about dying. Suicidal youth want to end the pain but wish that someone or something would change the situation so that their lives can continue.

- *Myth*—Discussing suicide with youth gives them the idea to commit the act.

  Reality—A suicidal child or teen already has the thought of suicide in his or her mind. Talking about suicide actually "… removes a child's fear that [he or she] is crazy or alone, takes away the guilt for thinking that way, and opens avenues for resolution of suicidal thoughts" ("Childhood Suicide," 1998, p. 4). Explained the California

"The young man who in a fit of melancholy killed himself today might have wanted to live had he merely waited a week!"

—Voltaire, 1746

> "… [S]taff members [should] inquire directly and ask whether students who give … clues are thinking of harming or killing themselves. A staff member needs to give a clear message: 'I am here to help you and I care about you.' School staff members may be very concerned that they might say the wrong thing. They need to let the basic helping desire that brought them into education in the first place guide their inquiry. They need to act from the heart and show concern, and must not dismiss or minimize the suffering [their students] are experiencing."
>
> (Poland, 1989, p. 53)

> "Three years ago I jumped off the Golden Gate Bridge. The moment I let go of the rail I knew I had made the biggest mistake in my life."
>
> —California youth who survived a suicide attempt ("An Interview," 1998, p. 17)

Association of School Psychologists (1998, p. 14), "Asking a child or adolescent whether he or she is depressed or thinking about suicide can be helpful. Rather than 'putting thoughts in the child's head,' such a question will provide assurance that somebody cares and will give the young person the chance to talk about problems."

- *Myth*—Suicide is inherited or destined.
- *Reality*—Certain children may have a genetic predisposition to suicidal behavior ("Suicide Facts," 1998, p. 10), and chronic parental depression has been shown to be "… a strong predictor of adolescent suicide" ("Suicide Facts," 1998, p. 10). However, in the large majority of cases, youth suicide is situational, and situational variables (e.g., the use of alcohol and other drugs, gun availability) are important factors. As an example, one Houston teenager who committed suicide left a note to her parents that said, in part, "Why did you make this so easy by leaving me this gun!" Most suicidal young people are ambivalent about death and swing back and forth between wanting to live and wanting to die. Thus, most suicides can be prevented.

- *Myth*—There are particular times when suicides are more likely to happen.

  Reality—There is no compelling evidence linking youth suicide with any particular days of the week, seasons, or holidays (Poland, 1989). (There is a higher incidence of suicides for adults during the Thanksgiving and Christmas holidays, however.)

- *Myth*—Suicide is a white male problem.

  Reality—Although most suicides are committed by males (by a ratio of 5:1, according to the American Foundation for Suicide Prevention [1996a]), the suicide rate for white females has more than doubled since 1950 (American Foundation for Suicide Prevention, 1996a). The suicide rate for young African-American males has risen by two thirds in the past 15 years (American Foundation for Suicide Prevention, 1996a), and suicide rates are higher in the western states with a large Native American population (Poland, 1995). Suicide crosses every racial, ethnic, and socioeconomic boundary in our society.

- *Myth*—There are usually no warning signs of suicide.

  Reality—According to the American Foundation for Suicide Prevention (1996b), three quarters of the people who have committed suicide gave some warning of their intentions to a friend or family member. Other suicide interventionists believe there are *always* warnings but that the people close to the suicide victims often do not recognize them and/or take them seriously. (Unfortunately, experience shows that most youth tell their friends of their suicidal plans, rather than an adult. The peers often do not share these plans with an adult helper, either because they do not take the threat seriously or because they want to "protect" the friend or friendship by maintaining this confidence.)

"Kids don't wake up suicidal. They get there after traveling a long road."

—Richard Lieberman, NCSP, consultant to the Los Angeles Unified School District's Suicide Prevention Unit (CASP, 1998, p. 14)

- *Myth*—There is nothing anyone can do to prevent a suicide.

  Reality—One suicide interventionist (Lieberman, 1999) pointed out that often suicide is perceived by young people as "fate" or "destiny"—something that has to happen. But as noted previously, suicide is almost always situational, and most suicides can be prevented. Children and teens attach a permanence to the situation that does not really exist, and because they believe suicide is destined, they do not become involved and take action to save the life of their suicidal peer.

- *Myth*—Children under the age of six do not commit suicide.

  Reality—Suicide in this age group is very rare, probably because very young children are much more involved with their parents/caretakers, much less involved with alcohol and other drugs, and have less gun access than older children (Poland, 1995). However, evidence has shown that children three, four, and five years old have been clearly suicidal. As noted in "Childhood Suicide" (1998, p. 4), "Children often regard themselves with the same hostility and criticism as their parents do, thereby forming a nucleus of a bad self-image." A study of suicidal preschoolers found four primary reasons for their suicidal ideation: self-punishment, escape, reunion with a significant other, and rectification of an unbearable life situation (Rosenthal & Rosenthal, cited in "Suicide in Children," 1998).

- *Myth*—When the mood of a depressed child improves, the suicide crisis is over.

  Reality—As stated in "Childhood Suicide" (1998, p. 4), "When a child's mood or behavior 'picks up,' it may be because the indecision concerning suicide is over. A decision has been made and the anxiety is past, but that decision could be for suicide."

- *Myth*—Once a youth contemplates suicide, he or she should always be considered suicidal.

  Reality—When the crisis and precipitating problems are resolved, suicidal ideation generally stops. If the youth's coping skills fail in the future, however, suicide could again become an option he or she considers.

Liability Issues Pertaining to Suicide

If one of your students has committed suicide, and if you did not take the steps expected of you to prevent this death from happening, your school and its employees may have a serious liability issue on your hands. (*See "Liability and Litigation" in Chapter Twelve for tips on preparing for a possible lawsuit.*) School districts and their employees have been sued for failing to notify parents when their children were suicidal, for inadequately supervising suicidal students, and for failing to obtain psychological help for suicidal students. Many such districts have lost the cases and have been directed to pay monetary damages to the parents of deceased students. The liability issues are *foreseeability* and *negligence*. That is, if a child writes or talks about suicide, adults (particularly trained adults such as school counselors and psychologists) should be able to foresee a potential suicide. It is negligent on the part of a school not to notify parents/guardians when students are known to be suicidal and to supervise the students closely (e.g., removing a lethal weapon) until the parents assume responsibility. Schools may also be found negligent for failing to recommend appropriate counseling assistance for suicidal students and for inadequately training their staffs on suicide prevention.

> "The key issue is not whether the school somehow caused the suicide, but whether the school failed to take reasonable steps to prevent it."
>
> (Poland, 1997, p. 148)

The role of the school pertaining to youth suicide is essentially the following (Poland, 1990, 1995):

- To detect potentially suicidal students. (For example, in numerous cases teachers and schools have been found negligent for failing to obtain assistance for and/or for failing to notify the parents of students who, prior to committing suicide, talked about suicide or wrote about suicide in class essays.)

- To assess the severity of the risk level of the suicidal student. (School psychologists and counselors should have had special training in this area.)

- To notify the parent(s)/guardian of a suicidal student. It is not enough to tell only the police. (It is good practice to document in writing that the parents have been notified and encouraged to obtain psychological assistance for their child within the community and to have two school representatives present when the parents are notified.)

- To work with the parent(s)/guardian to secure the needed supervision and services for the suicidal student.

- To monitor the suicidal student and provide ongoing assistance. (In some states, such as Texas, if parents are resistant to obtaining needed psychological assistance for their children, school psychologists may provide services to suicidal minors without the permission of their parents. Check the statutes for your state.)

In summary, school staff members (e.g., counselors and psychologists) are legally bound to tell the parent(s)/guardian if a student talks or writes of plans to kill himself or herself. *No adults* at school, including teachers, administrators, support staff, and bus drivers, should keep a secret about suicidal behavior. Everyone must listen to and really hear what suicidal youth are saying and take definite actions to get them help. In case after case, school staff have been found negligent for failing to take such actions. Students, however, have traditionally not been held liable for failing to report the suicidal ideation of their peers, but this trend could certainly change, as they have been named as parties to lawsuits after a homicide. Students should be taught to tell an adult when they become aware that a friend or classmate may be contemplating suicide.

Any such failure to alert parents/guardians on the part of school staff will certainly be considered negligence by the courts in the event of a lawsuit, as the following case ("District Held Liable," 1997; "Student Suicide," 1997) illustrates. In October 1989 a 13-year old student, Shawn Wyke, attempted suicide by hanging himself with a football jersey in a boys' restroom at his junior high school. Another student (named Jonathon) interrupted the suicide attempt, talked Shawn out of it, and convinced him to leave the room.

That evening Jonathon told his mother about what had happened. His mother called the dean of students, Jim Bryan, who allegedly told her he would "take care of it." The next day Bryan called Shawn into his office. There he read and discussed with Shawn some Bible verses. Bryan later said he believed Shawn felt better after this discussion, so he took no additional action related to the suicide attempt (including calling Shawn's mother).

Later that day Shawn encountered a school custodian as he was leaving the boys' restroom. He told the custodian that if he "… had stayed in there any longer, he would have killed himself" ("District Held Liable," 1997, p. 8). Upon inspection of the restroom, the custodian found a coat hanger and cord hanging from the ceiling. Naturally concerned, the custodian told the vice principal of the school that a student had been talking about killing himself. She was told "… to find something better to do" ("District Held Liable," 1997, p. 8). Later that night, Shawn was successful in his attempt to kill himself, at home.

A federal district court dismissed the plaintiff's constitutional duty to care claim. However, the jury in the case *Wyke v. Polk County School Board* (11th Cir., 1997)—a suit filed by the parents in which Dr. Poland provided expert testimony—found the Florida school district partially liable on a wrongful death claim and ordered the district to pay $165,000. As explained in "District Held Liable" (1997):

> "'Shawn did not merely seem unhappy,' wrote the court. 'Shawn did not merely talk about committing suicide. He twice tried to hang himself from the rafters in the school's restroom. The workings of the human mind are truly an enigma, but we do not believe (and neither did the jury) that a prudent person would have needed a crystal ball to see that Shawn needed help and that if he didn't get it soon, he might attempt suicide again.'"
>
> ("District Held Liable," 1997, p. 8)

It was not the administrator's failure to place the student in protective custody or provide him with suicide intervention services after a dean of students learned of the attempt [although this would have been the correct course of action] that hurt the district's case. Nor was it expert testimony that said Polk County had failed to adequately train its employees on suicide prevention [which also would have been a good idea]. It was school officials' failure to notify the student's mother or grandmother of the suicide attempt that crossed the line into negligence, the court said, and allowed the district to be held accountable by a jury in a wrongful death suit ... (p. 8).

Discipline and school troubles are known to be precipitating events in many youth suicides (*see "Suicide Statistics, Causes, and Myths" previously in this chapter*), and a trend school administrators need to be aware of is that it is not unheard of for students to commit suicide after being disciplined (e.g., suspended or expelled). The disciplinary action could be the last straw that causes a student to follow through with previous suicide plans. A few students have gone directly from a suspension/expulsion conference and killed themselves. In a 1992 case in the Cypress-Fairbanks Independent School District in Houston, Texas, for example, a junior high school student who was suspected of selling drugs on campus was called to the office by the assistant principal. The administrator talked to the student about the school's suspicions and told her that she was in serious trouble. The student's mother arrived, was told that her daughter was being suspended, and was advised of the next steps (that the student had rights, that there would be a hearing process, etc.). The mother dropped her daughter off at home and went back to work. A half hour later, the girl shot herself with the family pistol. She left a note to her mother saying, "I lied. I did sell the drugs."

In this case, because the student had made no mention of suicide during or after the suspension conference, there had been no suicidal writing or plans, and the school had no reason to suspect suicidal ideation, the district was exonerated in the wrongful death suit filed against it. Unfortunately none of these warning signs occurred, or the suicide might have been prevented.

This case illustrates the point that every student involved in a serious discipline sequence (i.e., suspension or expulsion) should be questioned about suicide, even though many school administrators will be uncomfortable conducting such discussions with students. If they are uncomfortable in this regard, administrators should enlist the assistance of a school counselor or psychologist. These sorts of discussions will not plant the idea of suicide in the mind of students, as many administrators worry will happen (CASP,

1998). In fact, many secondary students in particular are thinking about suicide at any given time. While such discussions have not been ruled essential by the courts, they will save lives!

Of course, most suicidal students are not as subtle as this Houston, Texas, student was. Following school or discipline troubles, and especially when there is a reason to suspect suicidal intent, the supervision of a student becomes extremely important. Consider what happened with Kelson, a 14-year old student in Springfield, Oregon. Kelson brought a gun to school and robbed a teacher at gunpoint in 1985. The vice principal took Kelson to the office and called the police. While waiting for the police to arrive, "… Kelson handed over a suicide note he had written and asked to see his favorite teacher. The request was denied, so he asked instead to go to the restroom" ("Are School Psychologists Liable," 1994, p. 1). Can you guess the rest of the story? Allowed to go to the restroom unsupervised, Kelson "… killed himself with the gun that the school administrators [had] never asked him to hand over" ("Are School Psychologists Liable," 1994, p. 1).

Kelson's parents sued the school, and the 9th Circuit Court of Appeals ruled that the school had been negligent. As noted in "Are School Psychologists Liable" (1994, p. 1), "The court found that school administrators breached the duty of care entrusted to them, resulting in Kelson's death." This tragedy could have been averted if the administrator had been sensitive to the very real danger of suicide and had supervised Kelson appropriately. By "appropriate supervision," we do not mean wrestling Kelson for the gun! Instead, the administrator could have calmly bargained with the student, saying, for example, "Please tell us where the gun is and then you can see your teacher." Slenkovitch (1986) cautioned against taking an authoritarian approach with suicidal students, and recommended that schools document a "good faith" effort on their part to prevent youth suicide.

Accounts of schools held liable for negligence in the suicides of students would fill volumes, and space does not allow us to enumerate them here. Most concern the failure of school staff to take some basic, commonsense actions when they have firsthand (and in many cases, quite obvious) knowledge that students are suicidal. We do want to cover one final case, however, since it delves into a different aspect of liability—that of *secondhand* information.

In a 1988 case in Montgomery County, Maryland, an eighth grade girl threatened to commit suicide to her friends. These responsible girls told their school counselor about the threat. Two counselors called in the suicidal student, and when they questioned her about her suicidal plans she denied making the threat. So they sent her on her way and took no further action. This student died a month later in a murder-suicide with another 13-year old girl (Owens, 1992).

The Maryland Supreme Court ruled that the school counselors had breached a common law duty to prevent the murder-suicide of the two girls, although they were not required to pay damages (deGroot, 1994). This ruling came after seven years of litigation and after the counselors had lost in a lower court. In hindsight, it's easy to see that the counselors might have used an assessment to determine the student's level of suicide risk. The counselors certainly should have called the student's parents that day and told them, "Your daughter's friends are concerned. They say she's planning to kill herself. When we talked to her personally, she denied it. But mom and dad, you need to know that." The counselors also could have made a referral for psychological assistance at that time, and they should have closely monitored the student in the following days and weeks.

Suicide Postvention

After the suicide of a school community member (whether student or staff), you must focus on two primary tasks: (1) assisting your students and staff in processing their reactions to the crisis, and (2) working to prevent additional suicides by attending to at-risk students.

Discussing and Processing Reactions to Suicide

Take the following steps after the suicide of a school community member:

See "Getting the Facts" in the "Verifying Information/Crisis Fact Sheet" section of Chapter One.

- Verify the suicide.

  Unless the suicide occurred at school, the Crisis Coordinator and a member of your school's or district's mental health staff (e.g., the Counseling Liaison or a school psychologist) will need to contact the family of the deceased to verify the suicide. This contact should occur in person (see "Task List" in Chapter Two for details).

  If the circumstances sound like a suicide but the family members maintain that the death was accidental (or know it was a suicide but plan to tell others that it was an accidental death), this conversation can be uncomfortable. Rather than pressing the issue with the family, a helpful term to use is "suicide equivalent" behavior. Consider the following: A Houston, Texas, junior high school student shot herself in the stomach with her father's gun one evening while her parents were at home. She then begged with her parents not to let her bleed to death, but she died before help could arrive. Was it an accident? Was it suicide? Most certainly it was "suicide equivalent" behavior, because rational people do not point a loaded gun at their stomach unless they wish to harm themselves. (In this instance, suicidal writing was later found and the girl's friends all knew about her suicidal ideation.)

In such cases the term "suicide equivalent" can be helpful in assisting the members of your school community. You would then treat the situation like it may have been a suicide and address it accordingly. You would use the word suicide, saying, for example, "We don't have all the facts and details but (the deceased's) behavior sounds very suicidal." Or you could use whatever language the parents request in the acknowledgment of the death as long as it does not conflict with the coroner's or medical examiner's ruling (American Association of Suicidology [AAS], 1998).

At no time should you lie about the cause of death, even if the parents request you to do so (AAS, 1998). Let the parents know that lying is against school policy and, anyway, would not work because some students would probably know the truth and would discuss it among themselves. Advised the American Association of Suicidology, "Rumor creates more anxiety than truth. Students' concerns must be dealt with honestly. Reveal to the students that the parents do not accept the ruling of the cause of death and help them understand how difficult it is for parents when a child commits suicide" (AAS, 1998).

- Create a Crisis Fact Sheet.

  Be sure to include on the Crisis Fact Sheet the most common warning signs of suicide (*see "Suicide Statistics, Causes, and Myths" previously in this chapter*) and sources of assistance in your community (e.g., the school counselor/psychologist, a crisis or suicide prevention hotline, your local hospital, and private mental health practitioners). If you have no local or statewide suicide prevention number to provide to students and their parents, provide the toll-free number for the "National Adolescent Runaway and Suicide Hot-Line" (1-800-621-4000). This number is staffed 24-hours per day, and the crisis responders will be able to refer callers to a helping agency in their state.

See "Verifying Information/Crisis Fact Sheet" in Chapter One for details and a sample Crisis Fact Sheet.

- Tell your students and staff about the suicide when the news is confirmed.

  Many administrators without training in suicide prevention and postvention try to pretend that a suicide has not happened and simply hope that no other suicides occur (Poland, 1989). However, the suicide must be acknowledged, and your students and staff must be given the opportunity to express their emotions and ask questions. Crabb (cited in Poland, 1989, p. 135) stressed that students need "… open and honest communication that confronts the crisis, not false assurances that everything will be alright."

  The forum in which this information is shared is important. School staff members can be notified as a group (but preferably will be notified individually before they arrive at school using your preestablished

See "Telling the Facts" in the "Verifying Information/Crisis Fact Sheet" section of Chapter One for guidelines.

calling tree, if you have one). Educate your entire staff (including support staff, bus drivers, etc.) about suicide "contagion" and suicide postvention recommendations so that they will feel comfortable speaking with the students about the crisis and will be able to do so in an appropriate manner.

In contrast, *students should not be given news of any crisis—and particularly of a suicide—in an assembly format.* Student discussions should take place in groups of their own classroom or homeroom or smaller, preferably with their teacher and a member of the counseling staff and/or an administrator present. This format allows the students to receive the news of the crisis in familiar surroundings and with people they know and trust (Stevenson, 1994). In a larger group, dealing with the intensified emotional responses of students is not easy, and the situation could quickly get out of hand. Further, large-group presentations are less beneficial for individual students needing special attention (Stevenson, 1994).

One Houston, Texas, junior high school administrator learned the disadvantages of an assembly format the hard way. In 1991 a student at his school committed suicide. The school principal did not call the school psychologist at home to alert him of the crisis that evening, and before the psychologist arrived at the school the next morning the principal had already made an announcement over the intercom about the death. He had followed some outdated suicide postvention guidelines prohibiting the use of the word "suicide" and had instead asked that all students who wanted more information about the death come to the cafeteria. Then he had roughly 1,200 children assembled, and, using a microphone, he told them that this student had committed suicide.

Many students flew off the handle, and the situation quickly got out of control. Students were hyperventilating, turning tables over, and yelling, "We have to get her!" (The students were convinced it was the student's girlfriend's fault that he had committed suicide, and packs of students began roaming the halls looking for her. She had to be escorted by the school's constables out a back door and never returned to that school.) A large number of unruly students were suspended before the morning was over.

What you say (and do not say) when you tell your students about a suicide is as important as where and how you say it:

- Tell the truth about the suicide, but provide few or no details about the method. A specific statement such as, "He shot himself" or "She died of strangulation" is enough. This clarifies the method but allows the focus of the discussion to remain on how the school staff can help survivors with their thoughts and feelings about the death.

Do not provide unnecessary details about the cause of death (e.g., that it was painful, how the body might have looked, etc.).

- Stick to the facts provided on the Crisis Fact Sheet.

- Do not attempt to figure out (or spend time discussing with the students) why the person committed suicide. Students will invariably ask "Why?" and a helpful response is to say, "We're never going to know why (name) killed himself/herself. We need to talk about you and your thoughts, feelings, and emotions. You lost a classmate, and we need to focus on you because you're here."

- If the students ask "Why didn't God stop (name) from killing himself/herself?" explain that there are many different beliefs about this question and encourage the students to speak with their own clergy members and/or parents.

- Do not glorify the student in any way or communicate any approval of his or her actions (e.g., by romanticizing the action).

- Emphasize that suicide is avoidable and that the deceased student made a poor life choice. Say, for example, "(Name) made a very bad choice. How can we work together to make sure you do not make such a bad choice?" ("An Interview," 1998, p. 15).

- Do not portray the suicide victim as deviant or mentally ill, which may or may not be the case and would be difficult for students to accept if the suicide victim was well liked (Poland, 1989; "Suicide in Children," 1998). Instead, make clear that the student had problems that were unique to him or her, and emphasize again that the student "made a bad choice."

- Do not attempt to make the students feel better by saying, "There is nothing anyone could have done to prevent the suicide," because students need to understand that prevention is possible. Students, as well as staff, "… should be empowered with the belief that they can make a difference—that they can save a life and prevent a future suicide" (Poland, 1989, p. 140).

- However, be sure to also emphasize that no one except the suicide victim is to blame for his or her actions. As suicidologists have explained: "The message must be that everyone is hurting and everyone is angry—we are all survivors in the same boat. While we will probably never know fully why, we must stop blaming each other and stop blaming ourselves" (Lamb & Dunne-Maxim, 1987, p. 259).

- Focus on prevention—including recognizing warning signs—and explain that suicide is a major problem in our society. Emphasize the need to get immediate help for a suicidal person. Also explain to students the difference between "telling on" a peer (which is designed to get him or her into trouble) and telling an adult when a peer is talking about suicide (which is for the person's own protection and may save his or her life).

– Emphasize to students the help that is available to them both at school and in the community. Discuss what they could do and where they could turn if they felt they needed assistance with life problems or suicidal thoughts. Post a local crisis hotline number in each classroom ("Postvention," 1998). Also provide students with a card or handout listing the local crisis hotline number, the warning signs of suicide, and the message that they must not keep suicidal behavior or threats a secret from adults.

See "Why Process?" and "How Do You Process?" in Chapter Five for guidelines.

• Provide opportunities for your students and staff to process their reactions to the tragedy.

Processing will be particularly important in the suicide victim's classes. The Counseling Liaison (or another member of your school's mental health staff) should follow the victim's schedule and help the students and faculty in each of these classes cope with the death ("Postvention," 1998).

• Maintain the normal school schedule.

To avoid glorifying the suicide, do not dismiss school and, to the greatest extent possible, do not change the normal school schedule. Note that some time will likely be needed for students to process their reactions to the tragedy and ask questions. If many students are upset, you may need to modify or set aside the regular curriculum for a short time to address the emotionality of the situation (*see "Modifying the Curriculum" in Chapter Six for ideas*).

Some very upset students may wish to go home. These students should not be allowed to leave school on their own. Instead, a parent or caretaker should be called to come to school and escort them home. Give these parents/caretakers a copy of the Crisis Fact Sheet when they arrive at school, and encourage them to attend, with the students, the family/community meeting to be held that night (*see Chapter Two*).

See "Task List" in Chapter Two for details and a sample letter.

• Send a letter home to parents.

The American Association of Suicidology (AAS, 1998) recommends using the name of the suicide victim in correspondence to parents. However, many large school systems prefer not to provide the name on written communication outside the school (though they do tell their staff and students the identity of the victim). If the latter is your school or district's policy, simply indicate that "a sophomore male" or "sixth grade girl" committed suicide, for example.

Be sure to include in this letter the time and purpose of the family/community meeting to be held at the school that night, and encourage the parents to attend with their children and other concerned family members. Discuss the danger of suicide "contagion," and include the most common warning signs of suicide (*see "Suicide Statistics, Causes, and Myths" previously in this chapter*) and sources of assistance in your community (e.g., the school counselor/psychologist, a crisis or suicide prevention hotline, your local hospital, and private mental health practitioners).

Tell parents to request help immediately if their children express any desire to or hints about killing themselves or exhibit any of the warning signs of suicidal ideation. Also encourage them to safeguard their guns from the access of children, as guns are by far the most common suicide method used today (Poland, 1995). (Emphasize that it is not good enough for them to tell their children not to touch the guns. They must remove the guns from their home or lock them up very securely.)

- Plan and host a family/community meeting the night of the crisis.
- Provide counseling services to those who need them.

Provide counseling services to those close to the deceased (e.g., siblings, friends, teachers of the victim). They will likely feel anger and guilt in addition to grief. Other students may have irrational feelings of guilt about the suicide and need assistance in resolving these thoughts. It is best to begin working with those affected by the suicide as soon as possible, preferably within 24 hours of the tragedy (Schniedman, cited in "Suicide in Children," 1998).

- Address media concerns, if any. (*See "Media Coverage of Suicides" later in this chapter.*)
- Allow funeral attendance.

Any students (or staff) who wish to attend the memorial service or funeral of the suicide victim should be allowed to do so, but school should not be dismissed for this service. The best scenario is for the funeral to occur outside of school hours, so that the suicide is not glorified by hundreds of students leaving school to attend the service. The Counseling Liaison or Parent/Family Liaison might ask the family of the deceased if they could schedule the service after school or on a Saturday. Family members are usually understanding of the school's concern.

Any students who wish to attend the funeral should be prepared for what will happen there. Discuss with your students visitation/funeral procedures, including etiquette and appropriate denominational customs. Emphasize that the students have a choice about attending the funeral, and encourage those who plan to attend to go with their parents. (*See "Funerals" in Chapter Six for complete guidelines.*)

See "Task List" for tips on planning this meeting and "The Family/ Community Meeting" (both in Chapter Two) for information about its format and content.

See "Crisis Effects and Grief" and "Providing Counseling Services" in Chapter Seven.

- Do not memorialize the suicide victim at school.

Because of the danger of suicide "contagion," your school must be careful not to glorify or sensationalize the death in any way. For this reason, the suicide victim should not be memorialized at school, as a memorial places the deceased in the position of role model. Explained school psychologist Richard Lieberman, "When children think about suicide they are not thinking clearly. It is not a far stretch for a child who sees a beautiful tree, a yearbook dedication, or a memorial plaque to imagine he or she [would] receive such attention in death" (CASP, 1998, p. 14).

If your school is requested to dedicate yearbooks, dances, or other school events to the deceased, your answer should be no (Poland, 1989). There should be no physical memorial of any kind at school, and nothing permanent. If funds are donated, they should be allocated to a worthy cause, such as a suicide prevention effort or some sort of scholarship. One Houston school used donations to send a group of cheerleaders to a cheerleading camp. This was an appropriate use of such funds, as it was something "consumable" rather than a permanent memorial. Scholarship activities also meet another need after a suicide, which is to shift the focus from the suicide victim to the survivors. Explained suicidologists Lamb and Dunne-Maxim (1987, p. 249), "In general, the emphasis should be on ... avoid[ing] overdramatization. Instead, the focus must be on the needs of the living, the survivors."

Maintaining this "hard line" position on memorializing suicide victims is sometimes difficult for school administrators, because the victims' parents often are very "invested" in their children's memory and want some permanent memorial at school. If the suicide victim was popular, many of the students may want a permanent memorial as well. In such situations it helps to have a copy of the guidelines recommended by the American Association of Suicidology (summarized later in this section) to show the parents and students and to be prepared to explain why this ban on memorials in necessary (i.e., to prevent suicide "contagion").

If you make any exceptions to this policy, be sure to do so only after a great deal of thought and planning. For example, administrators at a high school in St. Paul, Minnesota, made an exception to their long-standing policy forbidding yearbook remembrances after friends of two deceased students (one a suicide victim) led approximately 400 of their peers in a "walk-out" to protest the ban ("Officials Agree," 1998). For the first time in more than 14 years, the ban on memorializing suicide victims would be lifted and the yearbook would include a page with pictures of the two students and some poetry. The negotiations involved in making this decision involved the parents of the two deceased students as well as the students' friends. Principal Walt Lyszak called the decision "a good compromise," although he acknowledged that he did have "'lingering doubts' about the effects of the memorial on teenagers at risk of suicide, which was the reason for the ban in the first place" ("Officials Agree," 1998, p. 4).

- Follow normal school procedures as with any death of a school community member.

While care should be taken not to glorify the suicide of a student or staff member, you also cannot pretend the death has not occurred. One school principal did just that by refusing to fly the school flag at half-mast after a student suicide (Dunne-Maxim, 1987). This decision upset many grieving students, because the flag lowering was a routine observance of a death at this school (and most others as well).

- Communicate with the family of the deceased.

School representatives may shy away from contact with the family members of a suicide victim because of their personal discomfort. However, it is important for your school to initiate contact with the family, not only to assist them but also to help in handling the postvention as smoothly as possible (a task made easier when there is open and ongoing communication between the school and the family).

In addition to formally expressing the school's condolences and returning personal items of the deceased, the Crisis Coordinator, Parent/Family Liaison, and/or Counseling Liaison should communicate with the family to:

- Discuss funeral and memorial concerns (*see "Funerals" in Chapter Six.*)

- Make a mental health referral and identify any survivor support groups available in the community (Poland, 1989). Family counseling is often helpful after a suicide, as the surviving family members may experience anger and guilt as well as grief. It is also important because, according to the American Association of Suicidology ("Understanding and Helping," 1997), "surviving family members not only suffer the trauma of losing a loved one to a suicide, but are themselves at higher risk for suicide and emotional problems."

- "Run interference" with the media, if the family welcomes this assistance. The media will generally not contact the family of a suicide victim for details, but the family may wish to make a statement (Ring, cited in Poland, 1989) via the Media Liaison. (The school should reserve the right to edit such a statement to ensure that its content conforms to the guidelines of the American Association of Suicidology or to decline to read the family's statement.)

- Emphasize to the family that confidentiality will be maintained (Ring, cited in Poland, 1989). That is, specify that no school personnel will comment or speculate on family problems or theories about why the victim committed suicide. This agreement can prevent misunderstandings between the family and the school.

– Assist the victim's sibling(s) within your school and area schools. These children have not only lost a brother or sister but may carry a weight of guilt and self-blame. Further, their family may be ostracized within the school and community because of the suicide (Poland, 1989). Siblings of suicide victims will have a difficult time escaping the effects of the tragedy, and they need your support. If a sibling attends another area school, contact the counselor at that school so that he or she can provide assistance ("Postvention," 1998). The parents will likely be very concerned about their surviving children and receptive to such assistance.

> "The stigma that our society has attached to the survivors of suicide [victims] will not go away easily, but a caring, reaching-out response from the school is a first step."
>
> (Poland, 1989, p. 140)

Any expressions of sorrow (e.g., cards or letters) from students who knew the suicide victim would also be appreciated by the family, and the school representatives could deliver these as well (Poland, 1989).

• Refer to and follow the suicide postvention guidelines of the American Association of Suicidology (AAS, 1998), summarized here:

– Don't dismiss school or encourage funeral attendance during school hours.

– Don't dedicate a memorial to the deceased.

– Don't hold a large assembly to notify the school community members of the suicide.

– Do verify the facts and treat the death as a suicide.

– Do give the facts to the students (while downplaying the method).

– Do emphasize prevention and everyone's role in preventing suicides.

– Do provide individual and group counseling.

– Do emphasize that no one else is to blame for the suicide.

– Do emphasize that help is available, that suicides can be prevented, and that everyone has a role to play in prevention.

– Do contact the family of the deceased.

The American Association of Suicidology (AAS) is composed of many mental health professionals who share an interest in suicide prevention. This 32-year old organization is recognized as the national leader in suicide prevention and postvention efforts. Explained one suicidologist, "… there is no federally funded research on suicide, [so] organized efforts at prevention rest largely with the AAS" (Colt, cited in Poland, 1989, p. 180). (*NOTE*: The Centers for Disease Control and Prevention also collect data and conduct research on youth suicide, although suicide is not their primary focus.)

Because suicide is such a disruptive and stressful crisis, school administrators would do well to have a copy of the AAS postvention guidelines to refer to and fall back on if questioned by others (e.g., parents, the media). With the guidelines in hand you can say, with confidence, "I've followed the guidelines from the leading suicide association in the country." (*NOTE*: The guidelines published by the AAS are not much more comprehensive than the summary provided in this chapter; however, it might be helpful for your school administrators to have an official copy to produce in a debate about what is appropriate after a suicide. The printed guidelines also include sample memos to faculty and letters to parents that might be helpful. To obtain a copy of the AAS manual, call [202] 237-2280.)

Some schools continue to use an older set of guidelines published by Phi Delta Kappa International (1988), which are in stark contrast to the AAS recommendations. For example, the Phi Delta Kappa guidelines specify a large assembly format for notifying school community members of a death, a technique that has been proven by both research and practical experience to be disruptive and potentially harmful to students' mental health. The Phi Delta Kappa guidelines also strongly recommend that schools not treat the death as a suicide. Not only would this policy lead to much confusion if the students know otherwise, but it would also cause the school to miss an important opportunity to work on the prevention of additional suicides. If you have these guidelines in your professional library, we recommend that you replace them with the proven AAS guidelines.

Preventing Suicide "Contagion" at Your School

To prevent "contagion" suicides from occurring at your school, you must focus on two main tasks: taking prevention steps with those known to be suicidal and identifying others at risk for suicide (Poland & Lieberman, 1998). School psychologists and counselors have training in suicide prevention and intervention, and we encourage you to follow their recommendations after the suicide of a school community member. It is beyond the scope of this book to outline comprehensive procedures for these prevention and intervention efforts.

> "Those previously suicidal are now more suicidal."
>
> (Poland & Lieberman, 1998)

However, a few of the most pertinent points follow ("Postvention," 1998; Stevenson, 1994):

- Immediately begin "networking" efforts to provide counseling assistance to two groups of students: those known to have been suicidal in the past and those who were close to the victim.

- Instruct all school staff to keep their ears open for any talk of additional threatened or attempted suicides among the student body.

- Make all staff members thoroughly familiar with exactly whom they should contact if they become aware of potentially at-risk students or a suicide attempt. (*NOTE*: Throughout this discussion, this contact person is referred to as the "designated school staff member.")

- If your school's mental health staff has not already done so, they should immediately familiarize themselves with the community resources available for assistance (i.e., police, medical, mental health, other relevant emergency personnel and agencies) and establish a relationship with them if one does not already exist.

- If *any* adult in the school becomes aware of the possibility that a student is suicidal, he or she should contact the designated school staff member, who will talk with (i.e., assess) the potentially at-risk student. (Using his or her professional judgment, this school official may then formally assess the severity level of the student's risk and/or refer the student for further assessment or treatment.)

- Students should be told to talk with *any* adult in the school community if they are concerned about the possible suicidality of a peer. That adult should then immediately contact the designated school staff member.

- *Take all threats of suicide seriously*. A student who writes or talks about suicide, or drops hints about suicide, is at risk!

- You must *always* contact the parent(s)/guardian of a potentially suicidal student, regardless of whether the knowledge of the risk is firsthand or secondhand information. The parent(s)/guardian must be contacted every time information concerning a student's potential suicide risk comes to the attention of school staff, and these contacts should be documented in writing. There are no exceptions to this rule. The parent(s) must be contacted, even if they are perceived by the school to be "the problem." (Your professional challenge is to elicit a supportive reaction from the parent[s].)

- Do not mince words with the parent(s)/guardian about removing guns and other potentially lethal instruments from the home of a suicidal student.

- Make a referral for the parent(s)/guardian of a suicidal student to a community agency or a private practitioner with experience counseling suicidal youth. Within the next day or two, call the parent(s)/guardian to ensure that they have followed through with obtaining the recommended mental health assistance for the student.

- In the presence of a second school representative, ask difficult parent(s) (i.e., those who are uncooperative, angry, or in a state of denial when informed about their child's suicidal intent) to sign a "Notification of Emergency Conference Form" documenting that they have been notified of their child's suicidal ideation and advised to seek mental health assistance. (*See the example following.*) If the parent(s)/guardian refuse to sign the form, the second school representative should sign the form as a witness that the conversation took place. Parent(s)/guardians who refuse to obtain mental health assistance for suicidal minor(s) leave you no choice but to call your local child protective services agency to report this negligence.

Notification of Emergency Conference Form

I, or we _____, the parent(s)/guardian of _____, were involved in a conference with school personnel on _____. We have been notified that our child is suicidal. We have been further advised that we should seek some psychological/psychiatric consultation immediately within the community. School personnel have clarified the district's role and will provide follow-up assistance to our child to support the treatment services from within the community.

_____   _____
(Parent or Legal Guardian)   (School Personnel/Title)

_____   _____
(Parent or Legal Guardian)   (School Personnel/Title)

Key points to tell parents

Key points you should communicate to the parent(s)/guardian of a suicidal student include the following (Cypress-Fairbanks Independent School District, 1998; Poland, 1989):

- "We have assessed the suicide risk and had your child sign a 'No-Suicide Contract.'" (*See the discussion of a "No-Suicide Contract" later in this section.*)
- "A local crisis hotline number was provided to your child." (Provide the parent[s]/guardian the number as well.)
- "We need you to work cooperatively with us to assist your child. It is important that you follow our intervention advice and act on the mental health referral we provide." (Depending upon the severity level of the suicide risk, your recommendations will range from immediate hospitalization to outpatient treatment.)
- "If your child refuses to see the mental health professional, you must insist that he or she does so and accompany your child to the

appointments." (Explain to the parent[s]/guardian that you can assist in convincing your child to attend these sessions, if necessary.)

- "For your child's sake, you must recognize the seriousness of this problem and act quickly."
- "You need to focus on your child's needs now. Providing him or her with assistance must be a priority in your family."
- "It's important that you increase your supervision and emotional support of your child." (A critical child should not, for example, come home to an empty house after school.)
- "Immediately remove any guns and other potentially lethal instruments (such as knives, ropes, and prescription medications) from your home. Telling your child not to touch your gun is not good enough!"
- "Be patient with your child. Try not to be angry with (him or her) because of the suicidal intent."
- "Offer help to your child with 'no strings attached.'"
- "Keep communication going with your child and try to prevent (him or her) from feeling isolation. Enlist the assistance of your family members and trusted family friends to interact with your child."
- "Show your child love, acceptance, and tolerance. This is not the time to 'get tough.'"
- "Take all suicidal threats and attempts seriously. If you believe suicide threats are attention-seeking and manipulative behaviors, then allow yourself to be manipulated!"

Key points when interacting with students

Key points for a mental health worker when interacting with suicidal students include the following (Poland, 1997):

1. Try to remain calm, and seek collaboration from a colleague.
2. Gather case history information from the student. Asking the student questions as if he or she were planning a "trip" (rather than suicide) can help to elicit concrete facts about his or her plans and alleviate some of the anxiety of the counselor or psychologist. For example, you might ask: "How long have you been planning this?" "Who have you told about these plans?" "Are you planning to take anyone else with you?" and so forth.
3. Ask specific questions about the suicide plan and the frequency and duration of suicidal thoughts. The most important question for the student to answer is, "How would you end your life?" The student's answer to that question will in large part determine your next steps. Consider the Houston student who told a school psychologist, in answer to that question, that he would shoot himself with his family's

.38 pistol, which was waiting for him in his bedroom, and that he had taken the gun out the previous night and had pointed it at his head. Obviously, a student with such a concrete suicide plan should not be allowed to leave the school psychologist's office except in the custody of his parent(s)/guardian, and the gun would need to be removed from the home immediately. In contrast, a student who answered, "I don't know how I'd do it. I'd just like to go to sleep sometime and not wake up," would not pose as severe a risk.

4. Emphasize that there are alternatives to suicide and that the student is not the first person to feel this way.

5. Do not agree to keep the student's suicidal thoughts or actions a secret. Explain your ethical responsibility to notify his or her parent(s)/guardian.

6. Ask the student to sign a "No-Suicide Contract" (*see the sample following*), and provide the student with the phone number of the local crisis hotline.

7. Supervise the student until his or her parent(s)/guardian have assumed responsibility.

8. Make a follow-up appointment at school with the suicidal student.

No-Suicide Contract

I, _____ agree not to harm myself. If I am having thoughts of
           (Student Name)

harming myself or committing suicide, I will do the following until I receive help:

• Get assistance from an adult, such as_____
                                 (Name and Phone Number)

_____

• Call the Crisis Hotline at _____

• Call the school psychologist or school counselor at _____
                                          (Name and Phone Number)

_____

I understand the contract that I am signing and agree to abide by it.

_____   _____
(Student Signature)   (School Personnel Signature)

Suicide Attempts

If a student attempts suicide at your school, you must take immediate steps to obtain assistance for the student (Stevenson, 1994). Those steps include the following:

- Call for professional medical and/or mental health assistance. If the suicide attempt necessitates medical attention, such as stemming extensive bleeding or pumping the stomach, the student will be taken to the hospital. If the attempt necessitates psychological intervention, immediate admittance to a psychiatric hospital is ideal but not always possible. In cases in which immediate admittance is not possible because of poor or no insurance coverage and/or limited beds in city and county facilities, a referral to another community mental health agency should be made.

- Remove all potentially lethal weapons and instruments from the student and the immediate area, if it is possible to do so without jeopardizing the physical safety of the school staff.

- Closely supervise the student until professional assistance arrives, including physically restraining the student if he or she poses a threat of imminent physical harm to himself or herself.

- Negotiate with the student, if necessary. However, you cannot promise to withhold information about the suicide attempt from his or her parents. Treat the student gently and with respect, maintaining a calm demeanor. Grant the student's immediate requests, such as a need to see a support person (e.g., a favorite teacher).

- Notify the student's parent(s)/guardian.

- Provide assistance, at the very least, to those in your school community who are aware of the attempt and preferably to your entire student body (because the students who know about the attempt will talk about it with many other students). (*See "Discussing and Processing Reactions to Suicide" previously in this section for guidelines.*)

See "Verifying Information/Crisis Fact Sheet" in Chapter One for more information.

If a student attempts suicide off school grounds, you must obtain the facts. If the school has not been notified of the suicide attempt but members of your student body are discussing such a situation, contact the family of the suicidal student to verify the rumor. The Crisis Coordinator, Counseling Liaison, and/or another member of your crisis response team should speak with the family in person. You may be uncomfortable making this contact, yet it is important to hear the facts from the family so that you can provide the appropriate intervention for the student and your school community.

If the parent(s)/guardian of the student being discussed are unaware of the rumored suicide attempt, follow the recommendations for communicating with parent(s) about their children's risk for suicide that were presented previously in this chapter (*see "Preventing Suicide 'Contagion' at Your School"*).

Media Coverage of Suicides

Media coverage of a suicide can be a causal factor in suicide "contagion" or "clusters." According to the American Foundation for Suicide Prevention (1998b), "After a film or news story on suicide, suicide rates tend to go up." There are also documented accounts of "… specific suicides that were committed shortly after seeing [coverage of] or reading about a suicide" (American Foundation for Suicide Prevention, 1998b). Thus, the nature of coverage of a suicide and the way in which you interact with the media after the suicide of a school community member are of concern.

Because youth suicide is so common, an isolated suicide at your school may not be considered newsworthy by your local press, especially if yours is a large school system or your school is in a large city. In contrast, any suicide in a small community will likely generate media interest. Clusters of suicides in one geographical area, and "pacts" between students who commit suicide together, will almost always be covered (Poland, 1989). If the media do arrive at your school to cover a suicide, you will be at odds with them to a certain extent: The media want a story, and you'd prefer as little publicity as possible (Dunne-Maxim, 1987).

> "The fact that [most youth suicides are] not news is a blessing but a sad commentary on the times."
>
> (Poland, 1995, p. 465)

All of the guidelines presented in this book for dealing with the media after a school crisis (*see especially Chapter Three, "Here Come the Media"*) apply after a suicide. However, when the crisis is suicide related, it is particularly important to convey a cooperative demeanor with the media, for three main reasons: (1) you will want to positively influence the coverage of the tragedy; (2) the school is the first place the media will come for information, preferring not to intrude upon the victim's family; and (3) your school will be closely linked with the suicide victim in the media coverage. (For example, the school the victim attended is usually included in headlines of suicide articles.) Thus, you will want your school to be portrayed by the media as "… concerned, responsive, and working on the problem of teen suicide" (Poland, 1989, p. 153).

The following recommendations (Poland, 1989) will increase the odds that any media coverage of the suicide (or suicide attempt) of your school community member is appropriate:

- Do not refuse to give an interview or simply read a prepared statement. The media may interpret such an approach as "… uncooperative and indicative of attempting to hide a lack of preparation for the problem of youth suicide" (p. 155).

- Approach the media in a positive manner, avoid becoming defensive, and be prepared for the interview. Remember the valuable role the media play in disseminating to the public important information about suicide warning signs and sources of assistance.

- The school spokesperson granting the media interview(s) should "... have a thorough understanding of the dynamics of youth suicide" (p. 154). If the Media Liaison (*see "The First Hour of a Severe Crisis" in Chapter One for information about this role*) does not possess this particular knowledge, someone from your school's mental health staff should conduct the interview(s) instead of, or in collaboration with, the Media Liaison.

- Encourage the media not to cover the story. Suggest, instead, they come back in a few weeks to do a story on suicide prevention. For example, they might report on teenagers who had struggled with problems but, with help, had chosen alternatives to suicide (with these survivors' prior permission, of course). The story of students who had intervened and prevented a friend's suicide would also be deserving of publicity.

- Honestly acknowledge the suicide or "suicide equivalent" action (*see "Suicide Postvention" previously in this chapter*).

- Provide brief identifying information about the victim such as age, grade, and gender. Make every effort to obtain parental permission before providing the name of the victim, even if other sources (e.g., the police) are already reporting the student's name.

- Answer the media's questions, but protect confidential information about the victim (and his or her family) and avoid discussing the circumstances/causation of the suicide and details of the victim's life.

- Downplay the method of suicide, withholding these details.

- Read any appropriate statement from the victim's family. (Reserve the right to edit this statement to ensure that it complies with the recommendations of the American Association of Suicidology—*see "Suicide Postvention" previously in this chapter*—or to refrain from reading it.)

- Express the sorrow of the faculty and student body.

- Emphasize the steps your school is taking to assist the other students in coping with the suicide. Explain that the students are being encouraged to continue with their normal school activities to the greatest extent possible.

- Outline the counseling services being provided by your school and within the community. Be sure to publicize the time and location of the family/community meeting to be held that night (*see "The Family/Community Meeting in Chapter Two*), and encourage all concerned parents to attend with their children.

- Acknowledge the widespread problem of youth suicide, citing appropriate statistics (*see "Suicide Statistics, Causes, and Myths" previously in this chapter*).

- Emphasize any prevention efforts your school or district has previously made in this area, providing the media with documentation. The media will likely be very interested in such positive steps and procedures. For example, media representatives in Houston, Texas, "… have even gone so far as to take photographs of written procedures and "'No-Suicide Contracts'" (p. 156).

- Ask the media to emphasize the warning signs of suicide (*see "Suicide Statistics, Causes, and Myths" previously in this chapter*) as well as the sources of assistance available within both your school and the community.

- Explain to the media the suicide "contagion"/ "clusters" phenomenon, and ask them, in their coverage, to follow the media guidelines proposed by the American Association of Suicidology (AAS, 1998) and summarized here:

  - Avoid details of the method.

  - Do not report the suicide as unexplainable or the result of simplistic or romantic causes.

  - Avoid making the story front-page news and avoid the word "suicide" in the headline.

  - Do not print a photograph of the deceased.

  - Refrain from coverage that excites or sensationalizes.

  - Do not imply approval of suicide.

  - Use simple language and review all statistics to ensure that accurate information is conveyed. Cite sources when appropriate.

  - Be cautious about contacting the survivors of a suicide victim or a person who has attempted suicide. It is preferable to have the school obtain approval from such people prior to your contact.

  - Avoid discussing the specifics of the situation and safeguard confidential information about the victim and his or her family.

  - Include, if possible, positive outcomes of suicidal crises.

  - Include information on the warning signs, sources of help, and what one should do if they become aware that someone is suicidal.

> "I would not want to be in the position of having to respond to the media coverage of a suicide without being able to produce evidence that the school system has worked on the problem …."
>
> (Poland, 1989, p. 156)

To prevent suicide "contagion," the second AAS point is critical. The suicide must not be portrayed as a "tragic, heroic, or romantic response to stress and pressure imposed by an uncaring adult world" (Shaffer et al., cited in "An Interview," 1998, p. 14), nor should it be portrayed in any sort of "mystical" terms.

Consider what has to be one of the worst-ever cases of reporting on a teen suicide, which appeared in 1985 in a Springfield, Missouri, newspaper (O'Dell, 1985). The headline read: "Bright, Popular Ozark Student Falls to

Dark, Lonely Thoughts." This article appeared on the front page, accompanied by the photo of a beautiful girl. It described in great detail how the suicide victim got her best black dress dry-cleaned, went to the cleaners to pick up the dress, put the dress on, drove to the Springfield Holidome, ordered a soft drink, dropped a cyanide tablet into the soda, drank it, and fell dead to the floor. The concluding sentence of the article read, "She was just too sensitive for this tough world of ours." Sending youth this type of message is quite harmful, as is providing them with a complete suicide plan to imitate! If your local media are ignorant of these dangers, you must educate them about the issues and strongly encourage responsible journalism pertaining to the coverage of suicides.

References

American Association of Suicidology (AAS). (1998). *Postvention guidelines for the schools: Suggestions for dealing with the aftermath of suicide in the schools* (2nd ed.). Washington, DC: Author.

American Foundation for Suicide Prevention. (1996a). *Suicide facts: Child and adolescent suicide.* Available online: http://www.afsp.org/suicide/children.htm

American Foundation for Suicide Prevention. (1996b). *Suicide facts: What to do if you suspect a loved one might be contemplating suicide.* Available online: http://www.afsp.org/suicide/whattodo.html

American Foundation for Suicide Prevention. (1998a). *Suicide facts: Firearms and suicide.* Available online: http://www.afsp.org/suicide/firearms.htm

American Foundation for Suicide Prevention. (1998b). *Youth suicide: Risk factors.* Available online: http://www.afsp.org/youth/riskfact.htm

American Foundation for Suicide Prevention. (1998c). *Youth suicide: The suicide act.* Available online: http://www.afsp.org/youth/act.htm

An interview with Scott Poland, Ph.D. (1998). *Child Therapy News, 6*(1), 11-17.

Are school psychologists liable for student actions? (1994, July). *American Psychological Association's Monitor, 25*(7), 1.

Bradshaw, D. E., & Kaslow, N. J. (1996). *Suicide facts: Danger signals.* Available online: http://www.afsp.org/suicide/danger.html

California Association of School Psychologists (CASP). (1998, November). Teen suicides: Life, after death. *NASP Communiqué, 27*(3), 14-15.

Centers for Disease Control and Prevention (CDC). (1989-1994). Death rates by selected causes: Suicides, by 5-year age groups. In *Morbidity and Mortality Data.* Atlanta, GA: Author.

Centers for Disease Control and Prevention (CDC). (1995). Suicide among children, adolescents, and young adults: United States, 1980-1992. *Morbidity and Mortality Weekly Report, 44*(15), 290-291.

Childhood suicide and myths surrounding it. (1998). *Child Therapy News, 6*(1), 4.

Children's Defense Fund. (1999, February). Moments in America for children. *NASP Communiqué, 27*(5), 6.

Cypress-Fairbanks Independent School District, Department of Psychological Services. (1998). *Suicide prevention is everyone's responsibility* [Brochure]. Houston, TX: Author.

deGroot, G. (1994, July). School staffs need training on suicide-warning signs. *American Psychological Association's Monitor, 25*(7), 58.

District held liable for student's suicide at home. (1997, December). *Today's School Psychologist, 1*(5), 8-9.

Dunne-Maxim, K. (1987, November). Postvention in the schools. In A. McEvoy (Chair), *Suicide prevention and the schools.* Symposium sponsored by Learning Publications, Orlando, Florida.

Egan, T. (1998, June 14). Killing sprees tied by string of youth rage. *Denver Post,* pp. 1A, 22A.

Fainaru, S. (1998a, October 18). Early detection sought for depression. *Boston Globe,* p. A35.

Fainaru, S. (1998b, October 20). Many struggle to put their world together. *Boston Globe,* pp. A1, A20-21.

Lamb, F., & Dunne-Maxim, K. (1987). Postvention in the schools: Policy and process. In E. Dunne, J. McIntosh, & K. Dunne-Maxim (Eds.), *Suicide and its aftermath* (pp. 245-263). New York: Norton.

Lieberman, R. (1999, January 22-23). *Crisis Intervention Workshop,* Walnut Creek, California.

O'Dell. (1985, January 6). Bright, popular Ozark student falls to dark, lonely thoughts. *Springfield News-Leader,* p. 1.

Officials agree to memorial. (1998, February 25). *Education Week, 17*(24), 4.

Owens, M. (1992, Summer). Student suicide and the civil liability that may be imposed upon school personnel as a result. *Journal of Law and Education, 21*(3), 487-490.

Phi Delta Kappa International. (1988, September). *Responding to student suicide: First 48 hours* (Current Issues Memo). Bloomington, IN: Author.

Poland, S. (1989). *Suicide intervention in the schools.* New York: Guilford.

Poland, S. (1990). Crisis intervention in the schools. *NASP Communiqué, 18*(5), 21, 26.

Poland, S. (1995). Best practices in suicide intervention. In A. Thomas & J. Grimes (Eds.), *Best practices in school psychology—III* (pp. 459-468). Washington, DC: National Association of School Psychologists.

Poland, S. (1997). School crisis teams. In A. P. Goldstein & J. C. Close (Eds.), *School violence intervention: A practical handbook* (pp. 127-159). New York: Guilford.

Poland, S., & Lieberman, R. (1998, June 15). *Crisis intervention.* Workshop sponsored by the Crowley's Ridge Education Cooperative, Jonesboro, Arkansas.

Postvention and the school. (1998). *Child Therapy News, 6*(1), 18.

Ross, C. (1985). Teaching children the facts of life and death: Suicide prevention in the schools. In M. Peck, N. Faberow, & R. Litman (Eds.), *Youth suicide* (pp. 147-169). New York: Springer.

Slenkovitch, J. (1986, June). School districts can be sued for inadequate suicide prevention programs. *The School's Advocate,* pp. 1-3.

Stevenson, R. G. (Ed.). (1994). *What will we do? Preparing a school community to cope with crisis.* Amityville, NY: Baywood Publishing.

Student suicide: Protecting your district from liability. (1997, January 24). *Today's School Psychologist (Bonus Report),* pp. 1-2, 4.

Suicide facts. (1998). *Child Therapy News, 6*(1), 10.

Suicide in children and adolescents. (1998). *Child Therapy News, 6*(1), 1-10, 24.

Understanding and helping the suicidal person. (1997, March). *NASSP NewsLeader,* p. 6.

U.S. tops in child murders: Federal study of industrialized nations shows country leads in homicide, suicide, other rates. (1997, February 7). *Rocky Mountain News.* Available online: http://www.insidedenver.com

chapter twelve

Is It Over?

Some time will need to pass—from days to weeks to months, depending upon the severity of the crisis you've just experienced—before you will be able to think objectively about the crisis. But eventually, you'll need to examine how well you did in responding to this crisis and to make some plans for the future. No matter how catastrophic or how painful the crisis was, your school will continue to educate students, and the lives of all the survivors—students, staff members, and their families—will continue.

Soon after you finish the initial crisis response (i.e., the hours, days, and/or the first few weeks following the crisis event) it is important to turn your attention to the future. You and the other members of the crisis response team will continue to play an important role in addressing the "fallout" of the crisis. In particular, if the crisis was severe, you will likely want to implement some changes in your school building and/or its crisis response policies (*see "Regrouping After a Crisis" later in this chapter*). You will need to be alert for similar types of incidents happening again either at your school or at other area schools (*see "'Copycat' Incidents" later in this chapter*). You will need to anticipate and plan to address the long-term effects for survivors, including continuing to provide counseling services and recognizing the anniversary of the crisis (*see "Long-Term Effects" later in this chapter*). Finally, you should prepare yourselves for possible litigation resulting from the incident (*see "Liability and Litigation" later in this chapter*).

Regrouping After a Crisis

Through your actions in addressing the crisis, your crisis response team has provided a valuable service both to your school community and the surrounding community. You deserve the thanks and praise of the community members. In the midst of a difficult situation, you did the best you could with the resources and knowledge available to you at the time. Through it all, you've no doubt learned a great deal about yourselves as well as your school and community and the character and strength of their members. In retrospect, you also can likely identify where there was room for improvement in your response. Once you are able to catch your breath and have time to reflect upon the incident and the crisis response, schedule at least one "regrouping" meeting with your team and the leaders from your school and district. Be sure to allow enough time for a lengthy, uninterrupted discussion.

Document—either by tape recorder or with very thorough notes—the discussion at this meeting. Among other topics, discuss:

- How are you and the other team members recovering from the effects of the crisis? Do you need more time or opportunities to process your reactions to the crisis? (*See Chapter Five, "Processing the Crisis," for complete instructions.*) Is there anything specific you need from your school and/or district to support your recovery and acknowledge your efforts?

- What worked well in terms of the school's crisis response? What do you have to be proud of? Specifically, think about:
  - The crisis response at the district level
  - The crisis response at the building and team level
  - How the staff responded and coped
  - How your students responded and coped
  - The response from the community

Be sure to acknowledge the contributions of all of your team members and participating staff, even those who were unable or unwilling (for whatever reason) to work directly with affected members of the school community. The crisis response was a team effort and all aspects of the response—including the administrative and the mundane (e.g., going for food)—were crucial to its success. Don't forget to say things such as, "We really appreciated how you wrote that letter and got it out quickly." Then each person will feel like he or she helped your school and community.

- What did not go as well as you would have liked during the crisis response? (*NOTE*: This part of the discussion is not intended to be a forum for blame, accusations, or finger pointing. Each member of your team did the best he or she could do at the time. The team members have probably mentally "replayed" the crisis and their actions repeatedly, and if something wasn't handled well, chances are they already realize that fact. They don't need your help to feel guilty after a crisis: People second-guess themselves enough as it is. Support your team members.) Specifically, *list in writing all of the factors you can think of* related to:

– Your school's crisis response plan (or lack thereof). Did the plan address only natural disasters, for example? Was the plan up-to-date? Could all staff members find and understand your plan? Did your plan actually help you deal with the crisis?

– Specific elements of the crisis response (e.g., media relations, communicating with parents, how long it took to alert other area schools, etc.).

– Safety shortcomings in your physical building and/or equipment or supplies. For example, perhaps you did not have a trauma kit or other appropriate first aid supplies available to you when you needed them. Perhaps your communications equipment was inadequate (e.g., no intercoms in portable classrooms) and hampered your school's crisis response.

– How the staff responded and coped. Were they able to locate their copies of the emergency procedures? Did they know how to follow them?

– How your students responded and coped. Did they follow the directions of the adults in charge as they had been taught? Would drills in emergency procedures be helpful for any future incidents?

– The level of collaboration and cooperation between your school and other agencies (e.g., the police, regional mental health organizations, the local media).

Make each problem you list an action item. The motivation to effect positive change will be unparalleled in the time immediately following a crisis. Use this energy to better prepare yourselves for future crisis incidents. (There *will* be other crises. They may not be as severe as the one you've just experienced, but a crisis of some sort will happen in your school again in the future.) You probably will not have enough time to come up with solutions during this meeting, so assign responsibility for rectifying each problem to either an individual or a committee. (In West Paducah, Kentucky, for example, the city and school leaders established a crisis committee for the county following the school shooting there.) Assign a reasonable time frame for completion of each task, and follow up!

> "My biggest disappointment is [that] we had an opportunity to make some [significant] changes [after our school shooting]. I just don't see that taking place."
>
> —Bruce Wegner, school librarian, Bethel Regional High, Bethel, Alaska (Fainaru, 1998b, p. A20)

• What were some of the root causes that may have contributed to the incident? For example, is there a "conspiracy of silence" at your school? That is, were there warnings of the crisis that went unrecognized by staff or were kept secret by your students? Does your school have a chronic weapons problem? Are drugs sold on your campus, or gangs active in the area? Do your students have somewhere to turn for advice and support? These are just a few of the many factors that might contribute to a school crisis, particularly a violent one.

After assessing the "big picture," talk about what you might do to begin to resolve some of these factors and/or improve the climate of your school. Ideas may be as simple as repainting your school's interior a more cheerful color, as they did in Bethel, Alaska, after the 1997 school shooting there (Fainaru, 1998b), or as ambitious as establishing a suicide prevention hotline. You might also plan an appropriate memorial to the victims of the crisis (*see "Memorializing Victims" in Chapter Six and "Suicide Postvention" in Chapter Eleven for guidelines*). Youth violence, in particular, is a complex problem with no easy answers. While these types of positive actions may not solve all of your school's problems, they are a means to both honor the victims of the tragedy and instill some hope for the future in survivors. Brainstorm any actions appropriate for your school, and make a concrete plan to implement the most feasible ideas.

"The Chinese symbol for crisis translates as 'Opportunity blowing on an ill wind.' Historically, we have learned much from those who have suffered tremendous injustice and loss. The opportunity for growth is upon us."

(Zenere, 1998, p. 39)

NOTE: For any major decisions, be sure to solicit input from everyone who will be affected by the plan (e.g., staff members, students, parents). Participation in making decisions affecting the school will be very important to those who work in the school as well as to older students who wish to contribute in meaningful ways. Involvement in decision making will also be beneficial for parents and other members of the surrounding community. Remember that participation breeds "ownership." People are more likely to "buy into" and/or abide by something they have helped create. For those involved, the policy becomes not "the school's policy," but "*our* policy." Consider forming ad hoc committees of interested parties from each of these representative groups when creating plans for change. At the very least, solicit input from the faculty and support staff, student council or government, and parent-teacher association.

In addition to reviewing the crisis response within your own school, schedule a meeting to share your experiences and what you have learned from them with the other schools in your district. You might schedule an inservice to share what you have learned to do well in terms of crisis response, so that other area schools might learn from your example and be well-prepared when they are faced with a crisis of their own. If your school's crisis was catastrophic, you might even work with your state's department of education and/or the state police to create a statewide inservice program on crisis response. Many states, including New York, Maryland, Florida, and

Delaware, have hosted statewide school safety planning conferences in recent years. The Department of Education and the state police in these states sponsored these events.

"Copycat" Incidents

After you have experienced the fear and horror involved in a severe school crisis, it may be unthinkable to you that what happened at your school could "inspire" someone to inflict the same kind of physical and emotional pain upon others elsewhere. Sadly, this "copycat" phenomenon is all too common. Both adults and children have committed atrocious "copycat" acts after hearing of tragedies in their communities or states or even elsewhere in the country.

Sometimes the perpetrators of "copycat" crimes acknowledge that they were influenced by similar crimes elsewhere. For example, in 1988 a gunman killed two people and wounded nine others at an elementary school in Greenwood, South Carolina. When he was interviewed after the shooting he admitted that he had been influenced by a similar shooting in Winnetka, Illinois, five months prior (Pitcher & Poland, 1992). More often, however, those who commit "copycat" crimes say they "don't know" why they did what they did, but their actions strike an eerie resemblance to crises that occurred elsewhere and were reported in the news. (*NOTE*: Other perpetrators seem to copy violent acts depicted in movies and television programs. For example, the movie *The Basketball Diaries*, in which a student shoots members of his Catholic school, has been linked to real-life violence, including the school shooting in West Paducah, Kentucky.)

Children, in particular, may be influenced by the news coverage of violent acts. Quite simply, hearing how a student elsewhere terrorized a school can give troubled children some very specific ideas about actions that they could take in *their* communities. Explained one researcher, "[Media coverage has] never, in my experience, turned a responsible youngster into a criminal. But a youngster who is already inclined toward antisocial behavior hears of a particular crime, and it feeds an already fertile mind" (Lacayo, 1998, p. 38). Commenting about the influence of the media on today's youth, Jack Levin, a sociologist at Northeastern University in Boston, said, "There is a fad that has swept the country and it goes way beyond sneakers or leather jackets. It is now murder. Maybe 20 years ago, teenagers would have imitated other teenagers down the block. But now, they imitate other kids in other towns, thanks to television" (Cannon, 1998, p. 10A). Agreed Alfred Blumstein, director of the National Consortium on Violence Research, "As they read about other kids doing this, that certainly can contribute to them doing it" (Cannon, 1998, p. 10A).

"A decade ago, the idea of shooting up a schoolyard wouldn't cross anyone's mind. Now young people have prior examples. [The child perpetrators in Jonesboro, Arkansas] probably couldn't spell Paducah, but they'd heard of it."

—James Fox, Dean of Criminal Justice, Northeastern University (Gegax, Adler, & Pedersen, 1998, p. 22)

"Authorities say the rise in 'copycat' crime is [a result of] teenagers playing a dangerous game of 'Top This.'"

(Dotson, 1999)

Besides providing a "game plan" for the act, the media's coverage can glamorize the perpetrators, which may excite other children, who are both impressionable and attention seekers. Seeing the pictures of child perpetrators—sometimes posed dramatically with a gun or sporting a jaunty smile—can make some children envious of the state-wide or national attention lavished by the press on these killers. What occurs is, in a sense, a twisted form of hero worship. After the school shooting near Jonesboro, Arkansas, for example, two 11-year old boys speaking with a reporter "… vied with each other for the title of Drew Golden's 'best friend'" (Labi, 1998, p. 37), hoping to call some attention to themselves. Speaking from prison after fatally shooting his school principal and another student at Bethel (Alaska) Regional High School in 1997, the student perpetrator admitted that he had initially planned to commit suicide after shooting the others. A friend he discussed his plan with beforehand had other ideas, however. Explained the murderer, "… James had some strong disagreements on that. He said lots of people will know about me. He said I should live the fame" (Fainaru, 1998a, p. A10).

Making sense of how a child could consider gunning down or otherwise hurting his or her peers and teachers a good idea, or how a child could find the notoriety associated with committing an act of violence glorious, is beyond the scope of this book. You must, however, be aware that these things do occur and anticipate and prepare for the following types of "copycat" threats and/or events. *The key is to take all such threats seriously:*

- *Threats or events at other area schools in the town or district*

  The day after the school shooting in West Paducah, Kentucky, telephone calls were received within the district indicating that "… something would happen at each of the McCracken County high schools [that] week" (Holliman, 1997). These threats frightened both students and parents, and the two other high schools in McCracken County increased their security. Fortunately, as Principal Bond predicted, the threats proved to be merely rumors.

- *Threats or events at other schools in the state*

  On December 15, 1997, a 14-year old boy hid in the woods outside his school in Stamps, Arkansas. He randomly shot two classmates, wounding both of them in the hip (Labi, 1998, p. 39). One wonders if news accounts of this sniper attack could have planted a seed in the minds of

Drew Golden and Mitchell Johnson, the perpetrators of a similar (yet more devastating) shooting near Jonesboro, Arkansas, three months later.

- *Threats or events at other schools nationwide*

When a school crisis is severe enough to be publicized nationally, schools around the country need to be aware of the potential for "copy-cat" actions by their students and heed any warning of such acts. When schools heed such warnings, tragedies *can* be averted. For example, in May 1998, three sixth grade students were arrested in St. Charles, Missouri. According to police, they "… had a 'hit list' and were plotting to kill fellow classmates on the last day of school in a sniper attack during a false fire alarm" ("At Least 13 Killed," 1998). As described in the *St. Louis Post-Dispatch* (Munz, 1998), "… rumors of violence had been circulating at the school for two weeks. A classmate told [Deputy Craig Ostermeyer, a DARE officer at the elementary school] about a student threatening to pull the fire alarm on the last day of school and open fire as students filed out of the building, similar to the incident in Jonesboro, Arkansas [two months prior]." This potential tragedy was averted, explained St. Charles County Sheriff Doug Saulters, because officials "… were privy to the information before it could actually be put together and executed" (Munz, 1998).

- *Suicide "clusters"/"contagion"*

Compelling evidence indicates that children and teens "… follow the suicidal actions of their peers, a trend known as suicide clusters or contagion" (Nemours Foundation, cited in California Association of School Psychologists [CASP], 1998b). For example, a week after a high school senior killed himself in Reed City, Michigan, in February 1998, a 13-year old student in the same school shot himself in front of his locker at the beginning of the school day with a .22-caliber rifle he smuggled into the school in a guitar case ("Michigan Student," 1998). While the reasons for suicide "contagion" are not entirely understood, it is thought that children who might already be contemplating suicide are influenced by the attention paid to another who has taken his or her own life.

If a suicide-related crisis occurs at your school, monitor closely any at-risk students (e.g., those who have previously threatened or attempted suicide and those who have suffered a recent loss) and "keep your ear to the ground" for suicidal talk. You should also send a note home to parents notifying them that there has been a suicide within the school community and explaining to them the potential for suicide "contagion." Urge parents to request help immediately if their children hint about or express any desire to kill themselves.

See "Suicide Postvention" in Chapter Eleven for guidelines on handling appropriately the aftereffects of a suicide within the school community.

For Concerned People Elsewhere …

"Copycat" Threats

After the April 1999 massacre and bombing at Columbine High School in Littleton, Colorado, there was a "… fevered week of 'copycat' incidents at schools across the continent. Authorities rounded up scores of kids for allegedly plotting to blow up their schools, sneaking guns onto campus, or threatening to 'off' their enemies" (Drummond, 1999, p. 29). Some incidents turned out to be hollow threats, yet many of them still struck terror in the minds of students and parents. "Nearly half of the 900 students at Scituate High School and Middle School in Scituate, Rhode Island," for example, "stayed home [from school at the end of April] after someone scrawled on a wall in the girls' bathroom Monday and Tuesday: 'You die on April 30th'" (Dotson, 1999).

Other "copycat" incidents were deadly serious. Eight days after the Columbine High killings, for instance, a 14-year old school dropout in the small town of Taber, Alberta, Canada, pulled a .22-caliber rifle from beneath his three-quarter length parka. He used it to kill a 17-year old boy and critically wound another in front of W.R. Meyers High School (Drummond, 1999).

Hypervigilant students and school staff likely averted other potential tragedies. In Bakersfield, California, some classmates of a 13-year old saw the student loading a .40-caliber handgun and reported him. When authorities removed the boy from class, they found a "hit list" in his possession naming 30 targeted victims. The words "they deserved to die" were written at the bottom (Drummond, 1999, p. 29).

The prevalence of "copycat" incidents after the news of a severe school crisis is publicized puts schools everywhere at risk and places school administrators in an uncomfortable position. "Now everyone has to be serious about everything," said Paul Houston, executive director of the American Association of School Administrators, "because they're afraid that if they aren't, they might be jeopardizing children" (Drummond, 1999, p. 29).

Yet while it is crucial to take prudent steps to ensure school safety, it is easy for schools to go overboard in the face of "copycat" threats. The school board in Allen, Texas, did just that. After receiving 11 bomb threats at various schools in a Dallas suburb following the Columbine tragedy, the school board canceled the remaining two weeks of classes for all 9,800 district students. Yet, no bombs were found, and one 15-year old middle school student was charged with calling in one of the bomb threats from within his school (Associated Press, 1999). According to an Associated Press (1999) article, "Parents were angry and students puzzled when they found the schools closed on Friday morning…. 'It's kids trying to test the system,' [one parent] said. 'I don't think they mean to hurt anybody, they just want to get out of school. I'm pretty ticked off. They got what they wanted.'"

Take the following steps to prepare your school for any "copycat" threats it may receive following a publicized school crisis elsewhere:

continued—

- Review your school's crisis response plan. (If you don't have one, review the first four chapters of this book and then schedule a school and/or district meeting to begin addressing your need for a comprehensive crisis response plan.)

- Alert all of your school staff that in the next few days your school may experience bomb threats; violent, attention-seeking actions by students; and imitations of the suspected student perpetrator(s)' dress and/or actions (e.g., students bringing toy—or real—guns to school or using threatening language).

- Instruct all of your school staff to immediately report any threats of violence or violent actions, both past and present. Take all such threats seriously, and fully investigate them.

- Whenever possible, provide extra security rather than canceling school. Take every precaution necessary to protect human safety while at the same time striving to maintain the regular schedule and a calm atmosphere. You might, for example, physically check all backpacks as students enter the building, scan students and their belongings with handheld metal detectors, and/or post security guards on a temporary basis.

- Bear in mind that if a bomb threat is received, "evacuations could make students feel protected, [but at the same time they could be potent] reminders that students and teachers all are vulnerable to violence" (Dotson, 1999). (*See "Bomb Threat" in the "Less Severe Crises" section of Chapter One for detailed recommendations.*)

- Involve the police in a timely manner whenever a crime is committed or is threatened. Follow their instructions.

- Communicate closely with your central office in the event of a "copycat" threat or action at your school. Your superintendent and/or school board may wish to become involved in the crisis response, and/or may need to notify other area schools of a potential threat to their safety.

- Make your school administration and security staff extra visible (e.g., positioning them in the hallways, common areas, and classrooms, as appropriate) in the days following a publicized severe crisis. Have teachers increase their visibility as well—for example, by meeting and greeting students as they arrive at school. The dual goals are to restore a sense of safety within your school and to watch closely for any potential "copycats."

- Have all the teachers explain to their students (perhaps reading a statement from the head administrator) that the school is taking all necessary steps to protect their safety. They should emphasize how important it is for students to immediately report to an adult in the school any rumors or threats of violence and that all such threats will be investigated. They should also tell students that any academic time lost due to bomb (or other) threats received by the school will be made up during a student holiday or in the summer, as necessary.

- Communicate to parents any extra security measures taken in the wake of a publicized severe crisis through a home letter. The purpose of the letter is to control rumors about any threats your school may receive and to reassure parents about the safety of their children at school. Encourage normal school attendance.

Long-Term Effects

The American Red Cross Disaster Services has a saying about the long-term effects of a crisis: "Everybody will be better, but no one will be the same." How long it will take for everyone in your school and community to get "better" will depend upon the severity of the crisis and how good the initial crisis response was. In every case of a severe school crisis, however, the crisis response team and school will have some work to do over the long term to continue to assist in the healing of the survivors. If your school crisis was severe, you can anticipate addressing its effects for many weeks, months, or even years to come.

"Suffering breaks our world, like a tree struck by lightning—splintered, shaken, denuded—our world is broken by suffering, and we will never be the same again. What will become of us is a mystery."

—Nathan Kollar ("What Is Grief?", 1998)

Mourning, in particular, may continue for years. If your school crisis involved the death of school community member(s), it is unrealistic to expect the grief to dissipate in a matter of weeks or months. As the mother of one child shot at an elementary school in Stockton, California, expressed, "There's some relief after nine years. But I still think about it" (Johnston, 1998, p. 31). Said the now retired superintendent of Westside School District, Grover Cooper, "I think it will be with me the rest of my life. That pretty much is how it will be with everyone out there [the day the shooting occurred at Westside Middle School near Jonesboro, Arkansas]" (Fugate, 1999, p. 2A).

"It's been nine years since our tragedy, and we still remember it with horror. But now we also see the good things that surround us every day of our lives. We hope that these feelings of comfort come to you soon."

—Text from a letter written to Westside Middle School near Jonesboro, Arkansas, by a high school class in Stockton, California, who lived through a school shooting as elementary students (Johnston, 1998, p. 28)

Emotional Effects on Survivors

As explained by the National Organization for Victim Assistance, "Not all victims/survivors [of a crisis] suffer from long-term stress reactions. But many victims may continue to reexperience crisis reactions over long periods of time," sometimes even years (NOVA, 1994a, 1994b). When long-term stress or crisis reactions occur, according to NOVA (1994a), they:

... [M]ay be made better or worse by the actions [or reactions] of others. When such reactions are sensed to be negative (whether or not they were intentional), [they] are called the "second assault" and the feelings are often described as a "second injury." Sources of the second assault may include:

- *The criminal justice system*
- *The media*
- *Family, friends, acquaintances*
- *Hospital and emergency room personnel*
- *Health and mental health professionals*

- *Social service workers*
- *Victim service workers*
- *Schools, teachers, educators*
- *Victim compensation system*
- *Clergy*

Obviously, you do not wish to cause a "second injury" to any member of your school community. Being aware of typical long-term crisis reactions will help you to behave in gentle and helpful ways toward crisis victims and survivors. The crisis effects that victims/survivors may experience in the long term include all those they felt immediately following the crisis (*see "Crisis Effects and Grief" in Chapter Seven for details*) as well as other new or intensified reactions.

Although the intensity of long-term stress reactions usually decreases over time (NOVA, 1994a), some stress reactions may either set in later or worsen as time goes by, if left untreated. These new or intensified reactions may include child abuse, spousal abuse, and/or substance abuse, behaviors that the American Red Cross has estimated increase 50-200% after a disaster or trauma. The effects of these behaviors will generally not improve unless help is received.

> "This spring, 54-year old Chun Keut died from complications related to heavy drinking his widow says began when their daughter Ram Chun, eight, was killed [in the 1989 school shooting in Stockton, California].... Friends say that he watched videotapes of his daughter's funeral for years. His wife says he began drinking after the shootings ...."
>
> (Johnston, 1998, p. 31)

Other severe reactions may involve post-traumatic stress disorder (PTSD). The following is a description of that disorder from the third edition of the American Psychiatric Association's *Diagnostic and Statistical Manual* (cited in NOVA, 1994b):

A. The individual has experienced an event that is outside the range of usual human experience and that would be markedly distressing to almost anyone, e.g., serious threat to one's life or physical integrity; serious threat or harm to one's children, spouse, or other close relatives and friends; sudden destruction of one's home or community; or seeing another person who is being (or has recently been) seriously injured or killed as a result of an accident or physical violence.

B. The distressing event is persistently reexperienced in at least one of the following ways:

(1) Recurrent and intrusive distressing recollections of the event (which may be associated with guilty thoughts about behavior before and during the event).

(2) Recurrent distressing dreams of the event.

(3) Sudden acting or feeling as if the event were recurring (includes a sense of reliving the experience, illusions, hallucinations, and

dissociative or flashback episodes, even those that occur upon awakening or when intoxicated) (in young children, repetitive play in which themes or aspects of the distressing event are expressed).

(4) Intense psychological distress at exposure to events that symbolize or resemble an aspect of the event, including anniversaries of the event.

C. Persistent avoidance of stimuli associated with the distressing event or numbing of general responsiveness (not present before the event), as indicated by at least three of the following:

(1) Deliberate efforts to avoid thoughts or feelings associated with the event.

(2) Deliberate efforts to avoid activities or situations that arouse recollections of the event.

(3) Inability to recall an important aspect of the event (psychogenic amnesia).

(4) Markedly diminished interest in significant activities (in young children, loss of recently acquired developmental skills such as toilet training or language skills).

(5) Feeling of detachment or estrangement from others.

(6) Restricted range of affect, e.g., unable to have loving feelings.

(7) Sense of foreshortened future, e.g., child does not expect to have a career, marriage, or children, or a long life.

D. Persistent symptoms of increased arousal (not present before the event) as indicated by at least two of the following:

(1) Difficulty falling or staying asleep.

(2) Irritability or outbursts of anger.

(3) Difficulty concentrating.

(4) Hypervigilence.

(5) Physiologic reactivity at exposure to events that symbolize or resemble an aspect of the event (e.g., a woman who was raped in an elevator breaks out in a sweat when entering any elevator).

E. Duration of disturbance of at least one month.

(1) Specify delayed onset if the onset of symptoms was at least six months after the distressing event.

It is natural for victims and survivors of a crisis to experience long-term stress reactions, and it is important to remember that "not all long-term stress reactions can be described as post-traumatic stress disorder" (NOVA, 1994b). PTSD requires treatment from a mental health professional (preferably one who specializes in trauma). It is recommended that such treatment be sought if symptoms persist for more than four weeks. It is optimal for all victims and survivors of a crisis to have received mental health assistance immediately following the crisis. If that was not possible, then those who have not previously sought treatment should do so whenever a severe crisis reaction continues in duration for a month. (The victims' advocate for your county would be an excellent referral source and would have information about low- or no-cost treatment.) Receiving needed mental health treatment will help survivors understand that it is not unusual to have long-term effects and to reexperience aspects of the trauma.

> "… Dr. Skaug [a Jonesboro, Arkansas, pediatrician who treated four of the injured survivors] predicted that many of the survivors would suffer from post-traumatic stress disorder and would require extensive counseling."
>
> (Associated Press, 1998, p. 29A)

Your school and community can do much to assist the majority of victims/survivors whose crisis reactions are less severe than PTSD. The California Association of School Psychologists (CASP, 1998a; Lieberman, 1998) has recommended that schools and communities provide the following types of support to victims/survivors of school crises (particularly following the departure of any outside crisis response team[s] that were assisting your school):

- Prepare staff to deal with their and their students' normal long-term reactions, such as the need to continue to discuss a shooting or other severe crisis incident.

  At the beginning of the school year following the shooting at Westside Middle School near Jonesboro, Arkansas, for example, Principal Karen Curtner said, "… [A] few [students] appear highly anxious with 'short fuses,' all seem to be more aware of their surroundings … hypervigilant … which has translated into an 'over reporting' of suspected behavior problems." As noted in Stockton (1998):

  > She further stated that this increase in reporting to teachers, administrators, and counselors probably goes along with an increase in telephone calls from parents expressing concerns about students' behaviors they have observed or heard discussed by their child. There is a uniformed "resource officer" permanently stationed on campus and it is not unusual for youngsters to ask a teacher his whereabouts if they missed seeing his presence. In addition, "the students seem to be more clingy with each other and move about in clusters as compared to last year," Mrs. Curtner said. One teacher also related that the faculty as a whole seems to be more open to physically touching the students "which seems to comfort [all] of us." Extra counseling support from the mental health community will continue throughout the year (p. 12).

- Continue to provide counseling support to school staff members.

One crisis interventionist (Kris Sieckert, personal communication, February 1999) noted that in Edinboro, Pennsylvania, many staff members have needed ongoing counseling support many months after a shooting death of their colleague.

- Let students know there will continue to be people who are willing to listen to them.

  Provide students with responsible, trained adult "listeners" and let students know that these people can provide long-term listening and counseling help. Tell them specifically who is available and when and where to find these people. Provide a list of local help resources (Zenere, 1998).

- Anticipate delayed effects and identify events or dates that might "trigger" those effects (see "Anniversaries and Significant Dates" later in this section for more information).

- Watch for pathological long-term stress reactions. Explained school psychologist Richard Lieberman (1998, p. 15), "Pathological long-term reactions are more severe than those experienced by most children." Pathological reactions to watch for include post-traumatic stress disorder symptomology, a drop in academic performance, truancy, drug use, and aggressive or suicidal behavior (Zenere, 1998).

Specifically, schools, parents, and communities should take the following steps to assist victims and survivors over the long term:

- Continue to provide counseling services to students for months and even years, depending on the severity of the crisis, the unique crisis history of the victims and survivors, and the students' personal connections with anyone who was killed in the crisis. Four months after the school shooting in West Paducah, Kentucky, for example, the students continued to attend weekly group counseling sessions with mental health professionals (Williams, 1998). After the 1998 shooting at Thurston High School in Springfield, Oregon, "the Thurston Assistance Center … was established to provide [long-term] counseling support and information to Springfield residents and families affected by the shooting" (Paine, 1998, p. 16).

A severe school crisis, particularly one that occurs in the spring, will likely necessitate that counseling services be provided over the summer, as was the case after the school shooting near Jonesboro, Arkansas. With any severe school crisis, it will also be necessary to provide services over extended school holidays (e.g., winter break). A Tennessee school counselor (Jane Williams, personal communication, December 1998) stressed how important it was for her school to make counseling available to school community members after a tragic car accident that occurred on the first day of the winter vacation.

See "Providing Counseling Services" in Chapter Seven for guidelines.

While it is crucial to continue to support victims/survivors emotionally, at some point you may want to deemphasize the location of the counseling services provided within your school building or relocate them. This deemphasis will help to refocus your school on education and will assist those who are not utilizing the long-term counseling services to put the crisis behind them and return to a state of normalcy at school. After the school shooting in Stockton, California, in 1989, "… a donated trailer was set up on campus to provide counseling services…. In some cases, services continued for several years" (Johnston, 1998, p. 30). Take your cue from the student body in timing this modification of services.

For the summer following the school year during which there was a shooting at Westside Middle School near Jonesboro, Arkansas, "specific counseling services were moved from the campus to lessen the association of grief and tragedy with the school building."

(Stockton, 1998, p. 12)

- Also support the students by communicating with their parents. The Parent/Family Liaison should send a letter home approximately one month after a severe crisis explaining long-term crisis effects to parents and providing guidelines for identifying pathological stress reactions. The Counseling Liaison should strive to identify students who are experiencing difficulties recovering over the long term and follow up with these students' parents, perhaps making a referral for private counseling.

Train school staff in post-trauma stress reactions so that they can better support the students. Your crisis response team, as well as the rest of your school's or district's mental health staff, can coordinate this staff inservice. You might also utilize the assistance of those specially trained in crisis response from outside your school or district (*see "Help to Request" in Chapter Four for suggestions*). (*NOTE*: If your school's crisis was catastrophic, this training in post-trauma stress reactions should take place on a district-wide or city-wide basis, as the long-term effects of the crisis will be far-reaching.)

After the May 1998 school shooting in Springfield, Oregon, for example, many from the school attended a symposium led by Dr. Robert Pynoos, the director of Trauma Psychiatry Services at UCLA. Trauma experts from UCLA came to Springfield to "… work with all district administrators and school board members" (Paine, 1998, p. 16), and trauma specialists from the Los Angeles Unified School District "… instructed [Springfield] teachers and school staff in post-trauma responses." Further, Dr. Marlene Young, executive director of the National Organization for Victim Assistance (NOVA) "… conducted a three-day crisis response workshop for 50 counselors, psychologists, and mental health workers" (Paine, 1998, p. 16).

- Provide ongoing opportunities for school staff to express their concerns and process their long-term reactions to the crisis. In West Paducah, Kentucky, Principal Bond held weekly faculty meetings for months after the school shooting at Heath High. These meetings were not mandatory, but Principal Bond felt these meetings were important enough to attend each one personally.

  If you do *not* make supporting the staff a priority, your school may lose some valuable educators. Teachers and administrators whose sense of security has been violated to a severe degree may lose their faith in education and change careers or take early retirement. However, with enough assistance they will begin to believe that they can overcome the effects of the trauma together. Nine years after the school shooting at Cleveland Elementary School in Stockton, California, for example, most of the teachers who were there at the time of the shooting are still there. Explained Principal Patricia Busher, "Everyone wanted to stay and heal together" (Johnston, 1998, p. 29).

- Continue to support the crisis response team members. School staff who assist with severe school crises need continued thanks and support from their administrators and school community three months, six months, even a year or more later. The superintendent or school board should write a complimentary letter to each member of the crisis team one to two weeks after the crisis. The superintendent should also visit the affected school every few months for a minimum of a year after a severe crisis. Particular attention should be paid to crisis response staff at the beginning of a new school year and on the anniversary of the crisis. (This support from the superintendent should be in addition to the ongoing support from the building principal.)

  Your crisis response team members (and other local caregivers who responded to the school's crisis) also must take good care of themselves (*see Chapter Ten, "Who Cares for the Caregiver?"*). Arrange for plenty of opportunities for your team to meet and process their long-term reactions to the crisis.

- Very young children who survive a crisis, or who have lost a loved one during a school crisis, will need ongoing assistance to understand what has happened. (*See "Crisis Effects and Grief" in Chapter Seven for details about children's developmental understanding of death*.) For example, the three-year old son of teacher Shannon Wright, killed in the school shooting near Jonesboro, Arkansas, will likely not fully understand the permanence of his mother's death for many years. When he does understand what happened to her, he may benefit from some form of counseling to address any feelings of anger, grief, or guilt. The long-term effects of a crisis may need to be dealt with throughout a young child's development.

Until young children *are* old enough to understand the finality of death, parents, other caregivers, and educators must be very careful about how they respond to the children's misperceptions. It is important to be honest and straightforward, even with young children. When confronted with a child's confused or "magical" thinking about a death (*see "Crisis Effects and Grief" in Chapter Seven*), adults can say, for example, "I know you believe that, but ...." If, instead, children are told something misleading, they might later remember what they were told and feel betrayed or angry.

- Create an appropriate remembrance of the victims of the crisis. These types of activities help to bring a sense of closure for survivors, and encourage healing.

See "Memorializing Victims" in Chapter Six and "Suicide Postvention" in Chapter Eleven for suggestions and cautions.

Anniversaries and Significant Dates

Some specific events or time frames—called "triggers"—remind victims/survivors of the trauma they've experienced. According to the National Organization for Victim Assistance (NOVA, 1994a), "triggering" events include:

- Sensing (i.e., seeing, hearing, smelling, tasting, touching) something similar to something the victim/survivor was aware of during the crisis.

  For example, the school shooting near Jonesboro, Arkansas, occurred after the perpetrators lured the students and staff onto the school grounds by pulling a fire alarm. The next time survivors of that tragedy (as well as people in other area schools and even some in schools across the country who had knowledge of this tragedy) heard a fire alarm, the experience was most likely traumatic for them.

- Hearing or seeing a news report about a similar event elsewhere.

- The proximity of significant family events, such as birthdays and holidays.

- Birthdays of the deceased.

- Involvement in the law enforcement process (e.g., identifying a suspected perpetrator in a police lineup).

- Involvement in the criminal justice system (e.g., providing testimony; news of a hearing, trial, sentencing, or appeal).

  When Principal Bond heard about the insanity defense being employed by the attorney of the student perpetrator of the school shooting in

"I walked outside the other day. It was really a nice day. The weather was warm, the wind was blowing a little, and I heard a bird, and suddenly, I began to tremble. It was like a panic attack. And I thought, 'Oh, my God, this is just like it was that day [of the killings a year ago] when I was walking across the schoolyard.' There was a wind, and there was a bird singing then."

—Pam Herring, mother of Paige Ann Herring, who was killed at Westside Middle School (Ashcraft, 1999, p. 14A)

West Paducah, Kentucky, for example, he worried about the effects on his school and community. He thought his community might need the assistance of a NOVA team (*see "National Crisis Response Teams/Organizations" in Chapter Four*) at the time of the trial and confided to a NOVA team member his concern that the effects on survivors would be significant if the perpetrator was not found guilty and sentenced appropriately.

The trial and appeals process can also result in ongoing stress reactions for victims/survivors, as the lengthy legal process can delay the sense of closure necessary after a crisis for many months and possibly years. After the sentencing of Michael Carneal (the shooter in West Paducah, Kentucky), which came more than a year after the tragedy, the father of one of the murdered girls said "... [my] family will attend the hearing when Carneal comes up for parole in 2023" (Oliver, 1998, p. 3A).

Survivors may need support throughout the legal process. After the school shooting in Springfield, Oregon, for example, plans were made in the Springfield School District "... to assist students and staff during the suspect's trial and the anniversary date of the shooting" (Paine, 1998, p. 16).

- Anniversaries of the event.

  First-, second-, and third-month anniversaries of the crisis remind many people of their losses and the trauma they experienced. The crisis reaction may continue on the crisis date each month thereafter and be particularly strong on the year anniversary of the event.

  While "triggers" vary by person, no matter what they are, they can "... bring back the intense emotion that occurred with the original trauma" (NOVA, 1994a). Further, "... [although] the intensity of the long-term reactions usually decreases over time, as does the frequency of the reexperienced crisis ... the effects of the trauma cannot be '*cured*' .... Even survivors of trauma who reconstruct new lives and who have achieved a degree of normality and happiness in their lives ... will find that *new life events* will trigger the memories and reactions to the trauma in the future" (NOVA, 1994a).

The following are actions you can take to assist your school and community in coping with significant dates and "triggering" events over the long term:

- Prepare your school community in advance for any known triggers.

In the case of the Jonesboro, Arkansas, shooting, for example, "Specific care was given to the planning of the first fire drill with teachers talking to the students within each classroom, a rehearsal of the change in routing, and the explanation of a 'no-bell' notification" (Stockton, 1998, p. 12). Schools have no choice but to perform mandated fire drills—a very important safety procedure—but in Jonesboro, following the shooting, this sensitive drill was not made a surprise. The school community was assured that this was a planned fire drill and that it was safe for everyone to go outside before the drill was performed.

- If news of a similar crisis elsewhere is publicized, address the effects this news may have on your school community.

Explained William Dodson, Pearl, Mississippi school superintendent, "Because we were [one of] the first [in a string of school shootings during the 1997-98 school year], we have been in a sense suffering longer. Each shooting brings it back up again" (Morello, 1998, p. 4A). Echoed a student from Bethel, Alaska, where a school shooting occurred in February 1997, "It was like this nightmare going on and on" (Fainaru, 1998b, p. A21). Even after several years, this effect may not have diminished. As noted in Pressley (1997), "Whenever something tragic happens in a classroom—or with children anywhere, the hurt comes back: 'When those kinds of things happen, it sort of reopens the wound,'" said Randall Cooper, former principal of a Kentucky high school in which a classroom was held at gunpoint by a student three and a half years prior.

Expect the stress reactions of your school community members to resurface or intensify when similar crises happen elsewhere, and temporarily reinstate or increase your offering of counseling services to help everyone cope.

> "I did have trouble sleeping last May, the night after I heard about those kids getting shot at their school in Oregon. I remember thinking it was too familiar."
>
> —Crystal Amanda Barnes, 13, school shooting victim from Jonesboro, Arkansas (Barnes & Martin-Morris, 1998)

You might also help your students feel better by encouraging them to take some sort of positive action after hearing about a similar crisis elsewhere. For example, the students at Pearl High School (in Pearl, Mississippi) created a posterboard of sympathy notes and cards for the students at Heath High (in West Paducah, Kentucky) after their school shooting. Heath High School students wrote "messages of hope on oversized cards" and mailed them to students at Westside Middle School (near Jonesboro, Arkansas) after the shooting there (Williams, 1998). Although these acts may sound like a macabre form of penpals, they are actually touching acts of sympathy "from one survivor to another" that help the survivors of crises feel less victimized by media accounts of other crises elsewhere.

- Be aware that *any type of tragedy* that occurs in your school or community soon after a crisis will exacerbate the effects of that crisis for victims/survivors.

Almost four months after the school shooting in West Paducah, Kentucky, two more traumatic incidents occurred in a single week. During that week an 11-year old elementary school student on the Heath campus was suspended for a "copycat" crime: "... threatening to bring a gun to school and 'shoot a bunch of people.' ... Word of the threat spread among students and teachers [and] 30 to 50 parents called the sheriff's department" (Williams, 1998, p. 22). (*See "'Copycat' Incidents" previously in this chapter for more information about this phenomenon.*) The next day, students at Heath High School learned that their homecoming king from the previous year, a 1997 graduate still popular at the school, had fatally shot himself (Williams, 1998). Principal Bond said that day "... turned into a horrible, horrible day....

"They're eventually going to be okay, as we're eventually going to be okay, but it will take time.... You've got to help them understand they're going to have some really bad days."

—Principal Bill Bond, Heath High School (West Paducah, Kentucky), when asked for advice for the survivors of the Jonesboro, Arkansas, school shooting (Williams, 1998)

It was more than the school could take.... [The students] had been getting by, but a lot of them just broke down." He said, "It set us back a lot." In response, Heath High School provided about six hours of counseling for students that day (Williams, 1998, p. 22).

- Note birthdays of the deceased and allow members of your school community to commemorate them if they wish to do so.

During the school year following the school shooting near Jonesboro, Arkansas, for example, several students of killed teacher Shannon Wright "... remembered her fall birthday by bringing individually vased flowers to place in her room. To accommodate this processing, the classes in that room were moved to another location allowing the students freedom to come and go in that room" (Stockton, 1998, p. 12). (*See "Modifying the Curriculum" and "Memorializing Victims" in Chapter Six for suggestions on other appropriate ways to remember victims of crises.*)

- Communicate with parents about the "anniversary effect."

Before significant anniversary dates, the Parent/Family Liaison should send a note home reminding families of the significance of the date and explaining its possible "triggering" effects. This letter should detail the stress reactions some parents might see in their children (or themselves or other family members) and encourage them to contact the school's counselor or psychologist for assistance if they become concerned about their children's stress reactions.

- Mark the year anniversary of the event appropriately.

Some school administrators might prefer to let the anniversary of a severe crisis pass unrecognized, believing that their school community will better cope if the event is not discussed. However, the long-term crisis reactions of the school community (and of the surrounding community as a whole) will be more severe if the date is ignored. If your school crisis was severe, few will forget the date, and the year anniversary of the trauma will be a difficult time for many.

There are as many ways to recognize the year anniversary of severe crises as there are schools that experience them. The key is to make sure that any activities that are planned will be meaningful for those who were affected by the crisis. To do so, you must involve those individuals in the planning process. The best course of action is to take your cue from your students and staff members, as well as their families. Allow them to lead the planning process and implement as much or as few remembrances as they feel they need. For the year anniversary of the school shooting in West Paducah, Kentucky, the students planned a choir performance. On the day itself, they extended their informal morning prayer group, and the school observed a spontaneous moment of silence at the time of the attack the year before.

The one-year anniversary of a crisis also is a meaningful time to unveil or dedicate any permanent memorial to its victims, whether it is a plaque, a flower garden, a ball field, or something else. (*See "Memorializing Victims" in Chapter Six for guidelines on appropriate remembrances.*)

In addition to marking the year anniversary within your school, it is important to not overlook the anniversary effects of a severe school crisis on your surrounding community. When a severe crisis occurs in your school, many in your community will be strongly affected and will benefit from participating with you in a commemoration of the anniversary date. On the year anniversary of the 1997 school shooting in Bethel, Alaska, for example, the high school sponsored a number of activities for the school and community, including a candlelight vigil, a formal memorial service, and a community dinner ("Conviction in Alaska," 1998). The school also held a "Celebration of Life" in the gymnasium on the anniversary day. A close friend of the slain student sang a tribute to the boy entitled "I'll Be Missing You" (Fainaru, 1998b).

In Jonesboro, Arkansas, both a private and a public memorial were held to mark the year anniversary of the shooting at Westside Middle School. By a proclamation made by Governor Mike Huckabee, all state flags were flown at half-mast on the anniversary day ("All State," 1999), and local government officials proclaimed March 24 a "Day of Prayer and Remembrance" (Hinkle, 1999, p. 1A). The brief private memorial, planned by Westside school administrators and held at the middle school on the anniversary of the shooting, was closed to all media

> "I am ready to get through it. I am looking at [the year anniversary day] as any other day, except that we will honor the memories of those lost and recognize those left behind. After the day has passed, we will continue to focus on the students, teachers, staff, and the whole Westside family. The focus has to remain there."
>
> —Westside Middle School principal Karen Curtner (Childress, 1999, p. 2A)

> "If people want to mark [the anniversary of the Westside Middle School shooting] they can have a prayer and create an awareness throughout the year that it can happen, and will continue to happen, until people say, 'We are tired of it. We are tired of burying our kids.' You can have all the little memorial services you want to, but until you do something positive, it won't mean a thing."
>
> —Pam Herring, mother of slain student Paige Ann Herring (Ashcraft, 1999, p. 14A)

except a small number of the local media. During the planning, Westside superintendent Dick Young said, "This will be a private moment for those who were personally touched and affected by this tragedy." He added that the service would not be a "spectacle or media event" (Hinkle, 1999, p. 15A). Classes were dismissed that day as a "flex day," or teacher planning day.

The public remembrance, sponsored by People Against Violence Everywhere (PAVE) and the Jonesboro Ministerial Fellowship, was held at the Craighead County Courthouse. The families of all five victims attended this service. A moment of silence was observed, and the victims were eulogized through songs and personal tributes. Additionally, a wreath for each slain victim was presented. The wreath for Shannon Wright was decorated with apples (because she had been a teacher); that for Paige Ann Herring, with butterflies and basketballs; the wreath for Britthney Varner, with daffodils; for Stephanie Johnson, ladybugs; and the wreath for Natalie Brooks, frogs—personal symbols representing some of the victims' favorite things (Hinkle, 1999, p. 15A). Approximately half of the audience members at this "well-done" community ceremony were media representatives, estimated school psychologist Betty Stockton (personal communication, April 1999).

You might also choose to mark the anniversary of a school crisis by focusing some energy on relevant prevention efforts. On the year anniversary of the shooting at Cleveland Elementary School in Stockton, California, for example, a teacher who survived the attack went to Washington, D.C., to testify before the U.S. Senate on gun control (Johnston, 1998, p. 29).

- If your school crisis was severe, plan the beginning of the following school year with care.

After the 1998 school shooting in Springfield, Oregon, a crisis responder summed up the long-term response in that community:

> *Long-term follow-up has required time, staff, and additional resources. The event was not over on May 22nd, the day after the shooting, or on June 12, the last day of school. Summer was filled with grant writing, summer activities at Thurston High, planning for ... the first days of school .....*
>
> *[The] Springfield School District ... made a commitment to enter this school year with thoughtfulness, planning, and training in*

response to this tragedy.... Our approach this year is two-fold: we will strive to recapture the school's normal activities, and at the same time, we want 100% of the students and staff to achieve a healthy recovery. Their reentry to Thurston High has been carefully planned and supported, beginning with [a] Memorial Day open house. The cafeteria has been painted and brightened in order to minimize the traumatic reminders....

Teachers asked students to be tolerant and patient with one another as they work through a broad range of reactions and reminded them that, while many students are ready to move on, some are not.

In her keynote address to [more than] 500 teachers as they returned to school this fall, Marleen Wong, head of District Crisis Teams for the Los Angeles Unified School District, noted, "Springfield will never be just any school district. It will be recognized and acknowledged, questioned and criticized, studied and consulted." She challenged us to "work hard to find that balance between mourning the past, treasuring the present, and keeping hope for the future." That has become our mission (Paine, 1998, pp. 16-17).

That eloquently stated mission is one your school would be wise to adopt after a severe crisis. In addition, continue to provide counseling services for at least six months, depending on the severity of the crisis (*see "Providing Counseling Services" in Chapter Seven for suggestions*). Utilize your building's mental health staff, the crisis response team, and other professionals both from within and outside your district and community (*see "Help to Request" in Chapter Four for more information*) to smooth the reentry into your school at the beginning of the new school year.

> "Though we were inevitably affected by tragedy, we are looking forward to what life has to offer us next. We have learned how very precious, yet circumstantial, life is. Now, more than ever, our eyes are open wide, our ambitions are high, and we are ready to live."
>
> —Senior at Thurston High School (Springfield, Oregon) on the first day of the new school year following their school shooting (Paine, 1998, p. 17)

When Victims or Perpetrators Return to School

Welcoming the student and/or staff victims of a school crisis—particularly a violent one—back into the school community must be handled with sensitivity. Your crisis response team should meet prior to the beginning of school (or prior to the anticipated return of injured victims) to make plans to assist them. Special attention should be placed on preparing their teachers. The Crisis Coordinator and Counseling Liaison should talk with the victims and their families before the victims return to school to assess their

> "Twenty of the injured students returned [on the first day of the new school year following the shooting] to Thurston High [in Springfield, Oregon]. Some still carry the physical evidence of scars and bullets within them and face lengthy rehabilitation. Some cannot yet return to the cafeteria and fear recurring violence."
>
> (Paine, 1998, p. 17)

emotional state and to alleviate as much anxiety associated with their return as possible. Their wishes should be accommodated whenever feasible.

The parents of student victims should be encouraged to accompany their children to school on their first day back and to stay as long as they wish. Your school staff should warmly welcome the victims when they arrive at school. There are no magic words for the staff to say to make the transition back to school much easier for victims. Simply communicate caring and concern and a hope that together you can move forward to begin a brighter chapter in their school experience.

Prior to the victims' return, your teachers should also "explain how students should treat [an injured, traumatized, and/or bereaved] student who is returning to school. Emphasize that trying to avoid or being overly solici-tous to the student will not help. Point out the need to return to normal relationships" ("Handling a Class," 1994). Advised Dr. Alan Wolfelt ("Helping Others," 1998), "How can you help? To begin with, be an active listener. Your physical presence and desire to listen without judging are your critical helping tools. Don't worry so much about what you will say. Just concentrate on listening to the words being shared with you. You should also strive to be compassionate. Give your friend permission to express his or her feelings without fear of criticism. Allow him or her to experience all the hurt, sorrow, and pain that he or she is feeling at the time."

> "When school starts this fall, I won't be the new girl anymore. Everybody knows who I am. I'll walk back in, without crutches, like everybody else."
>
> —Crystal Amanda Barnes, 13, school shooting victim from Jonesboro, Arkansas (Barnes & Martin-Morris, 1998, p. 110)

In a severe crisis in which a felony was committed, con-victed student perpetrator(s) will probably not return to your school, as they will likely be serving prison sen-tences. But following a less severe crisis, you may need to coordinate the reentry of a student returning from an alternative school, a juvenile detention facility, or a men-tal health facility. Many issues concerning the return to the school community of a previously removed student will need to be addressed, and your school should coordinate with the staff of the facility the student is returning from to make the transition as uneventful as possible (Dwyer, Osher, & Warger, 1998).

Within the school community, there is often much trepidation about a convicted student perpetrator returning to school. A Houston school super-intendent (Thornton, personal communication, March 1988), for example, stated that if a student who had shot an assistant principal there tried to reenroll, the school district would take every legal step possible to prevent his return. Likewise, parents and students in Jonesboro, Arkansas, have voiced fears about the two student perpetrators being released from jail and wanting to rejoin their classmates prior to graduation.

Often, rumors spread within a community that a suspected student perpetrator is going to make bail and be back in the community awaiting trial, causing community members much anxiety. If the rumors are true, your crisis response team must take steps to increase security and attempt to reduce the fear felt by staff and students. The Crisis Coordinator must give everyone the facts and stay in close contact with the prosecutor to ensure that accurate information about the status of the perpetrator is provided to school community members. Recent legislation has made such record sharing between the judicial system and schools easier (Poland, 1994).

When a student perpetrator is allowed to return to school, the most common strategy of schools is to transfer the student to another campus. This strategy may alleviate fears in an urban school system, but it does not work in a small community. It can also be difficult to transfer a student to another district. One school principal (Robert Williams, personal communication, November 1998) commented that when a neighboring county's superintendent asked him if he would allow a convicted student perpetrator to attend his school, he declined.

Often a student perpetrator will move to another location or attend a private school, but the problems don't necessarily end there. Former school principal Kate Stetzner (personal communication, November 1998) noted that when the boy who had murdered another student in her Butte, Montana, school when he was ten was released from custody a few years later and resurfaced in Missoula, Montana, community members there were outraged.

Our country is unfortunately now struggling with such complex issues as: How long do you lock up a ten-year old murderer, and where? Once those questions are resolved, we must figure out where children who commit violent crimes can go when they are released. Noted Gretchen Woodard, the mother of one of the convicted student perpetrators in the shooting at Westside Middle School near Jonesboro, "People have asked me if I think [my son] will come here" upon his release from Arkansas Division of Youth Services custody. "I say 'I don't think so.' Where in the world is he ever going to go where he's not known?" (Holmes, 1999, p. 9A).

Liability and Litigation

Ours is a litigious society. It seems that when people are injured in any way these days, even by spilling a hot cup of take-out coffee in their own lap, a lawsuit is filed. Certainly after a severe school crisis the possibility of litigation exists, and schools should prepare themselves for this possibility. As noted in Greenbaum, Gonzalez, and Ackley (1993, p. 35), "Lawsuits against schools are becoming increasingly common as individuals vent their frustration and demand significant financial damages for unsafe conditions on campus." Particularly if a school was grossly negligent in failing to prevent a crisis incident, or in its handling of the crisis event, a lawsuit may be filed by affected parties. For example, in an Oakland, California, case a school system was sued because an administrator had knowledge that a student was threatening to "beat up" another, but failed to take any preventative action. The parents of the beaten boy filed a lawsuit after the aggressor made good on his threats (Poland, 1994).

School officials have also found themselves in legal difficulty for failing to call children's protective services when they should have. The best advice we can offer is that if you have a question about whether there is a need to report suspected or confirmed physical or sexual abuse, then you should call the appropriate agency and ask. Not only have schools "... been found liable in lawsuits involving sexual misconduct by school employees, [and] personal injury or property damage to students and employees ..." (Greenbaum et al., 1993, p. 36), but schools have also been sued by the parents of students with Individualized Education Plans (IEPs) for disciplining the students inappropriately (e.g., changing their placement for longer than ten days without an IEP meeting). Schools have been sued, as well, for failing to warn parents about the suicidal intentions of their children (see "Liability Issues Pertaining to Suicide" in Chapter Eleven for details). Further, it is clear that schools have a responsibility to call for medical assistance when necessary and to notify police when a serious crime occurs at school. These are all commonsense issues that schools can be expected to address.

The issue of school safety and liability of educators, according to James (1994), will track closely with the model of "reasonableness." After reviewing the legal questions and suits filed against schools, James commented that the courts have supported the good faith efforts of schools to provide a safe and effective learning environment. Those school systems or administrators who were held liable after a school crisis had been extremely negligent and had failed to make any good faith effort to try to assist a troubled student or intervene in any preventative manner.

Sometimes a lawsuit is filed against a school months or even years after a crisis incident. Victims and/or their families generally file such suits to collect damages after suffering hardship associated with the crisis (e.g., medical bills, loss of income, etc.). Sometimes it seems that the families of victims decide to file a civil suit because they are dissatisfied with the outcome of the criminal trial. Even if the perpetrator(s) are found guilty and imprisoned, the grieving survivors still may be tortured by the

"... [D]oes the fact that Andrew [Golden] and Mitchell [Johnson] could be freed so quickly mean a person's worth is gauged by the age of the person who murders her? That's not right."

—Mitchell Wright, husband of teacher Shannon Wright, who was killed in the school shooting near Jonesboro, Arkansas (Casey, 1999, p. 12)

question of why the tragedy happened and believe that someone could have, or should have, done something more to prevent it. In such cases, they may feel that someone should "pay."

One year after the school shooting in West Paducah, Kentucky, the families of the three deceased victims filed a lawsuit seeking unspecified damages from 45 defendants. Those parties included the convicted student perpetrator and the parents of the shooter, as well as students, teachers, and administrators at Heath High School ("Prayer Deaths," 1998). The suit alleges that "... some people had noticed Carneal acting strangely before the attack but did nothing" and accuses school officials of "... having inadequate security measures" in place ("Prayer Deaths," 1998, p. 3A). After the December 1998 sentencing of Carneal, the mother of one of the victims noted, "The sentence does not give us any sense of revenge. We have never wanted revenge." What the families want, she explained, "... is an answer—one that perhaps would have come from a criminal trial." She said that the families intend to find out why the shootings happened (Oliver, 1998, p. A3).

While the magnitude of the grieving families' pain is immense, it is difficult to pinpoint what either the Carneal family or the school representatives could have done to prevent the tragedy from occurring. Everyone involved is very sorry about what happened, but are they liable? This lawsuit raises many questions that only the courts can answer. However, at first glance there does not seem to be a strong case against the administrators and staff at Heath High School. As James (1994) stressed, the courts will follow a doctrine of reasonableness in deciding whether schools are liable. School officials must act quickly in the aftermath of a crisis and must take preventative actions when they have strong firsthand knowledge of a potential crime, but they cannot be expected to read the mind of a troubled student.

School personnel often blame themselves unfairly, especially after lawsuits are filed, thinking, for example, "If only we had done something differently in third grade, just maybe the perpetrator wouldn't have murdered someone years later." The extra stress unreasonable lawsuits place on school staff after a trauma is unfortunate.

Nevertheless, you cannot prevent someone from filing a suit either against your school and/or individual members of your school community; there are always going to be lawsuits against the schools. Schools protect themselves by developing comprehensive crisis plans and by sharing information with other professionals, agencies, and especially parents. School administrators are encouraged to document their activities in writing, seek guidance from their supervisors, and call parents whenever there is a "duty to warn" issue. After a severe school crisis, it is also prudent to have your school system attorney present at all media interviews ("Control the

Media," 1998) as well as when any other attorneys interview teachers or other school staff ("School Officials," 1997). Your school system's attorney may also wish to depose all school community members who were involved in the crisis and the school's response to it shortly after the crisis event while the details are still fresh in their minds. If so, be sure your school community members have been given the opportunity to process their crisis reactions before they are deposed so they do not make emotional statements such as "I feel so guilty about ...."

References

All state flags to be at half-staff. (1999, March 23). *Jonesboro Sun*, p. 1A.

Ashcraft, H. (1999, March 21). Pam Herring's world fell apart in March of '98. *Jonesboro Sun*, pp. 1A, 14A-15A.

Associated Press. (1998, April 5). Doctor recounts treating Jonesboro victims: He says many of the injured will need counseling. *Dallas Morning News*, p. 29A.

Associated Press. (1999, May 14). Bomb threats shorten school year: Suburban Dallas school district closes two weeks early. *MSNBC*. Available online: http://www.msnbc.com/news/269740.asp

At least 13 killed in past months: Violence in U.S. schools. (1998, May 21). *ABCNEWS.com*. Available online: http://www.abcnews.com/sections/us/DailyNews/shooting

Barnes, C. A., & Martin-Morris, D. (1998, September). I was shot at school. *Teen*, pp. 108-110.

California Association of School Psychologists (CASP). (1998a, October). Schoolyard tragedies: Coping with the aftermath. *Resource Paper, 2*(4), 1-8.

California Association of School Psychologists (CASP). (1998b, November). Teen suicides: Life, after death. *NASP Communiqué, 27*(3), 14-15.

Cannon, A. (1998, May 22). Shootings at schools part of new trend that raises many questions. *Houston Chronicle*, p. 10A.

Casey, K. (1999, March). When the shooting stopped. *Ladies' Home Journal*, pp. 10-13.

Childress, A. (1999, March 23). "Terrible Tuesday" reminders, images are part of reality. *Jonesboro Sun*, pp. 1A-2A.

Control the media but provide information. (1998, November). *Practical Strategies for Maintaining Safe Schools: School Violence Alert, 4*(11), 1, 4-5.

Conviction in Alaska slaying. (1998, February 25). *Education Week, 17*(24), 4.

District School Board of Pasco County. (1994). Handling a class after a student dies [Handout]. Land O'Lakes, FL: Author.

Dotson, B. (1999, April 30). Alarming rash of school threats. *MSNBC*. Available online: http://www.msnbc.com/news/264186.asp

Drummond, T. (1999, May 10). Battling the Columbine copycats. *TIME*, p. 29.

Dwyer, K., Osher, D., & Warger, C. (1998). *Early warning, timely response: A guide to safe schools*. Washington, DC: U.S. Department of Education.

Fainaru, S. (1998a, October 19). Killing in the classroom: A tragedy was preceded by many overlooked signals. *Boston Globe*, pp. A1, A10-11.

Fainaru, S. (1998b, October 20). Killing in the classroom: Many struggle to put their world together. *Boston Globe*, pp. A1, A20-21.

Fugate, L. (1999, March 23). "Kind of like having a nightmare." *Jonesboro Sun*, pp. 1A-2A.

Gegax, T. T., Adler, J., & Pedersen, D. (1998, April 6). The boys behind the ambush. *Newsweek*, pp. 21-26.

Greenbaum, S., Gonzalez, B., & Ackley, N. (1993). *Educated public relations: School safety 101*. Malibu, CA: Pepperdine University, National School Safety Center.

Hinkle, B. (1999, March 21). Memorial services are scheduled Wednesday. *Jonesboro Sun*, pp. 1A, 15A.

Holliman, J. (1997, December 3). Kentucky County's schools increase security. *CNNinteractive*. Available online: http://www.cnn.com/US/9712/03/school.shooting.folo/

Holmes, P. (1999, March 22). "Craziness" returns for mother of Johnson. *Jonesboro Sun*, pp. 1A, 9A.

James, B. (1994). School violence and the law. *School Psychology Review, 23*(2), 190-203.

Johnston, R. C. (1998, May 27). Hope in the mourning. *Education Week, 17*(37), 26-31.

Labi, N. (1998, April 6). The hunter and the choirboy. *TIME*, pp. 28-39.

Lacayo, R. (1998, April 6). Toward the roots of evil. *TIME*, pp. 38-39.

Lieberman, R. (1998, Fall). Schoolyard tragedies: Coping with the aftermath. *School Safety*, pp. 14-16.

Michigan student shoots self. (1998, March 11). *Education Week, 18*(26), 4.

Morello, C. (1998, June 8). Pearl, Miss., sees chance for closure: Teen's trial begins Tuesday. *USA Today*, p. 4A.

Munz, M. (1998, June 12). School violence forum hears of local officials' success. *St. Louis Post-Dispatch*, p. 1.

National Organization for Victim Assistance (NOVA). (1994a). *Long-term crisis reactions* [Handout]. Washington, DC: Author.

National Organization for Victim Assistance (NOVA). (1994b). *Long-term traumatic stress reaction* [Handout]. Washington, DC: Author.

Oliver, J. (1998, December 17). Families comment after Carneal sentencing. *Paducah Sun*, p. 3A.

Paine, C. (1998, November). Tragedy response and healing: Springfield unites. *NASP Communiqué, 27*(3), 16-17.

Pitcher, G. D., & Poland, S. (1992). *Crisis intervention in the schools*. New York: Guilford.

Poland, S. (1994). The role of school crisis intervention teams to prevent and reduce school violence and trauma. *School Psychology Review, 23*(2), 175-189.

Prayer deaths. (1998, December 3). *USA Today*, p. 3A.

Pressley, D. S. (1997, December 2). Ryle principal feels the hurt: Memories of Shrout killings revived. *Cincinnati Enquirer.* Available online: http://enquirer.com/editions/1997/12/02/loc_kyshootryle.html

School officials in Pearl, Miss., help community cope with tragedy. (1997, November 11). *School Board News, 17*(21), 4.

Stockton, B. (1998, November). Back to school in Jonesboro. *NASP Communiqué, 27*(3), 12.

What is grief? (1998, January 12). *Journey of Hearts: A Healing Place in CyberSpace.* Available online: http://www.kirstimd.com/grief1.htm

Williams, L. (1998, March 28). West Paducah relives horror of high school shootings: Jonesboro killings upset fragile healing. *St. Louis Post-Dispatch*, p. 22.

Wolfelt, A. (1998). *Helping others with grief.* Available online: http://www.batesville.com/html/body_5c.htm

Zenere, F. (1998, November). NASP/NEAT community crisis response. *NASP Communiqué, 27*(3), 38-39.

conclusion

What Have We Learned?

A Message From Dr. Scott Poland

I have had the chance to talk with thousands of school personnel around the country about school crisis. Everywhere there are what I call "skeletons in the closet"—that is, all schools and communities have had crises and tragedies involving students and staff. My question is always: "What worked and went well, and what was problematic?" I never intend to make anyone feel badly, but I believe that we must learn from each tragic event so that we will be better prepared for the future. As the philosopher Dac once said, "the future is the past in preparation."

The tragic school shootings of the past year and a half, and my having personally gone to West Paducah, Kentucky, Jonesboro, Arkansas, and Littleton, Colorado, have changed me in some ways. I am absolutely committed to prevention. I have seen the pain of those communities. I have seen community members torture themselves with questions about how they failed to prevent the tragedy, and I've watched those on the scene second-guess themselves about whether or not their immediate response to the crisis was the best possible. This book was written so that others may learn from the experiences of those who have been through school crises. Specific chapters will assist schools and communities through every aspect of a school crisis and the upheaval in the community that accompanies one.

The most common reaction that schools have to a crisis is to ignore it, yet crisis theory and research indicate that it is essential to provide intervention as quickly as possible to all concerned after a crisis (Pitcher & Poland, 1992). The NOVA model outlined in this book provides a major part of that assistance. Specifically, it provides the opportunity for everyone who wants to do so to tell his or her story. Others listen to those crisis stories, and suddenly the school and community come together in their shock and grief. They then identify the many stumbling blocks ahead, and together they find the hope and resiliency to work through them.

After the school shooting near Jonesboro, Arkansas, Westside Middle School seemed like the epicenter of an earthquake. I faced hundreds of media personnel from around the world as the leader of the NOVA teams in both Jonesboro and West Paducah, Kentucky. Media representatives from other countries cannot believe what is happening in America. Citizens of the United States believe that we live in the best country in the world. I am not so sure—we live in the only country in the world where students bring guns to school and shoot their classmates and teachers. Timpane commented, "It's my suspicion that we are just at the beginning of a long road that will lead to safer schools" (cited in Jennings, 1989, p. 27). It is obvious that we have not traveled very far down that road.

Lieberman (1999) pointed out that when a crisis occurs you need to know "Who's on blood and who's on tears." Yet in the midst of a crisis, it is very difficult to know what to do without prior planning and guidance derived from the experience of others who have been through a severe crisis. A Bible passage illustrates this darkness and uncertainty: "I must work the works of Him that sent me, while it is day: the night cometh when no man can work" (Gospel of St. John, Chapter 9, Verse 4). There must be preparation and planning in place if you are to adequately fill the necessary roles, and practical ideas are provided for the development of an effective crisis response plan.

In this country, we have not put children first. Programs must be created to help troubled children and their families. In my state, Texas, when the prison expansion that is currently under way is completed in the near future, we will have more prison beds than any other *country* in the world. Where are the programs in Texas and other states to prevent a child from growing up to be a criminal? Prevention programs are much more cost effective than incarceration.

Many experts believe that the single greatest strategy to reduce violent deaths for children is as simple (and yet so complex) as keeping guns out of children's hands. Yet our society glamorizes violence and the perpetrators of violence. Pictures of Mitchell Johnson and Andrew Golden appeared on the cover of almost every magazine and newspaper after these boys gunned down four students and a teacher near Jonesboro, Arkansas. Millions of dollars were spent by the media to cover the tragic shooting. Yet how much is being spent on the prevention of the next school shooting? How much emphasis is there on helping the victims of such violence? A Houston television newsman commented to me that he was flown to Jonesboro by private jet on the same day as the Westside Middle School shooting. I and the other members of the NOVA crisis response team had to wait until the next day to travel there, flying coach.

What can be done to work on violence prevention in the schools? A national "accountability" movement has informed our nation's schools that all that matters are reading, writing, and arithmetic scores. Many educators would like to work on other essential skills for students, such as problem solving, anger management, violence prevention, the acceptance of diversity, and an appreciation of everyone regardless of race or ethnicity. But many schools do not have the time, resources, or mandate on these issues. We wonder if the schools and communities that have been affected by shootings by their own students would agree that the only job of schools is to teach the "three R's."

The events of the last two school years have made us absolutely committed to prevention and the examination of the societal factors that contribute to youth violence. There are many issues that our society must urgently address.

References

Jennings, L. (1989, October 4). "Crisis consultants" share lessons they learned from school violence. *Education Week, 9*(5), 1, 27.

Lieberman, R. (1999, January 22-23). *Crisis Intervention Workshop*, Walnut Creek, California.

Pitcher, G. D., & Poland, S. (1992). *Crisis intervention in the schools*. New York: Guilford.

appendix

Additional Resources

The following are brief lists of private organizations, government agencies, books, tapes, Web sites, and brochures that may be of assistance to schools, parents, and community caregivers after a school crisis. The resources listed focus on secondary intervention, although many will be useful for crisis planning and prevention as well. These lists are a good starting point for concerned schools and individuals but are by no means comprehensive. You are encouraged to explore the Internet; your school, local, and university libraries; independent and online booksellers; professional journals/memberships; and other sources of information when seeking additional assistance with and knowledge about school crises.

Organizations/Agencies

Administration for Children, Youth and Families
U.S. Department of Health and Human Services
330 C Street, SW
Washington, D.C. 20447
(202) 205-8051

- Provides an extensive grants program supporting gang prevention/intervention.

American Academy of Bereavement
2090 North Kolb, Suite 100
Tucson, Arizona 85715
(520) 721-3838

**American Academy of Child
& Adolescent Psychiatry (AACAP)**
3615 Wisconsin Avenue, NW
Washington, D.C. 20016-3007
(202) 966-7300
(202) 966-2891 FAX
www.aacap.org

- Makes available more than 60 fact sheets on youth issues such as children and firearms.

**American Association of School
Administrators (AASA)**
1801 North Moore Street
Arlington, Virginia 22209-1813
(703) 528-0700
(703) 841-1543 FAX
www.aasa.org

American Association of Suicidology (AAS)
4201 Connecticut Avenue, NW, Suite 310
Washington, D.C. 20008
(202) 237-2280
www.suicidology.org

American Red Cross
www.redcross.org

- Look in the business white pages of your telephone book for contact information for your local Red Cross chapter.

**Association for Death Education
and Counseling**
638 Prospect Avenue
Hartford, Connecticut 06105-4250
(860) 586-7503
info@adec.org (e-mail)
www.adec.org

Bureau for At-Risk Youth
645 New York Avenue
Rockville, Maryland 20850
(800) 99-YOUTH

- Staffed nationwide toll-free number for information and materials on drugs and violence.

**Bureau of Alcohol, Tobacco
and Firearms (ATF)**
U.S. Department of the Treasury
(800) ATF-GUNS

- Nationwide toll-free number for citizens to report illegal activity involving guns.

**Bureau of Justice Assistance (BJA)
Clearinghouse**
Box 6000
Rockville, Maryland 20850
(800) 688-4252

- Offers information and publications on BJA-funded crime, drug, and gang-related programs, including grants, technical assistance, and training.

Center for Loss and Life Transition
3735 Broken Bow Road
Fort Collins, Colorado 80526
(970) 226-6050
(970) 226-6051 FAX

**Center for the Study and Prevention
of Violence**
Institute of Behavioral Science
University of Colorado at Boulder
Campus Box 442
Boulder, Colorado 80309-0442
(303) 492-1032
(303) 443-3297 FAX

- This center maintains a database of violence-related research and publications, many pertinent to school safety.

Center to Prevent Handgun Violence
1225 I Street, NW, Suite 1100
Washington, D.C. 20005
(202) 289-7319
(202) 408-1851 FAX
www.handguncontrol.org

Committee for Children
2203 Airport Way South, Suite 500
Seattle, Washington 98134-2027
(800) 634-4449
www.chchildren.org

- Makes available violence and abuse prevention education and social literacy programs.

Community Crisis Response (CCR) Program
Timothy J. Johnson, Community Crisis Response
Office for Victims of Crime (OVC)
U.S. Department of Justice
633 Indiana Avenue, NW, Room 1352
Washington, D.C. 20531
(202) 305-4548
(202) 514-6383 FAX
www.ojp.usdoj.gov/ovc/help.ccr.htm

- A division of the U.S. Department of Justice, the Office for Victims of Crimes (OVC) established the Community Crisis Response (CCR) program to improve services for victims of violent crime in cases in which there are multiple victims. The CCR provides direct assistance and training to communities that have been significantly impacted by criminal incidents (and to the federal, state, and local agencies assisting them).

Drugs and Crime Data Center and Clearinghouse
1600 Research Boulevard
Rockville, Maryland 20850
(800) 666-3332

Federal Emergency Management Agency (FEMA)
500 C Street, SW
Washington, D.C. 20472
(202) 646-2500
www.fema.org

Gun Safety Institute
320 Leader Building
Cleveland, Ohio 44114
(216) 574-9180

Mothers Against Violence in America (MAVIA)
105 14th Avenue, Suite 2A
Seattle, Washington 98122
(800) 897-7697 or (206) 323-2303
(206) 323-2132 FAX
maviausa@aol.com (e-mail)
www.mavia.com

- A national grassroots network of mothers working to prevent violence by and against children and to promote safe schools, homes, and communities.

National Association for Children With AIDS
P.O. Box 15845
Durham, North Carolina 27704
(919) 477-5288

National Association of Elementary School Principals (NAESP)
1615 Duke Street
Alexandria, Virginia 22314
(703) 684-3345
(703) 549-5568 FAX
www.naesp.org

National Association of School Psychologists (NASP)
4340 East West Highway, Suite 402
Bethesda, Maryland 20814
(301) 657-0270
www.naspweb.org

National Association of Secondary School Principals (NASSP)
1904 Association Drive
Reston, Virginia 20191
(703) 860-0200
www.nassp.org

National Center for Death Education
Mt. Ida College
777 Dedham Street
Newton Centre, Massachusetts 02159
(617) 928-4711

The National Congress of Parents and Teachers
700 Rush Street
Chicago, Illinois 60611
(312) 787-0977

- Offers several documents on gangs and schools, highlighting successful initiatives that have been implemented locally by parents nationwide.

National Crime Prevention Council (NCPC)
1700 K Street, NW, 2nd Floor
Washington, D.C. 20006-3817
(202) 466-6272
www.ncpc.org

National Crisis Prevention Institute, Inc. (CPI)
3315-K North 124th Street
Brookfield, Wisconsin 53005
(800) 558-8976
(414) 783-5906 FAX

- Trains educators in the techniques of nonviolent crisis intervention, emphasizing deescalating potentially violent incidents.

National Education Association (NEA)
1201 16th Street, NW
Washington, D.C. 20036
(202) 833-4000
www.nea.org

National Emergency Assistance Team (NEAT)
Chair—Dr. Scott Poland, (713) 460-7825
Western Region—Richard Lieberman, (310) 472-4744. (Alaska, Arizona, California, Colorado, Hawaii, Idaho, Montana, Nevada, New Mexico, Oregon, Utah, Washington, and Wyoming)
Central Region—Kristine Sieckert, (414) 567-6632. (Illinois, Indiana, Iowa, Kansas, Michigan, Minnesota, Missouri, Nebraska, North Dakota, Ohio, Oklahoma, South Dakota, and Wisconsin)
Southeast Region—Dr. Phil Lazarus, (305) 348-2725. (Alabama, Arkansas, Florida, Georgia, Kentucky, Louisiana, Mississippi, North Carolina, South Carolina, Tennessee, Texas, Virginia, and West Virginia)
Northeastern Region—Dr. Ted Feinberg, (518) 785-5511. (Connecticut, Delaware, District of Columbia, Maine, Maryland, Massachusetts, New Hampshire, New Jersey, New York, Pennsylvania, Puerto Rico, Rhode Island, and Vermont)
Member at Large—Bill Pfohl, (502) 782-7288
Member at Large—Frank Zenere, (305) 995-7319

National Organization for Victim Assistance (NOVA)
1757 Park Road, NW
Washington, D.C. 20010
(202) 232-6682 (232-NOVA)—staffed 24 hours per day for those requesting information or assistance
(202) 462-2255 FAX
nova@access.digex.net (e-mail)
www.access.digex.net/~nova

National Runaway Switchboard
(800) 621-4000

- Toll-free, 24-hour hotline for runaway and homeless youth and their families.

National School Boards Association (NSBA)
1680 Duke Street
Alexandria, Virginia 22314
(703) 838-6722
www.nsba.org

National School Public Relations Association (NSPRA)
15948 Derwood Road
Rockville, Maryland 20855
(301) 519-0496
(301) 519-0494 FAX
nspra@nspra.org (e-mail)
www.nspra.org

National School Safety Center (NSSC)
4165 Thousand Oaks Boulevard, Suite 290
Westlake Village, California 91362
(805) 373-9977
(805) 373-9277 FAX
rstephen@pepperdine.edu (e-mail)
www.nssc1.org

- Offers print resources on many aspects of school safety, including pertinent laws, tips for safe facilities, weapons, bullying, and gangs. Also offers technical assistance to groups addressing a gang problem in a community or school setting.

National Youth Gang Center (NYGC)
P.O. Box 12797
Tallahassee, Florida 32317
(904) 385-0600, ext. 249, 259, or 285
(904) 386-5356 FAX
krosier@iir.com (e-mail)
www.iir.com/nygc/nygc.htm

- Funded by the United States Department of Justice.

North Carolina Center for the Prevention of School Violence
20 Enterprise Street, Suite 2
Raleigh, North Carolina 27607-7375
(919) 515-9397 or (800) 299-6054
www.ncsu.edu/cpsv/

Office for Victims of Crime (OVC)
Office of Justice Programs
U.S. Department of Justice
633 Indiana Avenue, NW
Washington, D.C. 20531
(202) 307-5983
www.ojp.usdoj.gov/ovc

- As authorized by the Victims of Crime Act (VOCA) of 1984, this office administers the Crime Victims Fund to support state-level services for victims of crime. Such funds are distributed through each state's Crime Victims Compensation Board, which is usually administered through the attorney general's office. In some states, the board is administered through the governor's office or state department of health.

Office of Juvenile Justice and Delinquency Prevention
810 Seventh Street, NW
Washington, D.C. 20531
(202) 307-5911
www.ncjrs.org/ojjdp

Partnership Against Violence Network
(301) 504-5462
www.pavnet.org

- Maintains a searchable library of information and data from seven federal agencies.

Safe and Drug-Free Schools Program
600 Independence Avenue, SW
#604 Portals
Washington, D.C. 20202-6123
(202) 260-3954
www.ed.gov/offices/OESE/SDFS

Safe Schools Coalition
(941) 778-6652
www.ed.mtu.edu/safe

Students Against Violence Everywhere (SAVE)
105 14th Avenue, Suite 2A
Seattle, Washington 98122
(800) 897-7697 or (206) 323-2303
(206) 323-2132 FAX
maviausa@aol.com (e-mail)
www.mavia.com

- Sponsored by Mothers Against Violence in America, 63 student-driven chapters nationwide (in elementary, middle, and high schools) assist students in finding innovative solutions to violence in schools and communities.

Survivors of Suicide
National Office
Suicide Prevention Center, Inc.
184 Salem Avenue
Dayton, Ohio 45406
(513) 223-9096

U.S. Department of Health & Human Services
Substance Abuse & Mental Health Services
   Administration
Emergency Services & Disaster Relief Branch
5600 Fishers Lane, Room 13-103
Rockville, Maryland 10857
(301) 443-4735

- Provides a number of films—several on natural disasters—about children, trauma, and how to assist children, at no charge.

Support Groups

The following are a few of the many support organizations available to crisis survivors and their family members. Additionally, you are encouraged to consult with a victims' advocate, mental health practitioner (e.g., at the school, in private practice, at a relevant county or state agency), the Red Cross, a local crisis hotline, or even the Internet to locate other sources of support after a tragedy.

The Compassionate Friend, Inc.
(630) 990-0010

- Supports parents who have lost a child to any type of death.

Families and Friends of Missing Persons and Violent Crime Victims
(206) 362-1081 or (800) 346-7555

Mothers Against Drunk Driving (MADD) National
(214) 744-6233
www.madd.org

- For survivors of people killed in vehicular accidents caused by drunk driving.

Parents of Murdered Children (POMC)
(513) 721-5683

They Help Each Other Spiritually (THEOS)
(412) 471-7779

- For individuals whose spouse has died from any cause.

Violence Project of the National Gay Task Force
(212) 714-1141

- For survivors of gay or lesbian victims of murder.

Books, Tapes, Etc.

The following resources pertain to many types of crises and crisis effects. School staff, mental health workers, parents/family members, children (preschool to adolescence), clergy members, crisis response teams, victims' advocates, law enforcement/juvenile justice personnel, and others will find these resources useful for coping with crises. "Crisis," however, is a broad topic, and space restrictions do not permit us to list every valuable resource. What we have attempted to do is provide a cross-section applicable for the various age and interest groups just listed, as well as for a variety of religious and philosophical beliefs. Bear in mind that what works for one family, school, or community may not be helpful for another, and select only those resources that address your specific needs/beliefs. (Note also that we cannot vouch for the accuracy or efficacy of materials produced by others; you are encouraged to judge the merits of such additional resources yourself.)

Abused, Exploited, and Missing Children

Alice Doesn't Babysit Anymore
By Kevin B. McGovern (1985, McGovern and Mulbacher Books)

- Grades K-5.

Anyplace But Here: Young, Alone, and Homeless—What to Do
By Ellen Switzer (1992, Atheneum)

A Book for Kids Who Were Abused
By E. Gil (1986, Launch Press)

- Grade 3 and above.

Child Lures: What Every Parent and Child Should Know About Preventing Sexual Abuse and Abduction
By Kenneth Wooden (1995, Summit)

Criminal Investigation of Child Sexual Abuse
National Criminal Justice (1997, NCJ 162426)
(800) 638-8736 voice and FAX-on-demand
www.ojjdp.ncjrs.org/pubs/98publist

- Offers suggestions for interviewing the child, other potential victims, and caregivers.

Do You Have a Secret?
By P. Russell and B. Stone (1986, CompCare)

- Grades 2-5.

Federal Resources on Missing and Exploited Children: A Directory for Law Enforcement and Other Public and Private Agencies
National Criminal Justice (1997, NCJ 168962)
(800) 638-8736 voice and FAX-on-demand
www.ojjdp.ncjrs.org/pubs/98publist

Getting Together
By E. Drake and A. Nelson (1983, Child Care Publications)

- For sexually abused girls.

Interviewing Child Witnesses and Victims of Sexual Abuse
National Criminal Justice (1996, NCJ 161623)
(800) 638-8736 voice and FAX-on-demand
www.ojjdp.ncjrs.org/pubs/98publist

Kidnapped: Child Abduction in America
By Paula S. Fass (1997, Oxford University Press)

Law Enforcement Policies and Practices Regarding Missing Children and Homeless Youth (Research Summary)
National Criminal Justice (1993, NCJ 145644)
(800) 638-8736 voice and FAX-on-demand
www.ojjdp.ncjrs.org/pubs/98publist

Margaret's Story: Sexual Abuse and Going to Court
By D. Anderson and M. Finne (1986, Dillon
Press)

  • Grades 1-4.

Missing and Abducted Children:
A Law Enforcement Guide to Case Investigation
and Program Management
National Criminal Justice (1994, NCJ 151268)
(800) 638-8736 voice and FAX-on-demand
www.ojjdp.ncjrs.org/pubs/98publist

Missing and Murdered Children (Impact Book)
By Margaret O. Hyde (1998, Franklin Watts)

My Body Is Private
By L. W. Girard (1984, A. Whitman)

  • Grades K-3.

No More Secrets for Me
By O. Wachter (1983, Little, Brown)

  • Grades 1-4.

Not My Child: A Mother Confronts Her Child's
Sexual Abuse
By Patricia Crowely (1990, Avon Books)

Outgrowing the Pain
By E. Gil (1983, Launch Press)

  • For older teenagers who have been sexually
    abused.

Please, No! Not My Child
By K. MacFarlane (1985)
Marshall Resource Center
Children's Institute International
711 South New Hampshire Avenue
Los Angeles, California 90005

Promise Not to Tell
By C. Polese (1985, Human Sciences Press)

  • Grade 3 and above.

Recognizing When a Child's Injury or Illness
Is Caused by Abuse
National Criminal Justice (1996, NCJ 160038)
(800) 638-8736 voice and FAX-on-demand
www.ojjdp.ncjrs.org/pubs/98publist

Something Happened and I'm Scared to Tell:
A Book for Young Victims of Abuse
By P. Kehoe (1987, Parenting Press)

  • Preschool through grade 2.

Something Happened to Me
By P. Sweet (1985, Mother Courage)

  • Grades 2-5.

Spiders and Flies: Help for Parents and Teachers
of Sexually Abused Children
By Donald Hillman and Janice Solek-Tefft (1990,
Free Press)

Teens & Sexual Harassment (Booklet #200-112)
BLR Publications
Business and Legal Reports, Inc.
39 Academy Street
Madison, Connecticut 06443-1513
(800) 727-5257
(203) 245-2559 FAX

  • A booklet for secondary students, available
    inexpensively in large quantities (also available
    with personal imprint).

When Your Child Has Been Molested:
A Parent's Guide to Healing and Recovery
By Kathryn Nagans and Joyce Case (Contributor)
(1988, Lexington Books)

When Your Child Is Missing:
A Family Survival Guide
National Criminal Justice (1998, NCJ 170022)
(800) 638-8736 voice and FAX-on-demand
www.ojjdp.ncjrs.org/pubs/98publist

Working Together
By E. Drake and A. Nelson (1986, Child Care Publications)

- For sexually abused boys.

Bombs

Bombs and Bombings: A Handbook to Detection, Disposal and Investigation for Police and Fire Departments
By Thomas Graham Brodie (1995, Charles C. Thomas Publications, Ltd.)

Explosives Identification Guide
By Mike Pickett (1998, Delmar)

Medicine Chest Explosives: An Investigator's Guide to Chemicals Used in Home Cooked Bombs
By Don McLean (1995, Paladin Press)

Pipe and Fire Bomb Designs: A Guide for Police Bomb Technicians
By Lee Scott (1994, Paladin Press)

Terrorism in America: Pipe Bombs and Pipe Dreams (SUNY Series on New Directions in Crime and Justice Studies)
By Brent L. Smith and Austin Turk (1994, State University of New York Press)

Bullying/Aggression/Fights

Administrative Intervention: A School Administrator's Guide to Working With Aggressive and Disruptive Students
By Donald D. Black and John C. Downs (1993, Sopris West)

Break It Up: A Teacher's Guide to Managing Student Aggression
By Arnold Goldstein, James Palumbo, Susan Striepling, and Ann Marie Voutsinas (1995, Research Press)

Bullies & Victims: Helping Your Child Survive the Schoolyard Battlefield
By Suellen Fried and Paula Fried (1998, M. Evans & Company)

Bully-Proofing Your School: A Comprehensive Approach for Elementary Schools
By Carla Garrity, Kathryn Jens, William Porter, Nancy Sager, and Cam Short-Camilli (1993, Sopris West)

No Bully 4 Kids, No Bully 4 Teachers/Grown-Ups
www.nobully.org.nz

- New Zealand Web site with information for both students and adults, including a "No Bully Game."

Set Straight on Bullies
National School Safety Center (NSSC)
(805) 373-9977

Clergy Members' Resources

Agents of Hope: A Pastoral Psychology
By Donald Capps (1995, Fortress)

All Our Losses, All Our Griefs: Resources for Pastoral Care
By Kenneth R. Mitchell, Herbert Anderson (Photographer) (1983, Westminster John Knox Press)

Baker's Funeral Handbook: Resources for Pastors
By Paul E. Engle (Ed.) (1996, Baker Book House)

Basic Types of Pastoral Care and Counseling: Resources for the Ministry of Healing and Growth
By Howard John Clinebell (1984, Abingdon Press)

Bereavement Ministry Program: A Comprehensive Guide for Churches
By Jan C. Nelson and David A. Aaker (1998, Ave Maria Press)

Comforting the Bereaved
By Warren W. Wiersbe and David Wiersbe
(Contributor) (1985, Moody Press)

Dying, Grieving, Faith, and Family:
A Pastoral Care Approach
By George W. Bowman III (1998, Haworth Press)

Hope in Pastoral Care and Counseling
By Andrew D. Lester (1995, Westminster John
Knox Press)

Praying Through Grief: Healing Prayer Services
for Those Who Mourn
By Mauryeen O'Brien (1997, Ave Maria Press)

The Skilled Pastor: Counseling As the
Practice of Theology
By Charles W. Taylor (1991, Fortress)

Spiritual Care of Dying and Bereaved People
By Penelope Wilcock (1997, Morehouse
Publishing)

Through the Eyes of Women:
Insights for Pastoral Care
By Jeanne Stevenson Moessner (Ed.) (1996,
Fortress)

Counseling/Therapy

A Child's First Book About Play Therapy
By M. A. Nemitoff and J. Annunziata (1990,
American Psychological Association)
• Preschool through grade 2.

Choosing to Live: How to Defeat Suicide
Through Cognitive Therapy
By Thomas E. Ellis and Cory F. Newman
(Contributor) (1996, New Harbinger)

Death and the Adolescent: A Resource Handbook for
Bereavement Support Groups in Schools
By Grant W. Baxter and Wendy J. Stewart (1998,
University of Toronto Press)

The Drawing Out Feelings Series Facilitator's Guide
for Leading Grief Support Groups
By Marge Eaton Heegaard (1993, Woodland
Press)

Effective Support Groups
By James E. Miller (1998, Willowgreen
Publishing)

Good Grief: Helping Groups of Children
When a Friend Dies (1985)
New England Association for the Education
    of Young Children
35 Pilgrim Road
Boston, Massachusetts 02215

Grief Counseling and Grief Therapy:
A Handbook for the Mental Health Practitioner
By James William Worden (1991, Springer)

Helping Bereaved Children:
A Handbook for Practitioners
By Nancy Boyd Webb (Ed.) (1993, Guilford)

Ignatius Finds Help: A Story About Psychotherapy
for Children
By M. Galvin (1988, Magination Press)
• Preschool through grade 6.

The Suicidal Patient: Clinical and Legal
Standards of Care
By Bruce Michael Bongar (1991, American
Psychological Association)

Treating Traumatized Children: New Insights
and Creative Interventions
By Beverly James (1990, Simon & Schuster)

Treating the Trauma of Rape:
Cognitive-Behavioral Therapy for PTSD
(Treatment Manual for Practitioners)
By Barbara Olasov Rothbaum and Edna B. Foa
(1998, Guilford)

When Your Child Needs Help
By N. Doft and B. Aria (1992, Harmony Books)
- Explains child therapy.

Death and Grief

For Adults

After Goodbye: How to Begin Again After the Death of Someone You Love
By Ted Menten (1994, Running Press)

After Suicide
By John H. Hewett and Wayne E. Oates (Eds.)
(1980, Westminster John Knox Press)

After the Darkest Hour the Sun Will Shine Again: A Parent's Guide to Coping With the Loss of a Child
By Elizabeth Mehren and Harold Kushner (1997, Fireside)

After the Death of a Child: Living With Loss Through the Years
By Ann K. Finkbeiner (1996, Free Press)

The Art of Condolence: What to Write, What to Say, What to Do at a Time of Loss
By Leonard M. Zunin and Hilary Stanton Zunin
(1992, HarperPerennial)

Bereaved Children and Teens: A Support Guide for Parents and Professionals
By Earl A. Grollman (Ed.) (1996, Beacon Press)

The Bereaved Parent
By Harriet Sarnoff Schiff (1978, Viking)

The Book of Eulogies: A Collection of Memorial Tributes, Poetry, Essays, and Letters of Condolence
By Phyllis Theroux (Ed.) (1997, Scribner)

Breaking the Silence: A Guide to Help Children With Complicated Grief—Suicide, Homicide, AIDS, Violence, and Abuse
By Linda Goldman (1996, Accelerated Development)

A Broken Heart Still Beats: When Your Child Dies
By Anne McCracken and Mary Semel (Eds.)
(1998, Hazelden Information Education)

Children Grieve, Too: A Book for Families Who Have Experienced a Death
By Joy Johnson and Marvin Johnson (1998, Centering Corporation)

A Child's View of Grief
By Alan D. Wolfelt, Lori Mackey (Illustrator)
(1991, Center for Loss & Life Transition)

The Courage to Laugh: Humor, Hope, and Healing in the Face of Death and Dying
By Allen Klein (1998, J. P. Tarcher)

Creative Grieving: From Loss to Enlightenment
By Arthur Samuels (1998, Stress Free Publications)

Cries of the Heart: Praying Our Losses
By Wayne Simsic, Michael McGrath (Illustrator)
(1995, St. Mary's Press)

Cry Until You Laugh: Comforting Guidance for Coping With Grief
By Richard J. Obershaw (1998, Fairview Press)

Death and Bereavement Across Cultures
By Colin Murray Parks, Pittu Laungani, and Bill Young (Eds.) (1996, Routledge)

Death and Grieving: Music, Meditation and Prayer
By Marianne Williamson (1998, Hay House)

Every Person's Guide to Death and Dying in the Jewish Tradition
By Ronald H. Isaacs (1999, Jason Aronson)

Everything You Need to Know When Someone You Know Has Been Killed (Need to Know Library)
By Jay Schleifer (1998, Rosen Publishing)

Explaining Death to Children
By Earl A. Grollman (1967, Beacon Press)

Five Cries of Grief: One Family's Journey to Healing After the Tragic Death of a Son
By Merton P. Strommen and A. Irene Strommen (Contributor) (1996, Augsberg Fortress Publications)

Good Grief: A Constructive Approach to the Problem of Loss
By Granger E. Westberg (1996, Fortress)

The Grief Recovery Handbook: The Action Program for Moving Beyond Death, Divorce, and Other Losses
By John W. James and Russell Friedman (1998, HarperCollins)

Grief's Courageous Journey: A Workbook
By Sandi Caplan and Gordon Lang (1995, New Harbinger)

The Grieving Child: A Parent's Guide
By Helen Fitzgerald and Elisabeth Kübler-Ross (1992, Fireside)

Healing After the Suicide of a Loved One
By Ann Smolin and John Guinan (1993, Fireside)

Heaven's Not a Crying Place: Teaching Your Child About Funerals, Death, and the Life Beyond
By Joey O'Connor (1997, Fleming H. Revell Co.)

Helping Children Cope With Separation and Loss
By Claudia L. Jewett (1982, Harvard Common Press)

Helping Teens Work Through Grief
By Mary Kelly Perschy (1997, Taylor & Francis)

How Do We Tell the Children? Helping Children Two to Teen Cope When Someone Dies
By Dan Schaefer and Christine Lyons (1993, Newmarket Press)

"I'm Grieving As Fast As I Can": How Young Widows and Widowers Can Cope and Heal
By Linda Sones Feinberg (1994, New Horizon)

Laughter, Silence and Shouting: An Anthology of Women's Prayers
By Kathy Keay (Compiler) (1994, HarperCollins)

Life After Suicide: A Ray of Hope for Those Left Behind
By E. Betsy Ross and Joseph Richman (1997, Insight Books)

The Mourning Handbook: The Most Comprehensive Resource Offering Practical and Compassionate Advice on Coping With All Aspects of Death and Dying
By Helen Fitzgerald (1995, Fireside)

No Time for Goodbyes: Coping With Sorrow, Anger, and Injustice After a Tragic Death
By Janice Harris Lord (1991, Pathfinder Publishing)

No Time to Say Goodbye: Surviving the Suicide of a Loved One
By Carla Fine (1997, Doubleday)

On Death and Dying
By Elisabeth Kübler-Ross (Rev. ed., 1997, Collier)

Remembrances and Celebrations: A Book of Eulogies, Elegies, Letters, and Epitaphs
By Jill Werman Harris (Ed.) (1999, Pantheon)

The Sacred Art of Dying: How World Religions Understand Death
By Kenneth Kramer (Ed.) (1988, Paulist Press)

The Seasons of Grief:
Helping Children Grow Through Loss
By D. A. Gaffney (1988, Plume)

Silent Grief: Living in the Wake of Suicide
By Christopher Lukas and Henry M. Seiden
(Contributor) (1997, Jason Aronson)

- Of special interest to parents and educators
  of teenagers.

Talking About Death:
A Dialogue Between Parent and Child
By Earl A. Grollman, Susan Avishai (Illustrator)
(1991, Beacon Press)

Talking to Heaven:
A Medium's Message of Life After Death
By James Van Praagh (1997, Dutton)

The Tibetan Book of the Dead
By Guru Rinpoche, Francesca Fremantle
and Chogyam Trungpa (Translators) (1992,
Shambhala)

- Ancient Tibetan Buddhist text that emphasizes
  the principle of birth and death recurring
  constantly in life.

What Happens to Good People
When Bad Things Happen
By Robert A. Schuller (1995, Fleming H. Revell)

- Reviews the blessings we experience in life
  even when life hurts and forgiveness is needed.

When Bad Things Happen to Good People
By Harold S. Kushner (1992, Avon)

When Goodbye Is Forever: Learning to
Live Again After the Loss of a Child
By John Bramblett (1991, Ballantine)

The Worst Loss: How Families Heal
From the Death of a Child
By Barbara D. Rosof (1995, Henry Holt)

For Children and Teens

After the Funeral
By Jane Loretta Winsch, Pamela Keating
(Illustrator) (1995, Paulist Press)

- Ages 4-8.

Badger's Parting Gifts
By Susan Varley (1992, Mulberry Books/William
Morrow)

- Ages 4-8.

Balloons for Trevor: Understanding Death
(Comforting Little Hearts Series)
By Anne Good Cave, Janice Skivington
(Illustrator) (1998, Concordia)

- Ages 4-8.

Daddy's Promise
By John T. Heiney, Michael J. Gordon (Illustrator)
(1997, Promise Publications)

- Ages 4-8.

Death (Preteen Pressures Series)
By Barbara Sprung (1998, Raintree/Steck Vaughn)

- Ages 9-12.

Death Customs (Comparing Religions)
By Lucy Rushton (1993, Thomson Learning)

- Ages 9-12.

Death Is Hard to Live With:
Teenagers Talk About How They Cope With Loss
By Janet Bode, Stan Mack (Illustrator) (1995,
Laureleaf)

- Young adult.

The Empty Place: A Child's Guide Through Grief
(A Small Horizon Book)
By Roberta Temes, Kim Carlisle (Illustrator)
(1992, New Horizon)

- Particularly applicable for a child whose sibling has died.

The Fall of Freddie the Leaf
By Leo F. Buscaglia (1983, Holt, Rinehart & Winston)
- Ages 4-8.

"I Wish I Could Hold Your Hand":
A Child's Guide to Grief and Loss
By Pat Palmer, Diane O'Quinn Burke (Illustrator) (1994, Impact)
- Ages 9-12.

The Kid's Book About Death and Dying
By Eric E. Rofes (Ed.) (1985, Little, Brown)
- Ages 9-12.

Lifetimes: The Beautiful Way to Explain Death to Children
By Bryan Mellonie and Robert R. Ingpen (Contributor) (1987, Bantam)
- Preschool through grade 3.

The Saddest Time
By N. Simon (1985, A. Whitman)
- Grades 1-6.

Sad Isn't Bad: A Good-Grief Guidebook for Kids Dealing With Loss
By Michaelene Mundy, R. W. Alley (Illustrator) (1998, Abbey Press)
- Ages 4-8.

Saying Goodbye to Daddy
By J. Vigna (1990, A. Whitman)
- Grades K-2.

Straight Talk About Death for Teenagers: How to Cope With Losing Someone You Love
By Earl A. Grollman (1993, Beacon Press)
- Young adult.

What Happens When We Die?
(Children's Bible Basics)
By Carolyn Nystrom, Wayne A. Hanna (Illustrator) (1992, Moody Press)
- Ages 4-8.

When a Friend Dies: A Book for Teens About Grieving & Healing
By Marilyn E. Gootman and Pamela Espeland (1994, Free Spirit)
- Young adult.

When Dinosaurs Die: A Guide to Understanding Death
By Laurie Krasny Brown, Marc Tolon Brown (Illustrator) (1998, Little, Brown)

Drugs

Addiction: The "High" That Brings You Down (Teen Issues)
By Miriam Smith McLaughlin and Sandy Peyser Hazouri (1997, Enslow Publishers)

The Addiction Workbook: A Step-by-Step Guide to Quitting Alcohol and Drugs
By Patrick Fanning (1996, New Harbinger)

Alcohol (Peer Pressures)
By Paula McGuire (1998, Raintree/Steck Vaughn)
- Ages 9-12.

Alcohol and You (Impact Book)
By Jane Claypool Miner (1997, Franklin Watts)
- Young adult.

The Berenstain Bears and the Drug Free Zone (A Big Chapter Book)
By Stan Berenstain and Jan Berenstain (1993, Random House)
- All ages.

Beyond the Bench: How Judges Can Help Reduce Juvenile DUI and Alcohol and Other Drug Violations (Video and Discussion Guide)
National Criminal Justice (1996, NCJ 162357)
(800) 638-8736 voice and FAX-on-demand
www.ojjdp.ncjrs.org/pubs/98publist

Buzzed: The Straight Facts About the Most Used and Abused Drugs From Alcohol to Ecstasy
By Cynthia Kuhn, Scott Swartzwelder, and Wilkie Wilson (1998, W. W. Norton & Co.)

Combating Underage Drinking: A Compendium of Resources
National Criminal Justice (1998, NCJ 168963)
www.ojjdp.ncjrs.org/pubs/98publist

Creating Safe and Drug Free Schools: An Action Guide
National Education Association
(800) 624-0100
www.nea.org/publications

Don't Let Your Kids Kill You: A Guide for Parents of Drug and Alcohol Addicted Children
By Charles Rubin (1996, Element)

- Focuses on the parents of addicts, rather than the addicts.

The Drug-Free School (Booklet #200-081), *Spanish Edition* (Booklet #200-082)
BLR Publications
Business and Legal Reports, Inc.
39 Academy Street
Madison, Connecticut 06443-1513
(800) 727-5257
(203) 245-2559 FAX

- Booklets for secondary students, available inexpensively in large quantities (also available with personal imprint).

Drug Recognition Techniques: A Training Program for Juvenile Justice Professionals (Update on Programs)
National Criminal Justice (1990, NCJ 128795)
(800) 638-8736 voice and FAX-on-demand
www.ojjdp.ncjrs.org/pubs/98publist

Drugs and Date Rape (Drug Abuse Prevention Library)
By Maryann Miller (1995, Rosen Publishing)

Helping Your Chemically Dependent Teenager Recover: A Guide for Parents and Other Concerned Adults
By Peter R. Cohen (1992, Johnson Institute)

Rising Above Gangs and Drugs: How to Start a Community Reclamation Project (3rd ed.)
National Criminal Justice (1995, NCJ 133522)
(800) 638-8736 voice and FAX-on-demand
www.ojjdp.ncjrs.org/pubs/98publist

Saying No Is Not Enough: Helping Your Kids Make Wise Decisions About Alcohol, Tobacco, and Other Drugs—A Guide for Parents of Children Ages Three Through Teen
By Robert Schwebel (1998, Newmarket Press)

Teens & Alcohol (Booklet #200-098)
BLR Publications
Business and Legal Reports, Inc.
39 Academy Street
Madison, Connecticut 06443-1513
(800) 727-5257
(203) 245-2559 FAX

- A booklet for secondary students, available inexpensively in large quantities (also available with personal imprint).

Urban Delinquency and Substance Abuse: Initial Findings (Research Summary)
National Criminal Justice (1994, NCJ 143454)
(800) 638-8736 voice and FAX-on-demand
www.ojjdp.ncjrs.org/pubs/98publist

First Aid

Baby & Child Emergency First-Aid Handbook: Simple Step-by-Step Instructions for the Most Common Childhood Emergencies
By M. J. Einzig (Ed.) (Rev. ed., 1995, Meadowbrook Press)

Smart Medicine for a Healthier Child: A Practical A-to-Z Reference to Natural and Conventional Treatments for Infants and Children
By J. Zand, R. Walton, and B. Rountree (1994, Avery Publishing)

Gangs

We encourage you to notify and work closely with your local police department concerning any gang threats or problems you may be experiencing. Particularly if your local police force has a special operations unit devoted to gangs, these professionals will be able to educate you on the known gang activity specific to your area—including warning signs of such gang activity—and recommended intervention steps.

Adolescent Gangs: Old Issues, New Approaches
By Curtis W. Branch (Ed.) (1998, Brunner/Mazel)

"Gang Assessment Tool"
(1992) National School Safety Center (NSSC)
(805) 373-9977

- Helps both schools and communities realistically measure youth gang activity in their area.

The Gang Intervention Handbook
By Arnold Goldstein and C. Ronald Huff (Eds.) (1993, Research Press)

Gangs and Schools
By R. Arthur and E. Erickson (1992, Learning Publications)

Gangs—Straight Talk, Straight Up: A Practical Guide for Teachers, Parents, and the Community
By Mary M. Jensen and Lt. Phillip C. Yerington (1997, Sopris West)

Gang Suppression and Intervention: Community Models (Research Summary)
National Criminal Justice (1994, NCJ 1482020)
(800) 638-8736 voice and FAX-on-demand
www.ojjdp.ncjrs.org/pubs/98publist

Gang Suppression and Intervention: Problem and Response (Research Summary)
National Criminal Justice (1994, NCJ 149629)
(800) 638-8736 voice and FAX-on-demand
www.ojjdp.ncjrs.org/pubs/98publist

My Posse Don't Do Homework
By L. A. Johnson (1992, St. Martin's Press)

Prosecuting Gangs: A National Assessment
By C. Johnson, B. Webster, and E. Connors (1995, National Institute of Justice [NIJ])

- Provides the findings of a nationwide survey of prosecutors' approaches to gang prosecution, including case studies.

Rising Above Gangs and Drugs: How to Start a Community Reclamation Project (3rd ed.)
National Criminal Justice (1995, NCJ 133522)
(800) 638-8736 voice and FAX-on-demand
www.ojjdp.ncjrs.org/pubs/98publist

Youth Gangs: An Overview
(Youth Gang Series Bulletin)
National Criminal Justice (1998, NCJ 167249)
(800) 638-8736 voice and FAX-on-demand
www.ojjdp.ncjrs.org/pubs/98publist

Miscellaneous Resources

AIDS and HIV-Related Diseases: An Educational Guide for Professionals and the Public
By John Powell and Amy Bourdeau (1996, Insight Books)

The Art of Forgiving: When You Need to Forgive and Don't Know How
By Lewis B. Smedes (1997, Ballantine)

Before It's Too Late: Why Some Kids Get Into Trouble—And What Parents Can Do About It
By Stanton E. Samenow (Rev. ed., 1998, Random House)

Carla Goes to Court
By J. Beaudry and L. Ketchum (1987, Human Sciences Press)
- Grades K-6.

Children in a Violent Society
By Peter Scharf (1998, Guilford)

Children in Danger: Coping With the Consequences of Community Violence
By James Garbarino, Nancy Dubrow, Kathleen Kostelny, and Carole Pardo (1998, Jossey-Bass)

Exploding the Myth of Self-Defense: A Survival Guide for Every Woman
By Judith Fein (1993, Torrance)

50 Ways to a Safer World: Everyday Actions You Can Take to Prevent Violence in Neighborhoods, Schools, and Communities
By Patricia Occhiuzzo Giggans and Barrie Levy (Contributor) (1997, Seal Press Feminist Publications)

The Gift of Fear: Survival Signals That Protect Us From Violence
By Gavin de Becker (1999, Dell)

How to Forgive When You Don't Know How
By Jacqui Bishop and Mary Grunte (1998, Talman Company)

Kids With Courage: True Stories About Young People Making a Difference
By Barbara A. Lewis (1992, Free Spirit Publishing)
- Children and teens who have overcome adversities and those involved in social action programs to help other kids and their communities tell their stories. A teacher's guide is included.

Let's Talk About Living in a World With Violence: An Activity Book for School-Age Children
By James Garbarino (1993)
Erickson Institute
420 North Wabash Avenue
Chicago, Illinois 60611
(312) 755-2250
- Workbook.

Lost Boys: Why Our Sons Turn Violent and How We Can Save Them
By James Garbarino (1999, Free Press)

Making Children, Families, and Communities Safe From Violence (Booklet)
National Crime Prevention Council
(800) WE-PREVENT
www.ncpc.org

A National Action Plan on School Violence and Kids From 2:00 to 8:00 PM (Free Booklet)
Ed Somers
U.S. Conference of Mayors
1620 I Street, NW
Washington, D.C. 20006
(202) 293-7330

100 Questions & Answers About AIDS: What You Need to Know Now
By Michael Thomas Ford (1993, William Morrow & Co.)
- Young adult.

On Playing a Poor Hand Well: Insights From the Lives of Those Who Have Overcome Childhood Risks and Adversities
By Mark Katz (1997, W. W. Norton & Co.)

Protecting Children From Danger: Building Self-Reliance and Emergency Skills Without Fear (A Learning by Doing Book for Parents and Educators)
By Matt Thomas and Bob Bishop (Contributor) (1993, North Atlantic Books)

Protecting the Gift: Keeping Children and Teenagers Safe (and Parents Sane)
By Gavin de Becker (1999, Dial Press)

Raising Children to Resist Violence
By the American Academy of Pediatrics
(847) 228-5005
www.aap.org/family/mnbrochure.htm

Reaching Out to Troubled Kids: 15 Helpful Ways to Bridge the Gap Between Parents, Teachers, and Kids (2nd ed.)
By Kathleen Fad (1996, Sopris West)

State Responses to Serious and Violent Juvenile Crime (Research Report)
National Criminal Justice (1996, NCJ 161565)
(800) 638-8736 voice and FAX-on-demand
www.ojjdp.ncjrs.org/pubs/98publist

Student/Staff Support Teams (SST)
By Vicki Phillips and Laura McCullough (1993, Sopris West)
- Presents a collaborative approach to solving student and building-level problems.

The Teacher's Encyclopedia of Behavior Management: 100 Problems/500 Plans
By Randy S. Sprick and Lisa Howard (1995, Sopris West)
- For grades K-9, problems covered include bullying, fighting, frequently victimized students, etc.

Teenagers & AIDS (Booklet #200-089)
BLR Publications
Business and Legal Reports, Inc.
39 Academy Street
Madison, Connecticut 06443-1513
(800) 727-5257
(203) 245-2559 FAX
- A booklet for secondary students, available inexpensively in large quantities (also available with personal imprint).

Violence: Reflections on a National Epidemic
By James Gilligan (1997, Vintage)

When Your Child Is Seriously Injured: The Emotional Impact on Families
Research and Training Center in Rehabilitation and Childhood Trauma
Department of Rehabilitation Medicine
New England Medical Center Hospitals
750 Washington Street
Boston, Massachusetts 02111

Natural Disasters

Aftermath: Communities After Natural Disasters
- This title is out of print, but you may be able to find it at the library, at a used bookstore, or through www.amazon.com (with an out-of-print order).

After the Clean-Up: Long Range Effects of Natural Disasters
- This title is out of print, but you may be able to find it at the library, at a used bookstore, or through www.amazon.com (with an out-of-print order).

The Berenstain Bear Scouts and the Really Big Disaster
By Stan Berenstain and Jan Berenstain (1998, Little Apple)
- Ages 9-12.

Coping With Natural Disasters
By Caroline Arnold (1988, Walker & Company)

Dangerous Planet: The Science of Natural Disasters
By Rob Nagel and Betz Des Chenes (1999, U*X*L)

Disasters
By Ned Halley (1999, Larousse Kingfisher Chambers)
  • Ages 9-12.

"Disaster Stuff for Kids"
www.jmu.edu/psychologydept/4kids.htm
  • This Web site contains reading material, links to other relevant sites, and a "My Story" page to allow children to post online their own experiences and thoughts about crises.

Emergency Procedures for Schools:
A Guide and Disaster Plan Framework
By Ralph W. Ritchie (1995, Ritchie Unlimited Publications)

Everything You Need to Know About Natural Disasters and Post-Traumatic Stress Disorder (Need to Know Library)
By Richard S. Lee and Mary Price Lee (1995, Rosen Publishing)

Helping Children Prepare for and Cope With Natural Disasters (Booklet)
Annette LaGreca, Ph.D.
Box 249229
University of Miami
Coral Gables, Florida 33124

Hurricanes and Tornadoes (When Disaster Strikes)
By Keith Greenberg (1995, Twenty First Century Books)
  • Ages 9-12.

I'll Know What to Do:
A Kid's Guide to Natural Disasters
By Bonnie S. Mark and Aviva Layton, Michael Chesworth (Illustrator) (1997, Magination)
  • Ages 9-12.

Managing Traumatic Stress: Tips for Recovering From Disasters and Other Traumatic Events (Brochure for the general public and in particular parents)
American Psychological Association's Practice Directorate
(202) 336-5500, ask for order department
www.apa.org

Natural Disasters (The World's Disasters)
By Tim Wood (1994, Thomson Learning)
  • Ages 9-12.

A New Species of Trouble: Explorations in Disaster, Trauma, and Community
By Kai T. Erickson (1994, W. W. Norton & Company)

Psychosocial Aspects of Disaster
By Richard Gist (1989, John Wiley & Sons)

School Buildings and Natural Disasters
(1982, United Nations Educational)

Surviving Natural Disasters: How to Prepare for Earthquakes, Hurricanes, Tornadoes, Floods, Wildfires, Thunderstorms, Tsunamis, and Volcanic Eruptions
By Janice McCann and Betsy Shand
  • This title is out of print, but you may be able to find it at the library, at a used bookstore, or through www.amazon.com (with an out-of-print order).

Wright's Complete Disaster Survival Manual: How to Prepare for Earthquakes, Floods, Tornadoes, & Other Natural Disasters
By Ted Wright (1993, Hampton Roads Publishing)

Nightmares

Go Away, Bad Dreams
By S. Hill (1985, Random House)
- Preschool through grade 3.

Jessica and the Wolf: A Story for Children Who Have Bad Dreams
By T. Lobby (1990, Magination Press)
- Grades K-3.

Night Light: A Story for Children Afraid of the Dark
By J. Dutro (1991, Magination Press)
- Preschool through grade 4.

Scary Night Visitors: A Story for Children With Bedtime Fears
By I. W. Marcus and P. Marcus (1990, Magination Press)
- Preschool through grade 2.

There's a Nightmare in My Closet
By Mercer Mayer (1968, Dial Press)
- Preschool through grade 2.

Rape

Dating Violence: Young Women in Danger
By Barrie Levy (Ed.) (1998, Seal Press Feminist Publications)

Defending Ourselves: A Guide to Prevention, Self-Defense, and Recovery From Rape
By Rosalind Wiseman (1995, Noonday Press)

Free of the Shadows: Recovering From Sexual Violence
By Caren Adams and Jennifer Fay (Contributor) (1990, New Harbinger)

A Guide to Rape Awareness and Prevention: Educating Yourself, Your Family, and Those in Need
By Robert Ferguson and Jeanine Ferguson (1994, Turtle Press)

Our Guys: The Glen Ridge Rape and the Secret Life of the Perfect Suburb
By Bernard Lefkowitz (1998, Vintage)

Quest for Respect: A Healing Guide for Survivors of Rape
By Linda Braswell (1993, Pathfinder Publications)

The Rape Reference: A Resource for People at Risk
By Maureen Harrison and Steve Gilbert (Eds.) (1996, Excellent Books)

Recovery: How to Survive Sexual Assault for Women, Men, Teenagers, and Their Friends and Families
By Helen Benedict and Susan Brison (1994, Columbia University Press)

Sexual Abuse Prevention: A Course of Study for Teenagers
By Rebecca Voelkel-Haugen (1996, Westminster John Knox Press)

When I Stopped: Remembering Rape at Thirteen
By Martha Ramsey (1997, Harvest Books)

School Safety and Crisis Intervention

Combating Fear and Restoring Safety in Schools
(Youth Out of the Education Mainstream Bulletin)
National Criminal Justice (1998, NCJ 167888)
(800) 638-8736 voice and FAX-on-demand
www.ojjdp.ncjrs.org/pubs/98publist

Coping With Crisis: Pertinent Points Checklists
By Scott Poland and Jami S. McCormick (in press, Sopris West, [800] 547-6747)

- Booklet of "Pertinent Points" checklists summarizing important information from this book, for use by crisis responders and volunteers.

Creating Safe and Drug Free Schools: An Action Guide
National Education Association
(800) 624-0100
www.nea.org/publications

Crisis Intervention in the Schools
By Gayle D. Pitcher and Scott Poland (1992, Guilford Press)

- Particularly applicable for school mental health staff.

Crisis Prevention & Response: A Collection of NASP Resources
National Association of School Psychologists
(301) 657-0270
www.naspweb.org

Early Warning, Timely Response: A Guide to Safe Schools
National Criminal Justice (1998, NCJ 172854)
(800) 638-8736 voice and FAX-on-demand
www.ojjdp.ncjrs.org/pubs/98publist

Effective Strategies for School Security
By P. D. Blauvelt (1991, National Association of School Principals)

Safe Schools: A Handbook for Violence Prevention
By Ronald D. Stephens (1995, National Educational Service)

Hands Without Guns Initial Workshop Guideline
Joshua Horwitz
(202) 544-2637
www.handswithoutguns.org/wksp1.html

- Youth workshop guide for teachers.

Keep Weapons and Crime Out of Your School
(Key #BC3)
BLR Publications
Business and Legal Reports, Inc.
39 Academy Street
Madison, Connecticut 06443-1513
(800) 727-5257
(203) 245-2559 FAX

- A booklet for secondary students, available inexpensively in large quantities (also available with personal imprint).

A Kid's Guide to Staying Safe at School (The Kids' Library of Personal Safety)
By Maribeth Boelts (1997, Rosen Publishing)

Reducing Youth Gun Violence: An Overview of Programs and Initiatives (Program Report)
National Criminal Justice (1996, NCJ 154303)
(800) 638-8736 voice and FAX-on-demand
www.ojjdp.ncjrs.org/pubs/98publist

Safe Schools Manual
By the National Education Association (NEA)
NEA Human and Civil Rights
1201 16th Street, NW
Washington, D.C. 20036
www.nea.org

School Safety 101
National School Safety Center (NSSC)
(805) 373-9977

School Violence Intervention: A Practical Handbook
By Arnold P. Goldstein and Jane Close Conoley (Eds.) (1997, Guilford Press)

Stopping School Violence (Free Brochure)
National Crime Prevention Council
(800) WE-PREVENT
www.ncpc.org

*Take Back Your School: Challenge Your Students
to Be the First Line of Defense in Their
School's Safety*
By Scott Poland and Donna Poland (1999,
Sopris West)
(800) 547-6747
www.sopriswest.com
- For use by teachers with secondary students;
  includes a workbook and three videos.

*Thinking About the Unthinkable: Seeking Solutions
to School Violence* (1998, Videotape)
National School Public Relations Association
15948 Derwood Road
Rockville, Maryland 20855
(301) 519-0496
(301) 519-0494 FAX

Weapons in School (Booklet #200-104)
BLR Publications
Business and Legal Reports, Inc.
39 Academy Street
Madison, Connecticut 06443-1513
(800) 727-5257
(203) 245-2559 FAX
- A booklet for secondary students, available
  inexpensively in large quantities (also available
  with personal imprint).

Suicide

Adolescent Suicide: Assessment and Intervention
By Alan L. Berman and David A. Jobes (1996,
American Psychological Association)

After a Suicide: Young People Speak Up
By Susan Kuklin (1994, Putnam)
- Young adult.

"Best Practices in Suicide Intervention,"
By Scott Poland
In A. Thomas and J. Grimes (Eds.), *Best Practices
in School Psychology—III* (1995, National
Association of School Psychologists)

*The Cruelest Death: The Enigma
of Adolescent Suicide*
By David Lester (1992, The Charles Press)

*Cry of Pain: Understanding Suicide
and Self-Harm*
By Mark Williams (1998, Penguin USA)

*Death by Denial: Studies of Suicide in Gay
and Lesbian Teenagers*
By Gary Remafedi (Ed.) (1994, Alyson
Publications)

*Depression and Suicide in Children
and Adolescents: Prevention, Intervention
and Postvention*
By Philip G. Patros and Tonia K. Shamoo (1988,
Allyn & Bacon)

*Depression in the Young: What We Can Do
to Help Them*
By Trudy Carlson (1998, Benline Press)

No One Saw My Pain: Why Teens Kill Themselves
By Andrew E. Slaby and Lili Frank Garfinkel
(Contributor) (1996, W. W. Norton & Co.)

Suicide Intervention in the Schools
By Scott Poland (1989, Guilford Press)

Team Up to Save Lives
By Ronald McDonald House Charities (1997)
McDonald's Educational Resource Center
(800) 627-7646

- Incorporating data from the Institute for Juvenile Research at the University of Illinois at Chicago, this free CD-ROM assists school caregivers at the middle/junior high and high school level in assisting suicidal students, communicating with parents, and formulating a crisis plan.

Trauma

*Childhood Trauma: Your Questions Answered
(The Element Guide Series)*
By Ursula Markham (1998, Element)

Children and Disasters (Series in Trauma and Loss)
By Norma S. Gordon, Norma L. Faberow, and Carl A. Maida (1999, Brunner/Mazel)

Children and Trauma: A Guide for Parents and Professionals
By Cynthia Monahon (1997, Jossey-Bass)

How to Survive Trauma: A Program for War Veterans & Survivors of Rape, Assault, Abuse or Environmental Disasters
By Benjamin Colodzin (1997, Barrytown, Ltd.)

Life After Trauma: A Workbook for Healing
By Dena Rosenbloom and Mary Beth Williams
(1999, Guilford)

Posttraumatic Stress Disorder: A Clinical Review
By Robert S. Pynoos (Ed.) (1994, Sidran
Publishers)

*Post-Traumatic Stress Disorder in Children
(Progress in Psychiatry Series)*
By Spencer Eth and Robert S. Pynoos (1985,
American Psychiatric Press)

Too Scared to Cry: Psychic Trauma in Childhood
By L. Terr (1990, Harper & Row)

Trauma and Recovery
By Judith Lewis Herman (1997, Basic Books)

Understanding Psychological Trauma
Baxley Media Group
110 West Main Street
Urbana, Illinois 61801
(217) 384-4838
(217) 384-8280 FAX

- Comprehensive five-videotape set reviews trauma effects on adults and children.

index

Goodwyn, W., 307

Gootman, Marilyn E., 154, 214, 239, 247, 251

governor, crisis assistance from, 138

Grace, J., 115, 116, 117

graduation ceremony, continuing with, 182

Graham, Dinah, 48, 277, 281

Graham, Linda Speer, 82, 131, 136, 147

grandparents, grief issues of, 245

Graves County High School, 118

Greenbaum, S., 3, 7, 385–386

Greenwood, South Carolina, 365

grenades, live, 30

grief, 235–248
  after suicide, 248
  assistance with, 242
  assisting surviving children with, 243–245
  common reactions, 239–241
  coping with, 241–242
  of family members of deceased, 239–245
  grieving process, 235–238
  guilt feelings and, 245–247
  issues for surviving grandparents, 245
  self-help groups, 243
  stages of, 235

Grimes, Carl, 120

Grollman, Earl, 240

guidance counselor, death of in Lowell, Massachusetts, 26

guilt, 241, 245–247, 345, 347

gun control, 5–6, 382

gun deaths, school, 1

gunshots, actions to be taken if fired, 29, 39–40

H

Haas, Dale, 13, 155

Hadley, Nicole, 116–117, 119–120, 197, 200, 211

Halupa, Paul, 182

Hamilton, Edith, 236

Hammond, Jane, 72

Hand, Kelly, 308

Harrisburg High School, 215

Hayes, Roger, 120

Heady, Ben, 116

Heath High School. *See also* West Paducah, Kentucky crisis
  aftermath of crisis, 172
  crisis intervention at, 120
  "feeder" school, feelings of guilt at, 246
  funds raised for, 217
  governor assistance at, 138
  memorializing victims, 181, 196, 212
  lawsuit, 387
  and the media, 112
  ongoing support of staff, 376
  processing session, 161
  security after crisis, 119
  shooting incident at, 115, 116
  subsequent traumas at, 380
  support for/from other schools, 190, 379

Heiman, Suzette, 110

help, summoning, 41–44. *See also* assistance, outside; resources for crisis assistance

Henry, T., 6

herbal supplements, to relieve stress, 322–323

Hereford, Thomas, IV, 211

Heritage Fellowship Assembly of God Church, 305

Herring, Mandy, 184

Herring, Paige Ann, 12, 13, 23, 184, 219, 308, 377, 382

Herring, Pam, 184, 219, 377, 382

Herzog, J. M., 236, 274

Hewitt, B., 117, 119, 126, 211, 298, 300

Higgins, Leonard, 314

Hines, Jeff, 127

Hinkle, B., 46, 213, 218, 381, 382

Hoehner, Thomas, 120

Hoffstein, Rev. Fred, 200, 311

Holliman, J., 117, 118, 181, 196, 366

Holmes, P., 299, 302, 304, 385

home schooling, and safety of children, 4

homicide, 1, 2, 232

honesty. *See* truth, importance of

hospital/medical representative, role in family/community meeting, 90, 92

hotlines
  as information source, 72
  suicide, 214–215, 243, 341, 364

Houston, Texas
  accidental shooting at school, 104
  multi-school violence in, 43

Howard, William, 297

Huckabee, Mike, 22, 381

humor, use of, 27, 84, 323

Hurricane Hugo, 265

Hutchinson, Tim, 215

I

identification badges, for crisis response team members, 70

identification of dead and injured, 39

Imber-Black, Evan, 208

Individualized Education Plans (IEPs), 252, 386

information about crisis, updating, 77

injury/death notification, 55–62
  clergy role in, 313
  missing/unidentified loved ones, 61–62
  in person at hospital, 59–61
  in person at school, 57–59
  as responsibility of Parent/Family Liaison, 35
  on the telephone, 56–57

intercom
  communicating facts of crisis, 52
  notifying staff of threat, 28, 29
  summoning medical assistance, 38

"Interference With the Peaceful Conduct of Educational Institutions" law, 46. *See also* legislation

Internet, 31–32, 195

interviews, granting to media, 106

intruder, armed, inside the building, 29–30. *See also* threatening person outside the building

J

Jacobson, L., 4, 116, 119

James, B., 386, 387

tornadoes, 61–62. *See also* natural disasters

tourniquets, use of in severe injury, 38, 39

traffic, controlling flow of, 46–47

translation, for non-English-speaking population, 53, 79, 262

transportation personnel, notifying about crisis, 42, 73–74

trauma
  additional, soon after crisis, 380
  addressing, 225–257
  cause of, 229
  four stages of emotional effects, 318–319
  immediate recovery from, 234–235

Trauma Psychiatry Services (UCLA), 221, 375

trial and appeals process, 378

"triggering events," 280, 377–378

Trump, Kenneth S., 3, 9, 129

trusts, establishing with donations, 144–145

truth, importance of, 50–52, 107–108

Tuckman, A., 153

Turner, Fred, 181

TWA Flight 800 explosion, 131, 174, 197, 306

Twain, Mark, 242

Tyson, P., 236, 274

U

United Way, 145, 217

University Heights Elementary School, 43, 44, 290–291

university/college psychologists, crisis assistance from, 136. *See also* Counseling Liaison; counselors, school

U.S. Bureau of the Census, population of schoolchildren, 110

U.S. Department of Education, 2, 3

U.S. Department of Justice, 15, 142, 145–146

V

Van Boven, S., 116, 118, 119, 120, 127, 200, 298, 303

Van Campen, T., 309

Varner, Britthney R., 13, 23, 176, 218, 236, 239, 300, 308, 374, 382

verbal intervention, 26, 38

verification of facts. See facts of the crisis

"vicarious victimization," 317–318

victims
  contacting families of, 288
  memorializing, 208–221
  photos of, 101, 102
  possessions of, 179
  releasing names of, 49, 101, 107
  returning to school, 383–385
  visiting, 82

victims' advocates
  help with grieving process, 242
  in Jonesboro, Arkansas crisis, 16, 20, 21
  locating mental health assistance, 135, 373
  role in family/community meeting, 90, 92
  role in injury death notification, 57
  services provided by, 137
  in West Paducah, Kentucky crisis, 120

Victims of Crime Act (VOCA), 145–146. *See also* legislation

violence
  curbing youth, 5–6
  definition of, 7
  effect on people, 7–8, 225
  increase in, 7
  self-inflicted (*see* suicide)
  toward teachers, 3

Violence Project of the National Gay Task Force, 243

Voltaire, 333

volunteers, 74, 82

W

Walker, K., 118, 126

"walkie-talkies," for alerting area schools, 44

Walliser, T. L., 2

Warger, C., 384

warning signal, to notify school staff of threat, 28, 29, 33

Watkins, A., 46, 245, 247, 304

weapons, protection from tampering, 45

Web sites, 72, 115, 189, 197

Wegner, Bruce, 363

West Paducah, Kentucky. *See also* Heath High School
  aftermath of crisis, 172
  caring for caregivers, 319–320
  case study, 115–128
  clergy's role in, 305, 309–310, 311, 312, 313–314
  communication with parents, 64
  concerns about trial, 377–378
  "copycat" threats, 365, 366
  crisis committee at, 363
  families of suspected student perpetrators, 298, 303
  family/community meetings, 120–121
  forgiveness in, 307–309
  financial support, 216–217
  funeral in, 200
  governor assistance, 138
  guilt, feelings of, 246, 247
  importance of religion in, 124
  lawsuit, 387
  and the media, 109, 112
  memorializing victims, 181, 196, 212
  NOVA team in, 139, 179, 320
  ongoing counseling, 374
  ongoing support of school staff, 376
  organ donations of victim, 211
  processing the crisis at "feeder" schools, 292
  processing session, 161
  student as hero in, 38
  subsequent traumas at school, 380
  support for families of suspected student perpetrators, 300
  support for/from other schools, 134, 135, 190, 379
  victims' advocates in, 137
  Web site, 197
  year anniversary, 381

"Westside Crisis Fund Committee," 217

Westside Middle School. *See also* Jonesboro, Arkansas crisis
  aftermath of crisis, 172
  anniversary of crisis, 219
  art therapy, 186
  canceling school, 71

feedback form

We would be pleased to hear from *Coping With Crisis* readers. Please contact us if you would like more information about other resources in this series, to request a training or workshop, or if you have suggestions that you believe would be useful to us. Send this page (or other correspondence) to:

Poland & McCormick, c/o Production Manager
Sopris West, Inc.
4093 Specialty Place
Longmont, CO 80504

Or e-mail your comments to: webmaster@sopriswest.com

Information to Share

1. Having used this book during an actual school crisis, the following are my comments about its practicality, ease of use, etc.: _____

    _____

    _____

2. Having used this book for crisis planning, the following are my comments about its level of detail, organization, etc: _____

    _____

    _____

3. The following is a description of a crisis situation I encountered that was not covered in this book or an innovative crisis response idea I would like to share: _____

    _____

    _____

    _____

    ❏ You have my permission to include this incident/idea in a future edition of this book, crediting me/my school or organization.

    ❏ You have my permission to include this incident/idea in a future edition of this book, anonymously.

continued—

4. Other comments: _____

_____

_____

_____

_____

❑ You have my permission to include these comments in promotional materials.

❑ You do not have my permission to include these comments in promotional materials.

Information to Request

❑ Please notify me when other books in this series become available.

❑ Please notify me of upcoming related conferences and other special events.

❑ I would like to arrange a training/workshop with Dr. Poland in my school/organization. Please contact me to discuss this opportunity.

Contact Information

I am a:

❑ Crisis Response Team Member   ❑ Parent

❑ School Psychologist/Counselor   ❑ Clergy Member

❑ School Staff Member/Teacher   ❑ Victims' Advocate

❑ Administrator   ❑ Law Enforcement/Justice Personnel

❑ Other Educator   ❑ Youth Leader

❑ Other (Please describe): _____

Name/Title: _____

Address: _____

_____

Phone: (w) _____ (h) _____

E-mail: _____

(*NOTE*: Contact information will be kept confidential and will not be sold or distributed to any other party.)

Thank you for taking the time to provide us with reader feedback.